}þp]{ on JavaScript

Peter-Paul Koch

Peachpit Press

ppk on JavaScript
Peter-Paul Koch

New Riders
1249 Eighth Street
Berkeley, CA 94710
510/524-2178
800/283-9444
510/524-2221 (fax)

Find us on the Web at: www.newriders.com
To report errors, please send a note to errata@peachpit.com

New Riders is an imprint of Peachpit, a division of Pearson Education

Editor: **Wendy Sharp**

Production Coordinator: **Andrei Pasternak**

Copyeditor: **Wendy Katz**

Compositor: **Kate Kaminski**

Indexer: **Patti Schiendelman**

Cover design: **Mimi Heft**

Interior design: **Maureen Forys Happenstance Type-O-Rama**

Original ppk logo by Beng, www.beng.biz

ISBN 0-321-42330-5

9 8 7 6 5 4 3 2

Printed and bound in the United States of America

Words of thanks

This book would never have been written if I hadn't gained a lot of experience by creating the 100 or so JavaScript pages on www.quirksmode.org and if they hadn't been appreciated worldwide.

Therefore first thanks go to my faithful readers who supported me mentally over the years, and who are now supporting me materially by buying this book.

Second thanks go to the editors of this book: Dean Edwards (general), Derek Featherstone (accessibility), and David Flanagan (Core), whose useful comments uncovered many mistakes and omissions; my development editor Wendy Sharp, who tightened the book considerably and more than once pointed out I forgot to explain something that's obvious to me but not to my readers; and my former colleagues Babette van Hardeveld, Marloes Hautmann, and Remco van 't Veer, who read early drafts of a few chapters and provided valuable feedback from the perspective of non-JavaScript programmers.

Third thanks go to my JavaScript fellow travellers who time and again wrote nifty scripts, explained obscure features, wrote great articles and books, criticized my wilder ideas and generally acted as peer reviewers; among others Cameron Adams, Erik Arvidsson, James Edwards, Aaron Gustafson, Christian Heilmann, Jeff Howden, Jeremy Keith, Stuart Langridge, Scott Andrew LePera, Dylan Schiemann, Bobby van der Sluis, Dori Smith, Dan Webb, and Simon Willison.

Also thanks go to Nick Finck and Jeffrey Zeldman, who over the years gave me plenty of opportunity to publish articles and columns on their sites www.digital-web.com and www.alistapart.com, who provided me with serious, enlightening feedback, and whose early encouragement proved to me that, though not a native speaker, I could write English well enough to get along in the world of Web development.

Special thanks go to E minor, the mysterious resident guru of the WDF mailing list who patiently explained the concept of object detection and why it's superior to browser detection to a bewildered newbie back in 1998. This explanation showed me how clueless the average JavaScript developer was, and since I was now slightly less clueless myself I decided to publish a few articles to explain this and other important JavaScript principles.

Contents at a Glance

Contents

Introduction

THE PURPOSE OF this book is to offer easy access to the basic JavaScript knowledge I've gathered since I've been a professional Web developer.

Since this book reflects my knowledge, it also reflects the limitations of that knowledge. I am a Web developer, not an application developer—which means I talk about browser incompatibilities, accessibility, low-level syntax, and cooperation with the HTML structural layer, instead of modules, design principles, and abstraction layers.

During the eight years that I've earned a living by making Web sites, I have used some JavaScript features extensively but largely ignored others. I always took the tools I needed to do the job I was paid to do, and it turns out that the JavaScript toolbox contains many features I don't need in my day-to-day use.

Obviously, I cannot teach you to use a tool that I myself don't understand. Therefore this book only treats those language features I work with. Object-oriented JavaScript, for instance, is conspicuously absent because I've never seen the need to use it. Besides, a book has a fixed length, and so I had to make choices—occasionally very difficult ones. In the end I selected those JavaScript features that I feel you must understand in order to use the language at competent intermediate to advanced level.

What you already should know

I expect you to be fluent in HTML and CSS. As we'll see in Chapter 4, integration with a clean and useful HTML structure is crucial for writing simple, effective scripts. Chapter 9 is incomprehensible without basic CSS knowledge.

In addition I expect you to have some JavaScript experience, even if only at copy/paste level. Take this code:

```
var x = document.getElementsByTagName('a');
for (var i=0;i<x.length;i++) {
    if (x[i].className != 'popup') continue;
    x[i].onclick = openPopup;
}
```

I expect you to vaguely understand that this code goes through all links in a page and defines a popup for those links that have a class="popup". You don't have to understand all the details (in fact, the purpose of this book is to explain those details), but you should have a general idea of what's going on.

Ideally, I want every beginning scripter to ascend to intermediate status by reading this book, while it should help every intermediate scripter well along the way to advanced understanding.

Companion site

My Web site, www.quirksmode.org, is a major JavaScript resource. At the directory www.quirksmode.org/book/ you'll find all example scripts, errata lists, and such.

You won't find compatibility tables in the book because they'd be outdated too quickly. Instead, such tables are online, where I can update them when browser compatibility patterns shift—or when I turn out to have made a mistake. Look for them at my site, which has been their natural habitat for the past five years anyway.

The book contains references to other Web sites: you can, of course, type the URLs into your browser's Location bar, but an easier route is to visit the companion site, where I've provided links to every site mentioned in the book.

Any JavaScript book needs example scripts. Once the writer has explained a bit of theory, he should show how to apply this theory in practice. An example script is the most obvious way of doing that.

Ideally, these scripts should be of practical value. It's all fine and dandy to create a script that lists your pets in alphabetical order and shows their fluffy images when you click on their cute names, but even if it illustrates the theory of, say, objects and popups, its practical value is essentially nil.

Therefore this book features eight real-world scripts that real-world clients paid me real-world money to write.

Each of the eight scripts was written for a specific client with a specific, commercial goal in mind, and each of the clients indicated he or she was happy with the script. In fact, six out of seven clients granted me additional business, and the only reason the seventh didn't is that he's a small business owner who needed just the one website.

You can't get much more real-world than that.

How the example scripts are used

The one disadvantage of using real-world example scripts is that it's impossible for me to treat one script per book chapter. I can't ask my clients to be content with a script that uses Core and Events but not DOM just because I haven't yet explained DOM to you.

Therefore the example scripts do everything in the book: They all use event handling, accessibility, DOM scripting, HTML structure, and CSS modification.

Essentially I chopped the scripts into pieces and then ordered these pieces thematically. You can find all example scripts at http://www.quirksmode.org/book/. Even if you're going to read this book somewhere other than in front of your computer, I advise you to familiarize yourself with the scripts beforehand. Throughout the book I assume you have an overall idea of what they do and why.

Textarea Maxlength

In September 2004 Website agency Lost Boys contracted me to create, among other things, a script that keeps track of the number of characters the user enters in a textarea. This was the Textarea Maxlength script. I subsequently discussed aspects of this script at great length in my "JavaScript Triggers" article at A List Apart, implemented it in the comment areas of my own blog, and added a description to QuirksMode. You can find my article at http://alistapart.com/articles/scripttriggers.

This is an extremely simple DOM script that slightly enhances the page it's on.

Usable Forms

In April 2003 the ING Bank contracted me to create a demo mortgage application form. Since this is one of the most complicated forms in existence, a way to hide irrelevant form fields until they're needed was mandatory. After all, a "Date of Divorce" field is only useful when the user indicates he is, in fact, divorced. In all other cases the field should remain hidden.

So I wrote Usable Forms, and to celebrate that fact I wrote "Forms, Usability, and the W3C DOM". You can find this article at http://www.digital-web.com/articles/forms_usability_and_the_w3c_dom/. You'll notice that the version of the script I discuss there is older than the one used in this book.

This is a moderately complex DOM script that continually restructures the document it's running in. It contains valuable lessons about working with custom attributes, the definition of relations between HTML elements, the use of markers, global events, and the advantages of the Level 0 DOM when working with form fields.

Form Validation

Form Validation was finalized in Spring 2004, when Website company SQR contracted me to create templates for a form-heavy site. Obviously, forms need validation scripts, and I created Form Validation, which hinged on the custom `validation` attribute and contained the—then major—innovation of displaying error messages next to the form field they apply to instead of in an alert.

Form Validation contains the basics of form handling, it generates a bit of HTML, and it uses JavaScript associative arrays in an interesting way.

Dropdown Menu

In January 2004 I was contacted by Orchid for Change which offers Websites to local organizations affiliated to the Democratic Party.

One script Orchid needed was an all-time classic: the dropdown menu. Even though its usability is somewhat suspect, it has been a favorite for years and is likely to remain one of the most requested scripts in the near future.

This script gives excellent examples of the close cooperation between CSS and JavaScript to ensure accessibility, making a script keyboard-compatible, the complete mess a mouseout event can cause, and a few more advanced topics.

Edit Style Sheet

The next example script was also written for Orchid.

Orchid has several HTML templates with main style sheets that define the positioning of the various items (masthead, navigation, main content, etc.). A client selects one of these pre-defined templates, and a site is created.

However, to make each site unique, the client should have the opportunity to fine-tune the styles, mainly the colors, background-colors, fonts and typographical styles. For that purpose, each site has a second style sheet that can be tweaked to accommodate unique parts of the design.

I wrote the Edit Style Sheet script to allow clients to change this second style sheet for themselves. The client enters the desired colors and typography into a form, and the style sheet is changed so that the results are immediately visible.

Unfortunately this script never left prototype phase. It therefore lacks a few features, notably a way of submitting the changed style sheet to the server and applying it to the entire site. Nonetheless the script provides an example of editing style sheets, as well as preparing your HTML forms to cooperate with a script.

Sandwich Picker

Of all the example scripts I like this one best.

In October 2004 I worked on a Website for my butcher, Keurslager Drost, who also owns a small but successful catering service. The site was meant to streamline catering orders, as well as give visitors an overview of his products.

Ordering sandwiches was to become a major feature of the site. Since a full database solution was out of the question for budgetary reasons, the 100 or so sandwiches would end up in one static HTML file, and users would have to be able to search through this huge list.

With this in mind I created the Sandwich Picker script. A large data table contains all sandwiches, and two, initially empty, tables would contain the search results and the order information. A search box at the top of the page allows users to search for sandwiches, and the script moves the correct <tr>s to the top of the page, directly below the search box. I added a tiny order system, containing an 'order' and a 'remove' button. Pressing these buttons would move the <tr> to the correct table. A price calculation script completed the page.

The script offers an interesting example of interacting with the user by modifying the document structure, and it illustrates a few key points in the cooperation between JavaScript and CSS.

XMLHTTP Speed Meter

In September 2005 Website company Eend contracted me to create a script for a ADSL download speed meter for the ISP Wanadoo. The plan was extremely simple: users would enter their postal code and house number in a form, and an XMLHttpRequest script would silently send this data to a server side script that returned a bit of XML with the rough download speed the client could expect.

The download speed was displayed as an animation that moved between the minimum and maximum speeds. Besides being graphically interesting, this animation would clearly show that the download speed was only an indication of what clients could expect, and not a definite promise. This was very important to Wanadoo, since an exact download speed is almost impossible to predict.

The script gives a simple example of working with XMLHTTP, shows how to read out the response, illustrates the principles of JavaScript animation, and gives an excellent handle to explain the difference between `setTimeout` and `setInterval`.

Site Survey

Shortly after the XMLHTTP Speed Meter was delivered, I started working on an unusual and interesting script for research company RM Interactive.

This company is hired by large Website owners to keep track of which pages their users visit, and to present an additional, and wholly voluntary, questionnaire after the user has left the site. All this is done by means of a popup.

The script that did all these things was old, couldn't handle popup blockers, and was inaccessible to noscript users. Since RM Interactive was about to be hired by the Dutch government, all accessibility issues needed to be solved.

So I rewrote the script from scratch, with emphasis on usability and accessibility. The script demonstrates circumventing popup blockers, keeping track of what happens in the main window, restoring communications between the popup and the main window, and finding out if the user has left the site.

Note that Site Survey is the only script that's spread out over two JavaScript files: survey.js in all pages of the host site, and popup.js in the popup.

Errors

Since these are real-life scripts they contain real-life errors. While writing this book I noticed two especially.

1. Sandwich Picker contains an accessibility error. Although in theory the page is accessible to noscript users, the usability of this noscript variant is severely hampered for reasons we'll discuss in 2G.

2. Form Validation works with the `validation` custom attribute (ie. an attribute that's not a part of any (X)HTML specification). While writing Chapter 4, I noticed that in contrast to Usable Forms and Textarea Maxlength, which definitely need custom attributes, Form Validation

could do without. Moving the information to the class attribute would result in a script that cooperates more closely with the CSS presentation layer. We'll discuss all this in 4B.

I decided not to correct these mistakes, since both are instructive and give insight in how JavaScript relates to HTML, accessibility, Web standards, and CSS.

The book's structure

In the first four chapters of this book we'll discuss high-level topics. The last six are devoted to technical topics.

Chapter 1 discusses JavaScript's purpose, gives a technical overview, and treats JavaScript history to show how its purpose has been redefined.

Chapter 2 discusses JavaScript's context: a usable, accessible, standards-compliant site in which structure, presentation and behavior are separated.

Chapter 3 discusses browser incompatibilities and strategies for dealing with them.

Chapter 4 discusses JavaScript's interaction with the HTML structural layer, initialization, and the <script> tag.

Chapters 5 to 10 discuss JavaScript's technical nuts and bolts: Core, BOM, Events, DOM, CSS modification, and data retrieval. 1B contains an overview of these topics.

Conventions in this book

Finally some words about the conventions in this book.

Sections

This book is divided into 10 chapters, each of which is divided into sections that are lettered A, B, C, etc.

The topics I cover are inextricably intertwined, but one of the disadvantages of the printed book format is that I cannot use hyperlinks. Therefore I did the next best thing: I created cross-references that use these chapter numbers and section letters. Example: "We're going to treat this in detail in 4B."

Code examples

Most chapters are heavily studded with code examples, which look like this.

```
var rows = document.getElementsByTagName('tr');
for (var i=0;i<rows.length;i++) {
    var cells = rows[i].getElementsByTagName('td');
}
```

If they're taken from one of the example scripts, I give the line numbers:

[Example script name, lines 14-17]

```
var rows = document.getElementsByTagName('tr');
for (var i=0;i<rows.length;i++) {
    var cells = rows[i].getElementsByTagName('td');
}
```

Occasionally I condense the example scripts because I want to focus on one feature and ignore everything else. In that case the message 'condensed' appears with the line numbers. The message 'changed' means that I changed the script a bit for reasons explained in the surrounding text.

Some lines of code are too long for this book, and are spread across two printed lines. In that case the line always ends with a special icon that means "the code on the next line really should be on this one". For instance:

```
var writerootRows = document.getElementById('writeroot'). ➡
getElementsByTagName('tr');
```

Sometimes JavaScript allows you to break the line at the indicated place; sometimes it doesn't. To avoid errors it's best to assume that all code is on one line in your source file.

Occasionally I give incorrect examples, which look like this:

```
var rows = getElementsByTagName('tr');
    for (var i=0;i<rows.length;i++) {
        var cells = rows.getElementsByTagName('td');
    }
```

The surrounding text always explains why these examples are wrong.

Sometimes a code example contains a text between square brackets:

```
    var rows = [get the rows in the start table];
    for (var i=0;i<rows.length;i++) {
        var cells = rows[i].getElementsByTagName('td');
    }
```

This always means: "we're going to do this-and-that first, but right now it doesn't matter how we do it". I want you to focus on the lines of real code in the example, and although they require some preparations I don't want to treat those in detail because they'd distract you from the subject I'm explaining.

You shouldn't confuse these square brackets with the square brackets that denote keys in (associative) arrays, as explained in 5K and 5L. Usually the difference is obvious.

A note on browser names

This book mainly focuses on four browsers, and I always name them "Explorer", "Mozilla", "Opera" and "Safari", followed by a version number where applicable.

"Mozilla" includes any browser based on the Gecko rendering engine, such as Firefox, Camino, and Netscape.

"Explorer" means Microsoft Internet Explorer on Windows versions 5 and up.

I decided to use this name long ago, and I have done so on www.quirksmode. org for the past seven years. Since I want to keep this book consistent with the site, it also uses "Explorer" throughout.

Although I know some people will retort that it really ought to be called Internet Explorer to distinguish it from Windows Explorer, I don't think anyone will confuse a WWW browser with a file manager — especially not when they're as tightly integrated as they are.

As we'll see in Chapter 3, the Windows version of Explorer is a completely different browser than the Mac version. Since the Mac version is on the way out and not a very good browser from a JavaScript perspective, "Explorer" without qualification always means the Windows version. I only refer to the Mac version when I explicitly add "on Mac".

Timestamp

The final version of this book was written in May 2006. Obviously, developments that occurred after that time haven't been covered.

During the writing of this book I tested my scripts in the following browsers:

Explorer 6.0 and 7.0 beta 2 preview

Mozilla 1.7.12 and Firefox 1.5

Opera 8.54 and 9 beta

Safari 1.3.2

Konqueror 3.0.5

iCab 3.0

Purpose

THE PURPOSE OF JavaScript is to add an extra layer of usability to a Web page.

That sounds simple, but this golden rule has frequently been misunderstood. Not all scripts add usability to a Web site; in fact, during several periods of JavaScript's checkered history, the creation of flashy-looking but useless scripts has been a significant cottage industry.

Even when writing useful scripts, JavaScript developers haven't always written them in their proper context: that of an accessible, modern HTML page that integrates the insights of the Web standards movement.

Worse, some scripts don't add a usability layer, they *are* the entire usability layer—and as a consequence the site falls apart when a browser doesn't support JavaScript.

We'll discuss usability, accessibility, and the Web standards movements in Chapter 2. The current chapter focuses on explaining JavaScript's purpose in more depth, so that you understand its role in a Web site. In addition, it discusses the constant redefinition of JavaScript's purpose throughout its history.

> **JAVASCRIPT IS NOT JAVA**
>
> Although the names suggest otherwise, JavaScript is not the same as Java. Granted, there are a few superficial syntactic resemblances, and both languages can be used to add usability to a Web page, but the differences are more important than the similarities.
>
> It's best to see Java and JavaScript as distant cousins. Occasionally you'll notice a family resemblance, but most of the time you're dealing with quite different languages. Knowledge of Java may help you learn the basics of JavaScript, but it may also hinder you, because some aspects of JavaScript, notably its dynamic typing and its use of prototypes instead of classes to support inheritance, are different from Java and require a different programming approach.

A: Conceptual overview

JavaScript is a scripting language interpreted by the browser. It adds usability to a Web site by handling certain bits of interaction, such as validating a form or creating a new menu, in the browser instead of on the server.

Handling interaction in the browser

To understand JavaScript's purpose, it's useful to take a quick peek at client-server communication.

A client is usually a program on the user's computer, while the server is usually a remote computer that holds interesting data. When the client needs data (a Web page, for instance) it sends a request to the server, and the server responds by sending the requested data. After getting this response, the client may send a new request, which leads to a new response, and so on.

1A

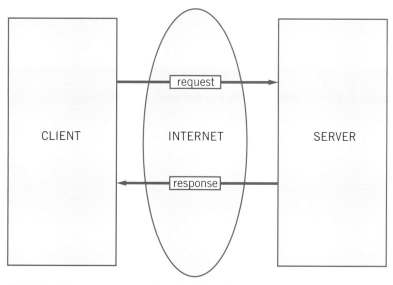

FIGURE 1.1   Client-server communication. The client requests something, and the server responds.

In the case of the World Wide Web, the client is a browser. When the user types in a URL or clicks a link, the browser sends a request to a Web server. The server responds by sending an HTML page. When the browser receives the HTML, it displays the page and awaits further instructions. When the user clicks a link or submits a form, the process is repeated. Every round of client-server communication requires a bit of time during which the user can't do anything, and may feel disoriented.

Less communication

This is where JavaScript enters the picture. JavaScript is a client-side programming language, which means it works in the client (the user's browser), not on the server. Therefore, any job that is handled by JavaScript doesn't require a round of client-server communication.

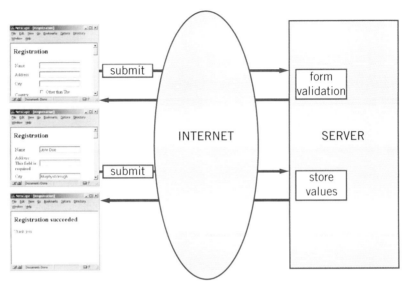

FIGURE 1.2   Form validation without JavaScript. The server receives the form, checks it, and generates a new page that's sent back to the client. When the user submits the form without mistakes, the server processes it and sends back a Thank You page.

For example, take form validation. Let's assume the user enters her data but forgets to fill out the Address field before hitting Submit. The incomplete form is sent to the server, where a server-side script notes the missing address and creates a new HTML page. This page, noting the error, is sent back to the client. After the user has entered the missing address, she submits the form again. Now the form is complete, and the server-side script can store the form data and send the user to a Thank You page.

With JavaScript to perform the form validation, you can skip the first request/response. When the user hits Submit, JavaScript checks the form. It sees that the address is missing, halts the form submission and generates an error message. When the user submits the form again, JavaScript again runs a check, doesn't find more problems, and allows the form submission to go forward. Only now does the browser send out a request, to which the server responds by storing the form data and sending back a Thank You page.

1A

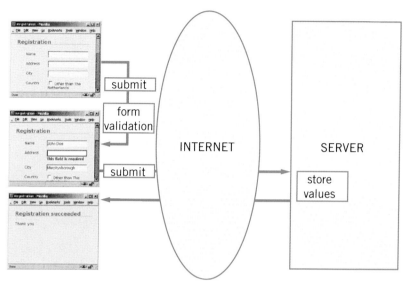

FIGURE 1.3   Form validation with JavaScript. The script checks the form on the client and halts the form submission if it finds errors. When the user submits the form without mistakes, the server processes it and sends back a Thank You page.

As a result, the script conveys a usability benefit—a smoother-working page— and JavaScript's purpose is fulfilled.

Fat vs. thin

Of course form validation is a simple example. It's been around since 1996, and although it's still one of the most popular scripts, it's not really challenging technically, or even conceptually. Nowadays JavaScript is capable of handling much, much more interaction.

That raises the question: How far should you take it? Should you create one giant JavaScript application to hold all your interactions and present your entire Web site in a single page? Or should you create separate and static HTML pages that use JavaScript only to add some subtle enhancements? In other words, should JavaScript be used as often as possible, or in a more restrained, limited way? Or, perhaps, not at all?

The answer depends on how you interpret JavaScript's purpose. Some say that nearly everything should take place on the client side, citing improved usability as their main argument. After all, any page refresh requires waiting, which might disturb a user's concentration. There's something to be said for that point of view.

Others maintain that as much interaction as possible should take place on the server, citing improved accessibility as their main argument. Some browsers do not support (enough) JavaScript to handle advanced scripts, and users of these browsers will not be able to use (or even see) script-heavy pages. There's something to be said for that point of view, too.

The first group embraces the idea of a *fat client*, the second group that of a *thin client*. (There are many more names for both, but for clarity's sake I'll stick to these two.)

A thin client relies totally on client-server communication. Basically, the logic of each round of interaction ("The user clicked here. What happens next?") is dictated by the server. When frequent page updates are necessary, this can lead to a slow and frustrating user experience.

A fat client, on the other hand, handles as much interaction as possible at the client. When the user does something, a script in the browser decides what to do next. Although no client can do entirely without communication with the server, the fat client tries to limit it to fetching extra bits of data, handling all other concerns itself.

Which approach is better?

Although the fat client certainly conveys some usability benefits, I feel that in the end the thin client is more likely to emerge as the "standard" way of using JavaScript, because of two fundamental imbalances between the thin and fat models.

The first is that the thin client is overall more in keeping with the Web's structure. The Web was conceived as a collection of documents, not as a collection of interfaces.

This conception of the Web has ruled the browsers' basic functions since the dawn of time. A browser has a Back and a Forward button to send you on to the previous or the next document, and not the previous or next step in an interface. A browser can bookmark documents, but not steps in an interface.

The second imbalance is about accessibility. Obviously, from an accessibility point of view, a thin client is preferable, because there's less to go wrong. Conversely, a fat client will fail much more spectacularly, since there's more functionality to fail.

Neither imbalance is unsolvable. It is possible to write complicated (hence fat) scripts that make sure the Back and Forward buttons, as well as bookmarks, continue to work in an advanced interface. It's also possible to write a perfectly accessible fat client. We'll discuss a few possibilities in 10D.

Nonetheless, all this takes a lot of extra work, for which not all projects have reserved time and money. Besides, writers of fat clients tend to focus on the usability problem (Back/Forward/bookmark) and ignore the the accessibility problem, thinking "This application is so advanced it's never going to be accessible anyway."

The purpose of JavaScript

In view of all this, is JavaScript's purpose best served by creating fat or thin clients?

The answer is, of course, "It depends." It depends on the site you're creating, on your target audience, and on your skills as a JavaScript programmer. This book will help you to improve the latter, but it doesn't (and cannot) say anything useful about your site or your target audience.

In the end, the choice between fat and thin is entirely your own. When in doubt, stay on the thin side, but in order to become a truly well-rounded JavaScript developer, you should create a fat client at least once.

B: Technical overview

The purpose of this book is to give an overview of all facets of JavaScript that are important in creating modern Web sites. I split JavaScript into six areas, each of which have their own purpose and problems, and each of which will be treated in its own chapter. The table below summarizes these six areas.

	Jobs	Treated in	Example scripts
Core	Making JavaScript a programming language. Allowing control structures, variables, functions, and objects.	Chapter 5	All
BOM (Browser Object Model)	Giving commands to the browser window, reading cookies, and communicating with other windows.	Chapter 6	Site Survey
Events Note: browser incompatibilities!	Finding out which actions the user takes, and defining functions that should react to these actions.	Chapter 7	All, but especially Dropdown Menu
DOM (Document Object Model)	Studying and changing the HTML document's structure.	Chapter 8	All, but especially Usable Forms, Sandwich Picker, Textarea Maxlength, Form Validation
CSS modification	Studying and changing the CSS presentation of the HTML document.	Chapter 9	Especially XMLHTTP Speed Meter and Edit Style Sheet
Data retrieval (XMLHttpRequest)	Downloading new data from the server without refreshing the page.	Chapter 10	XMLHTTP Speed Meter

All scripts use the Core language, Events, and the DOM, because all scripts must be a program (Core), must wait for the user to do something (Events), and must update the page somehow to give feedback (DOM).

Standardization

Standards-wise, JavaScript is a bit of a patchwork, and in order to understand the reasons for this you need a quick historical summary. (JavaScript's full story will be told in 1C.)

De facto Netscape 3 standard

JavaScript was invented and first implemented by Netscape, which back in 1996 was the leading browser. Then other browsers, such as Explorer, entered the market. In order to ensure that all existing Web sites functioned correctly, they were forced to copy Netscape's JavaScript implementation exactly.

Therefore, even today all JavaScript browsers support the de facto Netscape 3 standard. It consists of Core 1.1, BOM, the traditional event model, and the Level 0 DOM. Back in those days CSS modification and data retrieval weren't invented yet, so they're not part of this standard. Nowadays the standard is distinctly antiquated, but since millions of Web pages still use old-fashioned Netscape 3 scripts, no browser can afford to relinquish this standard.

Then followed the Browser Wars, during which Microsoft and Netscape struggled for pre-eminence in the browser market and made a distinct point of being as incompatible as possible. It took JavaScript many years to recover from this ordeal, and we're still suffering the consequences, especially in event handling.

Modern standards

In order to understand the modern standards we first have to discuss a fundamental distinction between Core and the DOM (which includes event handling and CSS modification).

Although JavaScript is best known for its function as a client-side scripting language in Web browsers, it can be implemented in a variety of other environments. Adobe's ActionScript, for instance, implements JavaScript Core in Flash movies, and Netscape once had its own brand of Web servers that used JavaScript as their primary server-side language.

Flash movies and Web servers are fundamentally different environments than Web pages. Nonetheless, they all use the JavaScript Core language in order to create a programming environment.

DOM, on the other hand, is specific to XML documents (including HTML pages). Its view of a document as a hierarchical collection of nodes (see 8A) is excellently suited to Web pages, but largely useless in a Flash or server-side environment.

That's why there are separate standards for Core and the DOM.

The European Computer Manufacturers Association (ECMA) has standardized JavaScript Core, and this standard is (supposed to be) used in any JavaScript implementation, be it Flash, Web browsers, Web servers, or one that is yet to be invented.

On the other hand, XML and its numerous offshoots are the domain of the World Wide Web Consortium (W3C). W3C created the DOM specification, which includes event handling and CSS modification.

The BOM and data retrieval have not yet been specified officially. The Web Hypertext Application Technology Working Group (WHAT-WG) is working on the BOM, while at the time of writing W3C has created a first draft of an XMLHttpRequest specification for data retrieval. The BOM still follows the old de facto Netscape 3 standard, while XMLHttpRequest is being used as originally specified by Microsoft.

Two tiers

JavaScript standards are therefore a two-tiered construct. The older, lower tier consists of the de facto Netscape 3 standard which is universally supported but rather restricted, while the newer, upper tier consists of standards coming from ECMA, W3C, Microsoft, and WHAT-WG, most of which are supported by most browsers.

The table below summarizes these two tiers:

	Netscape 3 standard	Modern standards
Core	Yes (1.1)	ECMA (1.5)
BOM	Yes	None (WHAT-WG)
Events	Yes (traditional)	W3C DOM and Microsoft
DOM	Yes (Level 0)	W3C DOM
CSS modification	No (not supported)	W3C DOM
Data retrieval	No (not supported)	De facto Microsoft, W3C draft

{ **STANDARDS**

Unfortunately there's no single documentation for the Netscape 3 standard any more, since the demise of Netscape's JavaScript guide.

At the time of writing you can find the various modern JavaScript standards here:

ECMA's JavaScript Core Specification: http://www.ecma-international.org/publications/standards/Ecma-262.htm.

W3C DOM Specification: http://www.w3.org/DOM/, (includes Events and CSS modification).

Web Hypertext Application Technology Working Group: http://www.whatwg.org/ (currently no direct link to the BOM specification).

http://msdn.microsoft.com/workshop/author/om/event_model.asp: Microsoft event model.

http://msdn.microsoft.com/library/default.asp?url=/library/en-us/xmlsdk/html/7924f6be-c035-411f-acd2-79de7a711b38.asp: Microsoft XMLHttpRequest. }

Although nowadays all browsers are serious about following all standards, we're still suffering from a few holdovers of the Browser Wars. Microsoft has not yet implemented W3C's Events specification, but instead uses its own proprietary event model. In order to write cross-browser event handling scripts you must therefore understand both the W3C and the Microsoft models, as well as the older Netscape 3 standard. We'll discuss all this in Chapter 7.

Versions

There are several JavaScript versions, ranging from the obsolete 1.0 to the 2.0 that's under development at the time of writing. It's important to note that these version numbers only apply to Core; other areas of JavaScript (notably the DOM) have their own version numbers.

Core version	Implemented in	ECMA specifications
1.0	Netscape 2 earlier Explorer 3 versions	
1.1	Netscape 3 later Explorer 3 versions	
1.2	Netscape 4 – 4.5	
1.3	Netscape 4.5+ Explorer 4 (slight upgrade in 5.0)	v1 (v2 contained some clarifications)
1.4	No browser, only Netscape servers	
1.5	Mozilla Explorer 5.5+	v3
1.6-2.0	Under construction	v4

Originally, the idea behind these version numbers was to allow Web developers to specify what level of JavaScript they were using. It was supposed to work something like this:

```
<script language="JavaScript1.2">
// scripts that use 1.2 features
</script>
```

Browsers that did not support JavaScript 1.2 were supposed to ignore the entire <script> tag, so that the scripts would only be executed in browsers that could handle 1.2.

The advent of Netscape and Explorer 4 relegated this well-intentioned idea to the dustbin. Both browsers claimed to support JavaScript 1.2, but not even the most powerful fantasy can imagine them supporting the *same* JavaScript 1.2. Besides, this idea was only truly implemented in Netscape 2 and 3, though specifying "JavaScript1.2" triggers special and exciting incompatibilities in Netscape 4.

Therefore these version numbers play no role in modern JavaScript development, and I advise you not to specify any version in the language attribute (in fact, you shouldn't use that attribute at all).

Towards JavaScript 2.0

As I write, JavaScript's inventor Brendan Eich is working on JavaScript 2.0. The purpose is to add new features to the Core language, including a better variable typing system, support for Java-like classes and interfaces, block scope for variables, and other innovations aimed at improving JavaScript as a programming language.

{
BRENDAN'S ROADMAP

http://weblogs.mozillazine.org/roadmap/ contains Brendan Eich's roadmap update for the deployment of Core 2.0.
}

Mozilla and Opera are expected to start supporting some of these features in 2007, and other browsers are expected to follow later. Adobe participates in this effort, so ActionScript is also likely to implement Core 2.0.

Security

The purpose of JavaScript is adding usability to a Web site, not breaching the user's privacy and security.

First of all, picture what happens when an innocent end user finds a Web page that contains JavaScript. He essentially downloads an unknown program written by an unknown person that's going to run on his computer. In general, executing unknown programs that do unspecified things on and to your computer is the fastest way to get infected with viruses, Trojan horses, and other malign entities.

In order to keep Web users secure from these hazards, as well as from breaches of privacy, JavaScript has strict security regulations. Its most important line of defense against malicious scripters is that it simply does not support certain actions.

No access to host computer

JavaScript cannot read from or write to the file system of your user's computer (with the exception of cookies; see 6G). Thus JavaScript cannot read password files from or write viruses to the user's hard disk.

Same-source policy

As we'll see in Chapter 6, JavaScript allows you to access and run scripts that are located in another frame or window. Nonetheless, without any restrictions this would be a serious security hazard, since it might allow, for example, malicious site owners to read out the password the user types in his online banking tool, and then submit this password to their own servers.

{ **EXCEPTION: TOP.LOCATION.HREF**

There's one exception to the same-source rule. If your site is caught in someone else's frameset, you are allowed to set (but not get!) `top.location.href`, or the location of the topmost frameset page. See http://www.quirksmode. org/js/framebust.html for more information. }

Therefore JavaScript has a strict same-source policy: Cross-window communication is allowed only when the pages in both windows come from the same Web domain. If that's not the case, the browser gives a security error.

This policy is very strict. Suppose I have two sub-domains, www.quirksmode.org and search.quirksmode.org. A page on the www domain opens a popup with a page on the search domain. Now the same-source policy kicks in and forbids any communication between the two windows, since they come from different (sub)domains.

document.domain

There is one way in which I'm allowed to mitigate the same-source policy somewhat. I can set the `document.domain` property in both windows to 'quirksmode.org':

```
document.domain = 'quirksmode.org';
```

Now both pages consider themselves to come from quirksmode.org without any subdomain, and the www page and the search page are allowed to communicate with each other.

Obviously, you may only set `document.domain` to a value that's part of the real domain. This doesn't work:

⊠ `document.domain = 'microsoft.com';`

The browser sees that my pages do not come from microsoft.com, but from quirksmode.org. Therefore the value is ignored and I cannot communicate with any page from microsoft.com.

Other restrictions

Apart from having no access to the host computer and the same-source policy, JavaScript has the following restrictions:

- JavaScript cannot read properties of the History object (which we'll discuss in 6C). Although you're allowed to send your users back in their browser history, you're not allowed to see to which page they'll return.

- JavaScript cannot set the value of a file upload field. Thus, malicious site owners cannot set the value to the location of a password file and then automatically submit the form in order to get a copy of the user's password file.

- If you try to close a browser window that has been opened by the user, the user is asked to allow this action. You may close windows opened by JavaScript without this restriction.

- Most browsers don't allow you to open new windows that are smaller than 100x100 pixels and/or that are located outside the visible computer screen. In addition, you may not produce new windows without title bars.

C: JavaScript history

During its checkered history JavaScript's purpose has been continually redefined, not only because every generation of browsers supports more JavaScript, but also because of the struggle for pre-eminence between the fat and the thin models of JavaScript programming.

A historical overview will therefore acquaint you with ancient and modern thinking about JavaScript's purpose, as well as provide perspective on the fat client vs. thin client question discussed earlier. You'll also begin to understand why JavaScript has been frequently misunderstood, especially by "hard" programmers.

False start

JavaScript was created by one man: Brendan Eich, then working for Netscape Communications Corporation. Its public history starts with the release of Netscape 2 in March 1996, but unfortunately it was a false start in more than one respect.

Eich's purpose in creating JavaScript was to give Web developers—not known for their technical prowess—an easy way to add bits of interactivity to pages. The idea was to copy scripts from other pages and tweak them a bit. In this respect he succeeded admirably: many JavaScript developers (including myself) started out as copy-pasters.

Unfortunately JavaScript had the wrong name and the wrong syntax.

Originally JavaScript was named LiveScript, but at the last possible moment its name was changed. This was done purely for marketing reasons: in 1996 Java was very popular, and Netscape thought it a good idea to hitch a ride on this popularity by choosing a similar name. Even worse, Netscape's marketing managers summarily ordered Eich to "make the language look like Java."

The result was a language that superficially resembles Java in name and syntax and that is easy to learn by copy-pasting. This inevitably led people to discount JavaScript as a "dumbed-down" version of Java, as a cute little scripting language you could do a few tricks with but that wasn't worth a serious programmer's attention.

We're still suffering the consequences of this fatal misperception.

De facto standard

Netscape 2, the first browser to support JavaScript, was a roaring success. Netscape 3 followed pretty soon, and to everybody's delight it supported even more functionality.

Netscape 3 also gave JavaScript its first de facto standard. Although this is not an official specification promulgated by an official body like W3C, it is no less real: every browser that supports JavaScript also supports the de facto Netscape 3 standard.

In 1996, Netscape 3 was the king of the hill. Web developers enthusiastically used its new functionalities and advanced features. Therefore, Netscape's competitors, such as Microsoft's Internet Explorer, had to support everything that Netscape supported. After all, who wanted a browser that didn't support the cool stuff used on thousands of Web sites? This copycatting is what made a de facto standard.

This is an important theme in the Web's history: once enough Web sites use a certain functionality, any browser must support that functionality and continue to support it indefinitely. If a browser doesn't, users notice that their favorite sites don't work, and they blame the browser they're using, whether that's fair or not.

The first thin phase

In those early days, the browser was still definitely a thin client. Form validation and mouseovers are fine and dandy, but they don't allow you to handle a significant amount of user interaction on the client. Users were forced to go back to the server time and again in order to truly interact with Web sites. Back then that was no problem; no user expected otherwise.

The Browser Wars

The browser market started to change rapidly. The first Internet hype began, and the Browser Wars were heating up. Who was going to rule the Web— Netscape or Explorer?

{ **WHAT DOES BROWSER WARS MEAN?**

The term "Browser Wars" is used exclusively to denote the era between 1996 and 1999 when Netscape and Microsoft waged their war for pre-eminence in the browser market. }

Neither party was confident of winning the Wars with its version 3 browser, and therefore both decided to create an upgraded and extended versions 4.

Unfortunately, Netscape's and Microsoft's CSS implementations did not match the standard—or each other's—and that set back the adoption of CSS by many years. Part of the reason was that the two competitors deliberately paid no attention to each other's implementation, a state of affairs that also hindered JavaScript in those days.

Both vendors implemented W3C's CSS specification, partly because they had helped shape the specification, and partly because they were afraid that the competitor would support CSS and gain an advantage.

A bunch of backgrounds and borders was not deemed sufficiently cool to win the Browser Wars. Both browser vendors therefore allowed JavaScript control over these CSS declarations. It became possible to use `position: absolute` to create a layer "on top of" the rest of the site, and then continuously change its `top` and `left` properties to make it move across the screen. This was *seriously* cool stuff.

LAYERS

In the Netscape 4 model, any absolutely positioned element was called a layer. Even though the Microsoft model didn't have an equivalent concept, it became customary to talk about layers when you meant absolutely positioned elements that moved across the screen.

The Netscape 4 model has died a slow and agonizing death, but the habit of talking about layers has remained. Nowadays it means an element that can be moved independently of the rest of the page's content.

> {
> DHTML
>
> Dynamic HTML (DHTML) is the changing of CSS properties by means of JavaScript. See 7A for more details.
> }

Collectively, these tricks became known as DHTML. They had little to do with actual HTML, and much to do with CSS and JavaScript, but a now-forgotten marketing genius coined the term, which has persevered even to the present day.

Competing standards

In order to make DHTML possible, the browsers needed to extend their JavaScript capabilities. In the past, Web developers could access only form fields, links, and images, but now it became mandatory to allow access to layers, too, so that they could be moved across the browser window. A DOM upgrade was necessary.

Unfortunately, in those days no specification existed for the improvement of JavaScript. Worse, both Netscape and Microsoft were trying to get a decisive advantage over the other, and therefore deliberately created totally incompatible DOM extensions. Both hoped that their DOM would become the new standard and the other DOM would be relegated to the ash heap of history.

Thus the proprietary DOMs (also known as "intermediate DOMs," since they came between Netscape 3's and W3C's DOMs) came into being. Netscape 4 supported the `document.layers` DOM, while Explorer supported (and still supports) the `document.all` DOM. They worked quite differently, but in the end Explorer's implementation was closer than Netscape's to the eventual W3C DOM, as well as easier to use.

> **DOCUMENT.LAYERS AND DOCUMENT.ALL: FORGET THEM**
>
> This book does not treat the intermediate DOMs because Netscape and Explorer 4 have all but disappeared. Nonetheless, you'll occasionally encounter these DOMs in older scripts. If you do, you can safely remove them and substitute modern W3C DOM calls, as explained in Chapter 8.

Managing these competing DOMs was the main challenge for Web developers during the Browser Wars. If you wanted to move a layer across the browser window—any Web developer's fantasy in those days—you had to write separate scripts to accommodate Netscape 4's and Explorer 4's DOMs and event models, as well as a bit of code that made sure older browsers would not try to execute either script.

Some Web developers thought this was great fun; others complained about a certain lack of standardization.

The first fat phase

Thanks to these new features, the client could now handle significant amounts of interaction. Animations, show/hide scripts, and other eye candy became possible overnight, and in the hands of a competent interaction designer these tricks could help users make more sense of a site and take more actions before being forced to load another page. Unfortunately, competent interaction designers were thin on the ground.

The fat model gained adherents, who began to redefine JavaScript's purpose. From a thin, simple language that could do a few tricks, it became a much more comprehensive construct that allowed developers to create true single-page interfaces.

Unfortunately, all this activity did not lead to the revolution promised by ecstatic gurus. Although a few experiments were interesting, most interfaces and libraries only offered variations on the moving layer and the dropdown menu.

JavaScript's redefined purpose was all about technology, and not about usability. This is a recurring theme in JavaScript history. Eight years later, we see essentially the same thing happening in JavaScript's next fat phase.

Browser Peace

Microsoft came out with Explorer 5 in 1999. It supported quite decent CSS, and the new W3C DOM standard. In contrast, Netscape 4 died, despite desperate last-resort attempts from both its parent company and Web developers to alleviate its suffering. Roughly at the same time, JavaScript's first fat phase broke down into its component parts: a bit of JavaScript and a lot of hot air.

This double demise of Netscape 4 and JavaScript's first fat phase allowed Explorer to win the Browser Wars and made room for the CSS revolution and a new way of thinking about Web development.

The CSS revolution

At the tail end of the Browser Wars, a group of concerned Web developers united in the Web Standards Project (WaSP). Their mission was to increase the standards awareness and compatibility of the various browsers and of Web developers themselves.

Back then JavaScript stood for all that was wrong with the old way of making Web sites. There was no standard; the average JavaScript-"improved" site was bloated, more likely than not worked only in one browser, and didn't consider accessibility at all. A fundamental re-think was necessary.

For those reasons among others, the WaSP, and Web developers sympathizing with its goals, focused on CSS. Many Web developers were tired of the hacks and workarounds that the Browser Wars era had given rise to and desperately wanted to clean the slate. CSS, and not JavaScript, gave them the best chance to radically break with the past.

The second thin phase

When the first fat phase of JavaScript ended, interest in the language dwindled, and its purpose became rather hazy. Some developers reverted to the pre-Browser Wars form validation/mouseover school of thought; others continued to churn out fat (not to say obese) interfaces that pleased nobody; and many participants in the CSS revolution excluded JavaScript totally.

History could have proceeded differently from this point. Explorer 5.0 was already available, and it supported large swaths of the W3C DOM, as well as the XMLHttpRequest object that has come to play such a vital role in JavaScript's second fat phase. But fat clients had gone out of fashion and simply stopped evolving.

A new start

From about 2003 onwards, a few pioneers began to write JavaScript in a new style that was heavily influenced by the ideas of the CSS revolution. For the first time it was tightly embedded in a comprehensive theory of Web development, and the identification and solving of accessibility issues was taken seriously.

{ ENHANCING MARKUP WITH JAVASCRIPT

One of the prime examples of this new coding style is Simon Willison's 2003 article "Enhancing Structural Markup with JavaScript" at http://www.sitepoint.com/article/structural-markup-javascript.

The example scripts are extremely, almost laughably, simple, but that's the whole point of this coding style. It doesn't focus on large amounts of code, but on close cooperation with the HTML structural layer, and thus on Web standards and accessibility. }

The resulting scripts were thin, and mostly concerned themselves with subtly enhancing HTML pages and adding light touches of functionality. If the browser does not support JavaScript, little is lost except for a bit of usability. This coding style is known as *unobtrusive scripting*, and we'll discuss it in detail in Chapter 2.

Unobtrusive scripting didn't immediately conquer the world. In progressive Web-development circles, JavaScript still had a bad name for being inaccessible, while developers of Browser Wars-style bloatware were mostly unaware of the new approach.

The second fat phase

Then JavaScript's second fat phase started with a big bang. One article crystallized slumbering technical and usability notions by showing that modern techniques allow the creation of a single-page interface that silently loads little chunks of data from the server.

The article was a resounding success, which in itself indicates that people were ready, even eager, to start a new fat phase of JavaScript use. And it's true: a site can become much, much more usable if a few smart scripts make sure that one single page contains everything the user needs and allows her to take all actions she wants. Thus JavaScript's purpose was again redefined. Fat clients became fashionable overnight.

The Ajax wave brought new blood into the JavaScript community—an infusion of people from other disciplines, most importantly the server-side languages, with fundamentally different ways of looking at JavaScript.

{
AJAX

Jesse James Garrett's article "Ajax: A New Approach to Web Applications" started the Ajax hype. It can be found at http://www.adaptivepath.com/publications/essays/archives/000385.php.
}

1C

These developers are interpreting the purpose of JavaScript in different ways. Put (too) simply, traditional Web developers heavily influenced by the CSS revolution create thin, accessible JavaScripts in spaghetti-code, while "hard programmers" coming from server-side development create fat, inaccessible Ajax clients in impeccably object-oriented code.

In some respects Ajax resembles DHTML too closely for comfort. Accessibility, for instance, is hardly an issue for many Ajax applications. And the hype tends to concentrate on technical issues (how Ajax?), while usability and interaction issues (why Ajax?) remain underreported. Finally, bloatware libraries (called "frameworks" nowadays) are on the rise again.

Fortunately, there has been one significant change since the first fat phase: browser vendors and JavaScript developers agree that standards are there to be followed. Although browser problems will always exist, the deliberate incompatibilities that characterized the Browser Wars era have gone.

What's next?

At the time of writing, the Ajax hype is still running at full speed. Nonetheless I believe that it will end just as DHTML did: people will simply lose interest and it will fall apart into a bit of JavaScript and a lot of hot air—though I don't know when this will happen.

{ **134 AJAX FRAMEWORKS AND COUNTING**

A May 2006 count revealed that there were no less than 134 Ajax frameworks available. Although some view this state of affairs as proving Ajax's health, personally I feel that it means the hype has gone over the top. Who needs 134 programs that do essentially the same thing?

http://ajaxian.com/archives/134-ajax-frameworks-and-counting }

JavaScript will swing back to a thin phase in which its purpose is again redefined and large-scale solutions make place for smaller, simpler scripts.

Of course, in due time this third thin phase will be followed by a third fat phase, in which an as-yet-uninvented acronym will and redefine JavaScript's purpose for the sixth time.

This movement between fat and thin phases seems to be one of the few "laws" of JavaScript history. Can we break these cycles somehow? Essentially that's only possible if everyone would agree to a single purpose for JavaScript.

Therefore I hope that by the time the third fat phase comes around, JavaScript developers, including those coming from "hard" programming backgrounds, will have learned to look beyond cool code and slick libraries/frameworks, and will base their actions on the context their scripts run in: standards-compliant, accessible Web pages.

Context

JAVASCRIPT IS USED in the context of a Web page. This is obvious, but it has a few consequences that haven't always been properly appreciated. JavaScript is embedded in an environment that also uses HTML and CSS, and in which usability and accessibility are essential elements. After all, a script must add something useful to a site, and the site must continue to work when JavaScript is disabled or entirely absent.

This chapter—in fact, my entire approach to JavaScript programming—is heavily influenced by the standards-compliance CSS revolution that has changed Web development. Therefore it's fitting to start this chapter with a quick summary of the CSS revolution and its impact on JavaScript.

A: The CSS revolution

As we saw in 1C, in 1998 (when Netscape and Explorer 4 couldn't agree about anything), a group of concerned Web developers united in the Web Standards Project (WaSP), to do something about the ludicrous proprietary elements of JavaScript and to promote the use of CSS for defining the presentation of Web sites. Their main message was "Follow the standards," and they aimed this message at both browser vendors and Web developers.

At first, WaSP and its sympathizers concentrated on promoting CSS. There were various reasons for this, the most important being that using CSS in Website creation formed the clearest break with the past. JavaScript didn't really enter the equation yet, both because CSS was enough of a challenge to occupy the best minds in Web-development land for years, and because back in 1998 the average JavaScript was badly written, badly thought out, and completely inaccessible.

ABOUT WASP

A quote from their site: "The Web Standards Project is a grassroots coalition fighting for standards which ensure simple, affordable access to Web technologies for all."

The great standardization battles have been fought and largely won, but there are plenty of details that still have to be worked out. For that reason, WaSP has created a number of task forces that focus on specific areas, for instance Education, Dreamweaver, Microsoft, Accessibility, and DOM Scripting. I am a member of that last task force.

Visit WaSP's site at http://www.webstandards.org to find out what you can do for the standards movement.

2A

Besides, it was relatively easy to get browser vendors to start working on their CSS implementation because it was a new technology that was not yet weighed down by millions of implementations on millions of sites. In contrast, JavaScript was hampered by the countless existing implementations of the browser-specific `document.layers` and `document.all` DOMs we briefly discussed in 1C. CSS offered the possibility of a clean slate.

One of the drawbacks of this focus on CSS was that, in the minds of some standards supporters, JavaScript became equated with "inaccessible." You'll still encounter this misconception every now and then, even though, as we'll see later in this chapter, JavaScript and accessibility can co-exist in harmony, as long as you take some precautions.

Unobtrusive scripting

In 2002, Stuart Langridge coined the term "unobtrusive scripting," which represented the first serious attempt to embed JavaScript in the new theory of CSS-based, standards-compliant Web sites.

An unobtrusive script should have all of the following traits:

- It should be usable, i.e., it should confer a definite usability benefit on the site.
- It should be accessible, i.e., if JavaScript doesn't work, the page should remain readable and understandable, although the loss of some usability is inevitable.

{
UNOBTRUSIVE DHTML AND THE
POWER OF UNORDERED LISTS

Read Stuart's original article at http://www.kryogenix.org/code/browser/aqlists/.
}

- It should be easy to implement; typically, a Web developer has only to include the script itself and add a JavaScript hook in the document, and the script works. We'll discuss JavaScript hooks in 4B.

- It should be separate; it resides in its own .js file instead of being scattered through the HTML.

In theory the first idea has been present since JavaScript's birth, but it has usually been disregarded by programmers eager to show off JavaScript's capabilities. Never mind if these capabilities don't confer a usability benefit—they're *cool*!

The other three ideas were new. Accessibility and JavaScript were generally held to be mutually exclusive, and most old-school JavaScript developers decided that their applications were too advanced to ever become accessible. That's nonsense, of course, but it is powerful nonsense that has held JavaScript in thrall for far too many years. We'll discuss JavaScript and accessibility in 2E.

Ease of implementation requires JavaScript hooks, and they became possible only with the advent of the W3C DOM. This was the sole idea that was new for technical rather than psychological reasons. See 4B for more information.

Separation, lastly, was an idea borrowed from the CSS revolution. If you should separate your HTML and CSS, it's logical to separate your JavaScript from both of them, too. Before we can discuss the three kinds of separation, we first have to study what we're going to separate.

The three layers

A Web page consists of three layers (and yes, these are the ones that need to be separated from each other):

1. HTML structure.

2. CSS presentation.

3. JavaScript behavior.

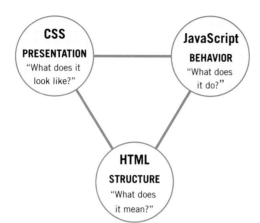

2A

FIGURE 2.1
The three layers of a Web page. The HTML structural layer is the required basis, and the CSS presentation and JavaScript behavior layers are built on top of it.

The HTML structural layer is the most basic part of the page. The HTML tags form the structure of the page and give meaning to its content. For instance, if a certain text is marked up with an <h1>, it's a header and should be treated as such. Browsers (or, more generally, user agents—programs that interpret HTML) are expected to distinguish this header from the surrounding normal text, for instance by displaying it in bold and in a larger font, or by pronouncing it louder or slower. Once you've created structurally correct HTML, you can be reasonably certain that most user agents, hence most users, will recognize a header as a header.

The purpose of the CSS presentation layer is to define how your HTML should be presented. CSS allows you to specify colors, fonts, leading, and other typographical elements, as well as the general layout of the page, for instance, "The navigation block goes next to the content block."

The JavaScript behavior layer adds interactivity to an HTML/CSS page. As soon as you want something to happen when the user mouses over an HTML element, you need JavaScript to implement the effect.

Every Web page needs an HTML structural layer—without HTML, there is no Web page. However, the CSS and JavaScript layers are optional. Old, obscure, or unusual browsers may not support CSS and/or JavaScript, in which case one or both layers may go missing—the presentation or behavior instructions are never executed.

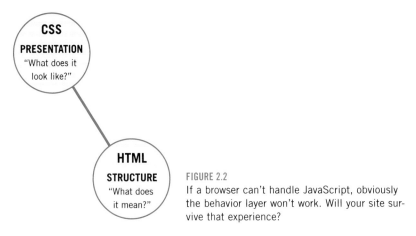

FIGURE 2.2

If a browser can't handle JavaScript, obviously the behavior layer won't work. Will your site survive that experience?

The consequence of this state of affairs is obvious. Any site must be able to survive the demise of the behavior layer (or the presentation layer, but that's a much rarer occurrence). In other words, a site may not totally rely on JavaScript, but must remain accessible when JavaScript doesn't work. We'll get back to this in 2E.

Separation of concerns

Another point raised by the division of client-side code into three layers is the separation of concerns. In general, it's best to manage each of the three layers separately. At the most basic level, this is done by making sure of the following:

- The HTML is structural, not too complex, and makes sense without CSS and JavaScript.
- The CSS presentation layer and the JavaScript behavior layer reside in separate .css and .js files.

Separating concerns makes for easy maintenance. When you use separate CSS and JavaScript files, it's easy to link to these files from all pages in your site. This has obvious maintenance advantages: if you open the .css file and change, say, the font size from 12px to 0.8em, this change will immediately be propagated to all HTML pages that link to that .css file.

Besides, separation allows you to change the entire CSS presentation layer to give your site a new design, without having to recode either the HTML structural or the JavaScript behavior layer.

The three separations

As you see, separating concerns makes your site's code cleaner and easier to maintain. In the next section we'll discuss the gory details of the three separations:

- Separation of presentation and structure (CSS and HTML);
- Separation of behavior and structure (JavaScript and HTML);
- Separation of behavior and presentation (JavaScript and CSS).

All three influence the way we should write JavaScript.

B: Separation of presentation and structure

The basic idea of separation of presentation and structure is to make sure the HTML defines structure, and only structure, and that all presentation is defined in a separate CSS file. No more `<font>` tags or presentational tables in your HTML! If you need to specify a font or a grid, do so in CSS.

A discussion of the separation of CSS and HTML seems to have no place in a JavaScript book. Nonetheless, there are a few aspects of this separation that influence the way you should code JavaScript.

CSS modification

JavaScript allows you to modify CSS; i.e., you can make a link red in the CSS, and later on overrule this style with JavaScript and make the link green. Sometimes this is quite useful, since style changes allow you to pull the user's eyes to the HTML element you need her to focus on—an error message, for instance.

We'll discuss the ins and outs of CSS modification in Chapter 9, and we'll see that CSS modification becomes much harder without a properly separated CSS presentation layer.

As we'll see in 9E, the changing of the `className` of an element is usually the best way to effect CSS modification. For instance, if Form Validation finds a user error in a form field, it changes the CSS class of that field:

```
// obj is the form field
obj.className += ' errorMessage';
// in CSS
input.errorMessage {
    border: 1px solid #cc0000;
}
```

The point is that this trick only works if you have properly separated presentation and structure. The class errorMessage has to be defined in CSS in order for the style to change, and that in turn is only possible (or, at least, workable) if you started out with a proper CSS presentation layer.

Modify structure or presentation?

JavaScript allows you to change the presentation of your Web site and also allows you to change the structure of your HTML document—in fact, most example scripts do so.

Usually it's clear whether a script should change presentation or structure. Sandwich Picker, for instance, is all about moving the `<tr>`s that contain sandwiches the user selected to the correct table—the search results table at the top of the page or the order table just below it. This is an example of a pure structure change.

XMLHTTP Speed Meter contains an animation; it changes the CSS `width` of the element holding the gray background image, while the document structure stays the same. This is an example of a pure presentation change.

In a few cases, though, you can change either the HTML or the CSS. Usable Forms is the clearest example. The purpose of that script is to hide form fields until the user needs them. You can hide form fields in two ways: make them invisible by CSS (`display: none`) or remove them entirely from the document structure.

The user doesn't care which of the two we choose; in either case the form fields appear only when they're needed. Nonetheless there are a few differences between the two methods.

First, I feel that changing forms in response to user actions is a change in structure, not in presentation. The form fields should not just be hidden from view, but should be entirely removed from the document. Once the user has checked or unchecked several form fields, and the script has reacted by showing or hiding form fields, every visitor will eventually see the unique document structure he or she needs.

Of course this is a theoretical consideration, and you should feel free to disagree with me, even though I don't think a similar case can be made for hiding the form fields by CSS.

There's a practical component, too. When a form is submitted, the browser creates name/value pairs for all form fields, and sends them to the server. If we hide the unnecessary form fields by means of CSS, the fields themselves are still part of the form—they're just hidden. Therefore they, too, are sent to the server, even though that's not necessary.

Conversely, if, as in Usable Forms, these form fields are entirely removed from the document structure (hence also from the HTML `<form>` tag), they aren't sent to the server, for the simple reason that they aren't part of the form at the moment it is submitted.

I found these two reasons sufficient to make Usable Forms operate by changing document structure instead of presentation. Although you may disagree with me, you should spend some time thinking about such issues when you encounter them.

C: Separation of behavior and structure

Separation of behavior and structure is easy to understand: just don't put any JavaScript code in your HTML page. This takes two steps:

1. Put all JavaScript functions in a separate .js file that's linked to from all HTML pages that need it.

2. Remove all event handlers from the HTML and put them in the same .js file.

Functions in separate file

JavaScript code belongs in the .js file, and not in HTML files.

Therefore, this is wrong:

```
<script type="text/javascript">
function doAllKindsOfNiftyThings()
{
    // JavaScript code
}
</script>
</head>
<body>
<h1>My HTML page</h1>
[etc.]
```

But this is right:

```
<script type="text/javascript" src="nifty.js"></script>
</head>
<body>
<h1>My HTML page</h1>
[etc.]
```

```
// in nifty.js
function doAllKindsOfNiftyThings()
{
    // JavaScript code
}
```

We'll discuss the technical aspects of <script> tags in 4D.

Remove event handlers from HTML

The second step in separating behavior and structure is to move all JavaScript calls within your HTML to the separate .js file. In fact, 99% of the JavaScript code in HTML pages consists of inline event handlers.

Here, the handlers are in the HTML, where they don't belong:

X
```
<a href="home.html"
    onMouseOver="mOv('home')"
    onMouseOut="mOut('home')">Home</a>
```

Instead, define them in the separate .js file:

```
<a href="home.html">Home</a>

// in separate .js file
var nav = document.getElementById('navigation');
var navLinks = nav.getElementsByTagName('a');
for (var i=0;i<navLinks.length;i++)
{
    navLinks[i].onmouseover = [code];
    navLinks[i].onmouseout = [code];
}
```

The script takes the element with id="navigation" (a <ul>, for instance) and accesses all of its links, then assigns onmouseover and onmouseout event handlers to them one by one.

> {
> ### HOOKS AND EVENT-HANDLER REGISTRATION
>
> In order to fully understand the code on the previous page, you have to understand JavaScript hooks—the hook here is the ID that says "deploy the behavior here"—and the various ways of registering event handlers. We'll discuss hooks in 4B and event-handler registration in 7C.
>
> All example scripts separate behavior and structure, so you can take a look at the way they define event handlers if you prefer to study some practical examples right away.
> }

The javascript: pseudo-protocol

Occasionally you'll see javascript: pseudo-protocol links like the following one:

 `<a href="javascript:doAllKindsOfNiftyThings()">Do Nifty!</a>`

This complicated and dirty code is secretly meant as an onclick event handler: when the user clicks on this link, we want to execute doAllKindsOfNiftyThings(). Therefore you should remove the javascript: call from the link and replace it with an onclick event handler in the separate .js file:

```
<a href="somepage.html" id="nifty">Do Nifty!</a>

// in separate .js file
document.getElementById('nifty').onclick =
doAllKindsOfNiftyThings;
```

As to the href, it should contain either a URL that noscript users can follow, or the entire link should be generated in JavaScript. We'll get back to this in 2F.

{ **NOSCRIPT USERS**

When I talk about "noscript users" I mean those users whose browser, for whatever reason, does not support enough JavaScript to use a scripted interface. This may be because their browser doesn't support JavaScript at all, or because their browser supports some JavaScript, but not enough. Netscape 4 is a good example of the latter category. }

2D

D: Separation of behavior and presentation

The third separation, that of behavior and presentation, is unfortunately much more complex than the previous two. Don't expect clear answers in this section; this separation is one of the areas of modern JavaScripting that has not yet crystallized into a set of easily learned and understood rules. Right now we have more questions than answers.

The basic question is: which effects should you define in CSS and which ones in JavaScript? Although the answer might seem obvious—presentation goes in the CSS and behavior in the JavaScript—there are gray areas where CSS and JavaScript overlap, and where it's unclear if a certain effect is presentation or behavior.

Dropdown Menu—:hover or mouseover/out?

Dropdown Menu's purpose is to show submenus when the user mouses over a main menu item and hide them when the user mouses out again, and since time immemorial (1997, to be exact) we've used JavaScript to obtain this effect. Back then there were no other options; if you wanted a dropdown menu you needed JavaScript.

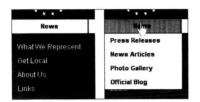

FIGURE 2.3
Dropdown Menu. When the user mouses over the News link, the submenu becomes visible. Do we code this in JavaScript or in CSS?

However, you can now create this effect in CSS, without any need for JavaScript:

```
<li><a href="#">News</a>
  <ul>
    <li><a href="#">Press Releases</a></li>
    <li><a href="#">News Articles</a>    </li>
    <li><a href="#">Photo Gallery</a></li>
    <li><a href="#">Official Blog</a></li>
  </ul>
</li>

// in .css file
li ul {display: none;}
li:hover ul {display: block}
```

Any `<ul>` inside an `<li>`—in other words, any submenu—is initially hidden (`display: none`). When the user mouses over the `<li>`, though (`li:hover`), the submenu becomes visible (`display: block`).

Which solution is preferable? Most people will opt for JavaScript over CSS because Explorer 6 and earlier do not support `li:hover`.

Nonetheless, this eminently practical consideration does not answer the fundamental question. Let's for a moment suppose that all browsers support `:hover` perfectly in all circumstances, and that the CSS and JavaScript solutions are therefore equal in terms of browser compatibility. Which do we use?

The CSS code is a lot simpler than the JavaScript code, and that's of course an advantage. As we'll see in 7H, the JavaScript mouseout event, especially, is very obnoxious and needs a firm and masterful hand to keep it from playing up. In contrast, the CSS `:hover` selector just...works.

> **{ EVENTS EQUIVALENT TO :HOVER }**
>
> The JavaScript events that are equivalents to the CSS :hover selector are *not* mouseover and mouseout, but the Microsoft proprietary events mouseenter and mouseleave, which are available in Explorer but no other browser. See 7B.

In addition, the CSS code continues to work when JavaScript is disabled. Unfortunately, this does not necessarily mean that the CSS variant is more accessible than the JavaScript one.

Some people use a keyboard instead of a mouse. They use keystrokes (usually Tab) to put the focus on HTML elements (usually links), and then press Enter to activate the focused element. These keyboard users will not be able to use a CSS dropdown menu, since `li:hover` is a pure mouse selector that does not react to the keyboard focus. Besides, it's impossible to focus on `<li>`s— keyboard focus works only on links, buttons, and form fields.

In contrast, the JavaScript can be made to accommodate keyboard users, as we'll see in 7G. Therefore a CSS dropdown menu isn't inherently more accessible than the JavaScript version. Keyboard users will vastly prefer the JavaScript version.

In fact, both variants have their own unique problems, and from an accessibility standpoint neither is clearly superior. Accessibility alone doesn't help us to choose between CSS and JavaScript.

Let's take a more high-level theoretical perspective. Are dropdown menus presentation or behavior? The effect takes place only after a user action, which would argue for it being a behavior. On the other hand, the effect is about presenting the submenus, which argues for it being presentational.

Although personally I tend to lean towards the behavioral answer, the problem allows for more than one interpretation, and every Web developer should find his or her own solution to this theoretical conundrum—or just ignore it.

In conclusion, the single point on which a CSS :hover solution scores distinctly better than a JavaScript mouseover/out solution is the amount of code you need to write and maintain. Is this enough to say that the CSS solution is always better than the JavaScript one? It still boils down to a personal decision.

The same effect vs. a similar effect

In a dropdown menu, you want to deploy the same effect on any <li> that's eligible for it. "If this <li> has a nested <ul> (i.e., a submenu), show it when the user has his mouse over the <li>." As we saw, this rule is easy to summarize in two lines of CSS:

```
li ul {display: none}
li:hover ul {display: block}
```

The CSS is so simple because all <li>s are treated *the same*. Keep that in mind.

Now let's take a different example: a mouseover. When the user mouses over an image, the image changes, and when she mouses out, the image changes back to its original state.

Until today, all mouseover effects have been written in JavaScript, which is largely a matter of tradition. A JavaScript mouseover effect has been an all-time favorite since its inception in 1996, and it's one of the most copied scripts on the WWW. Since there are already a gazillion example scripts, nobody has ever ported it to CSS.

Nonetheless, in theory it's possible to create a CSS mouseover effect:

```
<a href="somewhere.html" id="somewhere">Somewhere</a>
<a href="somewhere_else.html" id="somewhere_else">Somewhere else</a>
a#somewhere {
    background-image: url(pix/somewhere.gif);
}
a#somewhere_else {
    background-image: url(pix/somewhere_else.gif);
}
```

```
a:hover#somewhere,
a:focus#somewhere,
a:active#somewhere {
    background-image: url(pix/somewhere_hover.gif);
}
a:hover#somewhere_else,
a:focus#somewhere_else,
a:active#somewhere_else {
    background-image: url(pix/somewhere_else_hover.gif);
}
```

You'll notice that every mouseover effect needs two CSS declarations—one for the normal state and one for the mouseover state. The reason is simple: every link has its unique normal and mouseover image, and these unique images need to be defined in the CSS.

In this case we're not deploying the same effect on all links, but a *similar* one. All links change images when the user mouses over them, but every link needs its own set of images. For every link we add to the document we have to create two new CSS declarations, and we have to do that manually. In fact, a pure CSS mouseover quickly becomes a maintenance hell, especially when you use dozens of links on your site.

This is, in fact, a general rule. CSS is extremely efficient when you want to deploy exactly the same effect on a number of elements, as in the dropdown example, but extremely inefficient when you want to deploy a similar effect on a number of elements, as in the mouseover example.

JavaScript allows you to write a script that can manage mouseover on an unlimited amount of links:

```
<a href="somewhere.html"
id="somewhere"><img src="pix/somewhere.gif" /></a>
<a href="somewhere_else.html"
id="somewhere_else"><img src="pix/somewhere_else.gif" /> </a>

function initMouseOvers() {
```

```
var links = document.getElementsByTagName('img');
for (var i=0;i<links.length;i++) {
        var moSrc = links[i].src.substring(0, ➡
        links[i].src.lastIndexOf('.'));
        moSrc += '_hover.gif';
        links[i].moSrc = moSrc;
        links[i].origSrc = links[i].src;
        links[i].onmouseover = function () {
                this.src = this.moSrc;
        }
        links[i].onmouseout = function () {
                this.src = this.origSrc;
        }
    }
}
```

Initially this solution requires more lines than a CSS solution, but this is more than offset by its versatility. If you need another mouseover, you simply add a link to the document, and it works.

Therefore, when creating similar-but-not-quite-the-same effects such as mouseovers, JavaScript is the most efficient solution. This is something to keep in mind when you're forced to choose between CSS and JavaScript.

Right now it's not possible to reach a definite conclusion about the separation of behavior and presentation. More research is necessary, and for now I'd like to ask you to spend a few minutes of thought on this problem whenever you encounter it—and if you find a good general rule, publish it! Maybe you'll lead the way in discovering the principles of the third separation.

E: Accessibility overview

I've already mentioned accessibility many times, usually coupled with some snide remarks about the general lack of it in JavaScript development. It's time for a more formal overview, as well as an accessibility test of the example scripts.

What is accessibility?

Accessibility means that your pages remain accessible to anyone, under all circumstances, especially when the user suffers from a condition she cannot change, for instance diminished eyesight, or has a browser that does not support (sufficient) JavaScript.

What does "remain accessible" mean in a JavaScript context? It means that the user must be able to read the content of the site, use the navigation, and perform common operations like submitting a form. Nothing less, but also nothing more.

Making every site perfectly accessible in all situations is rather a tall order, and we'll see that at the time of writing it is not yet possible because of some tricky technical issues with screen readers. Nonetheless, we should make a start, and since we are able to solve some accessibility problems, we should do so.

Noscript

The clearest accessibility problem, the one that everybody's able to name, is that some browsers will not support (sufficient) JavaScript. Your carefully crafted scripts don't work in these browsers, and their users will see an unscripted page.

Priority One of writing accessible scripts is, therefore, to make sure that the page functions without JavaScript. We'll discuss the gory details later, but first I'd like to point out two less well-known but still serious accessibility problems.

No mouse

Some users don't use a mouse, but instead navigate the Web through keystrokes. Some use the keyboard, but others might use widgets like on-screen keyboards, or devices that emulate a keyboard.

Their reasons for using keystrokes instead of mouse gestures may vary. I myself occasionally use the keyboard for some quick operations, and this is obviously my own choice. I could reach for the mouse, but sometimes I'm too lazy to do so.

Other users, though, may be forced to use the keyboard continuously for reasons they're not able to change. The most likely scenario is that these users are (partially) disabled in their hands and cannot perform the rather subtle movements necessary to guide the mouse. Keystrokes offer a good alternative for these users—except when a JavaScript developer has forgotten to take them into account.

Usually these users' browser is able to execute advanced scripts, and the user is able to see the results when they appear on the computer screen. Thus there's really no problem, except that the scripts don't react to keyboard input.

In order to make your scripts keyboard-compatible, you should define extra events in addition to normal mouse events. For instance, if you use a mouseover event you should also use a focus event, since without a mouse no mouseover event will ever take place. We'll discuss this specialized area of accessibility in 7B when we treat the available JavaScript events.

Screen readers

Some people cannot use a normal browser. Typically, these are blind or severely sight-impaired people who simply cannot read anything from a computer screen. Instead, they need a program that reads the content of the page out loud. These programs are known as screen readers.

JavaScript developers used to think that screen readers were essentially noscript browsers, and therefore accessibility for screen-reader users was an extension of accessibility for noscript users. As long as the page works without JavaScript, blind users would not suffer from JavaScript-related problems (though plenty of other problems like missing alt attributes still remained).

Unfortunately, this is a myth. Most screen readers are programs that run on top of an existing browser—usually Explorer, sometimes Mozilla. Since they use a normal browser to get their data, they also support JavaScript. When the underlying browser encounters a script, it tries to execute it normally.

{ **ACCESS MATTERS**

To delve deeper into the obscure realms of JavaScript support in screen readers, visit http://www.access-matters.com/. On this site, Bob Easton publishes the results of the research he conducted along with JavaScript/accessibility specialists Mike Stenhouse, James Edwards, and Derek Featherstone.

At the time of writing it's the only site about this subject that actually talks about the technical nuts and bolts instead of general principles. }

This seems to be good news. If screen readers also support JavaScript, there's no problem, right? Unfortunately, there are two very serious ones: the linear nature of screen readers, and their chaotic events support.

A screen reader offers only linear access to a page. When a sighted user with a graphic browser visits a site, she gets a quick overview of all possibilities simply by looking at it. The bunch of odd-color bits on the left will probably be the main navigation, the text in the middle is obviously the main content, etc. Thus the user can quickly determine which parts of the page she needs, and interact only with those parts. In addition, as soon as a script changes the document structure or presentation, her eye is drawn to this change and she can evaluate its meaning.

Not so with screen-reader users. A screen reader reads the page from top to bottom, usually in source code order. This is a severe problem to modern JavaScript. Even if all screen readers supported JavaScript perfectly (which they don't, not by a long shot), how would we alert their users to the fact that (parts of) the page have changed, especially when the screen reader has already read those parts?

Take Form Validation, in a hypothetical screen reader that supports perfect JavaScript. Screen readers allow their users to fill out forms and to submit them. Since JavaScript works fine, Form Validation runs when the user activates the Submit button, and if it finds errors, the script places error messages next to faulty form fields, alerts "Errors have been found," and halts the form submission.

The problem is that a screen-reader user may (usually but not always!) hear the alert and get an inkling of the problem, but since the reader has already read past the form fields themselves, he won't hear the error messages themselves.

To help screen-reader users, Form Validation scrolls back to the start of the form:

[Form Validation, lines 100-103]

```
<form id="startOfForm">
if (!validForm) {
    alert("Errors have been found");
    location.hash = '#startOfForm';
}
```

This is useful to both sighted and blind users; both groups will appreciate being sent back to the start of the form so that they can mend the errors of their ways. Nonetheless, it's important to note that this feature is a nice extra for a sighted user, but an absolute necessity for a screen-reader user.

Screen readers and events

Unfortunately, the events support of screen readers is extremely confused and chaotic. In theory you'd expect them to support interface events like focus and blur, but not mouse events like mouseover and mouseout, because screen-reader users use a keyboard (or an equivalent device) to give input.

{ SCREEN-READER EVENT SUPPORTS

The inimitable James Edwards has taken the time to actually test event support in some common screen readers. You can see the results of these tests at http://www.access-matters.com/results-for-javascript-part-2-navigating-forms/.

As soon as you view the data table you'll notice that "chaotic" is the best word to describe their support. Even if a certain screen reader supports a certain event under certain conditions, it may not always support that event. }

2E

Unfortunately, some (but not all) screen-reader vendors have seen fit to include mouse events anyway. The reason is, of course, that most sites use only mouse events because their creators never seriously considered keyboard accessibility. Screen-reader vendors want their programs to treat these pages correctly, too, and therefore added mouse event support. Of course this creates serious problems when an accessibility-aware Web developer wants to carefully separate screen readers from graphic browsers to give them special treatment.

I'm deliberately not going to give details; they'd just confuse you (and me), and screen-reader event support is likely to change when new versions are released. Suffice it to say that you cannot assume anything about screen-reader event support.

The situation is in fact so bad that I fear accessibility is just not possible in the generation of screen readers current at the time of writing. It was Derek Featherstone who drew the harsh but correct conclusion, "We can deal with JavaScript on or off, but we can't deal with in between," and therefore he feels it's better to ask users of older screen readers to disable JavaScript entirely. If they do, they'll fall back to a noscript page, and that's a situation we can handle.

At the moment, and speaking from the scant knowledge we have about screen-reader JavaScript support, I'm forced to agree with him, albeit reluctantly. Noscript screen readers are far easier to cater to than script-enabled screen readers.

{ **SHOULD USERS OF OLDER SCREEN READERS DISABLE JAVASCRIPT?**

Read Derek Featherstone's argument for yourself at http://www.boxofchocolates.ca/archives/2005/06/12/javascript-and-accessibility. }

Accessibility and usability

This brings us back to our starting point: any Web page should remain accessible when a browser does not support (sufficient) JavaScript. Before treating the practical accessibility of the example scripts, we first have to discuss a few general rules.

We should carefully consider JavaScript's purpose, which, as we saw in Chapter 1, is the addition of an extra layer of usability to a Web site. As soon as JavaScript is disabled, a Web site's usability will suffer—after all, an entire layer disappears. But the absence of this layer should not hamper the page's basic accessibility.

Take Usable Forms. When the script works, it makes sure that users will see certain form fields only when they actually indicate they need them. The "Date of divorce" field will remain hidden until the user indicates he is, in fact, divorced.

When the script does not work, the user sees all form fields he may possibly need. From a usability perspective, this is obviously undesirable: the more form fields the user sees, the more confused or irritated he becomes, and the more likely to decide not to bother with the form at all.

Nonetheless, the page remains perfectly accessible, and I've done my duty as a Web developer. The user is *able* to fill out the form and submit it to the server, even if without my nifty script the process will become more time-consuming and confusing. The user might be less *willing* to fill out the form because it's so huge and confusing, but that's something we can't help. When JavaScript is not supported, usability suffers.

Don't restrict usability

Accessibility should not restrict usability. If you have an excellent idea to increase your site's usability that won't work without JavaScript, use it—just make sure that it's *possible* (not necessarily easy, just bare-bones possible) to use the page without it.

2F

Perfect accessibility does *not* consist of offering exactly equal functionalities to script and noscript users. Sometimes that's flat-out impossible, and at other times the attempt will backfire with a vengeance.

For instance, let's try to create the Usable Forms effect without JavaScript. You could serve a form without the optional fields first, let the user submit it to the server, and send back an extended form with the "Date of divorce" field when your server-side scripts notices the user has checked the "Divorced" radio button. Technically, this could work.

However, from a user-experience point of view, it is far worse than the noscript form we just studied. Although that form may be confusing and is certainly less usable than the scripted version, at least it doesn't confront the user with extra downloads and fields at the moment he thinks he's successfully submitted the form.

In general, it's far better to accept the diminished usability of a noscript page than to try to work around it.

F: Rules of accessibility

Although it's nearly impossible to envision every situation that could hamper a scripted site's usability, I have found a few rules that will help you get the basics right. Don't treat them as the last word on JavaScript and accessibility. This is just a set of rules that will prevent a few of the most common problems. No doubt they'll be appended and amended by a next wave of thought and action, and one or more of these rules will likely misfire in some situations.

Always check these rules by applying your common sense.

Logical HTML

The most obvious way of preserving accessibility in a scripted environment is to make sure that the plain HTML page contains all the bare-bones necessities for successful browsing.

Content, navigation, and important forms should all be hard-coded in your HTML. Thus, whatever happens, any user will be able to access and use them.

Usable Forms is the prime example. When a browser doesn't support JavaScript, the form is nonetheless accessible, because all form fields and labels are hard-coded in the HTML. It's less usable, but as we've seen, that's inevitable.

Hard-coded links have an `href`

Any hard-coded link in your HTML should have an `href` attribute that leads to a useful page or other file. Therefore this is wrong:

☒ `<a href="#" onclick="showPopup('niceimage.jpg')">Nice image!</a>`

When a noscript user clicks on the link, nothing happens, and therefore the page is inaccessible. In addition, we saw in 2C that we shouldn't use inline event handlers any more.

Instead, an unobtrusive JavaScripter does this:

```
<a href="niceimage.jpg" id="nice">Nice image!</a>
document.getElementById('nice').onclick = function () {
    showPopup(this.href);
}
```

Now a noscript user follows the hard-coded `href` attribute, while a script user opens a popup. The site remains accessible, and the behavior is separated from the structure.

Generating content meant for script users

In some cases, generating content in JavaScript makes a site more accessible.

Links that trigger advanced scripts

Suppose you have a link that starts up a nifty Ajax script that fetches content and does other nice usable stuff, but that you don't have an HTML page for the link to lead to. As we've just seen, this is wrong:

☒ `<a href="#" onclick="startUpAjaxStuff()">Commence coolness!</a>`

We can't just apply the previous rule, though. Which page are we going to put in the `href` attribute if there is no obvious noscript equivalent for the Ajax script?

If adding an `href` to a link does not make sense, generate the link by JavaScript:

```
var link = document.createElement('a');
link.href = '#';
link.onclick = startUpAjaxStuff;
var linkText = document.createTextNode('Commence coolness!');
link.appendChild(linkText);
document.body.appendChild(link);
```

Now a noscript user does not see the link at all. That's good, because it wouldn't do anything if she clicked on it, and would just be confusing.

Note that the example script sets the `link.href` to `'#'`, even though we saw that using '#' as a href is generally not a good idea. We need it, though: most browsers define a hyperlink as an `a` element with an `href` attribute.

Fortunately, the previous rule doesn't apply in this situation, since the link is not hard-coded in the HTML, but generated by JavaScript. We can be certain that the user will encounter this link only when his browser supports sufficient JavaScript to also run the onclick event handler. The `href='#'` is therefore allowed.

Hide content in JavaScript

Hiding content is dangerous. In general, you hide content because you've decided the page becomes more usable when you don't show everything immediately. You wait until the user clicks on a link or a header, and start up a script that shows the content.

Without JavaScript, though, the content will never become visible, and the page is inaccessible. If you create a page that hides information until the user activates a script, you should always give the "hide content" commands in JavaScript, not in CSS.

For instance, Usable Forms initially hides all `<tr>`s that have a `rel` attribute. This can be done in CSS, but it's flat-out wrong to do so:

```
tr[rel] {
    display: none;
}
```

If a noscript visitor arrives at your page, he won't see these `<tr>`s and has no way of making them visible. Therefore the page is inaccessible.

Instead, Usable Forms hides the `<tr>`s in JavaScript (in fact, it removes them from the document entirely). If JavaScript is not enabled, they aren't hidden, and overall accessibility is preserved.

Redirecting your users

Occasionally, the best way to deal with an accessibility problem is to create both a script and a noscript version of your site. Although I don't like this solution and try to avoid it, it's nonetheless a trick that has proven its value in practice.

If you use this approach, you should follow two rules. First, the entrance page to your site should be the noscript page. Thus, all browsers, even those that support nothing but HTML, will get a page they can use.

Then, once a browser has arrived at the noscript page, you start a script that checks whether the browser supports your advanced scripts, and, if it does, redirects them to the scripted page using the `replace()` method.

```
<head>
<title>Noscript page</title>
<script type="text/javascript">
var isSupported = [check JavaScript support];
if (isSupported)
    location.replace('scriptpage.html');
</script>
</head>
```

Never ever use `location.href` in such situations. Using `location.href` creates a new entry in the browser's history (which we'll discuss fully in 6C). If the user arrives at the noscript page, she is redirected to the scripted page. Once she presses the Back button, however, she's sent back to the noscript page, where the script promptly fires up and sends her back to the scripted page. The Back button is effectively broken—one of the worst usability sins in existence.

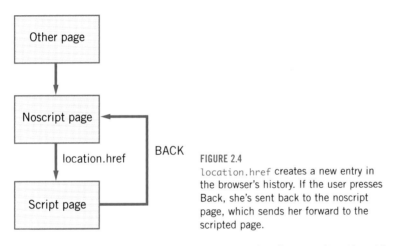

FIGURE 2.4
`location.href` creates a new entry in the browser's history. If the user presses Back, she's sent back to the noscript page, which sends her forward to the scripted page.

`location.replace()` also loads a new page, but it overwrites the old page in the browser's history. When the user presses Back, she's sent to the previous page in the history—the one she was on before entering the noscript page. As far as the user is concerned, the Back button continues to function correctly.

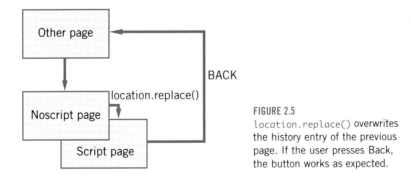

FIGURE 2.5
`location.replace()` overwrites the history entry of the previous page. If the user presses Back, the button works as expected.

Keyboard users

We already saw that keyboard users don't generate mouse events (unless they also use a screen reader). Therefore, you should always define an alternative to mouse events. Sometimes this is simple, for instance, pairing the mouseover event with the focus event; and sometimes it's more difficult, for instance, in a drag-and-drop script, where you'll have to write extra functions in order to cater to keyboard users.

We'll discuss this more fully in 7B.

Clickable items

Even if you create perfectly keyboard-accessible scripts, they are useless if the user cannot focus on the elements on which you've defined event handlers.

Take Dropdown Menus. It uses a mouseover event to trigger the dropdowns, and in accordance with the previous rule I added focus events for keyboard users. However, in order to trigger the focus event, the keyboard user has to be able to focus on the dropdown menus. If that's impossible, the script remains inaccessible.

The only elements that reliably gain keyboard focus in all browsers are links, form fields, and buttons. Therefore, any keyboard-friendly event or script should be set on one of these HTML elements.

Dropdown Menus does so; the focus events are applied to links. Since keyboard users can focus on links, the script remains accessible to them.

The <noscript> tag

Browser vendors realized that Web developers might want to offer special content to users without JavaScript. In order to allow this, they invented the <noscript> tag.

It works like this:

- Browsers that don't support any JavaScript don't know this tag. Since unknown tags are ignored by HTML parsers, these browsers show the content of the tag: the noscript content.

- Browsers that do support JavaScript check if JavaScript is enabled. If it is, they hide the `<noscript>` tag and its content from view; if not, the browser shows the content of the tag.

Unfortunately, the `<noscript>` tag doesn´t play an important role in modern accessibility. Plenty of browsers support antiquated versions of JavaScript, without the W3C DOM, XMLHttpRequest, or other modern goodies. These browsers will not show the content of the `<noscript>` tag because they support some (but not enough) JavaScript. Therefore their users, who should for all practical purposes be treated as noscript users, don't see the scripted interface, but they don't see the noscript extras, either.

Therefore, it's best not to use the `<noscript>` tag at all.

G: The example scripts

After all this theory, it's time to study the usability and accessibility of the example scripts.

Six out of eight example scripts offer significant usability enhancements over the unscripted page, and are therefore, I think, worthwhile to use. We'll treat the remaining two, Dropdown Menus and Site Survey, in due time, and you'll have to form your own opinion about their usability or lack thereof.

Seven out of eight example scripts are accessible, and the remaining one, Edit Style Sheets, doesn't have to be. Unfortunately, I made a few minor mistakes in Sandwich Picker that cause usability problems in the accessible noscript version. I could have removed them while preparing the script for this book, but decided not to because they highlight a few interesting accessibility solutions.

Textarea Maxlength

When the user exceeds the 1250-character maximum length, the counter warns him. In addition, he can see how many characters he's already typed. This is a small usability benefit.

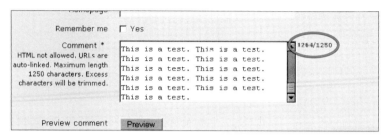

FIGURE 2.6   Textarea Maxlength with script enabled. The counter gives a warning when the user exceeds the maximum length.

If the script doesn't work, it doesn't warn the user. However, right next to the text area there is a text that states the 1250-character maximum length. In theory, a noscript user still has sufficient information. (In practice, users don't read such texts. That's not my problem, though. I've done what I needed to do to make the page accessible.)

Also, I generate the counter by JavaScript, since it would be confusing in the noscript version.

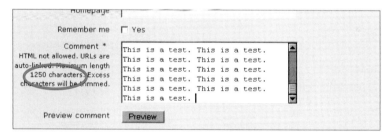

FIGURE 2.7   Textarea Maxlength noscript. The counter is gone, but the user doesn't know it's supposed to be there.

Usable Forms

From a usability perspective, it's a good idea to hide as many form fields as possible until the user indicates she needs them.

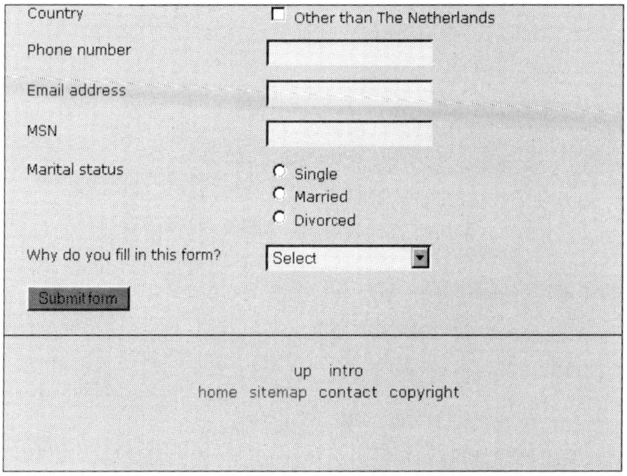

FIGURE 2.8
Usable Forms with
script enabled.
The user sees a
short form.

If the script doesn't work, the user sees the complete form with all fields. That's less usable than the scripted version, but still accessible. In addition, the form creator is allowed to add extra elements with class="accessibility" to the form. These elements are meant for noscript users and should contain useful help texts. If the script runs, it automatically generates an extra style:

```
.accessibility {display: none}
```

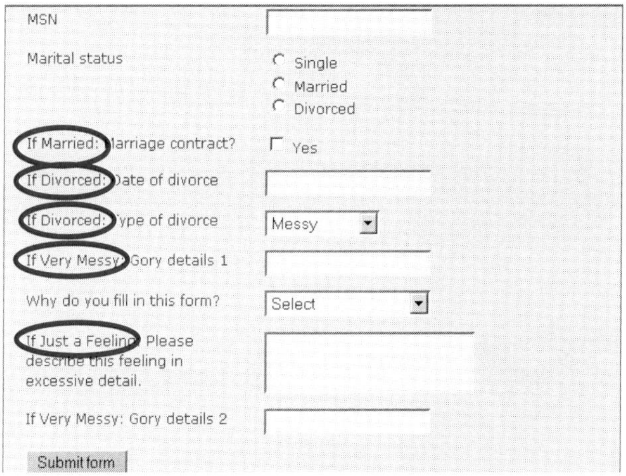

FIGURE 2.9
Usable Forms
noscript. The
user sees all form
fields. Fortunately,
many form fields
have an extra help
text, which is a must
in this confused
jumble.

This style hides the extra elements when the script works.

Form Validation

Validating a form is the oldest JavaScript effect in existence. Thus it's quite likely that a user has encountered it before. As we saw in 1A, this script saves the user a round-trip to the server if she makes a mistake. From a usability perspective that's always good. Then, the error messages are displayed right next to the form fields they apply to, which makes the whole process clear.

If the script doesn't work, the form is not validated. The only solution to this problem is installing a server-side form-validation script. This solution has been general knowledge since the dawn of time, but has always been disregarded.

The form fields contain attributes that define which validations the script should perform on them. The server-side script could use these same definitions.

Dropdown Menu

Are dropdown menus good from a usability point of view? I'm not going to get mixed up in that discussion; I will restrict myself to the observation that they're a golden oldie for which clients frequently ask. Besides, most Web surfers are used, or at least resigned, to them.

FIGURE 2.10 Dropdown Menu with script enabled. Does it make the navigation more usable?

Dropdown Menus offers an extreme example of diminished usability without JavaScript. I carefully crafted the CSS so that the menus would continue to be as user-friendly as possible in the absence of JavaScript, but in the end they remain huge lists of links that are hard to search through. Technically they are accessible—any user can activate any link—but finding the link you want to activate is another story altogether.

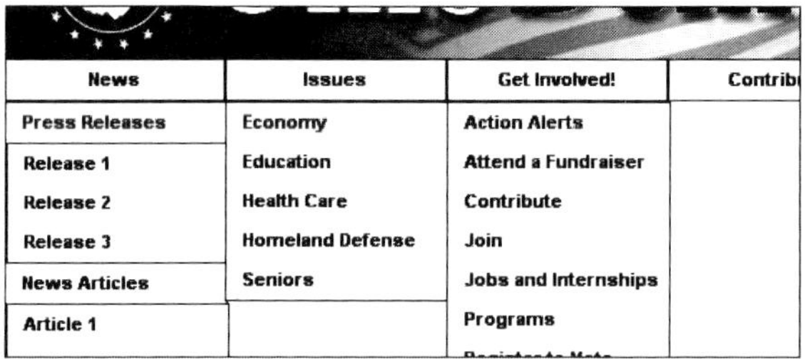

News	Issues	Get Involved!	Contrib
Press Releases	Economy	Action Alerts	
Release 1	Education	Attend a Fundraiser	
Release 2	Health Care	Contribute	
Release 3	Homeland Defense	Join	
News Articles	Seniors	Jobs and Internships	
Article 1		Programs	

FIGURE 2.11   Dropdown Menu noscript. All menus are permanently folded out. Not much usability, but accessibility is preserved.

Edit Style Sheets

This example script isn't meant for the average user. It's a site-administration script for Web masters; therefore, accessibility is not an issue. It's perfectly acceptable to say that all Web masters must use Explorer or Mozilla with JavaScript enabled in order to use the page.

As to usability, it's excellently suited for allowing people who don't know anything about CSS to edit a style sheet. They immediately see the result of their actions, and that's what counts.

Sandwich Picker

From a usability perspective, I consider Sandwich Picker the best script in this book. It's a simple, obvious way of quickly searching through a lot of items (and remember that the page I created for my client held about three times as many sandwiches as the example page I put on my site). Although it was born from necessity—the client didn't have the money for a database-driven solution—I feel that Sandwich Picker can also be used in database-driven search sites to fine-tune the results.

Unfortunately, I made a few errors on the page. Strictly speaking, it is accessible because the user can submit the form and thus order sandwiches—as long as he enters the sandwich names in the text area. Nonetheless, the usability of this noscript version suffers from a few problems.

First, I included a message for noscript users that offered an extra mailto link to get in touch with the site owner. It's correctly implemented: I hard-coded the message in HTML and then hid it by JavaScript, so that it is visible only if JavaScript is not supported. However, since the user can submit the form, this extra message was not really necessary and could confuse noscript users: "Do I use the mail link or the form?"

The second mistake is that I plain forgot to include `<label>` tags, which are a must for any accessible form.

The third mistake is even more insidious: I coded the form fields next to the sandwich names in exactly the wrong way. I had two other options, either of which would have resulted in better usability for the noscript page, but I chose the worst solution.

The HTML of one sandwich `<tr>` looks like this:

```
<tr>
    <td class="number"><input /></td>
    <td class="description">English sandwich</td>
    <td class="extra">bacon, cheese, lettuce, tomato</td>
    <td class="empty">freshly fried</td>
</tr>
```

Note that the `<input>` tag lacks all attributes. I did this deliberately, to keep the page easy to maintain. My client knew some basic HTML, and I trusted him to add a `<tr>` with new text for every sandwich to the document. However, I decided not to bother him with creating a unique `name` attribute for every `<input>`. Instead, I generated the necessary name by JavaScript.

When the page is loaded, these `<input>` tags are not part of the `<form>`. When the user indicates she wants to order a certain sandwich, the `<tr>` is moved to the order table, and only this table is part of the form.

```
<form method=post action="/cgi-bin/formmail/formmail.pl">
<table class="search">
    <tbody id="ordered">
    <tr>
```

```
                    <td colspan="3"><h3>Your order<h3></td>
                    <td class="extra" rowspan="200">
                            <div id="orderForm">
                            // name and phone fields
                            </div>
                    </td>
            </tr>
            // <tr>s of ordered sandwiches
            // are inserted here
            </tbody>
        </table>
        </form>
```

I did this because I wanted to send the server only those form fields that actually contain a value, i.e., only the sandwiches that the user really ordered.

It works fine in the scripted version. In the noscript version, though, users may think they can simply enter the desired number of sandwiches in the fields and submit the entire form. But the sandwich inputs are never sent to the server because they're not part of the form. Even if they were, they don't have a `name`, so my client would never know which sandwich the user has ordered.

This is clearly an error on my part. I could have solved it in two ways:

1. I could have hard-coded the form-field `name`s and extended the `<form>` tag to cover the entire page. Disadvantage: all empty form fields would be sent to the server, too. Besides, my client would have to remember to create a new `name` attribute for every new sandwich he inserted.

2. I could have generated the `<input />` tags by JavaScript. Disadvantage: none, really. Noscript users don't see any form fields in the sandwich table, but they don't know the fields are supposed to be there and will treat the table as a list of available sandwiches.

In retrospect, I should have generated the `<input />` tags.

XMLHTTP Speed Meter

This script is usable enough, even though I'd be the first one to admit that both the XMLHTTP call and the animation have mainly been added for the wow-effect, not to combat serious usability problems. It's perfectly possible to create a simple form, submit it to the server, and receive a page that shows the download speed.

In fact, the noscript version does exactly that. The database programmer created two PHP scripts: one to create XML for the scripted version, and one to create HTML for the noscript version.

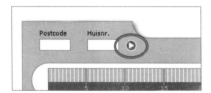

FIGURE 2.12   XMLHTTP Speed Meter noscript.

The only visible difference between the scripted and noscript versions is the Submit button. Note how it's being shown and hidden:

- The HTML contains a hard-coded `<input type="image">` that will work anywhere. It submits the form to the HTML-generating PHP.

- When JavaScript is supported, the input is hidden. The script also revises the form's `action` attribute so that it points to the XML-generating PHP.

Site Survey

People (especially Web developers) hate popups. Since Site Survey hinges on the clever use of a popup, some will question its usability. I knew that when I created the script, and the client and I quickly agreed on a few measures to maintain at least a semblance of user-friendliness:

- The popup would contain a short text that explained that a survey was in progress, and would they please leave the popup open. Thus it would at least be clear why the popup was present.

- The user would be allowed to close the popup at any time. The script would interpret this as a sign that the user did not want to participate in the survey. In addition to being user-friendly, this was also a coder-friendly decision: when the popup closes, do nothing.

As to accessibility, the popup won't open when JavaScript is disabled, and hence the script that follows the user in his journeys through the surveyed site won't work, either. Since the survey is not a necessary ingredient of any site, its demise is no problem; the host sites remain as accessible (or inaccessible) as they were.

The only accessibility problem is that noscript users are effectively barred from participating in the survey. Since they might conceivably use the survey to complain about the host site's inaccessibility, I offered them one loophole to enter it. The host site's homepage contains (or rather, is supposed to contain) a line of text with a link that leads directly to the survey. If the script kicks in, it is replaced by a text that warns that a popup is about to be opened.

chapter 3

Browsers

JAVASCRIPT IS A programming language interpreted by browsers. In order to run your scripts, a browser must contain a JavaScript interpreter—a module that reads and interprets the code you wrote.

But every browser has its own JavaScript interpreter, and there are differences between them, especially where the DOM is concerned. These differences cause the dreaded browser incompatibilities.

If you're unfamiliar with browser incompatibilities, I advise you to skim through 7E, especially the Mouse Position section. Don't worry about the technical details yet; just marvel at the incredible number of differences between the browsers (especially Explorer vs. the others).

Pretty bad, huh? Fortunately, this set of incompatibilities is by far the worst still in existence, and you'll rarely have to wade through such minefields. Nonetheless, browser incompatibilities are a fact of life and will remain so, even though the situation has improved vastly since the turn of the millennium.

This chapter discusses a few good and bad strategies for dealing with browser incompatibilities, but it does not contain lists of specific problems. For that information, go to www.quirksmode.org and study the compatibility tables there.

A: The browsers

Every browser contains a code engine (or rendering engine) that is responsible for interpreting the code on a Web page. A browser's JavaScript interpreter is part of this code engine, and therefore it's the code engine that really counts when it comes to JavaScript support.

It's impossible to test your scripts in all of the JavaScript-capable browsers. There are simply too many of them.

Nonetheless, I introduce a few important browsers (and code engines) in order of the excellence of their JavaScript support.

The Mozilla family

Netscape founded the Mozilla Project in 1998 after the miserable failure of Netscape 4. The idea was to create a code engine that anyone could use to build a browser. This code engine is called Gecko, and right now it powers the browsers marketed as Mozilla, Firefox, Netscape, and Camino (as well as a few others, I suppose). Mozilla and its numerous ilk are arguably the best browser family when it comes to JavaScript support.

In theory Gecko ought to work on every operating system, but in practice the Mac version usually contains a few minor bugs that are absent in the Windows and Unix versions.

Unfortunately, browsers are not required to include a new Gecko version as soon as it is released. Firefox and Mozilla do so, and Firefox contains an automatic update feature that makes sure users always have the latest stable version installed.

Netscape, on the other hand, poses a problem: it's rarely possible to find out which Mozilla version it uses (the 8.1 release says "based on Firefox," which is untrue as well as unhelpful). Besides, Netscape also offers the possibility of using Explorer's code engine, which muddies the waters even more. Fortunately, it has a tiny market share nowadays.

When bug reports start to come in, you'll usually find that one tester has an older version of Mozilla, Firefox, Netscape, or Camino installed, and it's hard to find out exactly which Gecko version runs under its hood. I generally ignore these complaints and tell people to upgrade to the latest Firefox. There are just too many Mozilla-based browsers to keep track of them all.

Fortunately, the trend is towards the adoption of Firefox; at the time of writing its user base is larger than the user base of all other Mozilla family members combined. This gives you a better chance of writing scripts that work in "all Mozilla versions."

Explorer Windows

Explorer (officially, Microsoft Internet Explorer for Windows) has had a market share of about 80 to 90% since 1999. The vast majority of Web users have Explorer 6.0 installed, but in the next few years they'll slowly migrate to Explorer 7.0.

Explorer's code engine is called Trident; Trident is not used for any other browser.

Explorer 5.0, released in March 1999, was the first browser to support the W3C DOM and XMLHttpRequest, but it was also the last Explorer version to contain a major JavaScript update. The 5.5, 6.0, and 7.0 versions only added a few JavaScript features and bug fixes. Essentially Explorer's JavaScript interpreter hasn't been updated for seven years, but even though that becomes noticeable here and there, its JavaScript support is still easily better than that of any browser except Mozilla.

Unfortunately, Explorer still uses quite a few proprietary methods and properties in certain areas, notably event handling. At the time of writing, the Microsoft Internet Explorer team is dedicated to following standards, as all other browser vendors do, but it hasn't fixed JavaScript yet.

3A

Safari

Safari is Apple's browser. Released in 2003 and using the KHTML code engine, it is well on its way to becoming the default browser for the Macintosh platform.

Safari has its share of bugs, and is slightly behind Mozilla and Explorer when it comes to JavaScript support. Nonetheless, it's a good browser that rarely gives me problems, as long as I don't try anything too fancy. When you write really advanced scripts, though, you'll encounter Safari's limitations. Apple is steadily working to make it a better browser, so I assume that Safari's JavaScript support will eventually rival that of Mozilla and Explorer.

Opera

Opera is an independent browser with a rather small market share (around 0.5%). It managed to survive—and even thrive—through the Browser Wars, without a large and prosperous corporation behind it. This achievement is not to be despised.

When it comes to JavaScript, Opera has always been slightly behind the other browsers. During the Browser Wars, it didn't implement DHTML (i.e., the Microsoft or Netscape proprietary DOMs), which in hindsight was an excellent decision.

Although it has largely caught up with the other browsers, it remains the most difficult browser to develop scripts for. It has its share of bugs, and its market share is so tiny that the temptation to just forget about it when you encounter a bug is difficult to resist.

Other graphic desktop browsers

A few other browsers support large parts of the W3C DOM: iCab is a small independent browser for Mac, and Konqueror is one for Linux/Unix. Both have good (though not excellent) JavaScript support, and I occasionally test my sites in them. Konqueror uses the KHTML code engine that drives Safari—in fact, KHTML was developed for Konqueror. Although code sharing takes place regularly between the Safari and Konqueror projects, there are differences between the two browsers.

Explorer for Mac is a wholly different story. Although it theoretically supports a quite decent amount of JavaScript, in practice it crashes with disturbing regularity when you try to run a script like Usable Forms. Tasman, the Explorer Mac code engine, was created in 1999 and 2000, and has hardly been updated since—effectively, it's a dead browser. In addition, when it was ported to Mac OS X, quite a few things went horribly wrong, and the 5.2 release for OS X is decidedly more buggy and crash-prone than the older 5.0 and 5.1 versions for Mac OS 9.

When I develop a script, I always test it in Explorer Mac, but as soon as it shows any sign of not being able to keep up, I add a browser detect to bar it from accessing the advanced interface (see 3D). I no longer bother to solve its bugs; it's too much work for too small a percentage of the browser market. Besides, they're usually unsolvable.

A minuscule percentage of Web users still use older browsers, for instance Netscape 3 or 4. These browsers haven't a prayer of executing any modern JavaScript, but as long as you use proper object detection, as we'll discuss in 3C, you won't encounter any problems.

Mobile phones

Mobile phones with an Internet connection are the Next Big Thing, and they'll change the market Real Soon Now.

Back in 1999, the company I worked for reached this conclusion when WAP became available in Europe. In 2002, the next company I worked for reached the same conclusion when former monopolist KPN tried to introduce the Japanese iMode system on the Dutch and German markets. Both attempts essentially failed.

In fact, everybody's mumbled the mantra so often that "Real Soon Now" has taken on the meaning "maybe year after next."

During one of the overheated 1999 meetings I made a strategic decision. I would start to pay serious attention to mobile phones as soon as a serious client turned up who was willing to pay serious money for mobile phone support.

Seven years have passed, and I'm still waiting for that client.

Frankly I don't believe that Internet over mobile phones will ever amount to much in Europe and North America—though Asia is another matter. The phone displays and keyboards are too tiny, especially when compared to the wide swaths of space people are used to having available on their desktop and laptop computers. I could be wrong, though. We'll see year after next.

From a testing perspective, mobile phones are an abomination, because there are far too many of them. I once heard a story about a testing protocol for mobile phones: an entire basketful is carried in and spread among the long-suffering Web developers, who spend their next few days catering to the phones' whims. I don't know if the story is true, but it could easily be.

This dark cloud has a silver lining: Mozilla, Microsoft, Apple, and Opera have meanwhile developed mobile versions that are being implemented in the next generation of phones. This is decidedly an improvement over the "browsers" cobbled together by the mobile-phone vendors themselves, which are generally unable to support even HTML properly, let alone CSS or JavaScript.

> ### { HTML SUPPORT IN MOBILE PHONES
>
> The incomparable Molly Holzschlag has gone to the trouble of summarizing XHTML support in a few mobile phones. Her conclusions—guaranteed to trigger an acute depression in any standards-aware Web developer—can be read at http://www.molly.com/2005/09/24/got-browser-woes-think-again. }

Screen readers

I discussed screen readers in detail in 2E. They are generally programs installed on top of an existing browser (most commonly Explorer), and their JavaScript support is chaotic and unreliable. There's nothing we can do about it.

Sight-impaired Web users won't be able to appreciate our clever scripts any time soon. All the more reason to keep our sites accessible.

3B

B: Incompatibilities

Which problems do these browsers have? How can we solve them?

Problems

Roughly speaking, there are four categories of browser incompatibilities. The first three are on the way out, now that all modern browsers are serious about implementing the JavaScript standards discussed in 1B. The fourth category, unfortunately, will never disappear.

Not supported

Some browsers don't support some parts of JavaScript. For instance, Explorer and Mozilla allow you to access and change entire style sheets through the `document.styleSheets` nodeList. Safari allows read-only access, while Opera offers no access at all. (More on this in 9D.)

Browser vendors allocate resources and money to solve specific problems. Usually they have plenty of bugs to fix, and adding an extra feature may be just too much work. This is a perfectly understandable decision, and besides, all incompatibilities in this category are nice-to-have extras, not need-to-have basics.

It's easy to work around unsupported features as long as you start your script by checking whether or not they're supported. We'll discuss the technical nuts and bolts in 3C.

Legitimate differences of opinion

Browsers can have legitimate differences of opinion about vaguely specified areas of the JavaScript language.

The `defer` attribute of the `<script>` tag (see 4D for more) is an excellent example. Explorer has a unique take on this attribute, but its implementation can be regarded as a correct interpretation of the rather vague W3C spec.

Since it's impossible to say which browser is right or wrong, such incompatibilities will not be solved any time soon. They're not easy to work around, either, because checking whether a browser supports such a feature doesn't help; all browsers will proudly announce their support but interpret your code differently.

Fortunately, this is the rarest category of incompatibilities.

Deliberate incompatibilities

During the Browser Wars, Netscape and Microsoft each supported their own version of JavaScript, and both vendors deliberately added features the other browser didn't support, and chose not to add features that the other browser supported.

Since that time, the emergence of W3C standards has done much to alleviate the plight of JavaScript developers, but occasionally we still encounter relics from the ancient battlefields, especially in event handling.

Fortunately, these problems are rather easy to solve. Usually the various browsers use different names for the same thing—for instance, Explorer calls the event target `srcElement`, while standards-compliant browsers call it `target`. If you check for both names and use the one that's actually supported, you've solved most of the problems in this category.

Once Microsoft gets around to implementing the W3C events standard, we'll have overcome the last significant batch of deliberate browser incompatibilities, and the vendors will only have to do some minor mopping up.

Browser bugs

Browsers are created by humans, and humans make mistakes. These mistakes take the form of unexpected errors (yup, bugs). In fact, the majority of the cross-browser problems you'll encounter are due to bugs. For instance, Explorer 6 crashes on the (rather unimportant) `normalize()` method. Everybody will agree that this is not the desired behavior, but rather a programming bug that has to be solved.

It's while encountering this elusive and annoying bug category that scripters most commonly develop existential angst and premature hair-loss.

The problem is that it can take quite a while for these bugs to be fixed, because there are so many of them and because some bugs are easier to fix than others.

Not only is the problem unsolvable, it's even unmeasurable. In the technical chapters of this book I'll point out a few of the more obnoxious and well-known bugs, but the list is far from comprehensive. Neither are the compatibility tables on www.quirksmode.org even remotely complete. In fact, there will never be a list of all browser bugs, because creating and maintaining it would be just too much work.

Even if you learn all bugs enumerated in this book and on my site by heart, chances are you'll encounter a new one with the first script you write.

Solutions

With all that said, how bad is it?

For "hard" programmers, who unconsciously assume they have to deal with only one implementation of a language, browser incompatibilities generally come as a nasty surprise. Newbies can react pretty badly, too.

On the other hand, JavaScript is a bug-free haven compared to CSS. The current JavaScript incompatibilities are roughly comparable to the usual mid-level stuff that crops up all the time in CSS development, but without any of the really serious problems. CSS developers already have the basic mindset necessary to become efficient JavaScript browser herders.

Veterans of the Browser Wars don't see any reason to get excited. Today's stuff is distinctly small fry compared to the days when Netscape and Explorer fought their bitter war and browser incompatibilities were impossible to solve.

As you might have guessed, I share that last point of view. To me, browser incompatibilities are simple facts of life that won't disappear any time soon. My general advice is to get used (or at least resigned) to them as soon as possible.

Learning to work with browsers is a necessary component of becoming a good JavaScript developer. Even if you decide to use a library that works around the worst issues for you, you should experience, at least once, the frustration of handling a herd of obnoxious browsers by hand. I advise you to acquire that experience as soon as possible. It'll heighten your awareness of what browsers can do to your scripts.

My "secret"

Nowadays I hardly notice many browser incompatibilities. My "secret," apart from eight years of experience, is my writing.

Back in 1998, when I encountered my first incompatibilities, I set up a simple Web site to describe the problems and their solutions. For years, I kept adding new pages about new incompatibilities, and this has made QuirksMode.org what it is today. In addition, this process fixed problems and solutions in my head to the extent that I can still quote large swaths of obsolete Netscape 4 lore.

Apart from the obvious advantage of being able to look it up later, writing about browser incompatibilities forces you to think logically and order your thoughts so that other people will understand you. This extends your understanding of the problem. In addition, you usually create a few simple test pages to get to the bottom of the bugs, and this, too, extends your understanding.

So my advice is: when you encounter a browser bug, create a test page, write a coherent article, and put both online. It will help you to get a real grip on the problem, it will help other Web developers save their valuable hair, and once you've created enough pages you'll find yourself becoming something of a browser expert, both in your own eyes and those of others.

Day-to-day development

When I create a script, I constantly test every line I write in Explorer Windows and Mozilla. Explorer contains quite a few peculiarities that should be addressed immediately, while Mozilla is an excellent representative of W3C DOM-compliant browsers.

When I finish a script module, I start Safari and Opera (and occasionally Explorer Mac, iCab, and Konqueror) to check for problems. If I find any, I try to solve them, but the amount of time and trouble I take depends on the browser in question.

Essentially I'm willing to take a lot of time for Safari, but not for any of the other browsers. Opera bugs are either easy or impossible to solve, Explorer Mac is too old, and iCab and Konqueror have too little market share. Agree or disagree with my exact browser lineup, but I advise you to make similar decisions or risk total insanity.

Do not under any circumstance write a script for one browser first and add support for the other browsers "later on." This is the fastest way to hell. It's far better to solve nasty incompatibilities at the start of your project than at the end.

When a project starts, you usually have enough energy to spare for the browsers, and everybody expects you to be busy with serious coding, anyway. Conversely, at the end of the project you're tired, and your time is increasingly taken by the small changes that always crop up when deadlines approach. If you still have to solve your browser issues at that time, you probably won't solve them at all, and will instead resort to a browser detect.

Testing time

At testing time I always worry. Sure, right now my script works fine on my computers in my specific browser installs, but that does not mean it will work everywhere.

The obvious solution is to test my script in as many browsers as I can lay hands on. The key is not numbers, but diversity.

Sometimes large testing sessions are performed in-house by employees of your corporate client. Unfortunately, these sessions rarely provide you anything of value. In 2005, I encountered a client who had arranged for no less than 60 people to test their new site. But by sysadministrative decree, they all used Explorer 5.5 on Windows NT 4, even though 6.0 and XP had been available for several years.

This setup was pointless. 5% of the testers saw a weird bug. I wasn't unduly worried by it, and it was a difficult one to solve, too, especially because I couldn't see it myself. I ignored it. My conclusion was that the site worked fine on 95% of the IE 5.5 Win NT 4 installs. That's good to know, but it's not what you'd call exhaustive browser testing.

What you really need is a wide range of browsers and operating systems—not hard to find in most Web-development companies. Ask your colleagues to test the site for you, and you'll usually get more varied bug reports than when clients test them. Especially try to get reports from different Windows versions; sometimes you'll uncover nasty problems.

If you're in a restricted environment yourself, first complain to your boss. You must have the tools you need to do your work, and that includes Macs and older Windows and Explorer versions.

Alternatively, ask for help at a Web-development mailing list. Usually these lists host quite a few helpful people who are willing to sacrifice a few minutes to check your site, and who more often than not can also give you a clue about the cause of the problem.

{ **MAILING LISTS**

Evolt, http://www.evolt.org, and Webdesign-L, http://webdesign-l.com/, are good general web-development mailing lists.

For specific JavaScript mailing lists, I can recommend my own list, at http://www.quirksmode.org/dom/list.html, and the JavaScript list at Louisiana Tech, https://lists.latech.edu/mailman/listinfo/javascript. }

You should develop a sense of when to stop taking obscure bugs into account. There's always one tester with an absurd browser ("Netscape 6.1 on Mac OS 9! Thousands of people use it!") and another whose Explorer install is corrupt. If you encounter such a situation, just ignore it. It's not worth your time.

Your scripts will never work in 100% of the browsers. Ever. Get used to it.

C: Object detection

Your best friend for avoiding browser problems is object detection. If your script uses an object, first check if the browser supports that object. If it doesn't, your script ends.

In contrast to browser detection (which we'll look at in 3D), object detection always works. Since it doesn't depend on browser identity but on browser capabilities, object detection is inherently superior to browser detection.

Once you know that your visitor's browser supports certain objects, you can safely start up your script. You don't need to know exactly which browser it is; you found the objects you need, so you know your script is going to work.

How object detection works

Let's continue with an example from the previous section: Opera doesn't support `document.styleSheets`. Therefore Edit Style Sheet, which relies on this object, should first check if a visitor's browser supports it. If not, the script should end.

That's why Edit Style Sheet starts out by detecting the presence of this object:

[Edit Style Sheet, lines 5-6]

```
function initStyleChange() {
    if (!document.styleSheets) return;
```

You can even pronounce this line: "if NOT document.styleSheets, return". The line checks if the object `document.styleSheets` is present, and if it isn't, it ends the function (`return`).

In fact, this is the general syntax of all object detections: you take the object(s) you want to use and check if they're there. If they aren't (if (!chosen.object)), you end the function.

Technically, object detection hinges on the conversion of an object to a boolean value. We'll get back to this in 5G.

W3C DOM check

By far the most common object detect is this one:

[Site Survey/survey.js, line 27. Most other scripts also use this line, or a variation on it.]

```
var W3CDOM = document.createElement && ➥
document.getElementsByTagName;
```

Often I want to check W3C DOM support before proceeding with a script. This line does so. It checks for the existence of document.createElement and document.getElementsByTagName, which, as we'll see in Chapter 8, are two vital DOM methods. Both have to be present (&&) for the browser to survive the check.

There are historical reasons why I use exactly this check and no other. Explorer 4, which doesn't support the W3C DOM, nonetheless supports document.createElement, though it has a different meaning. So merely checking for this object would allow Explorer 4 to pass. On the other hand, an old version of Opera supported getElementsByTagName but not createElement. That's why I check for both methods.

Event-handling test

In 7C we'll encounter my addEventSimple() function, which adds event handlers according to the W3C and Microsoft models (just nod wisely for the moment). This area of JavaScript contains a major browser incompatibility: the W3C model doesn't work in Explorer, and the Microsoft model doesn't work in Mozilla.

A bit of object detection is obviously in order:

[Usable Forms, lines 151-156. This function is also used in Site Survey, Dropdown Menu, and Edit Style Sheet.]

```
function addEventSimple(obj,evt,fn) {
    if (obj.addEventListener) // W3C
            obj.addEventListener(evt,fn,false);
    else if (obj.attachEvent) // Microsoft
            obj.attachEvent('on'+evt,fn);
}
```

The function checks for support of addEventListener() (W3C), and then for support of attachEvent() (Microsoft). If a browser supports one of these methods, the event handler is set and the function ends.

This object detection contains two interesting points:

- It checks for the W3C-compliant method first because the standard should precede any proprietary method. (Once Explorer supports the W3C standard, it's likely to retain support for the Microsoft model, too, in order to remain backward-compatible. Nonetheless I want this future version to use the standard, so the standards support check should come first.)

- If a browser supports neither method, no event handler is set. Thus this function also serves as a filter that allows most modern browsers to pass through, but excludes, for instance, Explorer on Mac.

Site Survey

A quick peek at Site Survey concludes the object-detection examples. Remember that this example script consists of two script files. Survey.js contains a few object detections—a standard W3C DOM check (line 27) and the addEventSimple() function (lines 86-91). Popup.js contains no object detection at all, even though it uses the W3C DOM to create new form fields.

A browser will only download popup.js if the popup opens. In turn, the popup opens only when the browser supports the W3C DOM and either advanced event-registration model, because that's what survey.js specifies.

3C

Thus, popup.js "hides" behind the object detections in survey.js; if the browser doesn't survive those detects, it never downloads popup.js. It's safe to use the W3C DOM event in the popup because without W3C DOM support the popup never opens.

This kind of object detection-once-removed is occasionally useful, but you should make sure that there's no way the user can directly open the "hidden" JavaScript file when you use it.

In the case of Site Survey, it's theoretically possible that the user could directly open the page popup.html. However, it's unlikely, since the file is not a regular part of the host site, and in any case the popup won't function correctly without out a main window from which to extract data. Therefore I judged it safe to "hide" popup.js behind the detects in survey.js.

How far should you go?

Sandwich Picker starts like this:

[Sandwich Picker, lines 1-12, condensed]

```
var IEMAC = (navigator.userAgent.indexOf('Mac') != -1 &&
navigator.userAgent.indexOf('MSIE') != -1);
var W3CDOM = (document.createElement && ➥
document.getElementsByTagName && !IEMAC);

if (W3CDOM) {
    var extraTD = document.createElement('td');
    // more stuff
    var extraButton = document.createElement('button');
    extraButton.appendChild(document.createTextNode('Collect all
orders'));
}
```

It first uses object detection similar to the one we just saw (except for the browser detect—see 3D). If the browser survives the check (if (W3CDOM)) it executes some extra code.

This code uses `createElement` twice, but since we just checked for its existence those lines are safe. However, the code also includes `appendChild`, and
our object detect hasn't checked if this method is supported. To be really finicky and precise we'd have to check for it first:

```
if (extraButton.appendChild)
    extraButton.appendChild([etc.]));
```

It's not wrong—theoretically, this is even safer than the actual Sandwich
Picker code. Nonetheless, nobody does it, because all browsers that support
`createElement` and `getElementsByTagName` also support `appendChild`. I experi-
mentally confirmed this conclusion by testing it in all available browsers. (Besides,
it wouldn't make sense for a W3C DOM-compliant browser not to support
something as vital as `appendChild`.)

Of course, this reasoning is not 100% watertight. Theoretically a browser could
be created that supports `createElement` and `getElementsByTagName` but not
`appendChild`, but it would be laughed out of business. Therefore, my scripts
use one general object detection right at the start, and from then on they
assume that the browser also supports related functionality, including other
vital W3C DOM methods.

When I need another area of functionality, such as XMLHttpRequest, I add
a second object detection to remove browsers that don't support it. After
all, the fact that a browser supports the W3C DOM doesn't necessarily
mean it also supports XMLHttpRequest. (See 10A for more on detecting
XMLHttpRequest.)

D: Browser detection

Occasionally it's possible to detect the browsers your visitors are using.
Unfortunately, this is the most abused feature of JavaScript, and if you're new
to JavaScript development I flatly forbid you to use it.

Why browser detection doesn't work

The idea behind browser detection is that you exclude those browsers in which you know your script will not work. Essentially you take a blurry snapshot of browser compatibility patterns at the time you create your script, and then assume that this snapshot isn't blurry and will remain accurate. But browser compatibility patterns are shifting constantly; what's true today can be false tomorrow.

Let's continue the `document.styleSheets` example. You have found out that Opera doesn't support it and that Safari has only read-only access, and you rightly decide to make sure that these browsers won't execute Edit Style Sheet.

This is wrong:

```
var browser = [detect browser];
function initStyleChange () {
if (browser == 'Opera' || browser == 'Safari')
    return
    // start initialization
```

Sure, Opera and Safari are now excluded from the script. But what about Netscape 4? It doesn't support `document.styleSheets`, but your browser detect doesn't stop it from trying to execute the script. So you have to add it:

```
if (browser == 'Opera' || browser == 'Safari'
|| browser == 'Netscape 4')
    return;
```

All fine and dandy, but iCab doesn't support `document.styleSheets` either. So here we go again:

```
if (browser == 'Opera' || browser == 'Safari'
|| browser == 'Netscape 4' || browser == 'iCab')
    return
```

This is getting ridiculous. You can never be certain that your browser detect will catch all browsers, because there are simply too many of them, and you can't test your script in all of them. As we've seen, one well-placed object detection takes care of the whole problem, making it obvious which method is better.

Nonetheless, suppose you create a 100% accurate browser detect that catches all browsers that don't support `document.styleSheets`. (Impossible—but suppose for a moment that it isn't.) Although you have solved your problem for the present time, the forward compatibility of your solution is essentially nil.

I fully expect Opera and Safari to start supporting `document.styleSheets` one day, although I cannot predict when and in which version. At that time, your browser detect will not allow Opera and Safari access to the script, even though by then they would be able to easily handle it. Your perfect browser detection has become an active bug that cheats your clients and users—very unprofessional.

Besides, you can't trust what browsers say about themselves. They routinely disguise their identity in order to bypass browser detects.

The browser-detect arms race

From the start of the Web, every browser has had a browser identification string. In JavaScript it's stored in `navigator.userAgent`, and it's also sent to the server as a HTTP header with every request the browser makes.

Back around 1995 there were Mosaic and Netscape, and of the two Netscape was decidedly the more advanced, since it supported exciting novelties like cookies and the `<center>` tag.

Along came a now-fortunately-forgotten fool who decided to use a browser detect in order to determine support for these features—and things went downhill fast from there.

How did these first browser detects find Netscape? They checked whether the browser identification string started with `Mozilla/`, which meant it was Netscape. Conversely, Mosaic's string started with `Mosaic/`. Thus Web sites did stuff like this (on the server, of course, JavaScript hadn't been invented yet) and early Web developers felt very clever:

```
<% if userAgent starts with 'Mozilla/' %>
    <h1><center>Welcome, <% read name from cookie %>!</center></h1>
```

```
<% else if userAgent starts with 'Mosaic/' %>
    <h1>Welcome, sort of</h1>
<% endif %>
```

An HTML parser will ignore tags and attributes it doesn't understand, so serving a `<center>` tag to Mosaic is no problem. Besides, an application that uses cookies must also provide for a no-cookie situation, since even Netscape users won't have one on their first visit.

From the very start of their existence, browser detects have been an unnecessary scourge inflicted on the world by Web developers who thought they understood browsers but were tragically wrong.

Browser vendors were forced to respond, and the only reasonable course of action was to make sure their identification strings matched the ones expected by the oh-so-clever detection scripts. The arms race had begun.

When Explorer entered the market, it too supported cookies and the `<center>` tag, and it wanted to end up on the right side of these browser detects. So its identification string starts with `Mozilla/`, too. It disguised itself as Netscape from the beginning of its career.

Other browsers followed suit. Nowadays any browser that's even remotely capable of more than just showing unstyled HTML starts its browser string with `Mozilla/`.

The Browser Wars upped the ante. As we saw in 1C, Netscape and Microsoft made sure that their version 4 browsers were totally incompatible. Reflexively, Web developers responded by creating yet more browser detects to separate the world into Netscape and Explorer.

Some developers decided to code their sites for one browser only—usually Explorer. Although back then there was some justification for this decision, they still used browser detection instead of object detection in order to decide whether to admit a visitor or not.

When the Browser Wars ended, countless sites had set up detection scripts that allowed access only to Explorer. History repeated itself: minor browsers

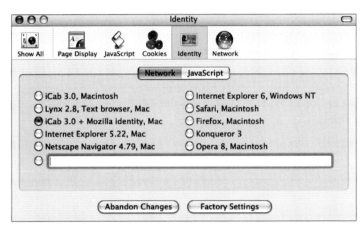

FIGURE 3.1   iCab offers its users a wide choice of identities to bypass browser detects written by clueless Web developers.

such as Opera could handle most of these sites but weren't allowed access. Therefore they changed their identification string to match Explorer's. They also started offering the user some control over the string.

Nothing has changed since then. Nowadays most browsers need to fuzz their identity in order to access many sites.

Unraveling the browser string

In light of the browser-detect arms race, treating the arcana of the browser string is essentially useless; every rule I mention can and will be broken by many browsers. Nonetheless I'll give you a few examples in order to show you that browser detection is an exercise in futility.

Here are a few browser strings. Try to unravel them:

```
Mozilla/5.0 (Windows; U; Windows NT 5.1; en-US; rv:1.7.12)
Gecko/20050915
Mozilla/4.0 (compatible; MSIE 6.0; Windows NT 5.1; SV1; .NET CLR
1.1.4322)
```

```
Mozilla/5.0 (Macintosh; U; PPC Mac OS X; en) AppleWebKit/312.8
(KHTML, like Gecko) Safari/312.6
Mozilla/4.0 (compatible; MSIE 6.0; Windows NT 5.2)
```

- The first one is Mozilla 1.7.12 (note how cleverly the Project hid the version number).

- The second one is Explorer 6.0 on NT 5.1 (which means XP, for reasons nobody outside Microsoft is allowed to know).

- The third one is Safari 1.3.2 (note that Apple included conflicting AppleWebKit and Safari version numbers).

- The fourth one is also Safari 1.3.2, but now in the disguise that allows it access to many sites otherwise closed to it.

Do you still want to deny access to certain visitors based on browser strings?

userAgent

The first rule of browser detection is to always use navigator.userAgent. Especially in older browsers, the value of this property may obey certain rules that, though never officially defined, may give some clues to a browser's identity. On the other hand, it may not.

In contrast, all other properties of navigator are unreliable. You should assume that navigator.appName, navigator.appVersion, and their ilk all lie. (Why? To bypass browser detects, of course.)

Mozilla/

As we saw, all browser identification strings start with 'Mozilla/' because that was the starting point of the arms race. The existence of this substring proves only that the browser has been released after 1994.

/[version number]

The slash is always followed by a version number, but unfortunately that, too, is useless. Every modern browser proclaims itself to be version 4 or 5 of the Mozilla code engine.

Netscape 1 through 4 were the only browsers that put their version number in this place in the string. You can use these version numbers as long as you're certain you're dealing with an old Netscape, not another browser in disguise.

(rambling string)

After the false version number comes a long and rambling string that is mostly enclosed in parentheses and contains complicated abbreviations (the reason and meaning of most of which have long since been forgotten).

But it may also hold a substring or two that actually give a clue to the browser's identity. On the other hand, it may not.

Opera

Let's treat our first positive identification. In Opera, `navigator.userAgent` always contains the string 'Opera', even when it's in disguise. It's instructive to take a quick peek at Opera's identification string. This is the default value for version 8.54:

```
Mozilla/4.0 (compatible; MSIE 6.0; Windows NT 5.1; en) Opera 8.54
```

Note the 'MSIE 6.0'. As you might guess, this is the disguise which lets Opera bypass all browser detects.

The presence of 'Opera' in the string could be a liability: a too-clever Web developer might use this substring to positively identify Opera and deny it access to his site. Fortunately, most browser detectors don't have the faintest idea what they're doing, and many have never heard of Opera anyway, so the possibility of this happening is slight. Nonetheless, Opera has taken a risk by including this substring.

Opera is the only browser that supports the `window.opera` property. If you must detect Opera, query this property.

Safari, iCab, and Konqueror

If the substring 'Safari' occurs in `navigator.userAgent`, the browser is obviously Safari. Unfortunately the reverse is not true; the absence of 'Safari' does

> { **NAVIGATOR.VENDOR?**
>
> Konqueror always has `navigator.vendor` 'KDE', and Safari's value always contains 'Apple'. Should we hope for a future browser detect based on `navigator.vendor`?
>
> No. Even if all browsers supported it, all browser detects would switch to `if (navigator.vendor == 'Microsoft')` and the whole thing would start all over again. It's far better to leave `navigator.vendor` in peace and forget about browser detects altogether. }

not prove that the browser is not Safari. If the user tells Safari to identify itself as Explorer 6 (or Mozilla 5.0 or even Netscape 4.77!), it plays this role to the hilt and doesn't give a clue about its actual identity.

The same goes for iCab and Konqueror; their strings might contain 'iCab' or 'Konqueror', but then again, they might not.

I hope that future versions of these browsers will take the same risk as Opera and carry their true name in every identification string, even when in disguise. On the other hand, I can't blame the vendors if they don't—we Web developers have made a mess of things.

Gecko

Mozilla's identification string usually contains 'Gecko.' Unfortunately, Safari's default string also contains 'Gecko.' (Why? To bypass browser detects, of course.)

In general, it's very hard to identify Mozilla positively. I go through all other options, and if I cannot identify the browser I assume it's Mozilla. But of course this assumption may be wrong.

MSIE

Explorer's string always contains the substring 'MSIE'. Most other browsers use this crucial passkey, too, so its presence proves nothing.

The version number

Explorer and Opera allow you to find their version number directly after the substring you were looking for ('Opera', 'MSIE'). Ignore the first character after the substring (it's always a space) and take the number that appears from the second character onwards.

See again Opera's string:

```
Mozilla/4.0 (compatible; MSIE 6.0; Windows NT 5.1; en) Opera 8.54
```

It disguises itself as Explorer 6, yet it really is Opera 8.54. Both version numbers are separated from the identification substring by a space.

Of course this rule does not work in any other browser. Putting the version number immediately after the browser name would be a dead giveaway, and navigator.userAgent is supposed to be shrouded in mystery.

The operating system

The Windows operating system can be identified by the string 'Win'. Note that some browsers say 'Windows', and others 'Win'.

The Mac operating system can be identified by the string 'Mac'. Here, too, some local variation is possible.

There is no general detect for Linux/Unix; I usually assume that any OS that's not Windows or Mac must be a flavor of Unix. That's not always true, but minor players like Amiga and BeOS are so rare that they can safely be discounted.

Of course these rules apply only if the browser hasn't disguised itself as another browser on another platform (such as Explorer 6 on Windows XP).

> **BROWSER DETECT SCRIPT**
>
> My browser detect script can be found at http://www.quirksmode.org/js/detect.html.

Correct use of browser detects

There are two situations in which a browser detect is the correct solution.

The first is when you actually want to know which browser a visitor uses, in order to store that information in a Web-site statistics program. Site Survey does so because my client wanted this information. Since the browser detect does not influence the script logic, it's perfectly safe.

The second situation is a lot messier and usually involves Explorer on Mac. This browser theoretically supports the W3C DOM, and therefore this object detection grants it access to the advanced scripts:

```
var W3C = document.createElement && document.getElementsByTagName;
```

Nonetheless, when you actually run complicated scripts in Explorer Mac, chances are it'll crash. This is a fact that no object detection will ever discover; object detection assumes that a method that is supported does not crash the browser.

There is no solution to this dilemma other than to browser-detect Explorer Mac out of existence. Sandwich Picker does so:

[Sandwich Picker, lines 1-2]

```
var IEMAC = (navigator.userAgent.indexOf('Mac') != -1 && ➥
navigator.userAgent.indexOf('MSIE') != -1);
var W3CDOM = (document.createElement && ➥
document.getElementsByTagName && !IEMAC);
```

If navigator.userAgent contains the strings 'MSIE 5' and 'Mac', then the browser is Explorer on Mac (or a browser disguised as such). The next line performs a standard object detection, but adds the clause "and if it's NOT Explorer Mac".

A filthy solution, but it's the only one possible.

E: Debugging

When a browser doesn't understand a certain JavaScript command, it produces a JavaScript error message. You need these messages for debugging, but unfortunately they're sometimes hard to read.

Occasionally the error messages won't help you, or aren't there at all, even though something is clearly wrong with your scripts. In these cases, you have to switch to other bug-hunting techniques.

3E

Error messages

First, you must make sure that you see error messages when they occur. In most browsers, this means opening the JavaScript error console:

- Mozilla: Tools > (Web Development >) JavaScript Console (the Web Development submenu exists in Mozilla, but not in Firefox).

- Explorer: Double-click on the yellow triangle in the lower-left corner. Then check the checkbox in the error message alert.

- Safari: Debug > Show JavaScript Console.

- Opera: Preferences > Advanced > Content > JavaScript Options > Open JavaScript console on error. (Valid for 8.54. Unfortunately, the Content menu is missing in my 9.0 beta 2. In general, Opera is prone to moving these options to other tabs and menus all the time.)

You'll notice that the error messages vary greatly in quality. Take this wrong bit of script:

```
var x = document.getElementById('tes');
alert(x.nodeName);
<div id="test"></div>
```

I accidentally forgot the last 't' of 'test', so the browsers don't know what I'm talking about. Let's see how they react.

FIGURE 3.2
Mozilla's error
message. Clear
and to the point.

Mozilla's message is the clearest: 'x has no properties' in line 9. Clicking on the link immediately takes you to the correct line.

FIGURE 3.3
Opera, too,
gives useful
information.

Although its 'could not convert' message is a bit cryptic, Opera shows not only where the error occurred, but also from where the function that contains the error was called. Essentially it follows this track until it finds a function called in response to an event. This is called a stack trace.

FIGURE 3.4
Explorer's line numbers
can't handle included
scripts.

Explorer, unfortunately, is vague. It says "Object required", but you see this message in about 60% of the problems, and Explorer never specifies which object it requires or why.

In addition, Explorer has trouble with included scripts:

```
<script src="included.js"></script>
```

If you add separate script files to your pages—and in 2C we saw that this is best practice nowadays—Explorer still considers the error to have occurred in the main HTML page. Therefore, its line numbers usually don't make sense.

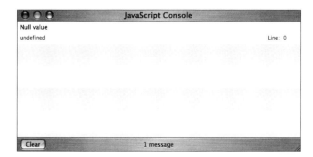

FIGURE 3.5
Safari's messages
are not very useful.

Safari, finally, gives the most cryptic error message of all: "Null value". True, but unenlightening.

Since Mozilla has the best error messages, whenever I encounter a problem I immediately switch to Mozilla to get a good, solid error message that actually tells me what's wrong. I advise you to do the same.

Of course, if the error occurs only in Explorer or Safari, you have a problem, and it's time for a more in-depth bug hunt.

{ **DEBUGGING TOOLS**

Mozilla and Microsoft both offer script-debugging tools that are rumored to be quite powerful. I have no experience with either, so I'll just provide the links.

The Venkman JavaScript debugger meant for Mozilla can be found at http://www.mozilla.org/projects/venkman/.

This IE Blog entry talks about the Microsoft Script Debugger: http://blogs.msdn.com/ie/archive/2004/10/26/247912.aspx. }

Dealing with browser bugs

Sometimes an error message will immediately reveal what's wrong and why. Sometimes, though, even Mozilla's errors don't help you any further—you just don't know what's going on. Especially worrisome are the occasions when something is clearly wrong, yet no error message appears.

In all these cases you have to isolate the bug by hand. This generally involves three steps:

1. If I'm not sure which function causes the bug, I turn off all functions in my script one by one by inserting a `return` statement as its first line. Now the function doesn't run any more, and if the bug also disappears I'm sure it's caused by this function. Note, however, that if you find a bug-triggering function, you should still check all other functions; the bug may be triggered by the combination of two functions.

2. When I've found the offending function, I add `alert` statements to it. I put the `alert` after the first block of statements and test again. If the bug occurs, the lines above the `alert` are to blame; if the bug doesn't occur I move the `return` or `alert` to below the next logical block. Once I find the block that causes the error, I use the `alert` to further fine-tune my search and isolate a specific line.

3. When I've succesfully identified the browser bug I create a bug report, complete with test page.

Using alerts

An `alert` statement stops the execution of the function it's in, which gives you the chance to check if the bug has already occurred. Take the wrongly spelled 'test' example we saw earlier. Assume that I haven't yet spotted the missing 't' and I'm still searching for the cause of the bug.

```
var x = document.getElementById('tes');
alert(x.nodeName);
<div id="test"></div>
```

The alert gives a definite clue, because it itself causes the bug. That will quickly lead you to suspect that the value of x is incorrect. In a real situation, I would change the alert:

```
alert(x);
```

Now an alert pops up that says 'undefined'. Now I'm certain that the bug is caused by x being not defined; I only have to study the assignment to x, and I'll probably spot the missing 't'.

Alerts and confirms

Sometimes alerts can be annoying. Let's say an error occurs somewhere in a long for-loop that goes through all <tr>s in an HTML page. I suspect it has something to do with the number of cells in one row, and I want to study the number of cells every row has. An alert allows me to do that:

```
var rows = document.getElementsByTagName('tr');
for (var i=0;i<rows.length;i++) {
    var cells = rows[i].getElementsByTagName('td');
    alert(i + ': ' +cells.length);
    var name = cells[1].firstChild.nodeValue;
}
```

This works, up to a point. I now see the index number of the row and its number of cells. Unfortunately, the alert pops up every time the script finds a new <tr> to work on, and if your HTML contains hundreds of <tr>s you'll see hundreds of alerts. That gets old in a hurry.

Instead, you could use a confirm:

```
var rows = document.getElementsByTagName('tr');
for (var i=0;i<rows.length;i++) {
    var cells = rows[i].getElementsByTagName('td');
    if (!confirm(i + ': ' +cells.length + '. Continue?'))
            break;
    var name = cells[1].firstChild.nodeValue;
}
```

3E

{ **ALERT AND CONFIRM**

We'll treat alert and confirm formally in 6E. }

The confirm contains exactly the same information as the alert, but in addition it offers you the choice of breaking off the function when you've found the faulty row. If the confirm returns false (i.e., if you press the Cancel button), the for-loop breaks off and you're not forced to wade through more alerts.

Error console

During complicated debugging sessions I occasionally create an error console:

```
function initConsole() {
    var console = document.createElement('div');
    console.id = 'errorConsole';
    document.body.appendChild(console);
}
function writeToConsole(message) {
    var newMessage = document.createElement('p');
    newMessage.innerHTML = message;
    var console = document.getElementById('errorConsole');
    console.appendChild(newMessage);
}
```

Now I can use writeToConsole() every time I need a debugging text:

```
function complicated() {
    var x = [an object that isn't what I expect it to be];
    writeToConsole('x is now ' + x.nodeName);
}
```

In the old days something similar was done with popups; 6F contains a code example.

Example

In order to explain how to deal with your daily dose of browser bugs, I'm going to give you a real example. When I was preparing Usable Forms for this book, I noticed that Mozilla behaved oddly when I soft-reloaded the page. After a soft reload (i.e., a reload during which the user does not press the Shift button) Mozilla and Explorer retain the values of any form fields.

However, Mozilla always checked the radio button above the one that was checked before the reload. It didn't give an error message; as far as it was concerned everything was fine. This was clearly a bug, either in my script or in Mozilla. I needed to find out more.

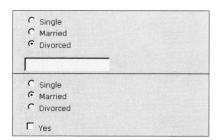

FIGURE 3.6
The Mozilla bug. Go to Usable Forms, check Divorced, and then soft-reload the page. Now Married will be checked.

From the outset I suspected this was a Mozilla bug, because Explorer uses exactly the same code and didn't have any problems. Therefore Mozilla misinterpreted a bit of code. But which bit? I needed to isolate the bug.

I started at step 1 and added a return statement to a function. For instance, here I turned off setDefaults():

[Usable Forms, lines 56-67, condensed and changed]

```
function setDefaults() {
    return;
    var y = document.getElementsByTagName('input');
    for (var i=0;i<y.length;i++) {
            if (y[i].checked && y[i].getAttribute('show'))
                    intoMainForm(y[i].getAttribute('show'))
    }
    // etc.
}
```

If the bug was caused by this function, it would not appear any more. Unfortunately, it did appear, so I was checking the wrong function. I moved the return to the next function and reloaded the page.

The bug stubbornly remained active until I closed down the initialization function prepareForm(). Now the bug disappeared. So, it appeared the error was somewhere in prepareForm().

To find the exact line of code that triggers the bug, I switched to alerts:

[Usable Forms, lines 16-19, changed]

```
function prepareForm() {
    if (!compatible) return;
    var marker = document.createElement(relatedTag);
    marker.style.display = 'none';
    alert('Made it to here');
```

I placed an alert after the first bit of code in prepareForm() and reloaded the page. The alert popped up, and to my amazement the wrong radio button was already checked. It seemed the bug was caused by the lines hitherto executed. That was odd, because these lines don't do anything to the form.

I moved the alert to the very first line of the function:

[Usable Forms, lines 16-19, changed]

```
function prepareForm() {
    alert('Made it to here');
    if (!compatible) return;
    var marker = document.createElement(relatedTag);
    marker.style.display = 'none';
```

Lo and behold, the wrong radio button was still checked. Apparently the bug wasn't caused by my script at all. It was already present before the script had had the chance to run.

Now what? Was this a native bug in Mozilla? Does Mozilla always check the wrong radio button? I disabled the script and soft-reloaded the page. The second time I did that, the correct radio button remained checked. Then I re-enabled my script, and the buggy behavior recurred, but only the *second* time I soft-reloaded the page, not the very first time.

This was worth a more detailed investigation. I disabled and enabled the script a few times, and found that the bug always occurred when the previous page ran my script. It didn't seem to matter whether the script ran in the current page.

Finding browser bugs is a matter of 99% perspiration and 1% inspiration. I'd already done the hard work, and I was now rewarded by a flash of inspiration. If my script was enabled, the previous page hid a few form fields!

I created a second form field before the radio buttons, made sure it was also hidden, and behold: the radio check now moved up not one, but two radio buttons. Therefore, the bug was caused by the hidden form fields in the previous page. Apparently Mozilla makes some indexing mistake when form fields are hidden.

Now that I had a definite handle on the bug, I created a test page. As I discussed in 3B, this step is absolutely crucial, since it forces you to create exactly those circumstances that trigger the bug, and leave out all irrelevant code, which in turn increases your understanding of the bug.

So I created a simple test page with one input and four radio buttons. I checked the last radio and reloaded. Nothing happened. Then I added a little script that removes the single input, and the bug reappeared in all its glory.

The bug was now successfully isolated and described. A search in Mozilla's Bugzilla database (see next page) turned up a similar one that has been known since 2002.

{ **BUG REPORT**

The bug report I created after these tests can be found at http://www.quirksmode.org/bugreports/archives/2005/11/radio_check_mov.html. }

3E

So, was I going to leave the bug as it was? Or should I try to solve it, for instance by setting a cookie that remembers the state of all radio buttons? In the end I decided not to bother, because solving the bug would make my script much more complicated, and because the bug affects only one browser in specific circumstances (how often will people reload a form page in Mozilla?).

Feel free to disagree with my decision in this specific situation, but sometimes solving a browser bug is more trouble than it's worth.

Reporting browser bugs

Once you've successfully isolated a bug, you should report it to the relevant browser vendor. All four major vendors offer bug reporting facilities.

Safari

Safari offers the easiest feedback mechanism. Just use its 'Report Bugs to Apple' feature and answer a few questions.

FIGURE 3.7
Safari's bug-reporting feature sends a bug report straight into Apple's database.

Opera

Opera makes it easy, too. Go to http://www.opera.com/support/bugs/ and carefully read the page, since it contains a useful summary of a proper bug reporting process.

Opera requires a good test case that has isolated the bug as much as possible. Once you've created that page, you can follow the links to the bug-report form.

Mozilla

Reporting a Mozilla bug is harder. The complete bug database of Mozilla is online at http://bugzilla.mozilla.org/, but you need some experience with Bugzilla in order to use it.

First you need to create an account. Then Mozilla requires you to check if the bug has already been reported. That's a reasonable request, but most bug reports are hard to read if you don't know Mozilla's and Bugzilla's internal structure. The few times I reported a bug it turned out that the bug was already known, but I couldn't find it because I didn't understand these structures.

Microsoft

The Microsoft bug reporting facilities are at https://connect.microsoft.com/feedback/default.aspx?SiteID=136 and they are only for Explorer 7 and later. Please do not report bugs in earlier Explorer versions. Note that you need a Microsoft Connect account in order to gain access.

QuirksMode

Finally, I have my own bug-reporting facilities at http://www.quirksmode.org/bugreports/. The reports here are primarily aimed at Web developers, although browser vendors occasionally go through these lists, too. A proper test page is required.

If you report your bugs here, other Web developers will be able to find them, and will thank you for saving valuable portions of their time (and hair).

Please be patient

You shouldn't expect a bug that you report to a browser vendor to be solved within a few weeks. Usually browser vendors address dozens of bugs simultaneously, and their time is limited. Besides, the bug you report may depend on other bugs, or it may not be important enough for immediate action. Patience is a virtue when dealing with browser bugs.

Preparation

A GOOD PREPARATION phase is a crucial step in creating simple, efficient scripts. Before writing a single line of code, you must make many decisions, most importantly about the cooperation between the HTML and CSS on the one hand and the JavaScript on the other. You also must know how to insert scripts in your HTML pages, and how to make sure they run at the right time.

The purpose of the preparation phase is to fix the basic outline of your scripts in your head (or on paper, or in a document, whatever works best for you). If you already know the rough shape your script is going to take, your actual coding hours can be spent on detail decisions and problems. Conversely, if you don't prepare, you might find after a few days of frantic coding that your fundamental approach is wrong or too complicated, and that you have to start all over again.

Don't skimp on the preparation phase! Even on a tight deadline in a chaotic project when using a few hours without coding a single line seems a waste of time, a good preparation will save you a lot of extra work a few days down the line.

A: HTML and CSS structure

The most important decisions in the preparation phase concern the HTML and CSS structure of your pages. Unfortunately, it's not really possible to give general rules for correct HTML and CSS structures; they depend on the purpose and context of the script. An HTML structure that works brilliantly in one case can be counterproductive in another situation.

This is an area where you have to make your own decisions. However, I can offer a few examples that will help you start thinking about good structures.

HTML structure

HTML structure is vital to some example scripts. The most obvious are Sandwich Picker, whose core is formed by the principle of "one sandwich one `<tr>`, " and Dropdown Menu, where the logical, semantic, nested `<ul>/<li>` structure is crucial.

Where does Sandwich Picker find the name of a sandwich? In the `<tr>`'s second `<td>`. How does Dropdown Menu know if an `<li>` has a submenu? It checks if the `<li>` has a child `<ul>`.

Obvious, isn't it?

In general, you should embrace such obviousness. Obviousness is the key to creating HTML structures that will help your script instead of hindering it. Besides, such HTML structures usually hold data that the script can use.

Whenever you can find the data your script needs by examining the document structure, you should do so, since it's always the simplest alternative. It's much easier to tell the script to look in the second `<td>` to find the sandwich name than to tell it to read it from an array or object that's defined elsewhere.

You'll see plenty of examples of this in 4F, where we discuss the HTML structure of the example scripts.

CSS structure

As with HTML, a good CSS structure can save you a lot of headaches.

The Order and Trash buttons in Sandwich Picker are excellent examples. They are created when the script is initialized, but the rules for their visibility and invisibility are complicated.

Initially both buttons are hidden. The Order button becomes visible when the user adds a quantity to a sandwich, since that's the first step in ordering it. When the sandwich is moved to the order table, the Order button should be hidden (the sandwich has already been ordered, after all), and the Trash button should appear (since only now has it become possible to remove the sandwich from the order form).

Of course you can write a script to arrange for all these show-and-hide actions. Hiding or showing a single button is trivial, but keeping track of which buttons are visible and hidden, and deciding which display changes are triggered by the latest user action, will most likely take a few dozen complicated lines of JavaScript.

Fortunately, you don't need JavaScript for this task. It's far simpler to define the display changes in CSS:

```
a.trash,a.order {
    display: none;
}
tr.highlight a.order {
    display: block;
}
#ordered a.order {
    display: none;
}
#ordered a.trash {
    display: block;
}
```

Initially both buttons are hidden. An order button in a `tr.highlight` is visible, except when it's in `table#ordered`, then it's hidden. A trash button is only visible in `table#ordered`.

As soon as the script takes action, the CSS associated with the buttons is re-evaluated and the buttons are automatically shown or hidden, without the need for complicated JavaScript functions that monitor user behavior and button placement.

Now the script only has to change the class of an ordered sandwich to `"highlight"`, and the Order button appears. When the script moves this `<tr>` to the Order table (which, unsurprisingly, has `id="ordered"`), the button disappears again, but the Trash button appears.

Obvious, isn't it? Again, obviousness is the key. Creating good, useful CSS structures that cooperate closely with your scripts will save you a lot of time and trouble.

B: Hooks

Many scripts don't work on an entire HTML page, but on specific HTML elements within the page. For instance, Dropdown Menu shouldn't convert every single `<ul>` in a page to a dropdown menu, but only the `<ul>`s that you indicate. Usable Forms should not hide all form fields in the document, but only the ones that you have marked as such.

In order to tell the script which HTML elements it should work on, you need hooks. A hook can be any kind of HTML structure, although an attribute, such as `id`, is the most obvious choice.

When the script starts up, it goes through the document in search of these hooks, and when it finds one it initializes the script for the HTML elements that contain the hook. Thus Dropdown Menu looks for `<ul class="menutree">`, and converts those elements to dropdown menus. Usable Forms searches through all `<tr>`s in the document and takes those with a `rel` attribute out of the document. Textarea Maxlength searches through all `<textarea>`s in the document and initializes those that have a `maxlength` attribute.

Let's discuss a few common hooks.

ID

The best known and most popular hook is id.

```
var x = document.getElementById('hook');
// initialize x
```

The script initiates the behavior on the element with id="hook".

This is the simplest way of creating hooks, because the getElementById method does all the dirty work for you. Unfortunately, you can use a certain id only once per document. Therefore id is only useful if a script needs a single hook.

Although that may seem restrictive, sometimes a bit of creativity and good HTML structuring will help you make the most of this single hook. Sandwich Picker does so when it has to find all sandwiches in the page. I could have added an attribute to every sandwich, but since all sandwiches reside in the same table anyway (good HTML structuring!), I decided to give this table an id (well, actually the <tbody> for reasons we'll discuss in 8E).

```
<table class="order">
    <tbody id="startTable">
    <tr price="1.75">
            <th colspan="5" class="header">&euro; 1,75</th>
    </tr>
    <tr>
            <td class="number"><input /></td>
            <td class="description">Ham</td>
            <td class="extra"></td>
            <td class="empty"></td>
    </tr>
    <tr>
            <td class="number"><input /></td>
            <td class="description">Cheese</td>
            <td class="extra"></td>
            <td class="empty"></td>
</tr>
// etc.
```

4B

[Sandwich Picker, lines 32-37, condensed]

```
var containers = document.getElementById('startTable').➡
getElementsByTagName('tr');
for (var i=0;i<containers.length;i++) {
    var y = containers[i].getElementsByTagName('td');
    if (y.length != 4) continue;
    // initialize trs
}
```

The script takes all <tr>s that are descendants of the element with
id="startTable". Any <tr> that does not contain 4 <td>s (i.e., that is a price
header) is filtered out, and the script initializes all other <tr>s, since it's
now sure they contain sandwiches. In this way, the id="startTable" hook is
enough to initialize the script.

class

If you want to initiate the same behavior on several elements, you need other
hooks. Take Dropdown Menus. The site I wrote it for had two separate dropdown
menus, and therefore I could not use an id. Besides, although the dropdown menus share an ancestor element, the main content area of the site
shares the same ancestor, and of course on some pages this area will contain
<ul>s, too, which should not become dropdown menus. Therefore I could not
use the descendant-of-id trick from Sandwich Picker.

Instead, I opted for a class="menutree". I convert only <ul>s with this class to
dropdown menus.

[Dropdown Menu, lines 7-9]

```
var lists = document.getElementsByTagName('ul');
for (var i=0;i<lists.length;i++) {
    if (lists[i].className != 'menutree') continue;
    // initialize dropdown menu on ul
}
```

If a certain `<ul>` does not have a `class="menutree"` the script ignores it and goes on to the next one.

Although the class attribute might seem the ideal hook, I have two problems with it:

- It already serves as the most important CSS hook.
- Sometimes you need a `name=value` hook, and that's pretty hard to pull off in a class.

The first point is extremely subjective, the second rather less so. In the past I strongly felt that class was a CSS hook, and that any JavaScript hook should use another attribute. It keeps presentation and behavior separated, and that cannot but lead to clearer Web sites where every attribute serves a clear goal.

Nonetheless, there's a lot to say in favor of using the class attribute. It already has a certain meaning, namely "Deploy styles here." It could just as well say, "Deploy behavior here." Essentially, the class can be both a CSS and a JavaScript hook.

Dropdown Menu's `<ul class="menutree">` is the best example. It serves both as a CSS and as a JavaScript hook. Thus you can initiate the dropdown menu behavior and also give the `<ul>` and its children the special styles any drop-down menu needs in order to be recognizable. As we'll see in a moment, Form Validation could also have benefited from a class hook.

Custom attributes

Textarea Maxlength, Form Validation, and Usable Forms all use custom attributes for hooks, i.e., attributes that are not part of any (X)HTML specification.

```
<textarea maxlength="300">
<input name="phone" validation="required numeric" />
<tr rel="othercountry">
```

The `maxlength` custom attribute tells Textarea Maxlength that the `<textarea>` has a maximum length, and also what that maximum length is. The `validation` custom attribute tells Form Validation which checks should be performed on this form field. The `rel` custom attribute tells Usable Forms that the `<tr>` should be removed from the document, and also that it should be reinserted if the user checks/selects the form field with a matching `rel` attribute.

I call them custom attributes because I custom-created them for the job. As a result, they are not valid HTML; the `validation` attribute is not a part of the HTML specification at all. `rel` is, but only on `<a>` and `<link>` tags. `maxlength` is valid, too, but only on an `<input>` tag.

This does not matter to JavaScript. The W3C DOM method `getAttribute()`, which we'll discuss in 8G, allows you to get the value of any attribute, whether it's part of the HTML spec or not.

Nonetheless, it might matter to you as a Web developer. If you have decided your pages should be perfectly valid (X)HTML, you cannot use custom attributes since the validator would choke on them.

What's more important? Valid (X)HTML or a custom attribute that closely cooperates with your script? This important decision is one you should make for yourself. To aid you in this process, let's discuss possible alternatives to the custom attributes of the three scripts.

Form Validation does not need a custom attribute. The `validation` attribute can easily be rewritten as a class attribute:

```
<input name="phone" class="required numeric" />
```

This approach has clear advantages, although I didn't realize that when I wrote the script back in 2003. Once you have a `class="required numeric"` you can easily add an extra style to the form field—for instance, an icon that communicates that the form field expects numeric input. You now have available a series of class names that contain useful, semantic information about the form fields, such as "This field is required" and "This field is numeric."

Therefore, if you move the values of `validation` to `class`, and then change `.getAttribute('validation')` to `.className` in Form Validation, the script works better than before.

name/value pairs

Unfortunately, Textarea Maxlength's and Usable Forms' custom attributes are less easy to convert to classes, because I conceived these custom attributes as name/value pairs. Let's discuss Textarea Maxlength first:

```
<textarea maxlength="300">
```

The `maxlength` custom attribute contains two bits of data:

- The fact that this textarea has a maximum length.
- The value of this maximum length.

The script uses the first bit of data during initialization: it adds event handlers to the textarea, so that its user input can be checked. At this point, the exact value doesn't matter.

[Textarea Maxlength, lines 2-11, condensed]

```
for (var i=0;i<textareas.length;i++) {
    if (textareas [i].getAttribute('maxlength')) {
    // administration
    textareas[i].onkeyup = textareas[i].onchange = checkMaxLength;
        }
}
```

When the `checkMaxLength()` function is executed, it needs to know how many characters the textarea may contain. That's no problem; the value of the `maxlength` attribute contains this information.

[Textarea Maxlength, lines 17-18]

```
function checkMaxLength() {
    var maxLength = this.getAttribute('maxlength');
    // compare
}
```

4B

Let's port this to a class.

```
<textarea class="maxlength=300">
```

Now the CSS selector for this textarea becomes not `textarea.maxlength`, but `textarea.maxlength=300`, which does not work.

Nonetheless, the first job is easy: in order to find out if the script should be initialized for a textarea, find out if its class contains "maxlength":

[Textarea Maxlength, lines 2-11, condensed and changed]

```
for (var i=0;i< textareas.length;i++) {
    if (textareas[i].className.indexOf('maxlength') != -1) {
    // administration
    textareas[i].onkeyup = textareas[i].onchange = checkMaxLength;
        }
}
```

But what about the value of maxlength? This value is present in the class attribute, but it's not easy to find. If we can be absolutely certain that the value `"maxlength=300"` is the last one in the class, we do this:

[Textarea Maxlength, lines 17-18, changed]

```
function checkMaxLength() {
    var maxLength = this.className.➥
    substring(this.className.indexOf('maxlength')+10);
    // compare
}
```

This is not an example of clear and concise JavaScript, but neither is it extremely complicated. However, suppose now that `"maxlength=300"` is not last in the class attribute. Our script grows more complex:

[Textarea Maxlength, lines 17-18, changed]

```
function checkMaxLength() {
    var index = this.className.indexOf('maxlength');
```

```
    var maxLength = this.className.➥
    substring(index+10,this.className.indexOf(' ',index));
    // compare
}
```

This, in turn, does not work if "maxlength=300" is the last part of the class attribute after all. I could go on creating code examples, but you get the point: the value of a name/value hook cannot be easily read from the class attribute. Creating the hook as a separate attribute makes much more sense.

Usable Forms has the same problem. The hook `<tr rel="othercountry">` would have to be rewritten as `<tr class="rel=othercountry">`, and reading `'othercountry'` requires similar complicated substring statements.

All in all I feel that Textarea Maxlength and Usable Forms are better served by a custom attribute hook than by a class hook. Feel free to disagree with me and use class, but be aware of the difficulties of reading out the value of a name/value pair in the class.

C: Preparing the page

After you've made decisions on the HTML and CSS structure and the hooks you're going to use, it's time to write the initialization function that prepares the page for the script to come.

We'll discuss the mechanics of initialization in 4E. Here, I'd like to concentrate on the purposes of the initialization script, and the high-level decisions you make while writing it.

In this section we'll go through the most important actions the example scripts take during the initialization phase. The emphasis will be on the purpose of these actions, and not on the technical nuts and bolts (most of which are treated in later chapters).

4C

Setting event handlers

The most important action the initialization function takes is registering event handlers. As far as the user is concerned, the script starts when he takes action and the page responds. But which action should he take?

Usually, the correct event is obvious. Form Validation clearly needs the submit event: the script starts up when the user submits the form. Dropdown Menu clearly needs the mouseover and mouseout events: the menus should become visible when the user moves the mouse over them, and be hidden when the mouse moves out again.

Nonetheless you could face some tricky decisions, too. What if a Dropdown Menu user doesn't use a mouse? Which events does Site Survey use? Exactly when do we read out the length of the text area's content in Textarea Maxlength?

Usable Forms is a difficult case. The most logical event would be the change event: The script fires whenever the user changes a form field. Unfortunately there are technical problems that preclude its use.

The most important thing you must do in this phase is clearly picture what the user should do to start up the script. Once you've made that decision you can go through the available events (see 7B) and decide on the best, or, in some cases, the least confusing one to use. We'll study the event handlers of all example scripts in detail in 7G.

Determining visitor status

Occasionally you need to determine exactly what's going to happen when a visitor enters your page. Site Survey is the prime example here.

First, the script determines the survey status. Is it still active, i.e., does the current day fall between the start and end dates of the survey? If not, the script ends.

When a new user visits the site, a script draws a random number that decides whether or not the user is selected for the survey, and stores this information in a cookie. If she isn't selected, she should not be bothered with the survey for at least another day; technically that's done by setting the cookie to expire in a day's time. If she is selected, the survey popup should appear.

When a user returns to the site, the script discovers the cookie from the previous visit and does nothing. The client and I decided that a user who has already gone through the selection process is never led to the survey.

This is not especially difficult, but it has to be taken care of during the initialization. We'll study this example of cookie use in 6G.

Setting up access

Sometimes a script needs access to a certain resource. Edit Style Sheet, for example, needs access to the style sheet it's going to edit.

Therefore the initialization function starts by finding out whether the user's browser supports the editing of entire style sheets, and then creates a variable which points to the correct style sheet. We'll discuss this in 9D.

Generating content

Sometimes it's necessary to modify the HTML document. As we saw in 2E, it may be useful to generate HTML elements such as links or buttons in JavaScript when they are useless without JavaScript support.

Take Sandwich Picker. A lot has to be prepared before the user can start picking sandwiches. Every sandwich `<tr>` needs an Order and a Trash button, and since they make no sense without JavaScript support I use the W3C DOM to add them. The script first creates template nodes, and when the initialization script goes through all `<tr>`s it inserts clones of these nodes into the first `<td>` that also holds the form field.

We'll discuss the technical details in 8E, but the point here is that the initialization script is the only correct place to create the buttons, since they should be available at the moment the user starts interacting with the page.

Defining relations

Occasionally, I define relations between one HTML element and another if an event on the first element should trigger changes in the other element. Thus I don't have to search for the other element when the event takes place: this bit of data has already been defined.

Textarea Maxlength is a good example. When the user enters text in the text area, a counter should appear that shows the number of characters. If the user exceeds the maximum length, the counter should become red and bold. This counter is a <span> element.

In order to keep the script simple, I want to define the relation between a textarea and its counter element during initialization:

[Textarea Maxlength, lines 7-10]

```
// textareas[i] is the textarea currently being initialized
var counterClone = counter.cloneNode(true);
counterClone.innerHTML = '<span>0</span>/'+ ➥
textareas[i].getAttribute('maxlength');
textareas[i].parentNode.insertBefore(counterClone, ➥
textareas[i].nextSibling);
textareas[i].relatedElement = counterClone.➥
getElementsByTagName('span')[0];
```

I first create a new counter by cloning an element and adding text and a <span> tag to it. Then I insert it just after the textarea. (We'll discuss insertBefore() and cloneNode() in 8D and 8E, respectively.)

Finally I give the textarea a relatedElement property that points to the <span> that should be updated whenever the user types something. It is now very easy to access the <span> from the event-handling function on the textarea:

[Textarea Maxlength, lines 17-25]

```
// 'this' is the textarea the user has entered characters in
function checkMaxLength() {
```

```
var maxLength = this.getAttribute('maxlength');
var currentLength = this.value.length;
if (currentLength > maxLength)
        this.relatedElement.className = 'toomuch';
else
        this.relatedElement.className = '';
this.relatedElement.firstChild.nodeValue = currentLength;
}
```

First the script finds out if the maximum length has been exceeded. If so, it sets the class of the `relatedElement` (the `<span>`) to `'toomuch'`. Then it sets the content of the `<span>` to the current length of the textarea. In this way, `checkMaxLength()` has easy access to the `<span>` it should change.

Dropdown Menus uses the same trick, by the way. We'll study it in 7H.

Modifying document structure

The initialization function can also be used for large-scale modification of the document. For example, in Usable Forms, the script should remove all `<tr>`s that have a `rel` attribute. It should also make sure that they can be easily retrieved when the user clicks on a form field.

My solution creates an object, `hiddenFormFieldPointers`, that stores pointers to all `<tr>`s that are removed. These pointers are indexed by the value of the `rel` attribute. When the user clicks on a field that has `rel="othercountry"`, the script re-inserts the `<tr>`s that `hiddenFormFieldPointers["othercountry"]` points to.

Well discuss the technical nuts and bolts in 8K. Just note that such a setup requires careful planning as well as an initialization script that creates the necessary structures (such as `hiddenFormFieldPointers`) before anything else happens.

4C

D: The <script> tag

You have to include your scripts in the HTML page, and you have to start them at the right moment.

You include scripts in your page by means of a <script> tag. This tag can be used in two ways:

- You can give the tag an src attribute; the browser will automatically download the script from the indicated location.
- You can insert JavaScript code between the <script></script> tags.

Note that one <script> tag cannot fulfill both functions. It either imports an external file, or it contains JavaScript code.

Of these two methods, the first one is clearly preferable. As we saw in 2C, unobtrusive scripting requires your scripts to be totally separate from the HTML page, just as your CSS is totally separate. Therefore you should always import one or more .js files that contain the behavior layer of your site instead of directly writing your JavaScript commands in the HTML page.

This also allows you to write one script file and use it on many pages. For instance, Dropdown Menu was written to be used in all pages on my client's site, and was therefore included in all of them. Plus, if I change the .js file, these changes will automatically propagate to all pages in the site. This is a clear maintenance benefit.

Syntax

<script> tags, whether they import an external file or contain JavaScript code, go in the <head> of the HTML document by custom. The HTML specification allows a <script> tag anywhere, and in the bad old days, inserting them in the <body> of a page (for instance to document.write() a few lines of HTML) was common. Despite all this, I generally advise you to put all <script> tags in the <head>, along with all CSS <link> tags. It keeps your code clean.

This is the syntax for including a script:

```
<head>
<title>Example scripts - Sandwich Picker</title>
<link rel="stylesheet" href="sandwiches.css">
<script type="text/javascript" src="sandwiches.js"></script>
</head>
```

The <script> tag has an src attribute that points to the location of the script and a type="text/javascript" attribute that tells the browser you're importing JavaScript. It also requires a closing tag: </script>.

You can also include scripts from other domains. JavaScript's same-source policy (see 1B) doesn't apply to such scripts, since you, as the Webmaster, explicitly decide to include them and thus implicitly judge them to be safe.

language attribute

Sometimes a language attribute is added to the <script> tag. This attribute serves to specify the exact JavaScript version being used. As we saw in 1B, the JavaScript version number is not important, and you shouldn't use it.

defer attribute

The purpose of the defer attribute is rather vague: Officially it merely serves as an indication that the script being loaded does not contain any commands that change the HTML, most importantly document.write().

{ **DEFER IN EXPLORER**

Internet Explorer executes scripts with a defer attribute only when the page has been completely loaded. At the time of writing it is impossible to say whether that is a correct interpretation of http://www.w3.org/TR/html4/interact/scripts.html#edef-SCRIPT, since the definition there is rather vague. }

`<script>` tags with JavaScript content

As I said, you can also put your script directly between the `<script></script>` tags—but remember that unobtrusive JavaScripting calls for an end to this practice (see 2C). This is the syntax:

```
<script type="text/javascript">
alert('Hello world!');
</script>
```

Of course you can use as many lines of script as you need.

If you're using XHTML, the content of the `<script>` tag must be defined as CDATA, which tells the XML/HTML parser not to parse the contents, but to send it on as is to the script engine.

```
<script type="text/javascript">
//<![CDATA[
alert('Hello world!');
//]]>
</script>
```

Note the JavaScript comments `//`. It is necessary to hide the CDATA definition characters from the JavaScript interpreter. Since they are not JavaScript, but rather XHTML, the interpreter would choke on them.

Using multiple scripts

You're allowed to add an unlimited number of scripts to an HTML document. For instance, the Edit Style Sheet and Dropdown Menu scripts work on the same HTML page, and since I use separate .js files for the two scripts, I include both:

```
<script type="text/javascript" src="dropdown.js"></script>
<script type="text/javascript" src="editstyles.js"></script>
```

I created separate .js files for two reasons. First of all, they are independent scripts that should not influence each other, and which might be maintained by different programmers at different times.

Second, Dropdown Menu is used throughout the entire site of my client, but Edit Style Sheet is only used in one administration page. Therefore I include dropdown.js in every page, but editstyles.js only in the administration page.

All scripts that you import end up in the global object of the HTML page. In practice, this means that if you define one variable in several script files, the last definition takes precedence. For instance, if dropdown.js and editstyles.js both contain a variable importantVariable, it gets the value defined in editstyles.js because that's the last script you imported.

E: Initialization

Once you've imported your scripts, you need to make sure they start at the right moment. In order to explain the problems here, let's take a detailed look at what happens when you include a script in an HTML page. We'll start with a very simple example:

```
<head>
<script type="text/javascript" src="hello.js"></script>
</head>

// hello.js contains
alert('Hello world');
```

When the browser encounters the <script> tag, it sends out an HTTP request to fetch the script file. The parsing and rendering of the HTML page is now halted until the script file has been loaded, or until the browser decides it doesn't want to wait any more (and the time at which it decides that depends on the browser). Therefore, if you import scripts from a slow server, page rendering may be delayed.

Once the script file has been received, it is parsed and the JavaScript statements are executed directly, if necessary. This means that the statement alert('Hello world') is executed as soon as the browser encounters it. Only after this has been done does the browser resume the normal HTML parsing.

Therefore users of this page will first see the alert, and the rest of the page only when they click OK.

Let's go to a more complicated example:

```
<head>
<script type="text/javascript" src="test.js"></script>
</head>
<body>
<div id="test">This is a test div</div>
</body>

// test.js contains
var test = document.getElementById('test');
test.onclick = function () {alert('Hello world!')};
```

A simple event-handler registration, you'd say. If the user clicks on the element, the alert pops up. That's true as far as it goes, but at the moment the browser executes these statements there is no element with id="test" yet. After all, the browser first loads the script file, then executes any statements, and only then continues parsing the HTML document. Therefore the element is not present at the moment the JavaScript code is executed, and the script generates an error message.

In order to prevent such problems, you enclose most of your statements in functions:

```
function initializePage() {
        var x = document.getElementById('test');
        x.onclick = function () {alert('Hello world!')};
}
```

Now the browser creates the function but doesn't execute it, because it hasn't yet received a command to do so. The trick, of course, is that you execute this function only when the page has been loaded.

The load event

The load event fires when the page has been loaded completely. Obviously this is exactly what we need for the initialization of our scripts. It works as follows:

```
function initializePage() {
        var x = document.getElementById('test');
        x.onclick = function () {alert('Hello world!')};
}
window.onload = initializePage;
```

This executes the `initializePage()` function when the page has been loaded completely. The script can now find the element with `id="test"`, and it sets the onclick event handler.

Most scripts start up only when the page has been loaded completely, because only at that time are all HTML elements on which the script wants to act present in the page. If the scripts started up earlier, they probably couldn't find most elements they need, and would give errors.

Unfortunately, the load event has two problems: correct mass initialization (i.e., initializing more than one script at the same time), and the exact timing of the event.

Mass initialization

`window.onload` (which we used above) essentially defines a method of the window object (see 5J). The problem is that if another script does the same, the `window.onload` value of the first script is overwritten, and the first script is never initialized.

4E

Let's return to the Dropdown Menus and Edit Style Sheets examples. Say that I'd initialize the scripts like this:

❌
```
// dropdown.js
window.onload = initNavigation;

// editstyles.js
window.onload = initStyleChange;
```

Only `initStyleChange()` will be executed, since it's the last defined value of `window.onload`. It overwrites the value given in dropdown.js, and Dropdown Menus is never initialized.

In order to execute both scripts, I need a better solution—one that allows me to set an unlimited number of event handlers on the same element. In order to do so I use my `addEventSimple()`/`removeEventSimple()` functions.

We'll discuss these functions in 7C, but by using them I can set several handlers for the same event on the same element. Now I can do this:

[Dropdown Menu, line 84]

```
addEventSimple(window,'load',initNavigation);
```

[Edit Style Sheets, line 104]

```
addEventSimple(window,'load',initStyleChange);
```

Now both event handlers are set. Better still, they don't overwrite each other.

Unobtrusive initialization

I created Site Survey and Usable Forms as independent modules that can be added to any site. Any Web developer who wishes to use them simply includes the correct script files, adds a bit of HTML, and the script works.

This means that I cannot use `window.onload` in the scripts. If I did that, my `window.onload` would either overwrite or be overwritten by the site's `window.onload`. Either case is unacceptable. Site Survey's general `document.onclick` event handler might overwrite or be overwritten by an existing `document.onclick` in the site, and that, too, would be unacceptable.

In these cases, I use the `addEventSimple()` solution, too. I add an extra onload event handler on top of any handler that may already exist.

Waiting for the load event

The load event fires when the page has been loaded completely, and that includes the images. This can cause a noticeable delay when a page contains huge image files.

When Dropdown Menu had been implemented on all of my client's sites, one clueless Webmaster added a 6 MB bitmap image to his homepage. This caused the site's usability to die a messy death. When a page appears ready, users expect to be able to use it, including its dropdown menus. Unfortunately, the mouseover events were not defined because they had to wait for the load event, which in turn had to wait for the 6 MB bitmap. That's confusing.

This problem is very hard to solve. Ideally, we'd want to have a sort of onLoadExceptForImages event that fires when the HTML page structure is loaded completely, but that doesn't wait for images. Unfortunately, such an event does not exist.

The DOMContentLoaded event comes closest. It fires when the DOM of the content is available, i.e., when the document has been parsed entirely, even though images may not yet be loaded. Unfortunately, at the time of writing this event is available only in Mozilla.

{ **ANOTHER SOLUTION TO LONG WAIT TIMES**

Dean Edwards describes a solution that works in Explorer and Mozilla, but no other browsers, at http://dean.edwards.name/weblog/2005/09/busted2/. }

4E

A solution would be not to use the onload event at all, but to simply include your script just before the </body> tag:

```
<body>
[all HTML]
<script type="text/javascript" src="dropdown.js"></script>
</body>
</html>
// at the end of dropdown.js
initNavigation();
```

This way, when the browser gets around to executing this statement, the entire page has already been loaded, and the script has access to all elements. It doesn't wait for the images, though.

The best way?

Unfortunately, all of them have drawbacks as well as advantages, and the context in which you write a script is of paramount importance in selecting an initialization method. I hope that this section has given you enough information to make your own decision.

In general, I myself still use the old window.onload, except when I have to initialize a script unobtrusively. In that case I use the addEventSimple() solution. We'll get back to this problem in 7C.

F: The example scripts

In order to gain a real understanding of the preparation phase, let's discuss the purpose and user interaction of my example scripts, and distill high-level decisions from them.

Below you'll find descriptions of the preparations I made for each of the example scripts. I start by defining the purpose, user actions, and the feedback on those actions. Then we'll take a quick look at script knowledge (what data does the script require in order to function) and maintenance considerations.

> **{** NOTE ON ACCESSIBILITY
>
> The preparation phase is also the proper time to consider accessibility issues. Since we already treated these in 2E, I'm not going to repeat the discussion here, but accessibility issues played an important role in the decisions I made. **}**

Textarea Maxlength

- **Purpose:** Give a warning when the length of the user input exceeds a certain limit.

- **User actions:** The user enters text in the text area.

- **Feedback:** When the user exceeds the limit, a warning is generated: the current length of the text gets a special style.

- **Script knowledge:** The script must know whether a certain textarea has a maximum length, and the value of this maximum length.

- **Maintenance:** The Webmaster should be able to add maximum lengths to other textareas, or to change the limit of a textarea.

HTML structure

Here, as in a few other scripts, the script knowledge and maintenance requirements can be combined. Every textarea that has a maximum length should get a custom attribute `maxlength`. The presence of this hook alerts the script to the fact that it should check this textarea, and its value is the upper limit of user input. In addition, this attribute is easy to change even for newbie Webmasters.

Example:

```
<textarea maxlength="300"></textarea>
```

Script structure

When the page is initialized, the script goes through all textareas and sees whether they have a maximum length. If they do, it sets an event handler.

When the event takes place, the script checks whether the user's text exceeds the limit. If it does, the script changes the style of the element that shows the current length of the text.

In order to do this, the textarea must somehow be related to this element: After it finds out which textarea is currently being edited, the script should be able to find the element that shows the current length. We already discussed the technical nuts and bolts in 4C.

Usable Forms

- **Purpose:** Hide as many form fields as possible until the user indicates she needs them.
- **User actions:** The user checks certain radio buttons or checkboxes, or selects a certain option.
- **Feedback:** The form fields appear at their proper place in the document.
- **Script knowledge:** The script must know if checking or selecting a certain value shows new form fields, and which form fields should be shown.
- **Maintenance:** The Webmaster should be able to define new actions: "If the user clicks on this checkbox, show that form field."

HTML structure

As with the previous script, the script knowledge and maintenance requirements call for clear definitions in the HTML itself.

Eventually the form would be modified by the bank's internal Web developers, and their JavaScript knowledge was insufficient to add complicated script structures every time new form fields were added. I created a simple, intuitive system to define which form fields should be shown in which circumstances.

I decided to give a rel attribute with the same value to each element that triggers a certain form change, and to each tag that contains form fields that should appear. Example:

```
<tr>
<td>[label]</td>
<td><input type="checkbox" name="country_other" id="country_other"
rel="othercountry"> Other than The Netherlands</td>
</tr>
<tr rel="othercountry">
<td>[label]</td>
<td><input name="other_country" id="other_country" /></td>
</tr>
```

This allows Webmasters to easily add or change relations, and allows the script to find related elements. Besides, the existence of the `rel` attribute serves as a hook.

Script structure

When the script is initialized, it removes all container elements that have a `rel` attribute. If the user clicks on form elements with a `rel` attribute, it returns the containers with the same `rel` value to their original position in the document, or removes them again. We'll study Usable Forms's associative arrays in 8K.

Form Validation

- **Purpose:** Validate form fields according to certain definitions.

- **User actions:** The user tries to submit the form.

- **Feedback:** Form fields with an erroneous value are highlighted. If there aren't any, the form is submitted.

- **Script knowledge:** The script must know what to check the individual form fields for, and must have a custom function for every sort of check.

- **Maintenance:** The Webmaster should be able to add existing definitions to new form fields, and to create new definitions and functions.

HTML structure

Form Validation needs an HTML attribute that serves as a hook, contains validation information, and can be updated by a newbie Webmaster:

```
<input name="phone" validation="required numeric" />
```

As we discussed in 4B, I could also have used class as a hook for this specific
script.

Script structure

Since I wanted Webmasters with JavaScript knowledge to be able to add new
validation definitions, the script structure should make it easy to add new bits
of script.

Therefore I decided to treat the values of the validation attributes as keys to
an associative array (we'll discuss those in 5K). If the script finds the value
"required", it looks up the function it should execute to handle this bit of validation, and then it does the same with the value "numeric":

[Form Validation, lines 9, 12, 15-32 (condensed), and 47-49 (condensed)]

```
validationFunctions["required"] = isRequired;
validationFunctions["numeric"] = isnumeric;
function isRequired(obj) {
    // check
}
function isnumeric(obj) {
    // check
}
```

If the Webmaster wants to add a validation function, he can write the function,
and add its name to the validationFunctions associative array and to the
validation attribute of the relevant form fields:

```
<input name="phone" validation="required numeric mustBeMobile" />
validationFunctions["mustBeMobile"] = checkMobile;
function checkMobile() {
    // check if phone number is a mobile number
}
```

If a form field is discovered to contain an error, the script automatically creates an error message next to it. I used the same naming system as with the
validation functions:

[Form Validation, lines 2-3]

```
validationErrorMessage['required'] = 'This field is required';
validationErrorMessage['numeric'] = 'This field requires a ➥
number';
```

In addition, I decided that any validation function could return one of three
values:

1. `true`; validation succeeded

2. `false`; validation not succeeded, show default error message

3. A string; validation not succeeded, show the string as error message.

This allows Webmasters to define special error messages for special cases.

Dropdown Menu

- **Purpose:** Show parts of a hierarchical navigation so that the user is not
  overwhelmed by all possibilities and options.
- **User actions:** The user selects a main navigation item.
- **Feedback:** The sub-items of the chosen main item become visible. Any
  other opened submenu becomes invisible.
- **Script knowledge:** The script must know which menu to show or hide.
- **Maintenance:** The Webmaster should be able to define new main items
  and sub-items.

HTML structure

The script must understand which sub-navigation to show when the user selects
a main navigation item. Obviously, the best way of doing that is to use nested
lists. If the user selects an item that contains a list, that list should become

visible. In addition, the root `<ul>` should get a class name that indicates "I'm a dropdown menu" and simultaneously serves as a JavaScript hook.

```
<ul class="menutree">
<li><a href="#">News</a>
  <ul>
    <li><a href="#">Press Releases</a>
        <ul>
                <li><a href="#">Release 1</a></li>
                <li><a href="#">Release 2</a></li>
                <li><a href="#">Release 3</a></li>
        </ul>
    </li>
  etc.
```

Script structure

In principle, the script structure is simple. If the user selects an item, make that item's nested list (if any) visible; if the user unselects the item, or selects another item, the nested list should become invisible again.

I didn't want to perform all kinds of complicated calculations in JavaScript, so I decided that the script would change only the `className` of the nested list. The CSS definitions for this new class name would take care of the actual visibility/invisibility.

We'll get back to Dropdown Menus in Chapter 7, especially in 7H.

Edit Style Sheet

- **Purpose:** Allow a Webmaster to edit parts of a style sheet.
- **User actions:** The Webmaster indicates the desired style changes in a form.
- **Feedback:** The style changes are implemented immediately.
- **Script knowledge:** The script must know which styles to change when the user does something.

- **Maintenance:** The system manager should be able to define new styles that the Webmasters may change.
- **Special:** This script is meant for Webmasters, and is therefore part of the administrative module of the site. Normal users won't use it.

HTML structure

This script works with a form that contains fields that allow the Webmaster to change the styles. Since the script runs on an administration page, we have greater control than usual over its exact content. Therefore the script does not use a hook, but instead is hard-coded to use the second form in the page.

In order to keep everything simple, I decided to store the names and values of the CSS properties in the form fields:

```
<select name="textAlign" id="textAlign">
    <option value="">not specified</option>
    <option value="left">Left</option>
    <option value="center">Center</option>
    <option value="right">Right</option>
</select>
```

This select box is meant for setting the alignment of the text. Therefore, its name is textAlign (the JavaScript version of CSS text-align), and the values of the options are the CSS values: left, right, or center.

The script thus only has to read out the name and value of the form field the user changed in order to know which style it should change to which value. We'll discuss this further in 5K and 9D.

Script structure

The script first has to access the individual rules of the correct style sheet (colors.css in the example). Then it waits for the user to pick a rule, and to change a style of that rule.

As we saw, the style change itself is easy: Just take the name/value pair of the form field the user has changed, and use it as a CSS property/value pair.

Sandwich Picker

- **Purpose:** Allow the user to search for and order sandwiches.

- **User actions:** The user searches for sandwiches. The user can indicate she wants either to order or trash a sandwich.

- **Feedback:** The sandwiches the user searches for are moved to the search table. The ordered sandwiches are moved to the order table. The trashed sandwiches are returned to the start table at the bottom of the page.

- **Script knowledge:** The script must know where the sandwiches are located, and has to be able to search through the names of all sandwiches.

- **Maintenance:** The Webmaster should be able to add and remove sandwiches, and to set their prices. In this case the Webmaster was my client, and although he knew some basic HTML I didn't want to make things too difficult for him.

HTML structure

Each sandwich can be moved through the document. Since the list with all sandwiches and their descriptions is clearly a case of tabular data, it made most sense to give each sandwich its own `<tr>` and move these `<tr>`s through the document.

In addition, I put the price information in the table headers. Any sandwich below a certain header has that price. The element with `id="startTable"` initially contains all sandwich `<tr>`s, and therefore this `id` serves as the script's hook.

Script structure

The script's main job is to find out which `<tr>`s should be moved to which position, and then to do it. This is trickier than it seems; we'll discuss this problem fully in 8I.

The script should have easy access to the sandwich name and price, since they are needed for the search action and the total price calculation. Therefore I added these two bits of data as properties of the object that represents the `<tr>` (see 5J).

XMLHTTP Speed Meter

- **Purpose:** Show the estimated download speed as an animation.

- **User actions:** The user enters her postal code and house number.

- **Feedback:** An animation starts up and shows the estimated download speed.

- **Script knowledge:** The script must catch the download speed (or error message) that the server returns.

HTML structure

In all scripts we've discussed so far, I decided to store a significant amount of data in the HTML. This is not necessary with XMLHTTP Speed Meter; here, the data is pulled from the server by an XMLHttpRequest.

Therefore the only important point in the HTML structure was the animation. I decided to always show a grey background image, and to overlay it with an element that had a green background image. The animation would consist of changing the `width` of this element.

The script uses a few `ids` as hooks, and I assign a submit event to the only form in the page.

Script structure

This script has two distinct modules:

- The XMLHttpRequest module fetches data from the server.

- The animation module receives this data and shows it as an animation.

I developed each independently; their only point of connection is that the XMLHTTP module passes the data (the download speed) to the animation module.

We'll discuss the animation module in 9G and the XMLHttpRequest module in Chapter 10.

4F

Site Survey

- **Purpose:** Find out which pages of a site the user has visited, and redirect the user to a survey when she quits the site.

- **User actions:** The user browses a site in the normal way.

- **Feedback:** None visible. The popup remembers the pages the user has visited, but that information remains invisible.

- **Script knowledge:** The script must keep track of the pages the user visits, and be alerted when the user leaves the site.

- **Maintenance:** The client enters a few bits of data, notably the survey period and the project number. Nonetheless, there's no maintenance in the traditional sense.

- **Special:** Ideally, the users never notice that the script is there, until they see the survey being opened.

HTML structure

This script should be able to work on any page in any site. Therefore, I didn't prepare an HTML structure, except for defining an optional element with `id=" sitetrekText"`. If this element is present in the page the script is added to, the script creates a little help text that announces the popup that's going to open.

The popup contains a bit of text and a form. The script adds as many hidden fields to this form as necessary.

This script uses no hooks, since I can't predict how the pages it will work on will be structured. Besides, the script hardly changes anything in the document tree, so it doesn't really need hooks.

Script structure

The main challenge was keeping the communication between the popup and the main window open. The script reads out the necessary data (mainly the page URLs) and stores quite a bit of information in cookies for safekeeping.

We'll discuss these features in detail in 6B.

Detail decisions

These explanations focus on the high-level decisions I made while I was working out the scripts. These decisions allowed me to start writing the script, although during the writing I discovered many special cases and little extras that also needed to be addressed. For instance:

- Sandwich Picker needs a special function that converts a four-`<td>` `<tr>` to a three-`<td>` one or vice versa. The order table's fourth column is taken by the order form, so any `<tr>` I move to this table should have only three `<td>`s, and any `<tr>` I move to one of the other tables should have four.

- Edit Style Sheet needed a few functions to remember what the user was doing: if the page is reloaded the user should be able to continue working on the same rule, with his previous changes still visible.

- Usable Forms should scan all form fields after the page has been loaded— some may already be checked, and then the script should show the relevant `<tr>`s.

These are typical functionalities you add later on. Although they're important for the overall user experience of the scripts, you shouldn't worry about them much while making core decisions. Making sure that the basic functionality works is your first priority; once that's done you can start working on the extras. Besides, usually you'll discover the need for such extras only while you're writing the script.

4F

Core

ALL PROGRAMMING LANGUAGES have to contain structures that allow you to say, "If this is the case, then do that," or to perform calculations, or to define bits of code that should be run repeatedly. These structures—the structures that actually make JavaScript a programming language—are part of the JavaScript Core language.

In this long chapter, we'll discuss the Core syntax and structures you use most often. For beginners, Core is the most complicated area of JavaScript, partly because some features are technically dense, and partly because their practical use is not always evident. On the other hand, common Core functionalities such as operators, variables, and functions work pretty intuitively.

Although I tried to treat all topics in the (to me) most logical order, readers without programming experience might want to skip some advanced subjects until later. That's quite all right; this chapter isn't supposed to bog you down in details, but to enhance your understanding. If something doesn't work for you, just leave it be for the moment and return to it later on.

You might even decide to skip this chapter entirely, as well as Chapter 6, and move straight to event handling in Chapter 7. Later, when you have more experience, you can always return to Core.

In order to allow readers without previous programming experience to understand what this chapter is about, we'll start with a quick summary. Don't hesitate to return to this summary if you get lost in the dense technical woods, or to go through this chapter at your own pace and in your own order.

That said, here's the structure of this chapter:

Section A treats a few JavaScript basics. We'll first discuss the statement (one line of JavaScript that gives one specific command). We'll introduce a few important concepts such as operators (characters that give an instruction, like the * character that says "Now multiply this"). A short discussion of values ends this section.

In Section B we'll continue discussing values. From the outset it should be clear that everything in JavaScript, be it a string like "I am a JavaScript hacker!", a number such as 42, an object, or even a function (i.e., a list of JavaScript commands), is in fact a value and can be transferred from one variable to another.

Nonetheless, these values aren't exactly the same; even a non-programmer will see that there's a fundamental difference between the number 42 and a function. Therefore each value has a data type that defines what you can and can't do with it: number, string, boolean, or object.

The beauty of JavaScript is that it's very easy to convert one data type into another; if your script requires you to interpret the number 42 as the string "42", JavaScript silently converts it to a string.

Section C returns to operators and discusses a few important ones, notably those relating to arithmetic (*, / , -, +) and comparisons (==, <=, etc.).

Section D gives the basic rules for creating variables in JavaScript. It also discusses variable scope (i.e., in which area is a variable known—only in one function or in your entire script?).

Sections E, F, and G discuss working with numbers, strings, and booleans. All these data types have specific features and problems that you should be aware of. Section G gives a detailed overview of data-type conversion to boolean; this conversion comprises the core of object detection, as discussed in 3C.

Section H discusses control structures (`if`, `for`, `while`, `do/while`, and `try/catch`). You'll often use these structures for creating script logic, for example "If the user checks this checkbox, do that."

In Section I we'll take a close look at functions, which form the backbone of any script.

Section J discusses JavaScript objects, especially those objects that are created by the browser. For instance, each HTML element in your page is represented by a JavaScript object, and even the simplest script requires you to read out or change this object.

Section K shows that JavaScript objects are really also associative arrays; i.e., arrays that associate a value to a key. This is an important advanced topic; once you master associative arrays, you'll be able to write simpler and more elegant scripts.

Finally, Section L discusses normal arrays (collections of values that are associated with a number instead of a key).

A: The basics

Let's start with some JavaScript basics. Not only is this a useful exercise for learning JavaScript, it will help you understand how a programming language works.

Case sensitivity

Sacred tradition requires us to say "Hello world" before doing anything serious. Here goes:

❌
```
var test = 'Hello world';
   alert(Test);
```

We immediately encounter our first JavaScript error: `Test is not defined`.

JavaScript is case sensitive. The variable `test` is not the same as `Test`, so JavaScript doesn't recognize it.

Always take care to write names such as `getElementById` with exactly the right mix of upper- and lowercase characters. If you make even the tiniest mistake (such as `getElementByID`), JavaScript doesn't understand what you mean.

You'll learn this JavaScript lesson the hard way.

Statements and the ;

Every script consists of a list of statements—commands that tell JavaScript to do something. Take this script:

```
var test = 'Hello world';
alert(test);
```

It contains two statements. The first tells JavaScript to create a variable `test` and to assign the string 'Hello world' to it. The second tells JavaScript to create an alert box and display the value of `test` in it.

As you see, I terminate every statement with a semicolon. This tells JavaScript that one statement has ended and that any code that follows is part of a new

statement. This is important in cases where there are several statements on
one line:

❌ `var test = 'Hello world'; alert(test);`

Without the ; JavaScript would have no way of knowing where the first statement ends and the second begins.

It is customary to put every JavaScript statement on its own line, because that
keeps your code readable. In fact, JavaScript was designed with this best practice in mind. Whenever a line of code ends without a semicolon, JavaScript
automatically inserts one. The code below works fine:

❌
```
var test = 'Hello world'
   alert(test)
```

Nonetheless, neither of the two previous examples is considered good programming practice. Put every statement on its own line, and terminate the line with a
semicolon. CSS wizards have the advantage here, because in CSS every semicolon is required. They can port their semicolon discipline to JavaScript.

When to not use ;

You may not end a line with a semicolon when you use an `if`, `for`, or `while`
control structure. This is wrong:

❌
```
if (x == 4);
   {
       x = x * 2;
          alert(x);
   }
```

JavaScript understands this code as:

❌
```
if (x == 4)
   {
          /* nothing */;
   }
```

```
{
    x = x * 2;
        alert(x);
}
```

JavaScript is perfectly capable of doing nothing if `x` is equal to 4, and therefore this `if` statement generates no error message. Nonetheless, it's probably not what you want.

You'll also learn this nasty little JavaScript feature the hard way. I've wasted plenty of time searching for obscure browser bugs to explain a behavior that was really caused by an incorrect semicolon.

Comments

Some lines contain comments instead of code. Comments are ignored by the script interpreter and are meant for the human beings who are working with your code.

JavaScript has two ways of defining comments:

```
// This line is a comment
/*
    This block of lines is a comment
*/
```

The `//` characters make the rest of the line they occur on a comment. You may use them after a normal JavaScript statement:

```
if (node.nodeType == 3) // Safari bug!
    node = node.parentNode;
```

I often use `//` to temporarily disable lines of script. For instance, I disabled one line in the `addInput()` function of Site Survey:

[Site Survey/popup.js, lines 49-56]

```
function addInput(name,value) {
    var mainForm = document.forms[0];
```

```
     var newInput = document.createElement('input');
 //  newInput.type = 'hidden';
     newInput.name = name;
     newInput.value = value;
     mainForm.appendChild(newInput);
 }
```

In the real version, the script generated hidden form fields. However, in order to show you how the script works, I disabled this line so that you would see the form fields being generated.

The /* and */ characters define a multi-line comment, just as in CSS. Note that the */ is required: if you open a comment by /* but do not close it, all browsers give error messages.

Code blocks: {}

Curly braces {} define a block of code that counts as a single statement. These blocks usually run only in certain circumstances. For instance, take this function:

```
function highlight(obj) {
    obj.parentNode.className = 'highlight';
}
```

The curly braces define the code block that is the function body. The statements in the block are executed only when the function is called. The same happens with the if and for statements:

```
if (x == 4) {
    x = x * 2;
    alert(x);
}
```

The statements enclosed by the curly braces are executed only if x is equal to 4.

Omitting the {}

You may omit the {} when an `if`, `while`, or `for` block contains only a single statement. For instance:

```
if (x == 4)
    x = x * 2;
```

If `x` is equal to 4, x is multiplied by 2. This is valid JavaScript. However, omitting the curly braces may lead to problems. Take this code; it's not wrong, but it might not do what you expect:

```
if (x == 4)
    x = x * 2;
    alert(x);
```

Again, if `x` is equal to 4, x is multiplied by 2. Then, whether `x` is equal to 4 or not, `x` is alerted. In fact, JavaScript understands the code as:

```
if (x == 4) {
    x = x * 2;
}
alert(x);
```

To prevent this sort of error, it's best to always enclose `if` and `for` statements in curly braces.

Note that function bodies must *always* be enclosed in curly braces, even if they contain only one statement.

{

DO AS I SAY

When you go through the example scripts you'll see that I don't always follow this rule. I often omit the {} in an `if` with only one single statement; and yes, occasionally I encounter a bug because of that.

This is one of the few times I'd like to ask you to do as I *say*, not as I do.

}

Operators

Most statements contain at least one operator, a character that tells JavaScript exactly which operation should be performed. Take this code:

X a b;

Although you may have defined variables a and b, this pseudo-statement doesn't tell JavaScript what to do with them, and produces an error.

Instead, you should give explicit instructions:

```
var c = a * b;
```

This statement contains two operators: the * operator that performs the multiplication of a by b, and the = operator that assigns the result of that multiplication to c.

In general, you don't have to worry about operators. On the whole, you'll use them instinctively and correctly once you know what they mean. The most important exception is the + operator, and we'll discuss its problems in detail in 5B.

Operands

An operator needs operands—values on which to perform its operation. If we say a * b, the * operator commands a multiplication to take place. What do we multiply? The values of a and b. The * operator operates on a and b; therefore a and b are the operands of *. Most operators need two operands.

Operator precedence

Take this statement:

```
var a = x - y * z;
```

Which operator goes first: – or *? If you remember your math, you'll know that multiplication comes before subtraction. In technical terms, the multiplication operator has a higher precedence than the subtraction operator.

5A

Therefore, this statement first multiplies y by z, and then subtracts the result from x. The result of this last operation is stored in a. If you want the subtraction to take place first, you use parentheses, just as in normal math:

```
var a = (x - y) * z;
```

This would first subtract y from x, then multiply the result by z, and store the final result in a.

Note that the = operator has a low precedence: it executes only when all other operators have been evaluated. That's why the assignment of the final value of the calculation to a takes place last.

RETURN VALUE OF =

The = operator's return value is a bit tricky. Take this operation:

```
var a = 1;
```

This in fact does two things:

1. It assigns the value 1 to the variable a.

2. Once that's done, it returns this same value 1 to the next operator (if any), just as the * operator in the previous example returned the result of the multiplication to the = operator.

Usually there is no other operator in assignment statements, but occasionally you want to assign the same value to several variables:

```
var a = b = 1;
```

First JavaScript assigns the value 1 to b. Then it takes the return value of the = operator, which is still 1, and assigns it to a. In 5C we'll encounter one situation in which ='s return value is important.

Return value

Every operator returns a value, and it's this value that you want to do something with.

```
var c = a * b;
```

If we multiply a by b, the operation returns the result of this multiplication. The = operator takes this return value and performs its own operation with it: it stores the value in c.

Values

Getting and using values is the whole point of programming. Therefore we'll have to take a closer look at values in general. Take this line:

```
var a = b * 4;
```

4 is a value. b is a variable that contains a value (for instance, 3). If we multiply the value of b by 4 we get another value, 12, which is assigned to variable a. This is a simple example of value manipulation.

Functions as values

Now let's look at a more complicated example:

```
var test = function () {
    alert('Hello world!');
}
var otherTest = test;
otherTest();
```

In JavaScript, there is no fundamental difference between functions and other values. In this example, the variable test refers to a function. When the value of test is assigned to otherTest, otherTest becomes a function that when executed causes the 'Hello world!" alert to pop up.

Treating functions as values is quite common in event handling. We'll return to this subject in 5I and 7C.

Variables and literals

A value is commonly expressed as a variable or a literal. The difference is simple:

```
var a = 10;
var b = a * 4;
```

In this code example, a and b are variables, which means they may contain any value, though right now they contain 10 and 40.

The 10 and 4 are literals: they literally mean 10 and 4, and cannot mean anything else.

B: Data types

Every value has a data type to define what sort of value it is.

For example, 4's data type is number, "Hello world!"'s data type is string, and the function test()'s data type is object.

The six data types

JavaScript knows four important data types and two trivial ones. The important ones are number, string, boolean, and object; the trivial ones are undefined and null, which are two distinct ways of saying "It's not there."

Numbers

Numbers are pretty self-explanatory: they're numbers. You can add, subtract, multiply, and divide numbers, and when your script requires calculations, you always use numbers. Example:

```
var exampleNumber = 42;
```

We'll discuss numbers in 5E.

Strings

Strings are sequences of characters. When you define strings, you always sur-
round them by either single quotes ' or double quotes ". This tells JavaScript
that it's dealing with a string. Examples:

```
var exampleString = 'I am a JavaScript hacker';
var exampleString2 = '49';
```

Note that the second example string contains a number (or rather, two numerical characters), but since it is surrounded by quotes, as far as JavaScript is
concerned it's a string.

Strings are by far the most versatile data type JavaScript has to offer, and
pretty soon you'll notice that you use strings everywhere. For instance, most
of the times you read out something from the DOM—say, a text the user has
entered in a form field—you get a string.

We'll take a closer look at strings in 5F.

Booleans

Booleans know only two values: `true` and `false`. Real boolean variables are
only useful when you have to answer a simple Yes/No question ("Is this form
free of errors?" "Did the user check this checkbox?"). Example:

```
var exampleBoolean = true;
```

Note that there are no quotes around the `true`; if there were, it'd be a string,
not a boolean. We'll take a look at the boolean data type in 5G.

Objects

The object data type encompasses everything that's not a number, string,
or boolean. It differs from the other three types because objects are copied,
passed, and compared by reference, not by value.

What does that mean? Take the following lines:

```
var x = 1;
var y = document.getElementById('myName');
```

5B

```
var a = x;
var b = y;
```

Variables x and a both contain the value 1. However, y and b both refer to the object returned by getElementById('myName'), in other words, the HTML element with id="myName".

Any change to the real, underlying object that y and b refer to shows up in both variables. Take these two lines:

```
b.className = 'error';
alert(y.className);
```

The alert shows the value of the class attribute of the HTML element: 'error'. The fact that we used the variable b to access the element does not matter; y refers to the same object as b, and therefore it gets its data from the same source.

In contrast, x and a contain the same value, but they don't refer to any object. Anything done to the value of x does not affect a or vice versa.

We'll discuss many object data types throughout this chapter, such as arrays and functions. Although they differ in detail, they all are objects as far as data typing is concerned. We'll discuss objects in 5I.

undefined and null

Although undefined and null are closely related, they are not exactly the same.

null usually means "no object," but it may also be returned by a function if no other value fits. This is a rare occurrence, though.

For example, suppose there is no HTML element with id="test":

```
var x = document.getElementById('test');
alert(x);
```

x becomes null. You'll see how this comes in handy when we get to object detection (see 3C and 5G).

The `undefined` value is returned in three cases:

1. If you declared a variable but did not assign a value to it.

2. If you access an undefined property of an object (and in JavaScript you can see anything you like as a property of an object).

3. If you have defined a function argument, but no value is passed to it. (See 5I for arguments.)

Take, for instance, this code:

```
var x;
alert(x);
```

I declared variable x explicitly (see 5D), but it doesn't have a value. Therefore the alert gives `undefined`.

The second rule has odd consequences:

```
// y is not declared
alert(y);
alert(window.y);
```

As you'd expect, the first alert gives an error message: y is not declared. However, the second alert accesses y as a property of JavaScript's global object, the window (see 5I). Since undefined properties always have the value `undefined`, the alert doesn't give an error message, but instead shows "undefined."

The typeof operator

The `typeof` operator shows the data type of a value. Its syntax is:

```
typeof x;
```

Note two oddities:

- When used on functions, `typeof` yields "function". Nonetheless, as far as data types are concerned, functions are really objects.

- `null` evaluates to "object".

This operator is extremely useful for debugging. If you think a variable may hold a string instead of a number, you insert a `typeof` alert. In general, this is the first debugging tool you use when you think you've encountered a data-type problem.

Sometimes `typeof` is used for object detection. However, since object detection often tries to find out if a certain object exists, but `typeof` returns "object" whether an object exists or not (i.e., is `null`, which evaluates to `false`), it's not really useful in such situations. I advise you not to use `typeof` for object detection, but instead stick to the rules we discussed in 3C.

Data-type conversion

One of the beauties of JavaScript is that converting values from one data type to another is quite easy—in fact, it happens all the time. Take this code:

```
var a = 4;
var b = '4';
var c = a * b;
```

As you can see with your newly acquired data-type knowledge, `a` is a number and `b` is a string. The third line tries to multiply these two—an operation that obviously requires numbers.

Here's where data-type conversion kicks in. The multiplication operator needs numbers, so JavaScript tries to convert its operands to numbers, if at all possible. In this case it's easy: `b` is interpreted as the number 4, and c becomes 16.

It is important to realize that `b` does not *become* a number. It remains a string, but JavaScript *interprets* it as a number for the specific purpose of executing the multiplication.

On the other hand, the result of the multiplication (stored in `c`) is a number. This gives you the best of both worlds: your original variables don't change their data type, but the result of the operation has the correct data type.

Let's return to a previous example in order to show how pervasive data-type conversion is:

```
var x;
alert(x);
```

As we saw, the alert shows undefined, since x holds this value. However, alerts show strings, and therefore the value undefined is first converted to the string "undefined".

NaN

The success of data-type conversion depends on the raw materials, and that's particularly important when you convert strings to numbers. Take this example:

```
var exampleString = 'I am a JavaScript hacker';
var exampleNumber = 42;
alert(exampleString * exampleNumber);
```

In order to multiply these two values, JavaScript tries to interpret exampleString as a number. That's totally impossible, so the outcome of the multiplication is the special value NaN (Not a Number), which means "This value cannot be interpreted as a number."

{ **NAN AS A WARNING**

If you encounter NaN when you expect a number, you're certain to have made a data-type conversion mistake. One of the numbers you want to use is actually a string that is not convertible to a number. The error could be something obvious like a string that doesn't even contain a number, like "I am a JavaScript hacker". It could also be something more subtle, like the string value "7,000".

As soon as you see NaN appear, go through your variables and make sure they can all be interpreted as numbers. }

The + problem

In general you don't have to worry about data-type conversion; it just happens automatically. There's one case, however, where a more formal understanding is necessary: when you use the + operator.

The problem with the + operator is that it can mean two things. If it's used on numbers, it means add these two numbers together, but if it's used on strings it means concatenate or sew these strings together. Concatenation is an addition of sorts, but it's radically different from the mathematical operation.

Take this example:

```
var a = 4;
var b = '4';
var c = a + b;
```

You might think c has a value of 8, but in fact it contains the string '44'. JavaScript gives precedence to string concatenation above number addition. Therefore JavaScript interprets a + b as a string concatenation, not an addition. The number is converted to a string instead of vice versa.

Obviously, the solution to this problem is to make sure that both operands are numbers.

```
var a = 4;
var b = '4';
var c = a + (b*1);
```

If we multiply b by 1 first, JavaScript uses the value returned by this operation: a number. It subsequently interprets + as add, not as concatenate.

Adding and concatenating in one line of code

Occasionally you want to add some numbers and concatenate a string in the same line of code. Let's take a look at this example:

```
var amount1 = 42;
var amount2 = 24;
var message = amount1 + amount2 + ' apples is what you ordered';
```

`message` now becomes the string '66 apples is what you ordered'. This may seem odd, since we just saw that concatenation is stronger than addition. But it's the order of the variables and operators here that matters.

JavaScript first encounters `amount1 + amount2` and has to decide whether the + means addition or concatenation. It looks at the two operands `amount1` and `amount2`, sees that they're both numbers, and therefore adds them, resulting in the number 66.

Then it encounters the next +, which now means `66 + ' apples is what you ordered'`. It again looks at the operands, sees that one of them is a string, and interprets the + as concatenate. Therefore `message` becomes '66 apples is what you ordered'.

As you see, JavaScript goes through + operators from left to right, and decides on an individual basis whether they mean add or concatenate. Therefore, the next example will not do what you want:

```
var amount1 = 42;
var amount2 = 24;
var message = 'You ordered' + amount1 + amount2 + ' apples';
```

When JavaScript encounters the `'You ordered' + amount1` bit, it interprets the + as a concatenation, since one of the operands is a string. This results in the string 'You ordered 42'. Since one of their operands is a string, the second and third + also mean concatenate, and the result becomes 'You ordered 4224 apples'.

Fortunately, just as in mathematics, you can use parentheses () to say "Handle this operation first." Therefore, the solution is:

```
var message = 'You ordered ' + (amount1 + amount2) + ' apples.';
```

JavaScript handles the `(amount1 + amount2)` operation first, and in this context + clearly means add, resulting in the number 66. Then it goes through the other + operators from left to right, and they clearly mean concatenate. Now `message` reads 'You ordered 66 apples'.

Converting to boolean

JavaScript has rules to convert every data type into every other data type. You'll rarely need most of these rules—situations in which you want to convert an object to a number are not very common. However, converting the other data types to booleans forms the basis of object detection, as we discussed in 3C.

These are the rules for converting other data types to booleans:

- The values `null` and `undefined` become `false`.
- The numbers 0 and `NaN` become `false`.
- An empty string `''` becomes `false`.
- All other values become `true`.

We'll get back to this important conversion in 5G.

Explicit data-type conversion

I demonstrated this line of code earlier. It's an example of explicit data-type conversion:

```
var c = a + (b*1);
```

The idea is straightforward: perform the simplest possible operation that converts the variable to the desired data type. Multiplying by 1 is one simple way of converting a string to a number. Subtracting 0 is another:

```
var c = a + (b-0);
```

You can convert a variable to a string by concatenating it with an empty string:

```
var string = number_or_boolean_or_object + '';
```

Converting a variable to a boolean is best done by performing the NOT (!) operation twice:

```
var boolean = !!number_or_string_or_object;
```

We'll take a closer look at this operation in 5G.

TRICKY OPERATORS

Beware of the following two operators:

+ can mean both add and concatenate. (I discussed this in 5B.)

() executes a function. Sometimes, however, you want to transfer an entire function to another variable instead of executing it. In that case, you must omit the (). (See 5I and 7C.)

C: Common operators

Let's review a few common operators.

Arithmetic operators

The * operator, as you know, performs a multiplication. JavaScript also has the traditional − operator for subtraction and the / operator for division.

JavaScript offers an elegant shorthand for all mathematical operators:

```
c = c * a;
c *= a;
```

% OPERATOR

JavaScript also contains the little-used modulo operator %. This operator returns the remainder of a division:

```
var a = 5 % 2;
```

Now a is 1, because 5 modulo 2 is 1; after you've divided 5 by 2, 1 remains.

5C

Both of the statements above multiply c by a and then assign the result to c, but the second one is shorter, and is used quite a lot.

Of course, the +=, -= and /= operators also exist. They do the same thing: they take the value of the left-hand variable, then add, subtract, or divide it by the right-hand value, and assign the result to the left-hand variable.

Finally, there is the unary negation operator - which simply means "Make this number negative":

```
var a = -3;
```

Now a contains the value –3.

++ and --

JavaScript contains a shorthand for adding or subtracting 1: the ++ and -- operators. As we'll see in 5H, these are often used in for loops:

```
c++;
++c;
```

These statements do the same thing: They add 1 to c. But there's a subtle difference between the two. If you put ++ before the variable name, the variable is first incremented (1 is added to it) and the new value is passed to the next operator. If you put the ++ after the variable name, the variable's old value is passed to the next operator, and it is incremented afterwards.

Take this example:

```
var c = d = 1;
var a = c++;
var b = ++d;
```

Initially c and d are both 1, and the ++ operator increments both to 2. However, a is 1 and b is 2:

* var a = c++ means "Assign the (old) value of c to a, and then increment c."
* var b = ++d means "Increment d, and then assign the (new) value to b."

The `--` operator works in the same way, but it decrements the variable: it sub-tracts 1.

You'll instinctively use the `++` and `--` operators correctly 99% of the time. In the remaining 1%, the subtle difference between `c++` and `++c` will trip you up.

=, ==, and ===

The `=` operator (used liberally in all code examples) means assign and *only* assign. This is an assignment:

```
var x = y * 2;
```

JavaScript multiplies `y` by 2 and assigns the result to variable `x`. You can also assign the same value to several variables:

```
var a = b = c = 1;
```

Now `a`, `b`, and `c` all have the value 1. That's because the `=` operator returns the value it just assigned. `c = 1` is executed first, and its return value (1) is assigned to `b`, after which the return value of this operation (still 1) is assigned to `a`.

`=` does *not* mean compare. If you want to compare two values, you must use the equality operator:

```
if (x == 4) {
    // do something
}
```

This statement is a correct comparison. `if (x == 4)` means "If `x` equals 4". If `x` is indeed equal to 4, then the code block delimited by curly braces `{}` is executed. If not, it's not executed. The `==` operator always returns a boolean `true` (values are equal) or `false` (values aren't equal). We'll discuss this in more detail in 5G and 5H.

Let's do it wrong:

```
❌  if (x = 4) {
        // do something
    }
```

This is not a comparison. The statement x = 4 does not return a boolean, but rather the value that you just assigned to x (which in this example is 4). So this really reads:

❌
```
if (4) {
    // do something
}
```

As we saw in 5B, any number except for 0 or NaN is converted to boolean true, and therefore the if statement would always be executed.

The important distinction between = and == is, once again, something you're going to learn the hard way.

The === operator looks like the two previous operators, but is the identity operator, the stricter version of the equality operator. It requires that its operands have not only the same value, but also the same data type.

Take this code:

```
var x = 4;
var y = '4';
if (x == y) {
    alert('x and y are equal');
}
if (x === y) {
    alert('x and y are identical');
}
```

x is the number 4, and y is a string that contains only the character '4'. JavaScript is quite relaxed about this difference, and interprets the string '4' as the number 4 if necessary. Therefore, x == y is true: x is equal to y, since they can both be interpreted as the number 4 (or the string '4', for that matter).

x === y is false, though, since the === operator requires both comparison values to have the same data type. In this example, they don't: x is a number and y is a string. Therefore, x is not identical to y.

In practice, you don't need the === operator; it's rarely necessary to compare data types in common scripts. If you accidentally type one = too much, though, weird things may happen.

!=, <, >, <=, and >=

Sometimes you want to know if one value is *not* equal to another. This is when you need the inequality operator:

```
if (x != 4) {
    // do something
}
```

If x is not equal to 4, do something.

JavaScript also has less-than, greater-than, less–than-or-equal-to, and greater-than-or-equal-to operators. They all return a boolean: comparison correct or incorrect.

```
if (x < 4) {
    alert('x is is less than 4');
}
if (x > 4) {
    alert('x is greater than 4');
}
```

5C

{
!==

As you might have guessed, there's also a non-identity operator (!==), which is the strict version of the != operator. Two values are not identical if they have different data types, even though they might be equal because they can be interpreted as having the same value.

You rarely need this operator.
}

```
if (x <= 4) {
    alert('x is less than or equal to 4');
}
if (x >= 4) {
    alert('x is greater than or equal to 4');
}
```

If both operands can be interpreted as numbers, the two values are compared numerically:

```
var x = '100';
var y = '1000';
if (x < y) {
    alert('100 is less than 1000');
}
```

Even though x and y are strings, they can both be interpreted as numbers, and therefore JavaScript compares them numerically.

If one of the operands cannot be interpreted as a number, the comparison is alphabetical. Take this example:

```
var a = 'apple';
var b = 'window';
if (a > b) {
    alert('apples are greater than windows');
}
else {
    alert('windows are greater than apples');
}
```

JavaScript determines that windows are greater than apples, because the string 'window' comes after the string 'apple' in normal alphabetical order.

Note that uppercase characters are 'less' than lowercase characters:

```
var a = 'apple';
var b = 'Window';
if (a > b) {
```

```
    alert('apples are greater than Windows');
}
else {
    alert('Windows are greater than apples');
}
```

Apples are now greater than Windows, since the string 'Window' comes before the string 'apple' in alphabetical order.

The conditional operator ? :

The conditional operator is unusual, because it works with three values, while all other operators work with one or two values. It performs a check and assigns one of two values to a variable based on that check. For instance:

```
var a = (b == 0) ? 0 : 1;
```

This means "If b is equal to 0, assign 0 to a; otherwise, assign 1 to a." Of course, this code gives the same result:

```
var a;
if (b == 0) {
    a = 0;
}
else {
    a = 1;
}
```

> **{ TERNARY OPERATOR**
>
> The conditional operator is occasionally referred to as the ternary operator, since it works with three operands instead of the usual one or two. As far as I'm concerned, this name is not useful, since it highlights a bit of its syntax instead of its purpose. **}**

The conditional operator is one of the useful shorthands that JavaScript provides, and I always use it for simple checks like the previous one. For instance, in 9F we'll encounter a simple show/hide script. If an element currently has `display: block`, I want to set its `display` to `none`, and vice versa:

```
var currentValue = this.relatedTag.style.display;
var newValue = (currentValue == 'none') ? 'block' : 'none';
```

That closes our preliminary study of operators. We'll encounter many more as this chapter progresses.

D: Variables

Variables are nothing more than useful containers to hold a value that's going to be used and/or changed in your script. In fact, every script uses variables to store and manipulate data, and anyone who has even the least bit of JavaScript experience will intuitively use them correctly.

Variable names

JavaScript variable names must consist of letters, numbers, underscores, and dollar signs. The first character may not be a number. Remember that JavaScript is case-sensitive: the variable `test` is not the same as the variable `Test`.

A custom in JavaScript development is to spell longer variable or function names in camelCase so that they're easier to read. The name starts with a lowercase character, but whenever a new "word" begins, you use an upper-case character. Sandwich Picker, for instance, uses the variable `currentPrice` instead of `currentprice` or `current_price`.

The W3C DOM uses the same system, for instance, `getElementById` or `createElement`. If you do the same with your variable names, you'll get comfortable with the system quickly, and lessen your chances of making mistakes with inner capitals.

RESERVED WORDS

You may not use the following words as variable or function names, because they already mean something in JavaScript:

break, case, catch, continue, default, delete, do, else, false, finally, for, function, if, in, instanceof, new, null, return, switch, this, throw, true, try, typeof, var, void, while, with.

The following words are reserved for future extensions of JavaScript, such as the upcoming 2.0 specification:

abstract, boolean, byte, char, class, const, debugger, double, enum, export, extends, final, float, goto, implements, import, int, interface, long, native, package, private, protected, public, short, static, super, synchronized, throws, transient, volatile.

At the time of writing, Mozilla and Safari give an error if you use any of the above words as variable or function names, although Explorer and Opera allow them.

5D

The var keyword

The first time I use a new variable, I precede its name by the keyword `var`. This is an explicit variable declaration: I take the time and trouble to explain that I am declaring a new variable.

You don't have to assign a value to the new variable:

```
var x;
```

You have now explicitly declared variable `x`, but you haven't assigned it a value yet, and as we saw in 5B it now holds the special value `undefined`. That's allowed, but it's best to assign a value as soon as possible, since you generally don't want the `undefined` value to mess up your scripts.

Implicit variable declaration

Using the var keyword is not required. If you start using a variable in your program without declaring it, JavaScript shrugs and creates it. This is called implicit variable declaration. An implicitly declared variable is always global in scope (see below).

The following two examples are both correct JavaScript:

```
var x = 10;
var a = x * 2;
alert(a);

// b has never been used yet
b = x * 2;
alert(b);
```

I do not use var to declare the variable b, but since I assign a value to it, JavaScript creates it automatically. Nonetheless, explicitly declaring your variables keeps your scripts clear and avoids scope issues, so I advise you always to do it.

Variable scope

Every variable has a scope: an 'area' inside which the variable is known, but outside of which it's unreachable. There are two scopes: global and local.

A global variable is defined throughout the JavaScript code (or, more correctly, throughout one global object) and can be used anywhere. A local variable is defined in only one function.

{
NO BLOCK SCOPE

Note that JavaScript has no block scope, as C++ and Java do. Any local variable is known throughout the entire function in which it's defined.
}

Use local variables

It's good programming practice to use as many local variables as possible. This prevents variables from interfering with each other, even if they share a name.

For instance, in Sandwich Picker I use the variable `price` to hold the total price of all sandwiches the user ordered. After all, it's a glaringly obvious name for a variable that holds a price, and other programmers will immediately understand its purpose.

If I had more price-calculation functions, I'd likely want to use `price` there, too. However, if `price` were a global variable, several functions would change its value. The result could be that `price` has an unexpected value and my calculations would go wrong.

It's far safer to define each `price` variable separately—to create one local variable `price` for each price-calculation function. Each function will be unaware of the `price` variables in the other functions, and there is no danger of interference.

Defining local variables

How do you define a local variable? There are two ways:

- You explicitly declare them with the `var` keyword inside the body of a function.
- You declare them as an argument when you define a function.

A variable that has been declared in any other way is global in scope. (We'll discuss functions in more depth in 5I.)

In the following example, `message` is a global variable, because it's defined out-side of any function body:

```
var message = 'Error!';
function doSomething() {
    alert(message);
}
```

In this example, it's a local variable, because it's defined in a function body:

```
function doSomething() {
    var message = 'Error!';
    alert(message);
}
```

In this example, it's global again. It's used in the function body, but it isn't declared by the var keyword:

```
function doSomething() {
    message = 'Error!';
    alert(message);
}
```

Here, finally, it's local again, because it's a function argument:

```
doSomething('Error!');
function doSomething(message) {
    alert(message);
}
```

E: Working with numbers

Numbers are fairly straightforward to work with. Note that JavaScript makes no distinction between integers and floating-point values; they're both numbers. Calculations work as expected, and you can influence their order by the use of parentheses:

```
var sum = var1 + var2 * var3;
var sum = (var1 + var2) * var3;
```

The first line of code multiplies var2 and var3, and then adds var1 to the result. The second line adds var1 and var2, and multiplies the result by var3. No surprises here.

ROUNDING ERRORS

When you perform calculations with decimals, you may come across the infamous rounding error. For complicated reasons, the simple calculation 0.05 + 0.01 does not yield 0.06, as you'd expect, but 0.060000000000000005. Similarly, -0.07+0.05+0.02 does not yield 0, but -3.469446951953614e-18.

Solution: round the result in one of the ways described below before showing it to the user.

The upcoming JavaScript 2.0 specification will address this problem.

Octal and hexadecimal numbers

JavaScript also allows you to use octal and hexadecimal numbers. Any number that starts with a 0 is octal; any number that starts with 0x is hexadecimal. Take this example:

```
var test1 = 042;
var test2 = 0x42;
alert(test1 + ' ' + test2);
```

The alert now says '34 66', since the octal number 42 is decimal 34, while the hexadecimal number 42 is decimal 66.

OCTAL ERRORS

People will never add 0x to their numbers accidentally, but adding an accidental leading 0 is possible. When I created Site Survey I was asked to add an extra variable to hold the project number. I duly did so, but the client complained that it didn't work as expected. It turned out that he'd entered the (octal) number 042, which was returned to the server as 34. I told him to either remove the leading 0 or to make the variable a string.

5E

{
THE MATH OBJECT

Instead of treating the complete Math object, I'll just highlight a few methods that are useful in everyday Web development. For a complete overview, see http://www.w3schools.com/jsref/jsref_obj_math.asp.
}

The Math object

JavaScript has a Math object that contains methods for more complex mathematical operations (e.g., Math.sqrt(4) gives the square root of 4) and properties for constants (e.g., Math.PI holds the number pi). Although the Math object allows many mathematical calculations, you'll rarely need those in a Web site—well, maybe if you want to calculate the path of a circular animation, but how often does that happen?

Math.round(), Math.floor(), and Math.ceil()

The Math object contains three methods for rounding numbers: Math.round(), Math.floor(), and Math.ceil().

Math.round() always rounds to the nearest integer:

```
alert(Math.round(1.4)); // yields 1; the nearest integer
alert(Math.round(1.6)); // yields 2; the nearest integer
```

Math.floor() always rounds down (including when working with negative numbers):

```
alert(Math.floor(1.6)); // yields 1
alert(Math.floor(-1.6)); // yields -2
```

Math.ceil() always rounds up (including when working with negative numbers):

```
alert(Math.ceil(1.6)); // yields 2
alert(Math.ceil(-1.6)); // yields -1
```

Although these methods work on numbers, you can also specify a string as the argument. As usual, data-type conversion makes this possible:

```
alert(Math.floor('1.6')); // also yields 1;
```

Math.random()

Math.random() gives a random number between 0 and 1. I use it in XMLHTTP Speed Meter to generate a random animation:

[XMLHTTP Speed Meter, line 111]

```
var fluctuationDirection = (Math.random() < .5) ? 1 : -1;
```

If the random number is smaller than 0.5, the animation should take one step in the positive direction; if it's larger, it should take one step in the negative direction.

If you need a random number between 0 and 10, simply multiply the value of Math.random() by 10:

```
var randomNumber = Math.random() * 10;
```

Math.abs()

Math.abs(x) gives the absolute (i.e., non-negative) value of the number x. I use this in XMLHTTP Speed Meter, too, because I want to calculate the direction of an animation:

[XMLHTTP Speed Meter, lines 84-86]

```
var distance = Mbit - currentMbit;
var direction = distance/Math.abs(distance);
if (!direction) return;
```

currentMbit is the current position of the animation, and Mbit the desired position. Subtracting one from the other yields the distance the animation has to go. But I also want to know the direction of the animation, so I divide distance (which may be positive or negative) by the absolute value of distance (which is always positive). This division yields 1 or –1, which gives me the direction of the animation.

If the outcome is 0 (i.e., the current and desired position are the same) I end the function.

toFixed()

The `toFixed()` method converts a number to a string with the specified amount of decimals. This is especially useful when working with prices; for example, `price.toFixed(2)` gives output that's suitable for a price.

Contrary to the `Math` methods we just discussed, `toFixed()` is a method of a Number object. This doesn't work:

> ❌   `var x = '4';`
>   `alert(x.toFixed(2));`

`toFixed()` cannot be used on strings, and therefore this code gives an error message.

I use the method in Sandwich Picker. I want to show the total price of the user's order in the correct place, and I want it to have two decimals and no weird rounding errors. I wrote a function `createReadablePrice()` that takes care of this operation:

[Sandwich Picker, lines 204-208]

```
function createReadablePrice(price) {
    price = price.toFixed(7);
    price = price.replace(/\./,',');
    return price;
}
```

The function receives a price and makes sure it has two decimals. Then it replaces the dot with a comma. (In Dutch, the comma is the decimal separator.)

Note that this function receives a number but returns a string.

parseInt() and parseFloat()

Two global methods wrap up this quick overview: `parseInt()` and `parseFloat()`. Both receive a string as an argument and extract a number: an integer and a floating-point number, respectively.

The real power of these methods is that the strings they receive may contain non-numerical characters, as in these examples:

```
alert(parseInt("3.54 apples")); // yields 3
alert(parseFloat("3.54 apples")); // yields 3.54
```

Both methods start at the left of the string. If the first character is not a number or a minus sign (or, in the case of `parseFloat()`, a decimal dot), they return NaN.

If the first character is valid, the methods continue reading out the string until they encounter a non-numeric character (or, in the case of `parseInt()`, a decimal dot). Once they encounter such a character, they return the number they extracted.

5F

F: Working with strings

Strings are JavaScript's most versatile data type, and you'll manipulate them often.

Quotes

A literal string is always surrounded by quotes. This alerts JavaScript to the fact that it's a string:

```
var exampleString = 'I am a JavaScript hacker';
var exampleString2 = '49';
```

As we already saw, the quotes make the second example a string, too, even though it happens to contain only numerical characters.

JavaScript also allows you to use double quotes. So this, too, is perfectly valid JavaScript:

```
var exampleString = "I am a JavaScript hacker";
var exampleString2 = "49";
```

> **{ CHOOSING BETWEEN SINGLE AND DOUBLE QUOTES**
>
> Long ago I decided that I'd always use single quotes for JavaScript and double quotes for HTML, even though both languages allow both types of marks. Therefore I nearly always use single quotes to delimit JavaScript strings.
>
> I advise you to make such a rule for yourself, since it'll make your code more readable and will occasionally prevent errors. **}**

But what if a string contains quotation marks? What if I need the string 'I'm a JavaScript hacker'? This doesn't work:

X `var exampleString = 'I'm a JavaScript hacker';`

JavaScript sees the second quote—the one being used as an apostrophe—as a string delimiter. Therefore it reads the string 'I', followed by a bunch of variable names it doesn't understand. The result is an error message.

One solution is to use double quotes as string delimiters:

```
var exampleString = "I'm a JavaScript hacker";
```

JavaScript sees that you're using double quotes to delimit the string, and therefore considers the single quote a part of the string.

The other solution is to *escape* the single quote. This is done by adding a backslash (\) just before the character. This backslash tells JavaScript to treat the next character as a character, not as a string delimiter. So this, too, is a valid way of defining the string:

```
var exampleString = 'I\'m a JavaScript hacker';
```

Now JavaScript treats the second quote as a part of the string.

Concatenation: +

As you learned in 5B, string concatenation means "sewing strings together."
The principle is simple:

```
var exampleString = 'I am a JavaScript hacker';
var exampleString2 = 'Hello world';
alert(exampleString2 + exampleString);
```

This yields "Hello worldI am a JavaScript hacker". You might want a space
between the two sentences. No problem:

```
alert(exampleString2 + ' ' + exampleString);
```

The shorthand notation also works fine:

```
exampleString2 += ' ' + exampleString;
```

Unfortunately, string concatenation uses the same + operator as does mathematical addition (as we saw in 5B).

The String object

As soon as you create a string it's made into a String object, which contains a
few useful methods and properties that allow you to quickly and easily manipulate the string. They are among the most important tools of every JavaScript
programmer.

length

A string has a length, and the length property allows you to determine it:

```
var exampleString = 'I am a JavaScript hacker';
alert(exampleString.length); // yields 24
```

Note that this is a read-only property.

indexOf() and lastIndexOf()

By far the most notorious String method is `indexOf()`. It returns the index number of a string within the main string, and is often used in browser detects (see 3D) to determine whether the user-agent string of a browser contains, for instance, 'MSIE'. Note that the first character in a string has index number 0, not 1.

For example:

```
var exampleString = 'I am a JavaScript hacker';
alert(exampleString.indexOf('JavaScript'));
// yields 7
```

This yields 7, since the substring 'JavaScript' starts at the eighth character (index number 7) in `exampleString`.

If the requested string does not exist, `indexOf()` returns −1:

```
var exampleString = 'I am a JavaScript hacker';
alert(exampleString.indexOf('PHP')); // yields -1
```

Now let's look at a slightly more complex example:

```
var exampleString = 'I am a JavaScript hacker';
alert(exampleString.indexOf('a')); // yields 2
```

In fact, there are five 'a's in `exampleString`. Without further instructions, `indexOf()` always returns the index number of the first character that matches the substring. Therefore, the previous example will yield 2 (which is the index number of the third character).

But suppose you want to look for the second 'a' in the string. You have to give `indexOf()` extra instructions by adding an argument:

```
var exampleString = 'I am a JavaScript hacker';
alert(exampleString.indexOf('a',3)); // yields 5
```

Now `indexOf()` starts its search at the fourth character (with index number 3) and returns 5, since the first 'a' after the fourth character is the sixth character (with index number 5) in the string.

More generally, the following code always returns the position of the second 'a' in any string:

```
var secondA = exampleString.indexOf('a', ➡
exampleString.indexOf('a')+1);
```

The `lastIndexOf()` method works the same as `indexOf()`, except that it searches backwards from the end of the string:

```
var exampleString = 'I am a JavaScript hacker';
alert(exampleString.lastIndexOf('a')); // yields 19
```

Here, too, you can define a second argument that says where the search should start:

```
var exampleString = 'I am a JavaScript hacker';
alert(exampleString.lastIndexOf('a'),18); // yields 10
```

charAt()

The `charAt()` method allows you to find a character at a certain position in the string:

```
var exampleString = 'I am a JavaScript hacker';
alert(exampleString.charAt(9)); // yields 'v'
```

The tenth character in the string (with index number 9) is a 'v', so that's what the alert shows.

{ **EXAMPLE WITH LENGTH, INDEXOF(), AND CHARAT()**

I occasionally use a combination of `indexOf()` and `charAt()` to find out if a user enters valid input. (Yes, I could also use a regular expression, but I'm bad at them and avoid them whenever possible.) Suppose the user is only allowed to enter vowels in a form field and I have to check each character to see if it's a vowel. I do that as follows:

```
var vowels = 'aeiouy';
var inputString = [read out form field];
```

continues

```
for (var i=0;i<inputString.length;i++) {
  if (vowels.indexOf(inputString.charAt(i)) == -1)
      // notify user of error
}
```

The definition string `vowels` contains all the vowels. The script goes through the string the user has entered (`inputString`) character by character (`i` goes from 0 to the `length` of the string). It takes the character at each position (`inputString.charAt(i)`) and tries to find its position in the definition string `vowels` (`vowels.indexOf(...)`). If the character doesn't occur in the test string (`indexOf(...) == -1`), the user has entered a disallowed character.

substring()

The `substring()` method allows you to take a substring from a string. Of course, you have to specify the start and end point of the substring:

```
var exampleString = 'I am a JavaScript hacker';
alert(exampleString.substring(5,8));
```

The start character (index 5) is part of the substring, but the end character (index 8) is not. The sixth character (with index 5) is an 'a', and the eighth character (with index 7) is a 'J'. Therefore, this yields the string 'a J'.

You can also leave out the second argument, in which case the substring continues until the end of the string:

```
var exampleString = 'I am a JavaScript hacker';
alert(exampleString.substring(5));
```

Now the alert says 'a JavaScript hacker'.

split()

The split() method allows you to split a string into several parts. The argument of the function defines the character(s) the string should be split on, and split() returns an array. For instance:

```
var exampleString = 'I am a JavaScript hacker';
var splitString = exampleString.split('c');
```

Now exampleString is split wherever a 'c' occurs. All parts of the string become a new string, and splitString becomes an array that contains all these strings. (We'll discuss arrays in 5L.) The 'c' characters themselves are removed entirely.

So splitString becomes this array:

```
['I am a JavaS','ript ha','ker'];
```

An excellent example of how to use split() is contained in Form Validation. This script allows the Web developer to define a custom validation attribute on form fields that tell the script which checks it should run on the form field. For instance:

```
<input name="phone" validation="required numeric" />
```

The validation script does this for all form fields:

[Form Validation, lines 80-98, condensed heavily]

```
// els[i] is the form field currently being investigated
var req = els[i].getAttribute('validation');
var reqs = req.split(' ');
for (var j=0;j<reqs.length;j++) {
    // run check
}
```

It takes the validation attribute of the field. Then it splits this string by spaces and stores these strings in the array reqs. In the case of the example form field, reqs holds two strings: 'required' and 'numeric'. Now the script goes through these strings (the for loop) and performs the checks 'required' and 'numeric'.

5F

toLowerCase() and toUpperCase()

The methods `toLowerCase()` and `toUpperCase()` make a string wholly lowercase or wholly uppercase:

```
var exampleString = 'I am a JavaScript hacker';
alert(exampleString.toLowerCase());
alert(exampleString.toUpperCase());
```

These alerts give 'i am a javascript hacker' and 'I AM A JAVASCRIPT HACKER', respectively.

These methods are occasionally useful when you compare strings. For instance, when you request the `selectorText` of a style rule (see 9D), some browsers return a lowercase string and others an uppercase string.

In Edit Style Sheet, I have to compare the returned `selectorText` with a string the user has chosen. Since I'm not certain whether either `selectorText` or the user string will be upper- or lowercase, I play it safe and convert both strings to lowercase before comparing them:

[Edit Style Sheet, line 52]

```
if (sheetRules[i].selectorText.toLowerCase() == ➡
selector.toLowerCase())
```

Of course, converting both to uppercase would work fine, too.

G: Working with booleans

Boolean values are simple to work with, but by themselves they're limited. Although you'll occasionally use a variable with a boolean value, the most important use of the boolean data type is with the `if` statement.

Variables with boolean values

A boolean value is either `true` or `false`. Variables commonly get a boolean value when they answer a Yes/No question like "Is this form valid?". Take `validForm` from Form Validation:

[Form Validation, lines 73-75, condensed]

```
function validate() {
    var validForm = true;
```

When the `validate()` function starts up, it sets the `validForm` variable to `true`, because initially it assumes that the form is valid:

[Form Validation, lines 89-92, condensed]

```
if (OK != true) { // if the form field contains an error
    // administration
    validForm = false;
```

When the script encounters an error in the form, `validForm` becomes `false`. At the end of the function, it's used to decide what to do next:

[Form Validation, lines 100-104, condensed]

```
if (!validForm) {
    alert("Errors have been found");
}
return validForm;
```

The `if` statement says "if NOT validForm", or "if validForm is false". Then `validForm` is returned to the submit event handler. If this return value is `false`, the form is not submitted to the server (see 7B). This is exactly what we want: the form should be submitted only if it contains no errors and `validForm` is `true`.

Boolean operators

The line `if (!validForm)` brings us to our next topic: &&, ||, and ! (also called AND, OR, and NOT). These are the three main boolean operators, and you'll use them in `if` statements and occasionally in other circumstances.

I'll use two test boolean values to demonstrate how these operators work:

```
var x = true;
var y = false;
```

The NOT operator !

The NOT operator reverses a boolean. If the variable is true it becomes false and vice versa:

```
var z = !x;
```

z is false, because x is true and the ! operator reverses that value.

The AND operator &&

The AND operator takes two booleans and returns true if *all* are true. Otherwise it returns false:

```
var z = x && y;
```

z is false because y is false. For z to become true, both x and y have to be true.

The OR operator ||

The OR operator takes two booleans and returns false if *all* are false. Otherwise it returns true:

```
var z = x || y;
```

z is true because x is true. For z to become false, both x and y have to be false.

{ BITWISE OPERATORS & AND |

JavaScript also contains the bitwise operators & and | (which perform bitwise AND and OR). If you don't know what bitwise AND and OR are, don't worry. You rarely need these operations in normal JavaScript.

Just make sure that you write && and || if you want to use the boolean AND and OR. **}**

Combining boolean operators

You can combine these three operators to define quite complex boolean expressions.

Let's add a third example value:

```
var x = true;
var y = false;
var z = false;
```

Now let's combine these variables and the three boolean operators:

```
var a = x && (y || !z);
```

What's a's value? Start by swapping in the values of x, y, and z:

```
var a = true && (false || !false);
```

Now resolve the NOT:

```
var a = true && (false || true);
```

Then resolve the part between parentheses (which, as usual, comes first). Since `false || true` is `true`, we get:

```
var a = true && true;
```

Now you know that a is `true`.

BOOLEAN GENERATOR

If you're not used to working with boolean logic, it's worth practicing. I have created a boolean generator that allows you to create and evaluate boolean expressions. You can find it at http://www.quirksmode.org/js/boolean.html.

5G

Testing if an object exists

The if() statement hinges on boolean values. The expression between the parentheses is evaluated as a boolean, and data-type conversion makes sure that all parts of such an expression are interpreted as booleans.

Remember the rules of converting a value to a boolean?

- The special values undefined and null become false.
- The numbers 0 and NaN become false.
- An empty string becomes false.
- All other values become true.

The conversion of an object to a boolean forms the core of object detection that we discussed in 3C. Let's repeat the example:

[Edit Style Sheet, lines 5-6]

```
function initStyleChange() {
    if (!document.styleSheets) return;
```

document.styleSheets is supposed to be an object, but the browser might not support it. In any case, the if() statement forces data-type conversion from object to boolean:

- If the browser supports document.styleSheets, the object exists and is converted to boolean true.
- If the browser does not support document.styleSheets, the object does not exist. As we saw in 5B, an object that does not exist has the value null, which in turn converts to boolean false.

The NOT operator reverses this value. Therefore, the browser ends the function (return) if the if() statement returns true, i.e., if document.styleSheets evaluates to false: if the browser does not support the object.

A more complicated example is my favorite line of object detection, which
checks if the W3C DOM is supported:

```
var W3CDOM = document.getElementsByTagName && ➡
document.createElement;
```

It checks if the browser supports `getElementsByTagName` and `createElement`.
The principle is the same: if these methods (with data-type object) exist, they
evaluate to `true`; if they don't exist, they are `null` and evaluate to `false`. If a
browser supports both of them (&&), it supports the W3C DOM.

Advanced uses of boolean operators

The value returned by the && and || operators is unusual. To show why, let's
look at a case that involves strings and numbers:

```
var x = '2';
var y = '3';
var z = x * y;
```

As we saw earlier, the strings `x` and `y` are interpreted as numbers, the multiplication is executed, and the value the operation evaluates to (which is a number)
is stored in z. Therefore, z now becomes a number, though `x` and `y` remain strings.

Now let's look at our last object-detection line:

```
var W3CDOM = document.getElementsByTagName && ➡
document.createElement;
```

Both objects are interpreted as booleans in order to perform the operation
&&. Now you'd expect `W3CDOM` to become a boolean, too, just as z became a
number in the previous example.

But that doesn't happen. The boolean operators && and || don't return `true` or
`false`, but rather the *value* of the last expression they evaluated. This is very
much an exception to the general rule:

```
var W3CDOM = document.getElementsByTagName && ➡
document.createElement;
alert(W3CDOM):
```

The alert now displays:

```
function createElement() {
[native code]
}
```

The `document.createElement` expression was evaluated last, hence `W3CDOM` now contains its value (which is a native browser function).

However, the last expression that was evaluated doesn't have to be the last expression in the statement. In order to discuss this potentially confusing feature, we have to take a closer look at how boolean operators work. Take this example:

```
var z = x || y;
```

As we saw, the expression `x || y` becomes `true` if either x or y (or both) are `true`. The point is that if x is `true`, the expression automatically becomes `true`, too. Therefore JavaScript doesn't have to evaluate y; its value doesn't matter any more.

In other words, if x evaluates to `true`, JavaScript doesn't evaluate y because it isn't necessary to do so. The `||` operator returns the value of the expression that was evaluated last, and therefore z now contains x's value.

The reverse happens here:

```
var z = x && y;
```

As we saw, `x && y` becomes `true` if both x and y are `true`. Therefore, if x is `false`, the expression automatically becomes `false`, too. JavaScript doesn't have to evaluate y any more.

Using the && and || oddities

We can use these facts in interesting ways. As we'll see in 7F, most browsers store the event target in `evt.target`, but Explorer uses `evt.srcElement` instead. Therefore, any function that wants to use this target first has to find out where the browser stores it. I use this line:

[Usable Forms, line 71]

```
var evtTarget = evt.target || evt.srcElement;
```

What happens? JavaScript encounters a || operator and starts evaluating the first expression (evt.target). If the browser is W3C DOM-compliant, evt.target exists, i.e., it is not undefined, and JavaScript has found an expression that evaluates to true. It doesn't have to go on to the next expression, so it breaks off the || operation.

Nonetheless, || doesn't return true, but the *value* of the expression that was last evaluated, i.e., evt.target's value, which is the target of the event. That's exactly the bit of data we need.

If the browser is Explorer, evt.target is undefined, which converts to boolean false. Therefore JavaScript proceeds to the second expression, and since evt.srcElement exists, it evaluates as true. Again, || doesn't return true, but the value of the expression that was last evaluated (evt.srcElement), which is again the target of the event.

In other words, evtTarget now contains the target of the event, whether that information is found in evt.target or evt.srcElement. You'll often use this trick when there are several possible locations for one bit of data.

{

USING && AS ON-THE-SPOT OBJECT DETECTION

It's possible to use the && operator in a similar way, although I never do so:

```
var x = document.createElement && document.➥
createElement('div');
```

This statement first evaluates document.createElement. If it doesn't exist, it returns the value null, which converts to boolean false. Now it stops, since it knows enough (&& can never return true if one of its operands is

continues

`false`). That's a good thing, since the second expression would give an error message if a browser that doesn't support `createElement()` tried to execute it.

If `createElement` does exist, it evaluates `document.createElement('div')` (in other words, it creates a div) and returns its value (the div) to `x`.

This is a sort of on-the-spot object detection: "I want to use `createElement`. Does it exist?" The problem is that if you use this kind of object detection, you have to repeat it on every single line that uses a W3C DOM method. The object detection described in 3C is easier to write and maintain.

H: Control structures

In the previous section we took a quick peek at the `if` statement. It's time to treat it, and its fellow control structures, officially.

The if statement

An `if()` statement always needs an expression between its parentheses. This expression is interpreted as a boolean value. If the expression is `true`, then the `if`'s script block is executed; if the expression is `false`, then the script block isn't executed:

```
if (this expression returns true) {
    // this block is executed
}
```

For instance:

```
if (x == 4) {

    alert('x is 4. Oh joy!');

}
```

> ## { COMMON ERRORS IN IF STATEMENTS
>
> As we saw in 5A, there are two nasty little errors to avoid in your `if` statements. Both examples below will always show the alert, even if `x` is not 4:
>
> ```
> if (x = 4) {
>    alert('Hurray');
> }
> if (x == 4);
> {
>    alert('Hurray');
> }
> ```
>
> The first example does not compare `x` to 4, but assigns 4 to `x` and also returns this value. Since 4 converts to boolean `true`, the alert always pops up. The second example has a semicolon in exactly the wrong place, and therefore says "if `x` is equal to 4, do nothing. Afterwards, show the alert." }

The comparison `x == 4` returns a boolean `true` or `false`. If `true` is returned, the alert pops up.

Now take this `if` statement from Textarea Maxlength. When the script initializes, it goes through all textareas in the page and sees if they have an attribute `maxlength`. If one does, the textarea is initialized:

[Textarea Maxlength, lines 10-19, condensed heavily]

```
if (textareas[i].getAttribute('maxlength')) {
   // initialize textarea
}
```

`textareas[i]` is the current textarea. I use the `getAttribute()` method to search for the attribute `maxlength`. If the attribute exists, then `getAttribute()` returns its value, which is a string, such as "300". If there is no `maxlength` attribute, it returns `null`.

The `if` statement interprets this returned value as a boolean, which is `false` if the value is `null`, and `true` otherwise. Therefore the textarea is initialized only if it has a `maxlength` attribute.

You can also use several boolean operators within the `if` statement. This allows you to perform quite complicated checks. For instance, take a look at the most complex `if` statement in the example scripts, from Usable Forms:

[Usable Forms, lines 70-81, condensed]

```
var e = [event object];
var tg = [target of event];
if (!(
    (evtTarget.nodeName == 'SELECT' && e.type == 'change')
    ||
    (evtTarget.nodeName == 'INPUT' && ➡
evtTarget.getAttribute('rel'))
)) return;
```

If the user clicks anywhere on the page or changes any select box, a function is called. I want it to actually do something in only two cases:

- If the user has changed a select box, i.e., a `change` event has fired and its target is a select box.
- If the user has clicked on an input that has a `rel` attribute.

If neither is the case, the function should end immediately (`return`), and that's what the `if` checks for. Let's take it apart:

```
(tg.nodeName == 'SELECT' && e.type == 'change') // case 1
```

This bit is `true` if the target of the event is a `<select>` element AND the type of the event is `change`. Let's call it 'case 1'.

```
(tg.nodeName == 'INPUT' && tg.getAttribute('rel')) // case 2
```

This bit is `true` if the target of the event is an `<input>` element AND it has an attribute `rel`. Let's call it 'case 2'. So the `if` becomes:

```
if (!(case 1 || case 2)) return;
```

If both cases are `false`, the expression says:

```
if (!(false || false)) return;
```

`false || false` is `false`, so it becomes:

```
if (!false) return;
```

The `!` operator reverses this value to `true`. Therefore, the function ends if neither of my requirements is met. That's exactly what I want.

Now suppose case 2 is `true`: the user has clicked on an `<input>` with a `rel` attribute. The expression says:

```
if (!(false || true)) return;
```

or:

```
if (!true) return;
```

Again, the `!` operator reverses this value to `false`. Now the `return` statement is not executed and the function does not end. That's also exactly what I want.

else if and else

`if` statements can be extended with `else if` or `else`. Both are executed *only* when the original `if` statement is not executed. `else if` means "Now try this `if`," while `else` means "In all other cases."

For instance:

```
if (x == 4) {
    alert('x is 4. Oh joy!');
}
else {
    alert('x is not 4. Too bad.');
}
```

If x is equal to 4, the first code block is executed and the second one is ignored. If x is not equal to 4, the first code block is ignored and the second one is executed.

else if works like this:

```
var x = 2;
var y = 3;
if (x == 4) {
    alert('x is 4. Hurray!');
}
else if (y == 3) {
    alert('y is 3. Hurray!');
}
```

The first condition x == 4 is false: x is not equal to 4. Therefore, the first code block is not executed. JavaScript now moves to the else if and evaluates the condition y == 3. Since it is true, the second alert is shown.

Of course you can use as many else ifs as you like. Take this example, again from Usable Forms:

[Usable Forms, lines 85-99, condensed]

```
if (evtTarget.type == 'checkbox') {
    // handle checkbox
}
else if (evtTarget.type == 'radio') {
    // handle radio
}
else if (evtTarget.type == 'select-one') {
        // handle select box
}
```

If the event target is a checkbox, the first block is executed. If it's a radio, the second one is executed, and if it's a select box, the third one is executed.

switch

I could also have used a `switch` statement for the last code example.

The `switch` statement takes a value and goes through a list of options, each of which is called a `case`. If it finds the right `case`, it starts executing the code block and doesn't stop until it reaches the end of the switch block or a `break` statement. It also ignores all other `case`s.

Take this bit from Edit Style Sheet. It isn't that different from the previous `if/else if` example:

[Edit Style Sheet, lines 74-86]

```
switch (relatedField.type) {
    case "text":
            relatedField.value = styles[i];
            break;
    case "checkbox":
            if (relatedField.value == styles[i])
                    relatedField.checked = true;
            break;
    case "select-one":
            for (var j=0;j<relatedField.options.length;j++)
                    if (relatedField.options[j].value == styles[i])
                            relatedField.options[j].selected=true;
}
```

The `switch` is performed on the value of `relatedField.type`, which, once again, gives the type of a form field.

If `type` is "text", the first line is executed, and then the `switch` encounters a `break` statement, which means "Stop operation." If `type` is "checkbox", the next two lines are executed, and a `break` is once again encountered. If `type` is "select-one" the last few lines are executed. There's no `break` statement after those lines because it's not necessary: the entire `switch` block ends.

{ NO DATA-TYPE CONVERSION

Note that the value after the case must have the same data type as the variable you use in the switch; no data-type conversion takes place. Take this code:

```
var x = '4';
switch (x) {
  case 4:
        alert('x is 4. Oh joy!');
        break;
}
```

The alert will not pop up, since the case expects the number 4, not the string
'4'. This is especially important when you use form-field values, which are
always strings, even when they contain only numbers. }

Common error

When your code is still in development, it's a good idea to insert the last
break anyway, in order to avoid the most common error in switch statements.
Suppose later on you add another case but don't pay enough attention to the
existing code:

```
case "select-one":
    for (var j=0;j<relatedField.options.length;j++)
          if (relatedField.options[j].value == styles[i])
                relatedField.options[j].selected = true;
    // note: no break statement
case "submit":
    // handle submit
```

Now if type is select-one, the switch executes the select-one case and then
continues to the 'submit' case, since there is no break statement to stop it.
This is usually not what you want.

Deliberately omitting a break

Sometimes, however, omitting a break can be exactly what you want. Take this example from Form Validation:

[Form Validation, lines 15-32]

```
function isRequired(obj) { // obj is the form field
   switch (obj.type) {
          case 'text':
          case 'textarea':
          case 'select-one':
                 if (obj.value)
                        return true;
                 return false;
          case 'radio':
                 var radios = obj.form[obj.name];
                 for (var i=0;i<radios.length;i++) {
                        if (radios[i].checked) return true;
                 }
                 return false;
          case 'checkbox':
                 return obj.checked;
      }
   }
```

I use a `return` statement instead of `break`, but the `return` serves the same purpose—it ends the `case`.

Note the start of the function:

```
case 'text':
case 'textarea':
case 'select-one':
   if (obj.value)
          return true;
   return false;
```

The form-field types ("text", "textarea", and "select-one") should be treated the same: we need to check if fields of those types have a `value`. Therefore, the three `case` statements all refer to the same bit of code.

For example, if the type of the form field is text, the function starts at `case: text`, and then continues until it finds a `return` (or `break`). Along the way, the function encounters two other `cases`, but it ignores those lines—they are irrelevant, since the `case` is text.

default

Neither example contains the final feature of a `switch`: the `default` statement. `default` is a `case`, too, and it simply means "In all other cases."

It's used as follows:

```
function isRequired(obj) { // obj is the form field
    switch (obj.type) {
            case 'text':
            case 'textarea':
            case 'select-one':
                    // handle
            case 'radio':
                    // handle
            case 'checkbox':
                    // handle
            default:
                    alert('Sorry, I don\'t know what to do');
        }
    }
```

If `obj.type` has none of the values defined in the `case` statements, the `switch` continues on to the `default` and executes it.

for, while, do/while

There are four loop statements in JavaScript, and although they differ in detail, they are all meant to repeat a code block until a certain condition is met. The most common one is the `for` loop, but occasionally you'll use `while` and `do/while`, too.

The fourth one, `for in`, loops through the properties of an object. Since it is hard to understand without treating JavaScript objects and associative arrays first, I will explain it in detail in 5K.

for

This is the structure of a `for` loop:

```
for (initialize; test; update) {
    statements;
}
```

A `for` statement always needs three arguments: an initial condition, a test (will the `for` continue for another loop?), and an update. The statements in the block are run repeatedly until the test becomes false.

By far the most common use of `for` is something like this:

[Dropdown Menu, lines 7-19, condensed heavily]

```
var lists = document.getElementsByTagName('ul');
for (var i=0;i<lists.length;i++) {
    if (lists[i].className != 'menutree') continue;
    // initialize <ul>
}
```

The loop goes through all `<ul>` elements in the page and does something with all of them. (We'll get back to the `continue` statement later.)

5H

Let's take a closer look at the three arguments:

1. `var i=0` is the initial condition. When the loop starts up for the first time, a local variable `i` is created and set to 0.

2. `i<x.length` is the test. Initially, and whenever the update has been performed, the `for` statement checks the test, and if the test returns `true` (if `i` is still smaller than `x.length`), it continues for another loop.

3. `i++` is the update. Every time the `for` statement finishes a loop, it performs the update. `i` is increased by 1.

The net result of all this is that the `for` loop goes through all `<ul>`s in the document. This is a best practice: as soon as you use `getElementsByTagName()`, (see 8B), you start up a `for` loop to go through the nodeList it returns.

while

A `while` loop takes only one argument: a test expression. The loop continues as long as the expression remains `true`.

I use `while` loops mainly when I want to go through an array and discard its elements one by one after doing something with them. Take this example from Usable Forms:

[Usable Forms, lines 41-51, condensed heavily]

```
while (hiddenFields.length) {
    // do stuff with hiddenFields[0]
    waitingRoom.appendChild(hiddenFields.shift());
}
```

`hiddenFields` is an array of `<tr>`s that should be removed from the document. The `while` loop takes the first of these `<tr>`s and removes it from the document. It simultaneously removes this `<tr>` from the array by means of the `shift()` method. We'll get back to this in 8I.

Once per iteration, the `while` loop tests for `hiddenFields.length`: in other words, it tests if the array still has elements in it. Once the `length` reaches 0 (which evaluates to `false`), the `while` loop quits.

In theory it's possible to rewrite all for loops as while loops. For instance, here's the for loop example rewritten as a while loop:

```
var lists = document.getElementsByTagName('ul');
var i = 0;
while (i<lists.length) {
    if (lists[i].className == 'menutree') {
        // initialize <ul>
    }
    i++;
}
```

There's a danger here, though. i must be updated within the while loop, or the loop will continue forever. The i++ does that, but I had to make sure it was executed every time, which means I had to change the class-name check.

Suppose I'd done it wrong:

```
var lists = document.getElementsByTagName('ul');
while (i<lists.length) {
    if (lists[i].className != 'menutree') continue;
    // initialize
    i++;
}
```

Say the second <ul> does not have class="menutree". The while loop faith-fully executes the continue statement, but i is not updated. That means that the next iteration of the loop again checks the second <ul>, which still doesn't have a class="menutree", and i is again not updated. This continues indefi-nitely. (Fortunately, most browsers recognize an infinite loop after a while, and allow the user to break it.)

In general, when using a while loop, you have to make sure that every iteration updates your test variable.

do/while()

The do/while() loop is almost, but not quite, the same as while(). It, too, takes one test expression and continues to loop as long as the expression remains true. The difference is that where while() first checks the test expression and then starts another loop, do/while() first performs a loop and then checks the test expression.

Take this example:

```
var x = 0;
while (x != 0) {
    alert('x is not 0');
}
```

The while() loop is never executed, since the very first test reveals that x is 0.

```
var x = 0;
do {
    alert('x is not 0');
} while(x != 0);
```

However, the do/while() loop executes before any test takes place and shows an alert. Only after the alert is shown docs the test reveal that x is 0, and the loop stops.

As with while loops, you should make sure that the test variable in do/while loops is updated in every loop.

> ### SEMICOLONS AND DO/WHILE
>
> You'll notice that I added a semicolon after the do/while loop. In this position it's perfectly safe, since the code block has already been defined. Semicolons are only dangerous when they're inserted between an if, for, or while statement and the code blocks they're supposed to execute.

So any code in a do/while() loop is executed at least once, while code in a while() loop may never be executed.

The animation functions of XMLHTTP Speed Meter contain a useful example of do/while(). I have to create an animation that goes from one point to another, but beforehand I have no idea what these two points will be, and whether the animation moves to the left or to the right.

Superficially, using a for loop seems to be possible. currentMbit is the current position, and Mbit the desired position:

[XMLHTTP Speed Meter, lines 79-95, condensed and changed]

```
function moveToNewSpeed(Mbit) {
    var distance = Mbit - currentMbit;
    var direction = distance/Math.abs(distance);
    if (!distance) return;
        for (var pos = currentMbit;pos != Mbit;pos+=direction) {
            // give animation orders
        }
}
```

The script first calculates the distance between the two points, and the direction the animation has to travel (+1 or -1). Then the variable pos goes from currentMbit to Mbit in steps of direction. pos now becomes all intermediate steps of the animation, and this is used to give the animation orders.

This seems to work fine, except for one tricky bit: the very last step, when pos becomes exactly equal to Mbit, is never made. As soon as pos becomes equal to Mbit, the test expression pos != Mbit becomes false, and the for loop stops. The animation stays stuck at the penultimate step.

I could solve the problem by changing the test expression to pos < Mbit or pos > Mbit. However, I don't know whether pos starts out as being larger or smaller than Mbit, because I don't know in which direction the animation is going. If I use pos < Mbit, animations from left to right would never work, and if I use pos > Mbit, animations from right to left would never work.

5H

Therefore I use a do/while() loop:

[XMLHTTP Speed Meter, lines 79-95, condensed]

```
function moveToNewSpeed(Mbit) {
    var distance = Mbit - currentMbit;
    var direction = distance/Math.abs(distance);
        do {
            pos += direction;
            // give animation orders
        } while (pos != Mbit)
}
```

Now the test pos != Mbit is executed after every loop instead of before it. When we reach the point where pos is equal to Mbit, the loop first executes the final step of the animation. Only when that's done does it conclude that it should stop.

break and continue

We already encountered two statements related to loops: break and continue.

break

The break statement can be used only within a switch or a loop statement. It means "End this code block immediately." It always refers to the innermost code block of which it's a part.

I use it in Form Validation. When I find an error in a form field I immediately want to create an error message and go on to the next form field:

[Form Validation, lines 85-96, condensed]

```
for (var j=0;j<reqs.length;j++) {
    var OK = validationFunctions[reqs[j]](x[i]);
    if (OK != true) {
            // generate error message
            break;
    }
}
```

The break statement works on the for loop. This loop goes through all values of the validation attribute, and each of these values has an associated function (see 5K).

If that function returns an error, an error message is generated. If that happens, the script breaks the for loop, because I don't want to continue with the other validations; more than one error message would only confuse the user.

As we've seen, break has a slightly different function in the switch statement.

continue

The continue statement can only be used in a loop, and it means "Go on to the next iteration." It always refers to the innermost loop of which it's a part.

Take this example:

[Dropdown Menu, lines 7-19, condensed heavily]

```
var lists = document.getElementsByTagName('ul');
for (var i=0;i<lists.length;i++) {
    if (lists[i].className != 'menutree') continue;
    // initialize <ul>
}
```

The script takes all <ul> tags in the document and loops through them. If the class name of a <ul> is not 'menutree', then it doesn't contain a dropdown menu, and the script must continue with the next <ul>. The continue statement does this: it skips the rest of the code block, goes back to the for statement, performs the update and the test, and continues with the next <ul>.

Labels

Occasionally you have nested loops and want to continue one that isn't the innermost one. For instance:

```
for (var i=0;i<x.length;i++) {
        for (var j=0;j<x.length;j++) {
            if ([something is the case]) continue;
    }
}
```

The `continue` statement now continues the inner loop (the `j`) because that is its default behavior. If you want it to continue with the outer loop (the `i`), you have to use a label:

```
outerloop: for (var i=0;i<x.length;i++) {
        for (var j=0;j<x.length;j++) {
                if ([something is the case]) continue outerloop;
    }
}
```

As you see, a label is nothing more than a bit of text plus a colon `:`. Repeating the bit of text after the `continue` tells JavaScript which loop to continue. I used the label text 'outerloop' in the example because it refers to the outer loop, but you can use any name you like.

You can also use a label after a `break` statement; it specifies which loop should break. Although you're allowed to add labels to any JavaScript statement, they're only really useful in combination with `continue` or `break`.

try/catch

The `try/catch` statement is not a loop. Its purpose is to make sure the user never sees an error message. It tries a few lines of code, and if they generate an error, the `catch` statement kicks in.

The general syntax is as follows:

```
try {
    // these lines may cause an error
}
catch (e) {
    // these lines are executed if an error occurs
}
finally {
    // these lines are always executed regardless of any errors
}
```

You may leave out the `catch` or the `finally` block if you don't need them. Note the `(e)` in the `catch` statement: it's required in some browsers. Using the variable name `e` is traditional, but you may use another name.

I am not a big fan of `try/catch` statements, since I don't like executing code that may cause an error. Nonetheless, it's sometimes necessary to use them. Site Survey contains an example:

[Site Survey/popup.js, lines 77-87, condensed]

```
function checkCommunication() {
    try {
            opener.testVar = true;
    }
    catch (e) {
            return false;
    }
    return true;
}
```

For reasons we'll discuss in 6B, the `opener.testVar = true` line may cause an error. The purpose of this function is to find out if that happens.

The function tries to execute the offending line. If that generates an error message, the `catch` statement executes and returns `false`. If the line works, the catch statement is ignored, and the function continues with the `return true`.

10A discusses another `try/catch` statement in XMLHTTP Speed Meter.

I: Functions

Functions are the backbone of any script. In general, about 95% of the code you write will be contained in functions. This makes functions one of the most important JavaScript structures.

Basic function syntax

This is a function from Site Survey. It is meant to add hidden fields to a form:

[Site Survey/popup.js, lines 49-56]

```
function addInput(name,value) {
    var mainForm = document.forms[0];
    var newInput = document.createElement('input');
//  newInput.type = 'hidden';
    newInput.name = name;
    newInput.value = value;
    mainForm.appendChild(newInput);
}
```

This example neatly highlights the most important syntactic requirements of a function:

- A function should be declared by using the `function` keyword. If you don't use that, JavaScript has no way of knowing that you're declaring a function.

- After the `function` keyword comes the name of the function. You use this name whenever you want to execute the function.

- After the name come required parentheses, which may contain arguments. Our example function has two arguments, `name` and `value`, but you may use as many arguments as you like. Arguments are separated by a comma.

- The statement(s) that comprise the function body are contained in a function block delimited by curly braces {}.

ALTERNATIVE SYNTAX

You may also create the function as follows:

```
var addInput = function (name,value) {
  // function body
}
```

The function is executed when you call it:

```
addInput('name','ppk');
```

The function is called by its name, addInput, followed by parentheses ().
These parentheses are the JavaScript operator that gives the actual command
to execute the function.

The parentheses contain the arguments (here 'name' and 'ppk'), separated by
a comma. These arguments are passed to the function. Now the function does
what it's programmed to do; it creates a hidden form field with the name and
value that were passed as arguments.

Arguments

When you call a function (or tell it to run), you may also need to provide
information for it to use. You pass these arguments to the function when you
call it, and the function receives them in the variable(s) declared inside the
parentheses.

```
addInput('name','ppk');
function addInput(name,value)
```

In the case of addInput(), the arguments contain the name and value of the
new form field, and they are used in the function body:

```
newInput.name = name;
newInput.value = value;
```

Of course you have to make sure that the function declaration and the calls
use the same number and order of arguments.

You can pass as many arguments to a function as you like, but in general
I advise you to use as few as possible. Function declarations and calls with
lots of arguments are generally hard to read, and decrease your code's
maintainability.

return

After a function has done its duty, JavaScript returns to the place it was called from and continues from there. Take this example:

[Site Survey/popup.js, lines 22-49, condensed heavily]

```
function trackMain(url) {
    if (url)
            addPage(url);
    // more stuff
}


function addPage(url) {
    // more stuff
    addInput('p' + pageCounter,url);
}


    function addInput(name,value)
```

`addInput()` is called from `addPage()`, and `addPage()` is called from `track-Main()`. When `addInput()` is ready, JavaScript returns to the `addPage()` function, sees that it is ready, too, and returns to `trackMain()`. This function is not yet complete, so now it continues where it left off, below the `addPage(url)` line.

This is an implicit `return`; the function ends because it's done.

return ends function

You can also explicitly order a function to return by using the `return` keyword. In fact, you'll do this quite often.

It's common to check for the existence of objects you're going to need before running a function. If the objects are not supported, you use a `return` statement to end the function. It shouldn't run any further, because it needs the missing objects and would give error messages when they don't exist.

We already encountered an example:

[Edit Style Sheet, lines 5-6]

```
function initStyleChange() {
    if (!document.styleSheets) return;
    // initialize page using document.styleSheets
```

If document.styleSheets is not supported, the return statement is executed and the function ends.

Returning a value

The function may also return a value. For instance, a function that calculates something should return the result of the calculation to the function that asked for it. Take createReadablePrice() from Sandwich Picker:

[Sandwich Picker, lines 193-208, condensed]

```
function calculateTotalPrice() {
    // calculate total price
    document.getElementById('priceDisplay').innerHTML = ➥
createReadablePrice(price);
}

function createReadablePrice(price) {
    price = price.toFixed(2);
    price = price.replace(/\./,',');
    return price;
}
```

calculateTotalPrice() calculates the total price, and createReadablePrice() makes sure that it has two decimals and a comma as decimal separator, so that it becomes human-readable for the Dutch market.

When that's done, the price is ready to be shown to the users of the site. Now createReadablePrice() returns the variable price to whichever function asked for it:

```
return price;
```

Of course, the function that called createReadablePrice() must do something with this return value:

```
document.getElementById('priceDisplay').innerHTML = ➡
createReadablePrice(price);
```

The return value of createReadablePrice(price) is assigned to the innerHTML of the element with id="priceDisplay".

Functions can return any value. createReadablePrice() returns a string, but it's also possible to return numbers, booleans, or objects.

Functions as values

Functions are values of a variable.

For example:

```
function addInput(name,value) {
    var mainForm = document.forms[0];
    var newInput = document.createElement('input');
//  newInput.type = 'hidden';
    newInput.name = name;
    newInput.value = value;
    mainForm.appendChild(newInput);
}
alert(addInput); // note: no parentheses after addInput!
```

The alert shows the entire function. In other words, we have created a variable addInput and its value happens to be (a reference to) a function. The variable addInput works like any other variable. You could, for instance, assign its value to yet another variable, so that it refers to the same function:

```
var testCall = addInput;
testCall('name','ppk');
```

testCall now has the same value as addInput: a reference to the function.

The () operator

You may have noticed that I left out the parentheses () in a few lines of the previous code examples. That's because () is actually a JavaScript operator: it's a command to execute the function, and we don't always want that to happen.

Let's take a closer look at this important operator:

```
function test() {
    return "Hello";
}
```

The variable test now refers to a function that returns the string "Hello":

```
alert(test);
alert(test());
```

However, these two alerts give different results. The first alert is commanded to show the value of the variable test, which happens to be a function. This is the first alert's result:

```
function ()
{
    return "Hello";
}
```

The second alert gets a quite different command: the parentheses () tell it to *execute* the function test and show its return value, as follows:

```
Hello
```

The key to good function use is knowing when to treat a function as a value and when to execute it. Treating a function as a value is important in event handling. Take, for instance, this line from Textarea Maxlength:

[Textarea Maxlength, line 16]

```
x[i].onkeyup = x[i].onchange = checkMaxLength;
```

The onkeyup and onchange event handlers now get a reference to the function checkMaxLength as their value, and that means "If the keyup or change event occurs, execute checkMaxLength."

We don't want the function to be executed when it is assigned to the event handlers, but only when the event actually takes place. Therefore, we don't include parentheses when we assign the event handler. We want to transfer the function itself, not the return value of the function.

We'll get back to this important topic in 7C.

Nested functions and variable scope

Functions can contain other functions. This is something you'll occasionally use in event handling. Take this function from XMLHTTP Speed Meter (we'll treat it completely in 10A):

[XMLHTTP Speed Meter, lines 121-139, condensed]

```
function sendRequest(url,callback,postData) {
    var req = createXMLHTTPObject();
    // administration
    req.onreadystatechange = function () {
            if (req.readyState != 4) return;
            // handle event
    }
}
```

The nested function is a normal function in all respects. It's executed when the readystatechange event occurs, and it works normally.

Nonetheless, one problem can arise when you use nested functions: variable scope.

Definition scope of functions

JavaScript functions run in the scope in which they are defined, not in the scope from which they are executed.

What does that mean? It means that a nested function has access to all the local variables of its parent function, even if the parent was executed long before the nested function is called.

The sendRequest() function creates an XMLHttpRequest object that fetches some data and stores it in req. When the data is returned to the browser, an event handler fires that does something with it (see 10B):

[XMLHTTP Speed Meter, lines 121-139, condensed]

```javascript
function sendRequest(url,callback,postData) {
    var req = createXMLHTTPObject();
    // administration
    req.onreadystatechange = function () {
        if (req.readyState != 4) return;
        if (req.status != 200 && req.status != 304)  {
            alert('HTTP error ' + req.status);
            return;
        }
        callback(req);
    }
}
```

req refers to the XMLHttpRequest object and is a local variable in sendRequest(), since it's declared within the function body with a var keyword. Since the nested event-handling function is defined within sendRequest(), this function also has access to all of its parent function's local variables, including req. Therefore, the nested function also uses req to refer to the XMLHttpRequest object.

The event handler fires long after sendRequest() itself has finished, but because it was defined within sendRequest(), it continues to have access to sendRequest()'s local variables.

51

Last value counts

It is important to realize that the nested function has access only to the *final* value of a local variable. The next example, which looks a bit like the previous one, doesn't do what you might expect:

```
X  function init() {
        var message = ' Clicked - ';
        var x = document.getElementsByTagName('a');
        for (var i=0;i<x.length;i++) {
                x[i].onclick = function () {
                        x[i].firstChild.nodeValue = message;
                }
        }
    }
```

Here, too, an event handler is defined within another function, and therefore has access to the local variables of that function. In the case of i, though, it doesn't work as expected.

The function init() defines event handlers on all <a> tags in the document. Let's say we have 10. During that process, i goes from 0 to 10, and when the function exits, it retains this final value 10.

The event handlers fire long after the function has exited, and by that time i has the value 10. Therefore, the event handler uses this value, and that causes an error. Since the tenth link in the document has index number 9, the event handler gives an error message: it can't find the eleventh link (with index 10) in the document.

The solution is to use the this keyword instead:

```
x[i].onclick = function () {
    this.firstChild.nodeValue = message;
}
```

In order to understand why this works, we have to study JavaScript objects.

J: Objects

Objects are useful storage units for variables and functions that are related to each other. For instance, in JavaScript every HTML element is represented by an object, which conveniently gathers all relevant information about the element in one place, where it is easy to access and change.

Take this form field:

```
<input name="name" value="ppk" id="myname" />
```

You can access it by doing this:

```
var formField = document.getElementById('myname');
```

In most other chapters, I'll say that "`formField` now contains the form field". In this section, though, we're going to be very finicky and precise, so instead I say that the variable `formField` now holds a reference to the JavaScript object that represents the HTML form field.

An object is nothing more than a collection of properties. Properties whose values are functions (such as event handlers) are called methods. In JavaScript there is no difference between variables and properties, and between functions and methods. Nonetheless, it's customary to speak of the methods and properties of an object.

Properties have a name and a value, and calling a property by name reveals its value. Let's read out a few properties of our object:

```
var formField = document.getElementById('myname');
alert('The form field with name ' + formField.name + ➡
' has value ' + formField.value);
```

The `name` and `value` properties of the form-field object coincide with the HTML `name` and `value` attributes. Reading out these properties reveals their values, which are shown in the alert. The alert faithfully reads "The form field with name name has value ppk".

We can also change these properties:

```
formField.name = 'author';
alert('The form field with name ' + formField.name + ' ➥
has value ' + formField.value);
```

Now the alert reads "The form field with name author has value ppk", and if the form is submitted to the server, the form field's name will be author.

We can also define methods on it:

```
formField.onclick = function () {
    alert('The form field with name ' + formField.name + ➥
    ' has value ' + formField.value);
}
```

Now the alert is shown whenever the user clicks on the form field.

Thus the formField object represents the HTML form field, and there's an object for every single HTML element in a page. Since these objects all contain useful information about the HTML elements they represent, and even allow you to modify the elements, you'll use these objects continuously in your scripts.

The dot

As you see in the code examples, every time I want to access a method or property of the object formField, I start with formField. and then add the name of the method or property. That immediately defines the purpose of the dot operator: it is used to access methods or properties of an object. The object itself is named on the left side of the dot, the method or property on the right side.

Therefore, any time you see a dot anywhere in JavaScript code, you know that an object is being asked for a method or property. This can be a simple operation, like formField.name ("access the name property of object formField"), or it can be something more complicated, like this:

```
var x = document.getElementById('test').getElementsByTagName('a');
```

This statement uses two dots, and therefore you immediately know that at least two objects are being accessed (in fact, there are several more involved). First we access the `getElementById` method of the `document` object (`document.getElementById`) and execute it (`('test')`).

This method returns yet another object (let's be precise: it's a reference to the object that represents the element with id="test"), and we access the `getElementsByTagName` method of this new object in order to get all `<a>` tags contained by this HTML element. The result is a nodeList object.

Although this may sound pretty complicated, you'll intuitively do the right thing whenever you use this sort of statement, and you rarely have to worry about the exact meaning. You now have access to all links in the element with id="test", and that's what counts.

Defining objects

Until now we worked with predefined objects. These come in two flavors: internal JavaScript objects (such as the String objects discussed in 5F), and host objects, or objects created by JavaScript's host (the browser). Host objects include those that represent each HTML element in your pages. The remaining chapters will focus almost exclusively on this herd of host objects.

There's a third flavor of object: those you define yourself. Although this book doesn't treat object-oriented programming, you should know how to create your own objects.

The following is perfectly legal (though a bit ponderous) JavaScript that creates an object:

```
var test = new Object();
test.a = 2;
test.b = '2';
test.c = function () {
    alert(test.a * test.b);
}
```

We first officially state that `test` becomes a new object. Then we define `a`, `b`, and `c` as properties of the object, and give them values. Since `c`'s value is a function, `c` becomes a method.

When we execute the method, an alert containing the number 4 pops up, just as if we'd used normal variables and functions:

```
test.c();
```

Object literals

JavaScript also allows you to use an object literal instead of how we did it in the previous code:

```
var test = {
    a: 2,
    b: '2',
    c: function () {
            alert(test.a * test.b);
    }
}
```

Executing `test.c()` alerts 4, just as in the previous example. Note that the syntax of an object literal is precise:

```
{
    propertyName: propertyValue,
    methodName: function () {
            // function body
    },
    propertyName: propertyValue // note: no comma
}
```

The entire object literal is enclosed in curly braces, and inside those braces all methods and properties are defined. First comes the property name, then a colon, then the property value (which of course may be a function), followed by a comma. However, this comma is forbidden after the very last property value.

We'll encounter a practical example of object literals in 10C.

Working with methods and properties

Whether you use internal JavaScript objects, host objects, or self-defined objects, they all contain methods and properties.

Many properties of host objects have predefined behavior. Take the `href` property of the `location` object that holds the URL of the current page. When you change the value of this property, the browsers interpret it as a command to load a new page (see 6C).

Predefined properties generally work as described: "If you set this property to that value, this will happen." Sometimes, though, the property works only in one browser.

You can create any property you want, just as you can create any variable you want. Even when some browsers interpret a change in a property's value as a command to do something while other browsers don't, setting the property doesn't hurt.

You can also access any property you want, even if it does not exist. In 5G we tried to access the `target` property of the event object, and saw that in Explorer its value is `undefined`, since Explorer uses the `srcElement` property instead. Nonetheless, accessing `target` is safe, as long as you don't mind the value `undefined` creeping up in your scripts.

Methods are another story, though. When you execute a method, you in fact do two things: first you access it, and then you try to execute it. Accessing the method is always safe, just as with properties, but executing it is not.

Example

An example will clarify these rules. As we'll see in 7D, sometimes it's useful to stop the propagation of an event (just nod wisely for the moment). The problem is that this functionality exists in two flavors: W3C-compliant browsers use the `stopPropagation()` method of the event object, while Microsoft uses a property of the event object: `cancelBubble`.

This is the correct way to handle the situation:

```
function stopProp(e) { // e is the event object
    if (e.stopPropagation)
            e.stopPropagation();
    e.cancelBubble = true;
}
```

e holds the event object. We first want to execute the `stopPropagation()` method, but we can't just go off and do it. In Explorer this method doesn't exist—and that really means that if you access the `stopPropagation` property of the event object, you get `undefined`. Executing this value as a method is obviously impossible and gives an error message.

Therefore we start out by checking if the event object has a method `stopPropagation` (if (e.stopPropagation)). If it does, we execute `e.stopPropagation()`.

Then we set Explorer's `cancelBubble` property to `true`. Since we don't use any kind of object detection, all browsers, including the W3C-compatible ones, execute this line of code. This does not lead to error messages. You can always define any property you like, so this action is legal. W3C-compliant browsers shrug and create a property `cancelBubble` with value `true`. Of course they don't do anything with this new value, because they're not programmed to do so. Only Explorer interprets this assignment as a command to stop the propagation of the event.

Creating your own properties

Creating your own properties is sometimes useful. Of course these properties don't have any predefined meaning in the browsers, so you have to write scripts that do something with the values they contain.

Let's take a look at an example from Sandwich Picker:

[Sandwich Picker, lines 193-202]

```
function calculateTotalPrice() {
    var price = 0;
```

```
var containers = [all trs in the ordered table]
for (var i=1;i<containers.length;i++) {
        var searchFields = [the input];
        var amount = searchFields[0].value;
        price += containers[i].price * amount;
}
document.getElementById('priceDisplay'). ➡
innerHTML = createReadablePrice(price);
}
```

Note that `containers[i].price` is a property of the object `containers[i]`.
Why do I use a property to store the price? While Sandwich Picker runs, `<tr>`s
containing sandwiches will constantly be transferred from one table to another
as the user searches, orders, and trashes them. Therefore I make sure that
every object that represents a `<tr>` holds a variable with the price of the sandwich, so that I always have easy access to this price, regardless of the exact
location of the `<tr>` in the page.

The this keyword

The `this` keyword is very powerful, provided you know how to use it. `this`
can be used in any function or method, and it always refers to the object the
method is defined on. Take a look at the simple `test` object we studied a
while back:

```
var test = new Object();
test.a = 2;
test.b = '2';
test.c = function () {
    alert(this.a * this.b); // was alert(test.a * test.b);
}
```

I replaced `test.a` and `test.b` with `this.a` and `this.b`. The method still works.
When it encounters the `this.a`, it takes the object it is defined on (`test`) and
goes to the `a` property.

We use the `this` keyword all the time in event handling. To understand why, let's look at an even older example:

```
formField.onclick = function () {
    alert('The form field with name ' + formField.name + ➡
    ' has value ' + formField.value);
}
```

Here we define an onclick event handler on a form field. It fires whenever the user clicks on the form field. With our newly acquired object knowledge we can easily see two important things:

1. The onclick event handler is in fact a method of the `formField` object.

2. The `this` keyword will refer to this `formField` object when used inside the event handler.

Therefore we can also do the following:

```
formField.onclick = function () {
    alert('The form field with name ' + this.name + ➡
    ' has value ' + this.value);
}
```

We'll discuss this important technique further in 7F.

The global object

If properties are really variables, it stands to reason that variables, even global ones, are really properties. But properties of which object?

The answer is: they are properties of the global object. JavaScript automatically creates a global object to hold all the variables, functions, and objects you define.

JavaScript Core does not state which object becomes the global object; specific implementations are left to make that decision. Client-side JavaScript uses the `window` object:

```
var exampleString = 'I am a JavaScript hacker';
alert(window.exampleString);
```

The variable `exampleString` is the `exampleString` property of the `window` object, and the alert works.

In itself this is not really useful. You'll rarely encounter situations in which saying `window.exampleString` is better than just saying `exampleString`. Nonetheless, it's correct JavaScript.

K: Associative arrays

We saw that `test.a` granted access to the `a` property of the `test` object. However, there is a second way of accessing the same property: `test['a']`. Similarly, `test.c()` can also be written as `test['c']()`. This is a very important bit of JavaScript lore.

The general rule is that the following two expressions are the same:

```
object.property;
object['property'];
```

The following two expressions are also the same:

```
object.method();
object['method']();
```

Note that the bit inside the square brackets is a string. The two examples above use the literal strings `'property'` and `'object'`, but it's of course possible to first create a string as a variable and then insert the variable name in the square brackets:

```
var iWantThisProperty = 'money';
var myHappiness = thingsToHave[iWantThisProperty];
```

This is the same as saying:

```
var myHappiness = thingsToHave.money;
```

Nonetheless, there's a difference in ease of programming. With dot notation, you must type the name of the property directly in your code. A script cannot change the literal code `thingsToHave.money` in any way; it always means "The `money` property of the `thingsToHave` object."

On the other hand, with square-bracket notation, changing the name of the property is easy as pie; you just create the string you need and put it between the `[]`. The code example above does so: it first creates the string `iWantThis-Property`, and then uses its value to call the correct property of the object `myHappiness`.

Square bracket vs. dot notation

In Edit Style Sheet, the form fields have the name and value of the style they should change. For instance, this is the form field where the user can specify the CSS `text-align` property:

```
<select name="textAlign" id="textAlign">
    <option value="">not specified</option>
    <option value="left">Left</option>
    <option value="center">Center</option>
    <option value="right">Right</option>
</select>
```

The select's name is `textAlign` (which, as we'll see in 9A, is the JavaScript equivalent to CSS `text-align`). The values of the options are the values this CSS declaration can take: `left`, `center`, or `right`.

When the user changes the select box, a function should start up that sets the correct CSS property (defined in the form field's `name`) to the correct value (defined in the form field's `value`). Suppose the user selects 'center'.

The dot notation doesn't work here. Suppose I did this:

[Edit Style Sheet, lines 57-64, condensed and changed]

❌ ```
function assignStyles() {
    var styleName = this.name;
    var styleValue = this.value;
    currentRule.style.styleName = styleValue;
}
```

Although extracting styleName and styleValue is easy, the currentRule.style.styleName doesn't work. The function therefore changes style's property named styleName:

```
currentRule.style.styleName = 'center';
```

You want to say "The property whose name is the value of variable styleName gets the value 'center'," but this statement always literally means "The styleName property of the object gets the value 'center'."

As we saw, you're allowed to define any property you like, so this statement is not wrong and doesn't give error messages. Nonetheless, it doesn't do what you want, either.

To solve this problem, you must use the square-bracket notation. This notation expects a string, and that's exactly what styleName contains:

[Edit Style Sheet, lines 57-64, condensed]

```
function assignStyles() {
    var styleName = this.name;
    var styleValue = this.value;
    currentRule.style[styleName] = styleValue;
}
```

Now the function takes the string that's the value of the variable styleName, and uses this string to determine which property of currentRule.style should get the value 'center'.

5K
```

Therefore, if the user changes the select box to 'center', the last line reads:

```
currentRule.style['textAlign'] = 'center';
```

Now we change the correct property, and the style change takes effect immediately.

Associative arrays

Associative arrays are arrays that allow you to find a certain value by using a string as the name of this value. These strings are called *keys*. A key now becomes associated with a certain value.

This is an example of a pure associative array from Form Validation:

[Form Validation, lines 8-13]

```
var validationFunctions = new Object();
validationFunctions["required"] = isRequired;
validationFunctions["pattern"] = isPattern;
validationFunctions["postcode"] = isPostCode;
validationFunctions["numeric"] = isNumeric;
validationFunctions["email"] = isEmail;
```

Note that we start out by making validationFunctions an object. This is required.

Now the validationFunctions object serves as a lookup table for the various form-validation functions. The trick is that I use the keys to this lookup table (required, pattern, etc.) as values of the custom validation attribute:

```
<input name="phone" validation="required numeric" />
```

The script reads out these values and uses them as keys to access the correct validation functions in validationFunctions.

[Form Validation, lines 82-88, changed and condensed]

```
var field = [form field];
var reqs = field.getAttribute('validation').split(' ');
for (var j=0;j<reqs.length;j++) {
    var isValid = validationFunctions[reqs[j]](field);
```

The function splits the `validation` attribute's value on spaces. As we saw in
5F, this yields an array, which it stores in `reqs`. Now the function loops through
all elements in this `reqs` array and uses the values it finds as keys.

Thus it finds the function it should execute: `validationFunctions[reqs[j]]`.
The return value of this function is used to determine whether the form field is
valid.

Another example of an associative array functioning as a lookup table can be
found in 8K.

The for in statement

The `for in` statement goes through all keys of an associative array (which is
the same as going through all properties of an object). In general, you use the
square-bracket notation when you do something with these keys.

Let's take our test object and use the `for in` statement on it:

```
var test = {
    a: 2,
    b: '2',
    c: function () {
            alert(this.a * this.b);
    }
}
for (var i in test) {
    alert(i + ': ' + test[i]);
}
```

Now you see three alerts: the first two show '2', and the last one shows the
entire function `c`.

Note that I use square-bracket notation (`test[i]`) to actually read out the value
of the properties. If I used dot notation (`test.i`) I'd encounter the same problem as before: It would mean "The `i` property of object `test`" (which is undefined), instead of "The property of `test` whose name is stored in `i`."

5K

Edit Style Sheet contains a practical example of `for in`. At a certain point I want to read out all styles that are currently contained in one style rule. `currentRule.style` is an object and contains a property for every style that can be defined:

[Edit Style Sheet, lines 68-70, changed]

```
var z = currentRule.style;
for (var i in z) {
    if (z[i]) { // simplified situation
                // store default styles
    }
}
```

The `for (var i in z)` loop now goes through every property of object z, which means every *possible* style that could be set on the style rule. Since that also includes all empty styles, I also check if the property has a value at all (`if (z[i])`).

If it doesn't have a value, I ignore it. If it does have a value, I store this value for future reference.

L: Arrays

Associative arrays use strings to access the data they hold, for instance `test['a']`. Real arrays use index numbers for this job, for instance `test[0]`.

An array is nothing more than a collection of values that are indexed numerically. Let's take a look at an array from XMLHTTP Speed Meter. Note that the index numbers of an array start at 0, and not at 1:

[XMLHTTP Speed Meter, lines 4-9]

```
var speedText = new Array();
speedText[0] = '0'
speedText[4] = 'till 4 Mbit/s';
speedText[8] = '4-8 Mbit/s';
speedText[15] = '8-15 Mbit/s';
speedText[20] = '12-20 Mbit/s';
```

Secretly I use this array as an associative array. When the script asks for a download speed, one of the values 0, 4, 8, 15, or 20 is returned. The `speed-Text` array defines the bit of text that should be shown next to the animation, and I really only need texts for 0, 4, 8, 15, and 20. Therefore I define only those elements of the array.

But what about the other elements? Since I did not define them, JavaScript does not create them. This is called a sparse array: an array that contains only those elements that are actually defined.

If I do `alert(speedText[11])` I get `undefined`, just as if `11` is a property that hasn't been defined.

Nested arrays

Array elements can be other arrays, in which case they're called nested (or two-dimensional) arrays:

```
testArray[5] = new Array();
testArray[5][0] = 'Nested array';
```

If you really want to, you can create three-, four-, or more-dimensional arrays by just repeating the process:

```
testArray[5][0] = new Array();
testArray[5][0][1] = 'A three-dimensional array element!';
```

Array notations

The `speedText` array works fine, but its creation is a bit ponderous. There are more elegant ways to create an array:

```
var testArray = new Array(0,1,'2','three',false); // hardly used
var testArray = [0,1,'2','three',false]; // array literal
```

The first notation is hardly used any more, though you'll occasionally encounter it in older scripts. The second notation is called an array literal, and as you see the syntax is quite close to the object literal, except that we use square brackets [] to enclose the entire array, and we don't use property names—after all, the arrays use index numbers.

Note that these notations don't give you the option of assigning the elements to specific indices: testArray now has five elements, numbered from `testArray[0]` to `testArray[4]`. If you want to define specific indices, you must use the notation we saw in the `speedText` example.

The `findPos()` function in Edit Style Sheet returns an array literal:

[Edit Style Sheet, lines 181-191, condensed]

```
function findPos(obj) {
    // calculate curleft and curtop
    return [curleft,curtop];
}
```

Of course, the function that `findPos()` returns this array to has to be ready for it:

[Edit Style Sheet, lines 140-141]

```
var coors = findPos(this);
colorPicker.style.top = coors[1] - 20 + 'px';
```

`coors` now becomes an array, and in the next line the function uses its second element (with index 1): the `curtop` from the function.

Use of arrays

A few JavaScript methods, notably `string.split()`, return arrays. Take this example from Form Validation:

[Form Validation, lines 80-85, condensed]

```
var req = els[i].getAttribute('validation');
var reqs = req.split(' ');
for (var j=0;j<reqs.length;j++) {
    // go through array elements one by one
}
```

The `split()` method of a string always returns an array, so `reqs` automatically becomes one. The `for` loop that's started up afterwards goes through the array elements one by one and does something to them.

Arrays and nodeLists

The example scripts contain a few more arrays, but most of them are meant to shore up the deliberate weaknesses of a data type that superficially resembles the array but is in fact quite different: the W3C DOM nodeList.

Take this bit of code:

```
var x = document.getElementsByTagName('p');
var y = x[2];
```

x is a nodeList that holds references to all <p> tags in the document, and just as in arrays, x[2] means the third element of array x, or the third paragraph in the document. I use this feature of the nodeList regularly.

Nonetheless, nodeLists are not arrays. For now it's best to see them as read-only arrays that lack all useful methods that the Array object defines. In 8I we'll see that, though nodeLists appear to be rather static and boring from an array perspective, they are in fact highly, even dangerously, dynamic.

length

Every array has a length property that holds the number of elements in the array. Let's return to our test array:

```
var testArray = [0,1,'2','three',false];
alert(testArray.length);
```

As you'd expect, the alert shows 5. testArray has five elements with index numbers 0, 1, 2, 3, and 4. The length property is automatically updated whenever you add or remove elements to or from the array.

You are even allowed to set the length property:

```
var testArray = [0,1,'2','three',false];
testArray.length = 0;
alert(testArray[1]);
```

Now the alert shows `undefined`, because we just set the length of `testArray` to 0, which means "Trash all elements." We could also set the `length` to another value:

```
var testArray = [0,1,'2','three',false];
testArray.length = 2;
alert(testArray[1]),
```

Now the alert shows 1. We set the `length` of `testArray` to 2, and therefore all elements with index 2 or higher (the third and subsequent elements) are removed from the array. The first two elements (with index 0 and 1) remain untouched.

push, pop, shift, and unshift

There are four methods for quickly adding and removing elements to and from the beginning or the end of an array: `push()`, `pop()`, `shift()`, and `unshift()`.

FIGURE 5.1
push, pop, shift, and unshift

As you see in the figure, `shift` and `unshift` work on the start of an array, and `push` and `pop` on the end. The syntax to add elements is as follows:

```
var x = [new element to be inserted in the array];
testArray.unshift(x); // x is now the first element
testArray.push(x); // x is now the last element
```

Note that the element to be added is an argument of the `push` and `unshift` methods.

Removing elements works slightly differently:

```
var x = testArray.shift();
var y = testArray.pop();
```

x now holds the first element of the array, and y the last. These two elements are now wholly removed from the array. Note that `shift` and `pop` don't accept arguments.

The `length` property is updated after each of these four operations.

I always use `push` and `shift` for my array manipulations, since this gives a First In First Out situation: the first element I put in the array is also the first element that leaves the array when the time comes to process them. In most situations this doesn't matter, but it's useful to have such a standard rule. I advise you to select one addition and one removal method and stick to them.

A few example scripts use `shift` and `push` on helper arrays, but I'll defer the practical explanations to 8I, since we first have to discuss nodeLists and find out why we need helper arrays at all.

Explorer 5 doesn't support these four methods. At the end of Usable Forms and Sandwich Picker, you can find the code I use to add support to Explorer 5.

5L

BOM

JAVASCRIPT HAS AN intermediate layer between Core (discussed in the previous chapter) and the Document Object Model, or DOM (to be discussed in Chapters 7-10). Commonly called the Browser Object Model, or BOM, this layer is specific to JavaScript's client-side implementation, so it's not part of Core. It does not work with the HTML document, so it's not part of the DOM, either. The BOM's most important task is managing browser windows (each of which have a separate window object) and enabling communication between them. Therefore, the window object stands at the center of the BOM.

Nonetheless, as you'll notice, BOM is also the catch-all category of JavaScript. There are many objects, methods, and properties that are not part of the document structure (for instance, the URL of the current page or the identification string of the browser), and these are defined on the window object.

Standards-wise, BOM is a bit of a problem. Core has been standard-ized by ECMA, and most aspects of the DOM have been specified by W3C. In contrast, the BOM has not yet officially been defined by any standards organization, although at the time of writing, WHAT-WG is working on a specification. Fortunately, the most important BOM features were all part of the de facto Netscape 3 standard, and are therefore supported by all browsers.

Site Survey is the quintessential BOM script. It's useful to compare it to the other example scripts, to highlight the difference between DOM and BOM.

All the other example scripts change an HTML document; for instance, by moving HTML elements through the document (Sandwich Picker, Usable Forms), changing the styles of elements (Edit Style Sheet, Dropdown Menu, XMLHTTP Speed Meter), or checking user input in a form field (Form Validation, Textarea Maxlength).

In contrast, Site Survey hardly changes anything in the document. The script sits quietly in its corner (a popup) and registers what users are doing in the site by storing the URLs of all pages they visit. Ideally, the user never notices it's there, until the script opens the survey page and politely requests the user to participate.

{

WHAT-WG

The Web Hypertext Application Technology Working Group (WHAT-WG) is an unofficial collaboration of browser vendors and other interested parties who work on the development of new, advanced technologies for delivering applications on the Web. Although WHAT-WG's specifications have no official status, some WHAT-WG members are also W3C members, while others are well-known Web developers; all of them support WHAT-WG's recommendations in word and deed. It is likely that WHAT-WG's ideas will eventually find their way into the official W3C specs and new browser versions.

WHAT-WG's best-known specification is Web Forms 2.0, in which the group defines new form widgets such as sliders and date/time fields, and proposes ways of adding these widgets to HTML.

Developers who are interested in innovating technologies that will make Web sites easier to use—and possible JavaScript implementations of these technologies—should take the time to acquaint themselves with the WHAT-WG's projects. Their Web site can be found at http://whatwg.org/.

}

The core tasks of Site Survey are to remember whether users are selected for the survey and to ensure that the popup stays in contact with the main window, even when the user requests new pages. Thus, Site Survey mainly concerns itself with window-related information such as the URL of the current page or cookies associated with it. It does not work with DOM information such as the existence and value of form fields. The window object is more important to Site Survey than the document object.

A: The window object

At the center of the BOM stands the window object. It serves four purposes:

- It is the global object that JavaScript Core needs to function.
- It represents the browser window that users see on their computer screen.
- It grants access to the HTML document loaded in the window.
- It contains miscellaneous information and functionality.

As JavaScript's global object, the window object contains all the variables and functions defined in your scripts. (We discussed the global object in 5J.)

As a representation of the browser window, the window object holds methods like `resizeTo` that allow you to change the window's dimensions, and objects such as `screen` that give information about the user's computer screen. In addition, it allows you to open and close new browser windows.

As the access portal to the HTML document, the window holds the document object, which in turn holds the entire HTML page the user is currently viewing.

Finally, as a holder of miscellaneous information and functionality, the window object contains the `location` and `history` objects, which are meant for navigation, a few interaction methods such as `alert`, and the browser's `userAgent` string.

6A

The window as global object

As we saw in 5J, JavaScript always creates a global object to hold all global variables and functions in your scripts. If you wish, you can explicitly invoke this global object, for instance:

```
var test = 'Hello world';
alert(window.test);
```

test is a global variable, and as such it's a property of the window object. Therefore window.test also accesses the variable.

Every browser window or frame is a global object in its own right. Although communication between these global objects is possible in certain circumstances, they remain separate.

New pages, new window object

In the course of a browsing session, one window object can contain many pages. Whenever the user loads a new page, the old page is thrown away and the new one is loaded into the same window object.

When that happens, JavaScript's global object is also cleaned rigorously. All variables and functions are destroyed, and if you still need them in the new page you have to redefine them by rerunning your initialization script and other functions.

Persistent window object

When the user loads a new page in a window, or even when he closes the entire window, the window object is wiped clean but is not destroyed. The most important consequence of this persistence of the window object is that any reference to it remains in force.

For example, when you open a popup, the browser creates an opener property in the popup that refers to the window it's opened from. This is an automatic, and very useful, feature that we'll discuss in detail in 6B.

When the user loads a new page in the main window, the window object is wiped clean. It is not destroyed, however, and therefore the opener property of the popup still refers to the same window object as it did earlier. (Of course, if the window now contains a page from another domain, JavaScript's same-source policy does not allow you to access this page. We'll get back to this problem in 6B.)

Even when the user closes the main window, opener still refers to the now-closed window. The window is gone from the computer's screen, but the window object still exists and can still be accessed, even though it doesn't contain any useful data any more.

I use this fact extensively in Site Survey, and we'll discuss it in more detail in 6B, when we treat cross-window communication.

Persistent data

Sometimes a page contains bits of data that you want to keep for future use, even when the page is removed. Suppose a page contains a module that calculates the user's yearly spending on insurance. In another page, you want to use the result of these calculations to show the user why it's advisable to insure herself with the company.

The result of the calculation is likely held by a global variable in the first page, and as soon as the user loads the second page, this global variable is lost. Somehow, you have to transfer the result of the calculation in the first page to the second page. You have to do this manually; there is no automatic way of taking care of it.

You have three options. You can store the data in a cookie. You can store the data in another window object. The new page can then retrieve the data from either of these sources. We'll treat these two scenarios in this chapter (6B and 6G, respectively).

The third option is that you send the data to the server for safekeeping. This is the most secure solution, since both cookies and other window objects can go astray and you run the risk of losing the result of the calculation. Nonetheless, sending data to the server is usually more complicated than storing it in a cookie or another window. It generally involves a form and a server-side script that catches and stores the data, and retrieves it later on.

In short, storing the data on the server is the safest solution, but it requires a bit of extra work. In Site Survey, I opted for storing some data in a cookie, and other data in another window.

New windows as new global objects

Your Web site may have more than one window, and thus more than one global object. If you use popups or frames, you effectively create several window objects, each of which is completely separate from all the others. These window objects are all global objects, and can contain variables or functions with the same names.

Suppose your site uses a main window and a popup, and suppose you define a variable message in each of them:

```
var message = 'Hello world'; // in main window
var message = 'Goodbye, cruel world'; // in popup window
```

These two variables message are completely independent, since they're properties of different global objects. If you add a line alert(message), it shows 'Hello world' in the main window, and 'Goodbye, cruel world' in the popup window. Both alert statements use the value of message as defined in their own global object.

Sometimes you need variables or functions from another window, as I do in Site Survey. In order to access them, you first have to access the other window (or rather, the other global object). Once you've done that, you can request its properties and methods, which are its variables and functions. For instance, this alerts "Goodbye, cruel world" in the main window:

```
// in main window
var popup = [open popup and create reference to its window
object];
alert(popup.message);
```

Using variables and functions that are defined in another window is therefore not very difficult, provided you can access the other window. As we'll see in 6B, gaining access to other windows is the most serious problem.

Availability of variables in other windows

But there's a catch we have to discuss right away. The last example, though correct in theory, does not work in practice:

```
// in main window
var popup = [open popup and create reference to its window
object];
alert(popup.message);
```

The second line correctly accesses the message property of the popup global object. Nonetheless, it'll likely give a JavaScript error.

The problem is that the popup is created in the first line of code, and the browser hasn't had the time yet to download the page. When the second line is executed, message is not yet available, and the second line results in a JavaScript error.

This problem also exists in Site Survey. The page in the main window calls a function in the popup when it is unloaded; i.e., when the user requests another page or closes the window. This popup is opened as soon as the user clicks anywhere in the main window. (Why? To defeat popup blockers. See 6B.)

These two things might happen simultaneously. In fact, it's quite likely that the user's first click takes place on a link. In that case, the click event causes the popup to be created, and immediately afterwards the main page unloads, which triggers the function call to the popup. Unfortunately, at that moment in time, the function is not yet available, since the HTML page for the popup hasn't yet been downloaded from the server. Without some extra safeguards, this routine would give a JavaScript error.

6A

The solution is a careful bit of checking and the creation of several cookies to hold window statuses. (We'll discuss cookies fully in 6G.) This is the function that's executed when the main window unloads:

[Site Survey/survey.js, lines 66-73, condensed]

```
// in main window
function ST_exit() {
    if (readCookie('ST_popup') == 'opened' && ST_newWindow)
            ST_newWindow.trackMain(location.href);
    else
            createCookie('ST_temp_store',location.href,1);
}
```

The script wants to execute the function trackMain() in the popup. It first checks if the popup has been opened by seeing if the ST_popup cookie exists. Then the script checks if the ST_newWindow variable, which should refer to the popup, has a value. If it does, the popup can be safely accessed and it calls trackMain().

If the popup creation takes place just before the main window is unloaded, the popup page isn't available yet, the cookie and the ST_newWindow variables don't yet exist, and the script goes to the else clause: it creates a cookie ST_temp_store that temporarily stores the page's URL (location.href).

When the popup page has been completely loaded, the script does the following:

[Site Survey/popup.js, lines 4-11]

```
// in popup
window.onload = function () {
    createCookie('ST_popup','opened',1);
    if (readCookie('ST_temp_store')) {
            trackMain(readCookie('ST_temp_store'));
            eraseCookie('ST_temp_store');
    }
}
```

First it creates the cookie ST_popup, so that the scripts in the main window know that the popup is available. Next, it sees if there's a cookie ST_temp_ store. If there is, it calls `trackMain()` to handle it, and erases the cookie.

Window properties

Every window object has a few miscellaneous properties.

window and self

The `window` and `self` properties refer to the window itself. Therefore, `window.innerWidth` accesses the `innerWidth` property of the window object, and `self.innerWidth` accesses the same property. I have no idea why we need two properties that refer to the same object.

name

The `name` property serves as a guide for the target property of HTML links, and also for popups. Initially it's empty, but you can always set it. Take this code:

```
window.name = 'ppk';
```

{

WINDOW AND SELF TRADITIONS

As you'll see throughout this chapter, I sometimes use `window` and sometimes use `self` to refer to the window. Although it doesn't matter which property you use, it is traditional to say `window.open()` but `self.innerWidth`. I suspect that these traditions go back to the very first people who described these properties: for unknowable reasons they chose `window` in one case and `self` in the other, and everybody else copied these code examples.

Feel free to switch `window` and `self` wherever you encounter them, but be aware that you're flouting tradition if you do, and that less experienced coders might not understand your script.

}

6A

Links with this target, such as `<a href="somepage.html" target="ppk">`, will open in this window.

In addition, you can use the name in the `window.open()` method we'll discuss in 6B:

```
window.open('somepage.html','ppk',[arguments]);
```

Now the browser checks for a window named 'ppk'. If it finds one, then somepage.html is opened in this window. If it doesn't find one, it opens a new window that is assigned the `name` "ppk".

status and defaultStatus

The `defaultStatus` and `status` properties allow you to write texts in the window's status bar. This used to be the height of cool, but in these more enlightened days we've become aware that users may not be entirely happy with potentially intrusive or arbitrary status-bar messages.

Status-bar texts are automatically generated whenever the user mouses over a link; the status bar shows the URL of the page the link leads to.

The `status` property directly accesses the status-bar text and rewrites it. The `defaultStatus` property defines a text that should be shown if the status bar is not otherwise occupied (i.e., if the mouse is currently not over a link).

Setting the status bar text works as follows:

```
window.status = 'Take a look at this wonderful site!';
```

Now the status bar contains this text until the user mouses over another link.

The `status` property is commonly used to show a message when a user mouses over a link, but it's not quite as simple as the line above, because the default action of a mouseover on a link is to show the `href` in the status bar. If you use the `status` property in this way, you need to cancel the default action, or else your status text will immediately be overwritten by the link's `href`.

```
link.onmouseover = function () {
    window.status = 'This is a GREAT link!';
    return true; // or, in some browsers, false
}
```

You typically prevent a default action by returning `false` from the event-handling function. In the specific case of status-bar messages, though, Explorer and Mozilla require you to return `true`.

B: Cross-window communication

How do you establish cross-window communication? We've glanced at the `opener` property of popups and the availability of functions and variables in other windows, but in general, communication between two windows is possible only if two conditions are met:

- Both windows contain pages that come from the same domain.
- One window contains a reference to the other.

The first condition is a result of JavaScript's same-source policy, as discussed in 1B. You are not allowed to spy on windows that contain pages from another domain, since that would invade the user's privacy.

The second condition is more complicated: essentially, one of the windows must already know of the other's existence. If neither of them is aware of the other, communication is impossible.

If a user opens two browser windows and loads your site in both of them, JavaScript's same-source policy is satisfied, but the windows don't know of each other's existence, and it is impossible to establish communication between them.

In practice, cross-window communication is possible only if one window opens the other, or, in other words, if you create a popup window.

Opening popup windows

You open a popup window with the `window.open()` method. It works as follows:

```
window.open('page.html','popup','width=300,height=400');
```

6B

> **WINDOW.OPEN() AND DOCUMENT.OPEN()**
>
> Although we've seen that you don't have to use `window.` when calling methods or properties of the window, `window.open()` is always written in full. That serves to distinguish this method from the `document.open()` method we'll discuss in 6F. Since an incorrect use of `document.open()` may wipe the entire page, this distinction is important.

As you see, this method takes three arguments:

- The first argument tells the browser which page to load in the new window. If you don't specify which page to load in the popup, the browser opens a blank window.

- The second argument sets the `name` property of the new window. We already discussed that property in 6A.

- The third argument contains instructions on the new window's features: its width and height, does it contain a location bar, etc.

In old browsers, the developer could control exactly how the popup would look and behave. The user could not resize it, and if the Web developer did not allow scrollbars, users would never see them, even if they were necessary. Basically the only thing the user could do was close the popup.

Modern browsers have given the user progressively more control over the popup. At this point, most browsers allow the user to resize popups, even if

> **POPUP FEATURES**
>
> See http://www.quirksmode.org/js/popups.html for a complete overview of all possible popup features and their browser compatibility.

resizable is set to 'no', and they always show scrollbars when they're necessary, even if scrollbars is set to 'no'.

Therefore, it's best to assume that the user can and will treat your popup as if it's a real window (which, in the end, it is).

References to other windows

The previous code example opened a popup window, but it didn't initiate cross-window communication. In order to do that, we must store the return value of the window.open() method, which is a reference to the newly created window.

Site Survey opens the popup as follows:

[Site Survey/survey.js, lines 30 and 62]

```
var ST_newWindow;
// more stuff
ST_newWindow = window.open('survey/popup.html',➡
'ST_window',[arguments]);
```

It opens a new window as described above, and it assigns the reference to the new window to variable ST_newWindow. Now this variable refers to the other window, and cross-window communication has been established.

opener

Remember, the popup window automatically creates an opener property that refers back to the main window, and if a new page is loaded into the popup (for instance, because the user clicks on a link), the opener property remains available. It's one of the very few properties that is not removed when a window object is wiped clean.

Therefore, even if the main page doesn't contain a variable like ST_newWindow, cross-window communication is still possible: You just use the popup's opener property.

Re-establishing contact

Unfortunately, the ST_newWindow variable in the main window is destroyed when the user loads a new page, which means that the new page in the main window cannot contact the popup.

That's a problem to Site Survey, since the ST_exit() function wants to call a function in the popup. When the main page unloads, it does this:

[Site Survey/survey.js, lines 67-73]

```
function ST_exit() {
    if (readCookie('ST_popup') == 'opened' && ST_newWindow)
            ST_newWindow.trackMain(location.href);
    else
            createCookie('ST_temp_store',location.href,1);
}
```

The trackMain() function stores the URLs of the pages the user views in the main window, but in order to call it, the main window needs access to the popup: ST_newWindow.trackMain().

Fortunately, the popup contains its opener property, which refers to the main window; thus cross-window communication is still possible. Thus the popup can restore the ST_newWindow variable in the main window:

[Site Survey/popup.js, line 30]

```
// in popup
opener.ST_newWindow = window;
```

The script goes to the main window (opener) and assigns to its ST_newWindow property (opener.ST_newWindow =) a reference to itself, the popup window (window). Now the main page is once again able to access the popup.

This re-establishment of contact with the main window is a job of trackMain(), and it's useful to take a detailed look at this function.

Before we start, let's pay close attention to the context. `trackMain()` is called at the moment the main page unloads, and it receives the URL of that page as an argument. Directly afterwards, the unload event takes place, which means either that the main window starts to receive a new page (which may or may not come from another domain), or that the user has closed the main window.

If the new page comes from another domain, JavaScript's same-source policy prevents the popup from re-establishing contact. We don't want error messages to appear, so we have to proceed with caution.

[Site Survey/popup.js, lines 22-24]

```
// in popup
function trackMain(url) {
    if (url)
            addPage(url);
```

First the easy bit. If the function receives a URL, it is stored through the function `addPage()`.

Now the hard work starts: finding out what has happened to the main window. Did the user leave the site? If so, I have to send the user on to the survey. If the user hasn't left the site, though, I should do nothing.

We're certain of one thing: the page that called `trackMain()` isn't there any more. But has the user requested a new page from the same domain, from a different domain, or has he closed the window altogether?

[Site Survey/popup.js, lines 26-27]

```
    if (!opener || opener.closed || !checkCommunication())
            startSurvey();
```

If the main window is closed or contains another site, the script immediately starts up the survey. To find out whether this is the case, I check three things:

1. If the `opener` property returns null (`if (!opener)`), even the window object of the main window doesn't exist any more. This is a rare case, but better safe than sorry, so I check for it anyway.

2. If `opener's closed` property is `true`, the main window has also been closed.

3. If the main window has not been closed, but communication is impossible (`!checkCommunication()`), the user has loaded another site.

[Site Survey/popup.js, lines 29-32]

```
else if (checkCommunication() && opener.ST_loaded) {
        opener.ST_newWindow = window;
        tryCounter = 0;
}
```

Then the script checks for the opposite. It uses `ST_loaded` in the main window to indicate that it has been loaded completely and that all scripts are ready for action. If it is possible to communicate with the main window, and if `ST_loaded` is `true`, the script re-establishes contact by means of the `opener.ST_newWindow = window;` line, and it sets `tryCounter` back to zero.

Note that the script checks the possibility of communication first. If `checkCommunication()` returns `false`, JavaScript doesn't even try to execute the second expression, as we saw in 5G. Therefore, the script does not try to access `opener.ST_loaded`, and that's a good thing, because that action would give an error if the main page came from another domain.

[Site Survey/popup.js, lines 34-37]

```
else if (tryCounter < nrOfAttempts) {
        setTimeout('trackMain()',waitingTime);
        tryCounter++;
}
```

If neither is the case (for instance, because the main window is busy loading a new page), I set a timeout to try again in a few milliseconds. I have set an upper limit to the number of attempts, since I don't want the script to spend ages trying to determine the status of the main window.

Note that this new call to trackMain() does not include an argument. The URL of the old page has already been stored, after all, and I want to avoid duplicates. When trackMain runs again, it ignores the addPage(url).

[Site Survey/popup.js, lines 39-41]

```
    else
            startSurvey();
}
```

If the status is unclear, or if the script already exceeded the maximum number of tries, it also starts the survey.

This is one way of re-establishing contact with the main window, and as you see, it can be pretty hard to find out the status of the main window.

Properties of closed windows

WARNING   Browser incompatibilities ahead

As we saw, when the user closes a window, its window object remains available. In order to indicate that the window is closed, its closed property is set to true. I use this fact in trackMain().

Unfortunately, at the time of writing, the closed property is unreliable in Opera. For that reason, among others, Site Survey doesn't work properly in Opera.

Obviously, a closed window loses all variables and functions that were defined in it. It's wiped clean, after all. But what about the default properties of the window object, such as location and navigator? Do they remain available, or are they destroyed, too?

Unfortunately, the browsers disagree on their exact status. When you try to read, for instance, the navigator.userAgent property of a closed window, some browsers give the browser string, while others give an error. Therefore, it's advisable to assume that a closed window has no properties except for closed.

6B

Attempting to communicate

If a window still exists but contains a page from a different domain, you are not allowed to access any properties of its window object. As we saw in 1B, this is a security feature: without it, malicious site owners could gather data on the surfing habits of their visitors.

Site Survey needs to know whether the main window still contains a page from the original site, or whether the user has surfed on to another site. In the first case, it re-establishes cross-window communication; in the second, it starts the survey.

How does it find out? We could try to read the `location.href` of the other window, but if it contains a page from another server, this property, too, is inaccessible. In fact, when a page comes from another server, we cannot glean any information whatsoever from that other window.

The solution to this conundrum is to try to set a variable in the other window. If an error occurs, the window contains a page from another domain. This is what the `checkCommunication` function does. Since "Can I communicate with the other window?" is a simple Yes/No question, the function returns a boolean value `true` or `false`.

[Site Survey/popup.js, lines 77-86]

```
function checkCommunication() {
    if (!opener) return false;
    try {
            opener.testVar = true;
    }
    catch (e) {
            return false;
    }
    return true;
}
```

First the function checks if the `opener` exists at all. If not, communication is obviously impossible, and the function returns `false`.

Then the function enters a try/catch statement, as discussed in 5H. It tries to set a variable in the other window (`opener.testVar = true`). If this causes an error, the `catch` statement catches it and returns `false`: communication is not possible.

If the function survives without error messages, it returns `true`: communication is possible.

Closing windows

Every window object has a `close()` method: calling it closes the window. Nonetheless, most browsers have a built-in safety catch that offers the user some control. Although every window can be closed by this method, in the case of windows that were opened by the user, some browsers refuse to execute `window.close()`, while others open a dialog box that asks the user if it's OK to close the window. If the user denies permission, the window stays open.

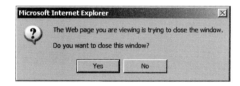

FIGURE 6.1
If you try to close a window that's opened by the user, Explorer shows this dialog box.

It is not possible to circumvent this security measure.

Windows that were opened by JavaScript can be closed without encountering this dialog box.

Popup blockers

Popup windows have a bad reputation, and not undeservedly. When purveyors of frontal nudity and similar undesirable types discovered that it was possible to confront any user with their products, popups became very popular over-night. Additionally, designers who were unable to create liquid layouts were determined to force users to view their sites at a certain width and height, and opening a popup was the simplest way of ensuring that.

In fact, the situation deteriorated to a point that the browser vendors decided to intervene by adding popup blockers to their browsers. Unfortunately, now that they have been around for a while, it has become clear that these popup blockers are insufficient. Sure, they block most of the old popups written by people who hardly know JavaScript, but they are in fact easy to circumvent, and Site Survey does so.

To understand how popup circumvention works, we must first understand how popup blockers work. Browser vendors did not simply disable the `window.open()` method, since popups can have legitimate uses. Instead, they blocked only unrequested popups.

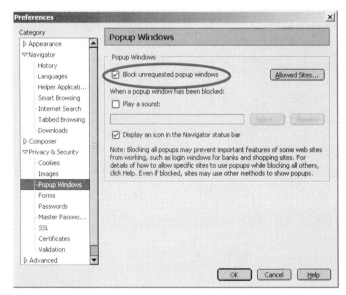

FIGURE 6.2   Like most other browsers, Mozilla allows you to block unrequested popups.

But how do you define an unrequested popup? The definition the browser vendors seem to have chosen is that any popup that is opened after a user click is a requested popup, and any other is an unrequested one.

So this simple script circumvents popup blockers:

```
var popup;
document.onclick = function () {
```

```
        popup = window.open('url','name','arguments');
    }
```

Whenever the user clicks anywhere in the document, the popup pops up, because the browser interprets the click as a user command to open the popup. Site Survey uses this principle.

It's only a matter of time before the dregs of the Internet catch up with this technique, at which point all current popup blockers will become worthless. And yes, the fact that this book mentions the technique will probably help speed up that process. I thought about leaving it out, but in the end decided not to. After all, depending on the circumstances, popups can be a valid part of JavaScript.

Besides, the fundamental problem is not one or another circumvention method, but the definition of unrequested popups, and this problem will not go away if we just refuse to look at it. Although the present definition is clearly insufficient, I can't think of a better one, and even if browser vendors create a new definition, this will only instigate a new round of the arms race, in which the browser vendors will operate at a disadvantage, since they have to leave a loophole for proper, valid popups to be opened.

Therefore I predict a popup-blocker arms race, the outcome of which will probably favor the malicious popup farms, unless browser vendors take the drastic step of disabling `window.open()` altogether.

C: Navigation

The window object contains two objects that have to do with navigation: location and history.

Location

The location object contains information about the current location of the page, aka the URL. This object has eight properties, seven of which contain parts of the current URL. The eighth, and most important, property is `href`, which contains the entire URL.

The figure below shows which parts of the URL are accessed by the properties
hash, host, hostname, href, pathname, port, protocol and search.

FIGURE 6.3   The hash, host, hostname, href, pathname, port, protocol, and search
properties of the location object.

All of these properties are read/write, although in practice you'll only write to
href and hash. I advise you to treat the other properties as read-only. In general it's not advisable to change, say, the port number of the current URL.

If you change the location.href of a document, the browser loads the new
page. Similarly, if you change the location.hash, the page jumps to the new
anchor (<a name="something"> or <element id="something">). The page is
not reloaded, since that's not necessary.

{

FINDING THE PAGE NAME

In general you need to know the page name, i.e., the path, the search, and
the hash. Unfortunately, no single property of location contains this information. pathname + search + hash can give incorrect results, since search
also contains hash.

Here the lastIndexOf() method of strings comes in handy:

```
var URL = location.href;
var pageName = URL.substring(URL.lastIndexOf('/'));
```

Take a substring of location.href, starting at the last /. Now you have
the page name, including any query strings and hashes.

}

The location object also contains two methods: `reload()` and `replace()`. The function of `reload()` is obvious: it reloads the current page from the server, which is occasionally useful if you work with dynamic data.

`replace()` commands the browser to replace the current page with the page on the URL specified in its argument:

```
location.replace('http://www.quirksmode.org');
```

Now the current page is replaced by QuirksMode.org.

href vs. replace()

Although it may seem that `replace()` has exactly the same function as `href`, this is not the case. If you change the `location.href` of a page, the browser loads the new page as if the user clicked on a link. The new page becomes a new entry in the window's history.

However, if you use `replace()`, the new page overwrites the old one in the window's history. In 2F we discussed the circumstances in which this difference is important.

History

The window contains a history object that gives limited access to its history.

Every window remembers which pages it has shown and makes these pages available through the Back and Forward buttons of the browser. This list of URLs is stored in the History object. For privacy reasons, however, it is not possible to read this list, with the sole exception of its `length`. You can send the user backward and forward in this list, but you cannot know for sure which page he'll end up in.

The history object has three methods: `go()`, `back()`, and `forward()`. The last two methods mimic the Back and Forward buttons of the browser.

The go() method allows you to specify how many pages you want the user to go forward (positive number) or backward (negative number). So this sends the user two pages backward:

```
history.go(-2);
```

There's rarely a reason to send the user back more than one page, especially when you cannot find out which page that was, so the go() method is seldom used.

History of separate windows

Every window has a separate history. If you send the user on to a new window, its Back button doesn't function, because the new window doesn't yet have any pages in its history. And of course history.back() doesn't work, either.

The history of frames is even more complicated. Each frame has its own history object, but so do the parent and top frames. When the user clicks the Back button, the browser window generally—but not always—undoes the most recent page change in one of its child frames. Unfortunately, this behavior is not totally reliable, and you shouldn't write scripts that assume history.go() of the parent frame will undo all recent page changes in its child frames in the correct order.

If you want to send the user back in the history of one specific frame, use the frame's own history object:

```
frames[1].history.back();
```

D: Window geometry

The window object represents the graphical browser window the user sees on her computer screen. As such, the window object contains a few objects, methods, and properties that allow you to read out information about, or even change, the graphical browser window.

The screen object

The screen object contains information about the user's computer screen. `screen.width` and `screen.height` properties give the screen resolution, while `screen.availWidth` and `screen.availHeight` give the available screen resolution, i.e., the screen resolution minus taskbars and such.

`screen.colorDepth` gives the number of bits per pixel the computer screen can handle. `screen.pixelDepth` gives the same information, but doesn't work in Explorer.

These properties are often a part of detection scripts, such as Site Survey, in which it is important to gather information about the computer and browser the visitor is using. Other than in such scripts, the screen object has no real use.

Window dimensions

A set of properties contains information about the window dimensions. The most important are `window.innerWidth` and `window.innerHeight`, which set the window dimensions.

Nowadays we don't need these properties, because all browsers have made this information available elsewhere. We'll discuss the right way to read out window dimensions in 9H.

Moving, resizing, and scrolling the window

The window object has two methods to move the window, two methods to resize the window, and two methods to scroll the window. They are `moveTo()`, `moveBy()`, `resizeTo()`, `resizeBy()`, `scrollTo()`, and `scrollBy()`. All these methods take two arguments: an x and a y coordinate.

The `To()` methods are absolute, i.e., the x and y coordinates give the new absolute position, size, or scrolling offset of the window. The `By()` methods are relative, i.e., they add the given x and y arguments to the current position, size, or scrolling offset of the window.

I use `resizeTo()` in Site Survey:

[Site Survey/popup.js, lines 59-63]

```
function startSurvey() {
    self.resizeTo(800,600);
    self.focus();
    document.forms[0].submit();
}
```

When the survey starts, the script resizes the popup to 800 × 600 pixels. `resizeBy(800,600)` would make the popup 800 pixels wider and 600 pixels higher than the current width and height.

Similarly, `moveTo(200,100)` means "Move the window to 200 pixels right of and 100 pixels below the upper left corner of the screen," while `moveBy(200,100)` means "Move the window to 200 pixels right of and 100 pixels below its current position."

Finally, `scrollTo(200,100)` means "Scroll to scrolling offset 200/100." `scrollBy(200,100)` means "Scroll the page by 200 pixels to the right and 100 pixels to the bottom, starting from the current scrolling position of the page."

> **RESIZEBY(0,1)**
>
> The most important reason for using `resizeBy()` is to defeat CSS rendering problems. Occasionally a browser doesn't respond correctly to a CSS change. It is supposed to reinterpret the CSS for the entire page, but due to some bug or other, it doesn't.
>
> Fortunately, all browsers reinterpret all CSS after the window has been resized. Therefore, resize the window minimally, for example: `resizeBy(0,1)`, to ensure that the CSS renders properly. A one-pixel resize is enough; it triggers the CSS reinterpretation and the bugs disappear.
>
> Ideally, follow this up with a `resizeBy(0,-1)` so that the window regains its original dimensions.

These methods also accept negative arguments: `moveBy(-100,-100)` means "Move the window to 100 pixels left of and 100 pixels above its current position."

focus and blur

Each window has a method `focus()` and a method `blur()`. `focus()` brings the window to the front of the stacking order; i.e., it becomes the uppermost window on the user's computer screen. The window also gains the keyboard focus; if you press Ctrl+R it's the focused window that reloads. `blur()` does the opposite: it hides the window behind the other windows.

As we just saw, I also use `focus()` in Site Survey. When the window has been resized, I focus on it. Then I submit the form, so that the newly resized and focused window contains the start of the actual survey.

E: Miscellaneous

We close our survey of the window object with a discussion of a few miscellaneous methods and properties.

navigator

The navigator object contains properties that say something about the user's browser. By far the most important one is `navigator.userAgent`, which

6E

{ **RESTRICTIONS**

In the past, `focus()` and `blur()` have been used for less-desirable actions, for instance opening a popup, blurring it, and then moving it beyond the edge of the computer screen—in effect, creating a hidden popup. Therefore, more and more browsers allow their users to switch off the `focus()/blur()` and `move/resize` methods. This means that you cannot assume that all browsers that your visitors might use will allow these actions. }

contains the entire userAgent string of the browser. The problem is not accessing this string, but interpreting it; in other words, detecting the user's browser. In 3D, we already discussed browser detection and why not to rely on it.

The navigator object contains other properties, including platform, appName, and appVersion, but they are less reliable than userAgent.

One other useful property, navigator.cookieEnabled, is covered in 6G.

alert, confirm, and prompt

The window object has three methods that cause dialog boxes to open: alert(), confirm(), and prompt(). The alert() method opens a dialog box with the argument as text. The confirm() method does the same, but gives the user an OK and a Cancel button. This method returns true (user clicked OK) or false (user clicked Cancel). The prompt() method allows the user to type in a string, and returns that string.

Example:

```
alert('Do you have a name?');
var hasName = confirm('Do you have a name?');
var name = prompt('Do you have a name?');
```

FIGURE 6.4
Alert, confirm, and prompt dialog boxes.

Now `hasName` contains `true` or `false`, while `name` contains the name the user typed in.

Note that the 'Do you have a name?' string shown in the dialog boxes is plain text, not HTML. Therefore, if you want a line break to occur in the box, you should use `\n` (newline character), not `<br />`.

```
alert('Do you have a<br />name?');
alert('Do you have a\nname?');
```

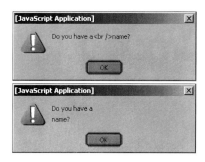

FIGURE 6.5
Dialog boxes contain plain text, not HTML.

In 3E, we discussed the use of `alert()` in JavaScript debugging.

`confirm()` and `prompt()` are rarely used, because, from a usability perspective, it's better to have users enter information in form fields and then read it out than to confront them with potentially confusing extra boxes.

Timeouts and intervals

Timeouts and intervals allow you to specify a bit of script that should be run after a certain time has elapsed. For instance:

```
setTimeout('myFunction()',1000);
```

Now the function `myFunction()` is executed 1000 milliseconds after the browser receives the `setTimeout` command. Note the two arguments this method requires:

1. A string, which is evaluated (interpreted as a JavaScript command) when the timeout runs out.

2. The waiting time in milliseconds.

It's also possible to use a function reference instead of a string:

```
setTimeout(myFunction,1000);
```

Now the same thing happens. The advantage of this method is that your code is cleaner (no complicated quotes), but the disadvantage is that you cannot send arguments to the function.

clearTimeout

It is also possible to cancel a timeout. To do this, you have to assign the timeout to a variable. After all, if you want to cancel it, JavaScript should be able to access the timeout.

```
var myTimeOut = setTimeout('myFunction()',1000);
```

This line of code does exactly the same thing as the previous line. However, since we assigned the timeout to a variable, we can use the `clearTimeout` method to cancel the command:

```
clearTimeout(myTimeOut);
```

If the timeout hasn't yet taken place, it's canceled, and `myFunction()` is not called.

Intervals

Intervals are timeouts that are run repeatedly. This line commands `myFunction()` to be executed in 1000 milliseconds, and to repeat it every 1000 milliseconds until further notice:

```
setInterval('myFunction()',1000);
```

Just as with timeouts, you can cancel the interval:

```
var myInterval = setInterval('myFunction()',1000);
clearInterval(myInterval);
```

Use of timeouts and intervals

Timeouts and intervals are useful whenever you want to defer the execution of code, or if you want a specific bit of code to run repeatedly. We already saw an example of the first situation in the trackMain() function of Site Survey.

[Site Survey/popup.js, lines 34-37]

```
else if (tryCounter < nrOfAttempts) {
    setTimeout('trackMain()',waitingTime);
    tryCounter++;
}
```

If the status of the main window is uncertain, the function should run again after a certain number of milliseconds, as defined in waitingTime.

Timeouts and intervals are crucial for JavaScript animations. We'll study those in 9G.

F: The document object

By far the most important object in a window object is the document object, which represents the HTML page the window currently contains. It holds a lot of information, and it also allows you to change the document on the fly. In fact, 80% of the scripts you write are concerned only with the document object and its numerous child objects.

The document object contains a node object for every single HTML element in the page. We'll discuss these W3C DOM node objects in detail in Chapter 8. In addition, the document has many more methods and properties, some of which are W3C DOM-compatible, others remnants of older, proprietary DOMs.

There are a few document methods and properties that are not a part of any DOM, and that give information about the document as a whole. In this section we'll take a look at a few of these miscellaneous methods and properties. (We'll treat one of them, document.cookie, in the next section.)

6F

lastModified

The `document.lastModified` property contains the last modification date of the document, provided that the server adds it to the document headers. If the server doesn't send this header, some browsers will decide the document was last modified today, while others maintain that it was last modified on 1 January 1970.

If the server does send a last-modified date, you initially receive it as a string. This string is browser-dependent. Here are a few:

```
01/22/2006 18:16:25 // Explorer Windows
Sunday, January 22, 2006 18:16:25 // Mozilla
Sun Jan 22 2006 18:16:25 // Safari
```

For this reason, among others, it's best to convert the last-modified time to a date object:

```
var lastMod = new Date(document.lastModified);
```

referrer

The `document.referrer` property contains the referrer to the current page, i.e., the URL of the page that brought the user to your page. If there is no such page, because the user typed in the URL or used a bookmark, then `document.referrer` is empty.

In general it's not a good idea to rely on `document.referrer` for security, since it can be spoofed by malicious surfers.

domain

The `document.domain` property allows you to circumvent the strictest part of JavaScript's same-source policy. We already discussed its use in 1B.

write()

The `document.write()` method allows you to write text to the page:

```
document.write('<h1>Hello world!</h1>');
```

Now the `<h1>` is inserted at the location of the `document.write()`. Although with the advent of the W3C DOM this way of creating dynamic HTML pages has become obsolete, `document.write()` was once the most important JavaScript method, and you'll often encounter it in scripts written before, say, 2002. Nowadays it's not important any more, except in one very specific situation that we'll discuss in 9C.

It is important to realize that a `document.write()` works properly only if it's executed while the page is being loaded. In addition, the written text appears exactly at the place the `document.write()` is called.

For instance, take this page:

```
<html>
<body>
<script type="text/javascript">
document.write('<h1>Hello world!</h1>');
</script>
<p>I am a JavaScript hacker.</p>
</body>
</html>
```

FIGURE 6.6
document.write() writes new content into the page.

The `<h1>` appears in place of the `<script>` tag: above the paragraph. If you want the `<h1>` to appear below the paragraph, you would do this:

```
<html>
<body>
```

```
<script type="text/javascript">
function sayHello() {
    document.write('<h1>Hello world!</h1>');
}
</script>
<p>I am a JavaScript hacker.</p>
<script type="text/javascript">
sayHello();
</script>
</body>
</html>
```

One warning: if you execute `document.write()` after the page has been loaded, the browser interprets it as a command to destroy the old document and to create a new one. To understand this behavior, we have to discuss two more methods.

open() and close()

You are allowed to create a new HTML document in JavaScript. To do that, you first have to open the document, then write in it, and then close it. For example:

```
<script type="text/javascript">
document.open();
document.write('<h1>Hello world!</h1>');
document.close();
</script>
```

First the document is opened, and at that point the old document is destroyed. Then you write something in the new document, and afterwards you close it.

The `document.open()` method is not required. If, after a page has been completely loaded, you command JavaScript to `write()` something, it assumes that you want to open a new document, and it destroys the current page.

Therefore, this doesn't work:

```
<a href="somepage.html" id="clickTest">
<script>
window.onload = function () {
document.getElementById('clickTest').onclick = function () {
        document.write('You clicked me!');
    }
}
</script>
```

The click event fires after the page has been loaded, and therefore the browser assumes that you want to open a new document, and destroys the old one. In its place, it shows a new document with the single line 'You clicked me!'

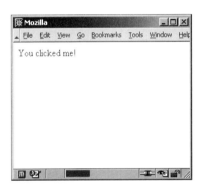

FIGURE 6.7
When document.write() is called after a page loads, it destroys the old page and creates a new one to write the message.

Writing into a popup

document.write() is occasionally used in combination with a popup:

```
var newWin = window.open('','newWin',[arguments]);
newWin.document.write('<h1>Hello world!</h1>');
newWin.document.write('<p>I am a JavaScript hacker!</p>');
newWin.document.close();
```

This used to be especially handy if you needed your own debugging window:

```
var debug = window.open('','newWin',[arguments]);
function addDebuggingMessage(msg) {
    debug.document.write(msg + '<br>');
}
```

Note that in this case you do not use the `document.close()` method. You want the popup to remain open for writing, because later on you're going to call the function from anywhere you need it:

```
function doSomething() {
    var x = [something complicated that's not
what you expected];
    addDebuggingMessage('x is ' + x.nodeName);
}
```

Nowadays it's also possible to embed such a debugging window in your document and use the `createTextNode()` and `appendChild()` methods we'll discuss in 8D and 8E to write your debugging messages. See 3E for an example.

G: Cookies

HTTP is a stateless protocol. This means that a Web server doesn't remember anything. If a user requests a page, the server has no idea if it is a new user, a user who visits the site several times a week, or a user who has been obsessively reloading every single page on the site for the past few hours. The server just sends the requested page and forgets about it.

Usually this is a good thing. Since it doesn't have any memory, a Web server can fully concentrate on serving Web pages, instead of also having to do tedious and time-consuming administration. HTTP was deliberately designed this way.

Nonetheless, sometimes you need to remember things about your visitors. Is this user logged in? Has this user requested the larger font size? Has this user already voted on the poll? To enable you to do this, Netscape introduced cookies back in the Internet's gray antiquity.

Cookies are small text files that are stored on the user's computer. They are related to certain directories in a certain Web domain, and when the user's browser requests a page from these directories, the cookies are automatically sent with the HTTP request. It's up to the server to do something with the information the cookies carry.

You can also set and retrieve cookies in JavaScript, and I do so in Edit Style Sheet and Site Survey. In both cases I want to remember certain information. In Edit Style Sheet I want to know which CSS selector the user was editing the last time he visited the page, so that I can automatically set the form to this selector, and the user can continue where he left off.

In Site Survey I want to know if the user has been selected for the survey or not. If a user comes to a page containing Site Survey for the first time, the script randomly determines whether or not the user is selected for the survey. If he is, the script makes sure that the popup appears in the way we've discussed in 6B.

name/value

The actual information of a cookie is contained in a name/value pair. The name is what makes a cookie unique for a given path: if you set a new cookie with the same name, the old cookie is overwritten.

In Site Survey, the name/value pair is "ST_status=yes" if the user is selected for the survey, or "ST_status=no" if he isn't selected.

Every subsequent time the user loads a page that contains Site Survey, the cookie is present, and the script uses the information contained in it to decide what to do next.

Expiry date

Cookies have an expiry date after which they are no longer associated with the site and are lost. If you don't define an expiry date, the cookie is lost when the current browser session ends; i.e., when the user closes his browser. If you define an expiry date in the past, the cookie is removed immediately.

6G

Expiry dates are set for GMT (Greenwich time) in the following format:

```
Tue, 23 Jan 2007 13:57:39 UTC
```

It's in this expiry date that the Site Survey "yes" and "no" cookies differ. If the user has been selected for the survey, the script sets the expiry date to the end of the survey period, so that the user is never bothered again. If he hasn't been selected, on the other hand, the script sets the expiry date to one day after the cookie was set.

I did this deliberately. The client and I agreed that if a user not already selected for the survey visits the site at least one day later, he is once again eligible for selection. In order to do this, the "no" cookie has to be removed after a day; i.e., its expiry date has to be set to one day after it was created.

domain and path

You can set cookies only for your site's domain, and by default they're only set for the path (usually the directory) of the page that sets them.

For instance, on www.quirksmode.org/js/cookies.html I set a few test cookies to help my readers understand them. If I did nothing, these cookies would only be associated with pages in www.quirksmode.org/js/ and its subdirectories.

Usually this is too restrictive. In general you want to associate your cookies with all pages on your site. All cookies have a `path` that contains the directory path they're associated with. If I set `path=/`, all cookies are associated with the Web root of the server and all its subdirectories—in other words, the entire site. This is usually what you want.

You can't associate cookies with another domain. For example, since I set my test cookies in the domain www.quirksmode.org, they cannot be associated with, say, www.google.com or www.microsoft.com: only Google and Microsoft are allowed to set cookies for their domains. This is a security feature.

Subdomains, however, are another matter. Suppose I had a domain search.quirksmode.org. Since my test cookies are set in the domain www.quirksmode.org, the pages in search.quirksmode.org do not have access to those cookies. I can change this by setting the cookie's domain. If I make it domain=quirksmode.org, the cookie would be associated with all pages in all subdomains of quirksmode.org, including www and search.

Setting a cookie

To summarize, a cookie consists of the following parts:

- A name/value pair that contains the actual information; this is empty by default.
- A GMT string with the expiry date; if not set, the cookie will expire when the user closes his browser.
- A directory path; by default the directory of the page the cookie is set to on.
- A domain; by default the domain of the page the cookie is set to on.

The syntax is as follows:

```
document.cookie = 'testcookie=yes; expires=Tue, 23 Jan 2007
13:57:39 UTC; path=/; domain=quirksmode.org';
```

This creates a new cookie with the name testcookie and the value yes, valid until 23 January 2007 in all directories of quirksmode.org and all its subdomains.

This syntax is very precise; note the semicolons and spaces that separate the various arguments and the strict form of the expiry date.

Once set, the cookie is immediately available for reading. When the user next requests a page from your site, the cookie is sent along in the HTTP headers and can be caught by server-side programs.

{

COOKIE RESTRICTIONS

Web browsers are not required to store more than 300 cookies. In addition, they are not required to store more than 20 cookies per domain. Finally, no cookie name/value pair may be larger than 4K.

I haven't personally tested the presence or absence of these restrictions in the various browsers, but in general you should assume that all browsers obey them.

}

document.cookie

The cookie is stored in `document.cookie`. This is a rather odd property that partially behaves as a string, but is not a string. You set a cookie by assigning it to `document.cookie`. If you read this property, though, it contains the name/value pairs of all cookies associated with the current page.

For instance:

```
document.cookie = 'testcookie=yes; expires=Tue, 23 Jan 2007
13:57:39 UTC; path=/; domain=quirksmode.org';
document.cookie = 'testcookie2=maybe; expires=Tue, 23 Jan 2007
13:57:39 UTC; path=/; domain=quirksmode.org';
alert(document.cookie);
```

Now the alert says "testcookie=yes;testcookie2=maybe".

Reading cookies

To read out a previously set cookie, you should take `document.cookie` and split it by semicolons. This gives you the name/value pairs of all cookies associated with the current page, and you can search them for the name of the cookie you're looking for.

For instance:

```
var searchString = 'testcookie'; // we're looking for this name
var cookieValue = '';
var cookies = document.cookie.split(';');
for (var i=0;i<cookies.length;i++) {
    if (cookies[i].indexOf(searchString + '=') == 0)
            // if name/value starts with the name we want
    {
            cookieValue = cookies[i].➡
substring(cookies.[i].indexOf('=')+1);
    }
}
```

Deleting cookies

You delete a cookie by creating a new cookie with the same name but with an expiry date in the past. For instance:

```
document.cookie = 'testcookie=yes; expires=Thu, 23 Jan 2003
14:32:04 GMT; path=/; domain=quirksmode.org';
```

Now the test cookie is removed, since its expiry date lies in the past.

6G

{ **MY COOKIE FUNCTIONS**

The syntax of all these actions is rather precise. Therefore I always use three helper functions to create, read, and erase cookies. They occur in Site Survey and Edit Style Sheets. See http://www.quirksmode.org/js/cookies.html for a line-by-line explanation of these functions. }

Example cookie use

In Site Survey I use cookies as follows (I left out a few lines of code):

[Site Survey/survey.js, lines 33-58, condensed]

```
function ST_init() {
    var currentStatus = readCookie('ST_status');
    if (currentStatus == 'no') return;
    ST_loaded = true;
    addEvent(window,"unload",ST_exit);
    if (currentStatus == 'yes') return;
    var ST_selectedForSurvey = (Math.random()*ST_sample < 1)
    if (!ST_selectedForSurvey)      {
            createCookie('ST_status','no',1);
            return;
    }
    createCookie('ST_status','yes',ST_surveyPeriod);
    addEvent(document,"click",ST_openPopup);
}
```

When the page is initialized, I read out the ST_status cookie to find out if the user has already visited the page and, if so, whether she was selected for the survey. If not (currentStatus == 'no'), I immediately end the function: nothing should happen.

If the user has been selected for the survey, or if it's her first visit, I set ST_loaded to true and set an onunload event handler to fire the function that stores the name of the current page in the popup window. We discussed both features in 6B.

If the user has already been selected for the survey (currentStatus == 'yes'), I end the function: we've done enough.

If it's the user's first visit, I now draw a random number to decide whether she is selected for the survey. If not, I set the ST_status cookie to 'no': user not selected. This cookie expires in one day; if the user returns after that time, she's again eligible for the survey. Then I end the function.

If the user is selected, I set the ST_status cookie to 'yes'. This cookie expires only at the end of the survey period; once a user has been selected, she gets the popup exactly once (on this page). Finally, I add an onclick event handler to the entire document, so that if the user clicks anywhere in the document, the popup is opened.

User control

Modern browsers allow users to manage their cookie permissions. They can choose never to accept any cookies, or not to accept third-party cookies, (meaning, they can choose to allow cookies only from the domain they're visiting.) In addition, all browsers allow the user to see and remove all currently active cookies. Because of these restrictions, you can never be 100% certain that a cookie-based system will work in all circumstances.

6G

DON'T TAKE COOKIES FROM STRANGERS

Third-party cookies are usually set by banner farms. If a site owner decides to add banners to his site, he adds a bit of (badly written) JavaScript code that imports an image, a Flash movie, or another file. Now the page also requests files from the banner farm's server, and therefore this server, too, is allowed to set cookies in the user's browser. Banner farmers love these cookies, because they allow the farmers to follow individual users over the entire Internet: whenever a user comes to a site that uses the same banner service, this fact is registered by the banner farm's server.

Since this clearly violates the privacy of Internet users, modern browsers refuse these third-party cookies by default.

Determining cookie support

With all that in mind, how do you find out if a browser supports cookies? Modern browsers all have a `navigator.cookieEnabled` property that is `true` if they support cookies. So you can do the following:

```
if (navigator.cookieEnabled) {
    // cookies enabled; set or read them
}
```

Frankly, I discovered this useful property only while doing research for this book. Therefore, Site Survey contains an old-style cookie detection that's also suited for older browsers. I set a test cookie and try to read it. If I can't, the browser doesn't support cookies:

[Site Survey/survey.js, lines 10-16]

```
var ST_cookiesSupported = false;
createCookie('ST_test','supported',1);
if (readCookie('ST_test')) {
    ST_cookiesSupported = true;
    eraseCookie('ST_test');
}
```

First I set `ST_cookiesSupported` to `false`. Then I create a test cookie and try to read it. If that's possible, I set `ST_cookiesSupported` to `true` and erase the cookie. I use `ST_cookiesSupported` in `ST_init`:

[Site Survey/survey.js, lines 33-35, condensed]

```
function ST_init() {
    if (!ST_cookiesSupported) return;
```

If it's still `false`, cookies are not supported, and the function ends immediately.

Events

AS AN EVENT-DRIVEN programming language, JavaScript does very little on its own; instead, it waits for the user to do something, and then reacts by executing a bit of script.

In order to find out what's going on in the HTML page, the DOM supports *events*. Every time the user takes an action—for instance, she clicks on a link, submits a form, loads a new page, changes the value of a form field, or presses a key—an event fires.

You can add *event handlers* to any elements. Event handlers are functions that are automatically executed when the event takes place on that element. If the script is well thought out, the page responds to user actions and interactivity is born.

All example scripts in this book are event-driven: they kick in only after the user takes an action that I, as the programmer, have decided is most logical in the context. For instance, Dropdown Menu waits for the user to mouse over or focus on certain links, Form Validation waits for the user to submit the form, and XMLHTTP Speed Meter waits for the user to enter a postal code.

A: Browser incompatibilities

As we saw in 1B, JavaScript standardization is a two-tiered construct, with the de facto Netscape 3 standard forming the lower tier, and the modern W3C specifications the upper one. This is also true in event handling, but there's one extra catch. There are two upper-tier specifications instead of one: W3C and Microsoft.

In contrast to the W3C DOM and XMLHttpRequest, which all browsers have honestly tried to implement, event handling is still plagued by deliberate incompatibilities that were introduced during the Browser Wars. Explorer sticks to the Microsoft way of doing things, while Mozilla follows the W3C specification faithfully. Safari and Opera support both systems. Although it's useful to see the combined W3C and Microsoft models as the advanced tier of event handling, you should be aware that there are differences between them, some of which are rather tricky.

You'll encounter most incompatibilities when you access the event object and its properties. For instance, W3C calls the target of the event `target`, while Microsoft calls it `srcElement`. If you need to identify the target of the event, you try both properties and use the one that contains a useful value—it's an inconvenience, but not a show-stopping problem.

Unfortunately, in addition to these easily solved problems, there still exist a few truly vicious incompatibilities—escapees, perhaps, from a Browser Wars Era malign-life-form exhibit. The mouse properties, especially, are infested with them. Solving these incompatibilities is difficult, and occasionally even flat-out impossible. We'll discuss these problems later in this chapter.

The traditional event-handling model, which is part of the de facto Netscape 3 standard, is supported by all browsers, but lacks a few functionalities of the W3C and Microsoft models. It's still possible to use this model instead of the advanced ones, and most example scripts actually do so, because the traditional model causes fewer browser incompatibilities.

Resolve case by case

You should resolve browser incompatibilities on a case-by-case basis; don't use one sweeping object-detection script to decide which event model you're going to follow. Consider this case:

```
if (W3C model) {
    // execute W3C compatible scripts
}
else if (Microsoft model) {
    // execute Microsoft compatible scripts
}
```

The problem is that there is no adequate general detect—no single object whose presence or absence conclusively proves that a browser supports or does not support a certain event model.

Besides, as I said earlier, browser incompatibilities mostly occur in the event object. Other areas of event handling are relatively problem-free, and don't usually require code branching. Therefore it's best to restrict your code branching to the scripts that really need it.

Overview

These are the most important topics in event handling and their browser compatibility:

Area	Description	Incompatibilities	Section
Events	The action that the user has to take to trigger the script.	Few	7B
Event handler registration	Defines which function is executed when the event takes place.	Some, especially between the W3C and Microsoft models	7C

7A

Area	Description	Incompatibilities	Section
Event bubbling and capturing	Determines which event handler fires first if an HTML element and its parent handle the same event.	Few	7D
Accessing the event object	The event object holds information about the event which your script may need.	Many, some of them unsolvable	7E
Targeting	Finding out which element you should do something with as a response to the event.	Few	7F

B: The events

During the preparation of your scripts, you have to decide which events to use. In this section we'll discuss all common events, and in 7G we'll take a look at the events I chose for the example scripts.

The events can be divided into three groups:

- Mouse events, caused by a certain mouse action.

- Keyboard events, caused by a certain key action.

- Interface events, which fire when something happens to the page, for instance, when a form is submitted or the page unloads.

> **TERMINOLOGY CLARIFICATION**
>
> If the user clicks on a link, a *click* event takes place. If you want a script to run when that click event takes place, you register an *onclick* event handler.

Mouse events

The common mouse events are click, dblclick, mousedown, mousemove, mouse-out, mouseover, and mouseup. They are available on all HTML elements. In addition, we'll discuss the Microsoft proprietary mouseenter and mouseleave events.

Mouseover and mouseout

When the user moves the mouse over an element, a mouseover event fires. When the user moves the mouse out of an element, a mouseout event fires.

Note that the mouse may move over and out of a lot of elements in a short time, especially when many elements have a visible (i.e., mouse-overable) part. The mouseout event, especially, can turn nasty in such environments. We'll discuss these problems in more detail in 7H, but the basic rule is to always carefully check the target of your mouseover and mouseout events before doing something.

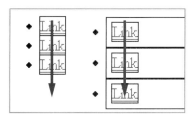

FIGURE 7.1

If you move the mouse on the path the arrow shows, the example on the left triggers one mouseover event for each of the three links. But the example on the right has an extra padding on the <li>, so following the same path triggers nine mouseover events (three for the links and six for the <li>s above and below each link). If your script doesn't expect mouseovers on <li>s, you have a problem.

Mousedown and mouseup

The mousedown event occurs when the user depresses the mouse button. The mouseup event occurs when the user releases the mouse button. They are very popular in drag-and-drop scripts (mousedown: user selects item, mousemove: user moves item, mouseup: user releases item), but otherwise you'll rarely need them.

Click

A click event occurs when one element receives a mousedown event followed by a mouseup event. It is by far the most common of the mouse events.

The click event also fires when the user has focused on an element and then presses Enter. Therefore, it is the only accessible mouse event.

On elements such as links and buttons, you can think of click as an activate event: the user activates a link or button, and it doesn't matter whether she uses a mouse click or a keystroke to do so.

Dblclick

The dblclick (double click) event occurs when one element receives two click events in rapid succession. In practice, you cannot use a click and a dblclick event on the same element—it's impossible to teach all browsers to distinguish between the two.

Mousemove

The mousemove event occurs when the user moves the mouse. In theory, every movement of 1 pixel counts as a mousemove event, so this event is likely to be fired many times over during even the smallest mouse movement.

This event is mostly used in drag-and-drop scripts.

Mouseenter and mouseleave

Two Microsoft proprietary mouse events are interesting enough to discuss, even though they're supported only by Explorer.

The mouseenter and mouseleave events are similar to mouseover and mouse-out, but with an important difference. Mouseover and mouseout events fire when a user mouses over or out of the element on which they're defined, *or one of its descendant elements*. In contrast, mouseenter and mouseleave fire *only* when the user mouses over or out of the element on which they're defined, and ignore any events on its descendants.

Take this example:

```
<p id="test">This is a <em>test</em> paragraph.</p>
document.getElementById('test').onmouseover = handleEvent;
```

When the user mouses over the paragraph, handleEvent() is executed. When she mouses over the <em> that's a child of the paragraph, handleEvent() is also executed, since the mouseover event bubbles up to the paragraph. (We'll discuss event bubbling in 7D.)

If we use mouseenter, the situation changes:

```
document.getElementById('test').onmouseenter = handleEvent;
```

Now handleEvent() is still executed when the user mouses over the paragraph, but nothing happens when she mouses over the <em>, since the event did not take place on the element on which the onmouseenter event handler is defined.

Mouseenter and mouseleave are therefore the true JavaScript equivalents of the CSS pseudo-class :hover. In addition, they're far easier to work with than mouseover and mouseout, especially in complicated dropdown/DHTML menus. I still have a secret hope that other browsers besides Explorer will start to support them.

Meanwhile, if you happen to work on an Explorer-only site, use mouseenter and mouseleave and forget about mouseover and mouseout. It'll save you a lot of headaches.

Accessible mouse events

Mouse events have a serious accessibility problem: except for the click event, they don't fire when the user doesn't use a mouse. If the user goes from link to link by keystrokes, no mouseover event will fire, since the mouse pointer is not placed over the elements.

Therefore, any script that relies exclusively on mouse events is inaccessible to keyboard users. The solution to this problem is, obviously, to use other events in addition to the mouse events.

Adequate non-mouse emulation events exist only for mouseover and mouseout. When the user tabs to links or form fields, these elements gain the focus, and when the user tabs away from them, the elements are blurred. Therefore, the non-mouse equivalents of mouseover and mouseout are focus and blur. We'll discuss these events later.

7B

The other mouse events are harder to emulate. If you wish, you can think of keydown and keyup as the equivalents of mousedown and mouseup, but be warned that these events are not the same, and that the equivalence is strained at best. For instance, the keyboard events fire when the user presses any key, while a perfect mousedown/up simulation requires these events to fire only when the user presses the Enter key.

The mousemove events cannot be emulated at all. If your script hinges on a mousemove event, you might add an extra script module that allows keyboard users to move an element by keystrokes.

Keyboard events

The keyboard events are keydown, keypress, and keyup. Generally they are available on all text-accepting HTML elements such as form fields, as well as on links, forms, and the document.

Keyup is the simplest of the three: it fires once when the user releases a key. Note that it fires after the character has been added to the form field.

Keydown and keypress fire continuously as long as the user keeps a key depressed. (Their frequency depends on the keyboard repeat rate the user has chosen in his computer settings.)

> **WARNING**   Browser incompatibilities ahead

If the user presses a key to enter text in a form field, the keydown and keypress events fire before the character has been added to the form field. Therefore, if you want to prevent the character from being added, you must use keydown or keypress. To make matters more complicated, Mozilla allows this prevention only on keypress, not on keydown.

Unfortunately, keypress is the most useless of the keyboard events, and you should generally steer clear of it. For instance, keypress does not always contain information about the actual key the user has pressed, and in some browsers doesn't fire at all if the user presses a key combination, such as Ctrl+C.

If you need a cross-browser script that detects the key the user has pressed and also prevents the character from being added to a form field, you have a problem. Detecting the key requires keydown or keyup, while preventing the character from showing up requires keypress. At the time of writing I don't have a solution.

Fortunately, you rarely need these two functionalities in the same script. All example scripts that use keyboard events just read out the text the user has typed. They don't need to know which key was pressed (that information is part of the text, anyway), and they don't want to prevent the user from typing more characters, either.

Interface events

> **WARNING**   Browser incompatibilities ahead

Interface events are indirect events: they take place after the user has performed a certain mouse or key action with "special meaning." For instance, if the user clicks a Submit button, a click event fires on the button. Afterwards, the submit interface event takes place, since a click on a Submit button has the special meaning "submit form."

The common interface events are blur, focus, change, contextmenu, load, unload, readystatechange, reset, submit, resize, and scroll. Their availability varies, as noted in their descriptions.

blur and focus

The focus event fires when an element gains the focus, for instance, because the user clicks on it or tabs to it. The blur event fires when an element loses the focus. These events are available on form fields, links, and the window.

These events serve as keyboard-accessible equivalents of mouseover and mouseout.

7B

{ **NO FORM VALIDATION FOR ONBLUR OR ONCHANGE**

Users often use tabbing to quickly navigate through a form so you might con-sider using the blur event for form validation (to validate a form field as soon as the user is done with it, i.e., when the field becomes blurred).

Don't do this   it's extremely annoying. The user generally doesn't want to be disturbed when he's busy filling out a form.

You could use the change event instead (and validate when the user has changed the content of a form field). It is somewhat less annoying than blur because it doesn't fire when the user enters nothing in a field.

Even so, I advise you to use onsubmit for all your form validation scripts. That's what the user expects, after all. First enter all data, and then validate all data. }

change

The change event fires when the user has changed the value of a form field. On select boxes, the event fires as soon as the user selects anything; on checkboxes and radio buttons, the event fires when the user checks or unchecks them. On text fields, the event fires when the field loses the focus after the user has changed its content.

The change event is not available on HTML elements other than form fields.

The change event's behavior on select boxes can have accessibility consequences. When you use the arrow keys to go through a list of options, the change event will fire for every option you encounter, even though it should only fire when you've reached the option of your choice.

Therefore it's best to use a separate Go button next to the select box. The user selects an option by mouse or by keyboard, and then uses this button to acti-vate that option.

{ **EXPLORER PROBLEM**

In Explorer, the change event on checkboxes and radio buttons fires when the field is blurred, not when the user checks or unchecks it. This matters when your interface needs to respond immediately to user actions, as Usable Forms does. In those cases, you might consider using the click event instead.

To see the problem, try Edit Style Sheet's checkboxes in Explorer. }

contextmenu

The contextmenu event—originally a Microsoft invention but currently supported by most browsers—fires when the user calls up the context menu, usually by right-clicking on the page. This event is typically used to disable the context menu so that users cannot choose the View Source command.

load and unload

The load event fires when the page has been loaded completely, including all external files such as images. We discussed this event in detail in 4E.

The unload event fires when the page unloads for whatever reason. It is not possible to distinguish between the various ways of unloading a page, i.e., clicking on a link, submitting a form, or closing the browser window. Neither is it possible to cancel the unloading of the page.

Both events are available on the window object. In addition, the load event works on images. When the image has been loaded completely, its load event fires.

readystatechange

The readystatechange event—originally a Microsoft extension but now supported by all browsers—is important when you use XMLHttpRequest, but rarely used outside such a context. We'll discuss this event in more detail in 10A.

In Explorer, the event applies to all elements, but the other browsers support it only on an XMLHttpRequest object.

7B

> ### OPERA LOAD/UNLOAD PROBLEM
>
> The load and unload events are unreliable in Opera: they do not fire when the user loads and unloads pages by means of the Back and Forward buttons or their equivalent keystrokes.
>
> A victim of this odd behavior is Site Survey. This script works with the unload event, but since it cannot be certain to catch every unload event in Opera, the script will never be guaranteed to work correctly.
>
> At the time of writing there is no solution to this problem.

reset and submit

The reset and submit events fire when the user resets or submits a form. onreset event handlers are very rare, but most form-validation scripts use the submit event to fire the validation functions. Both events are available only on forms.

Note that the submit event does not fire if JavaScripts submits the form, only when the user does.

```
document.forms[0].onsubmit = handleEvent;
document.forms[0].submit();
// event does not fire, so handleEvent is not executed.
```

> ### HASLAYOUT
>
> The hasLayout property has profound consequences for all kinds of CSS-related actions in Explorer. Discussing this property in full falls outside the scope of this book; you can read an introduction to the property and the problems it causes at http://www.satzansatz.de/cssd/onhavinglayout.html.

> { **MINOR RESIZE PROBLEMS**
>
> Mozilla fires the event once when the user stops resizing the window. Explorer and Safari fire it continuously as long as the user is busy resizing the window. Opera fires it a lot of times, but only when the user has stopped the resizing.
>
> This may matter if you write long and involved onresize event handlers. }

resize

The resize event fires when the user resizes the browser window, and therefore it is generally only available on the window. (In Explorer the event is available for all elements that "have layout.")

scroll

The scroll event fires when the user scrolls something. It does not matter whether the user drags the scrollbar, uses the arrow keys, or the mouse wheel. The scroll event is available on any element that has a scrollbar.

W3C events

W3C has defined a lot of potentially useful DOM events. The most general one is DOMSubTreeModified, which fires whenever any change occurs in the DOM tree below the element on which it's registered. Unfortunately, at the time of writing, this event is supported only by Mozilla, and even in that browser it doesn't work flawlessly.

> { **DOM EVENTS**
>
> Study the DOM events at http://www.w3.org/TR/2000/REC-DOM-Level-2-Events-20001113/events.html#Events-eventgroupings-mutationevents. As soon as their browser support becomes decent we'll use them a lot, since some of them are very handy. }

7B

> { **MICROSOFT EVENTS**
>
> Study the MS events at http://msdn.microsoft.com/workshop/author/dhtml/reference/events.asp. Obviously, most of them work only in Explorer. }

Microsoft events

Microsoft has also defined a lot of events, some of which could be useful. The most important ones are the mouseenter and mouseleave events discussed several pages back.

The default action

Many events have an associated default action. For instance, clicking on a link means the browser should load the page the link points to. Submitting a form means the browser should send the form to the server. Pressing a key means the browser should add the character to the text field the user is working on.

The general rule is that the event handler is executed first, and the default action takes place afterwards. This allows the event handler to cancel the default action.

Occasionally the purpose of an event handler is to find out whether the default action should take place or not. Form Validation is the most obvious example: it exists to decide whether the form submission started by the user should be allowed, or whether it should be aborted because the user has made a mistake.

> { **EXCEPTION: UNLOAD**
>
> The default action of the unload event (unload the page) is a special case: it cannot be cancelled. If it could be cancelled, you could prevent a user from leaving your site, and that's obviously undesirable. }

The return value of an event-handling function serves to allow or disallow the default action. If the function returns `false`, then the default action is cancelled. Any other return value will cause the default action to take place.

Take this simple example:

```
var x = document.getElementsByTagName('a');
for (var i=0;i<x.length;i++) {
    x[i].onclick = askConfirmation;
}


function askConfirmation() {
    return confirm('Are you sure you want to follow this link?');
}
```

We define an onclick event handler for all links in the document. The default action of a click event on a link is loading the page defined in the `href` property of the link.

However, before that happens, the click event takes place, `askConfirmation()` runs, and a confirm box (see 6E) is shown. The user can click OK (`true`) or Cancel (`false`). This boolean value is returned to the event handler by `askConfirmation()`, and it indicates whether the default action should take place (`true`) or not (`false`).

Form Validation contains a real-world example:

[Form Validation, lines 73-106, condensed heavily]

```
function validate() {
    var validForm = true;
    if (error found)
            validForm = false;
    return validForm;
}
```

The `validate()` function is the event handler of the submit event. It uses a variable `validForm` that's initially `true`, but becomes `false` when the script finds an error. It is returned at the end of the function. Thus the default action of the submit event (submit form) is cancelled when the function finds a mis-take in the form.

As we'll see in 7F, event handlers can become methods of the object you reg-ister them on—provided you register them correctly. `return false` works only from a function that is directly assigned as a method of an HTML element.

`return false` works in this case:

```
var x = document.getElementsByTagName('a');
for (var i=0;i<x.length;i++) {
    x[i].onclick = askConfirmation;
}
```

This, however, does not work:

```
var x = document.getElementsByTagName('a');
for (var i=0;i<x.length;i++) {
    x[i].onclick = function () {
                        askConfirmation();
    }
}
```

Now the onclick method of the link calls `askConfirmation()`, and although the function still returns `true` or `false`, this return value is not caught, and disap-pears without a trace.

A `return false` in an event handler works in the following cases:

```
x.onclick = askConfirmation;
x.addEventListener('click', askConfirmation,false);
x.attachEvent('onclick', askConfirmation);
```

It does not work in the following cases:

```
<element onclick="askConfirmation()">

x.onclick = function () {
    askConfirmation();
}
```

```
x.addEventListener('click', function () {
    askConfirmation();
},false);
```

An extra return statement will suffice to get these last examples in line:

```
<element onclick="return askConfirmation()">
x.onclick = function () {
    return askConfirmation();
}
x.addEventListener('click', function () {
    return askConfirmation();
},false);
```

W3C and Microsoft models

The W3C and Microsoft models also define ways to cancel the default action. In the W3C model, you have to call the preventDefault() method of the event object, while the Microsoft model requires you to set its returnValue property to false.

```
var evt = [the event object];
if (evt.preventDefault)
    evt.preventDefault();
evt.returnValue = false;
```

I never use such a construct, since return false is far simpler and completely cross-browser.

Event simulation

There are a few event-simulation methods you should know about. These methods simulate the occurrence of an event, and that can sometimes be useful.

- In 6D we encountered the focus() and blur() methods of the window. They also work on form fields, and, unsurprisingly, they set or remove the focus on the form field you use them on.

7B

- The `click()` method allows you to simulate a click on a form field. If, for instance, you use it on a checkbox, it changes from checked to unchecked or vice versa, just as if the user had really clicked on it. There's one exception: you cannot use the `click()` method on a file upload field in Mozilla or Opera.

- The `submit()` and `reset()` methods of a form submit or reset the form. Note that when you use the `submit()` method, the onsubmit event handler of the form will not fire.

C: Event-handler registration

Once you've decided which events to use, you need to tell the browser which function you want to run when that event takes place: "If the user clicks on this element, then run that function." For this, you want to register an event handler.

There are no less than four ways of registering an event handler. The oldest one works in all browsers but violates the separation of structure and behavior. The second one works in all browsers and is an excellent choice in many simple situations. The two remaining ways don't work in all browsers, but have a few important advantages over the other two.

Inline event handlers

The oldest way of registering event handlers is by adding an attribute to an HTML element:

```
<a href="somewhere.html" onclick="highlightNavItem()">
```
When the user clicks on the link, the `highlightNavItem()` function runs.

There's an HTML attribute for every event: onmouseover, onsubmit, ondblclick, and so on.

> { **CAMELCASE**
>
> In the past it was customary to write these attributes in camelCase: onClick instead of onclick. HTML is case insensitive, so in HTML pages this doesn't matter. XHTML, though, requires lowercase attribute names, so an onClick attribute does not pass validation. Making the attribute name lowercase solves this problem, and JavaScript doesn't care. }

As we discussed in 2C, inline event handlers violate the separation of structure and behavior, and should not be used. Therefore, this book will not treat them in detail. If you encounter them, you should convert them to one of the other event-registration models.

The traditional model

The traditional event-registration model is part of the de facto Netscape 3 standard, and all browsers support it.

Just as with `<img src>`, `<a href>`, or other important HTML attributes, JavaScript allows you to access all event-handling attributes as properties of the object that represents the HTML element. Let's port the inline event handler from the previous example to the traditional model:

```
<a href="somewhere.html" id="somewhere">

var x = document.getElementById('somewhere');
x.onclick = highlightNavItem; // note: no parentheses
```

x is the object that represents the HTML element, and we set its onclick property to the function `highlightNavItem()` (onclick now becomes a method of the object x).

7C

No parentheses ()

When registering an event handler in this way, you do not use parentheses ().
As we discussed in 5I, the () operator executes a function, and that's not what
we want here. Suppose we did this:

```
var x = document.getElementById('somewhere');
   x.onclick = highlightNavItem();
```

This code gives the command "Execute highlightNavItem() and assign its
return value to the onclick property of x."

That's not what we want. We want to execute the function only when the event
actually takes place. We want to say "If the user clicks on this element, execute highlightNavItem()."

In order to do that, we must assign the value of the variable highlightNavItem
(which is the function) to the onclick property. Now onclick refers to the function highlightNavItem(), and it's executed whenever the user clicks on the
HTML element.

```
   x.onclick = highlightNavItem; // note: no parentheses
```

We'll discuss this important matter further in 7F.

Executing event handlers directly

As we'll also see in 7F, event handlers are methods of the object they're registered on, and therefore you have the option of executing them directly instead
of waiting for the event to take place.

I use this trick in Textarea Maxlength:

[Textarea Maxlength, lines 16-17]

```
   x[i].onkeyup = x[i].onchange = checkMaxLength;
   x[i].onkeyup();
```

The checkMaxLength() function should be executed when a keyup or a change
event occurs on the textarea. However, the textarea may already contain text at
the moment the page is loaded. The length of this text should immediately be

shown next to the textarea, and therefore `checkMaxLength()` must be executed at once, without waiting for the event to take place.

Edit Style Sheet does exactly the same thing for the same reasons:

[Edit Style Sheet, lines 33-37]

```
var els = document.forms[1].elements;
for (var i=0;i<els.length;i++) {
    els[i].onchange = assignStyles;
    els[i].onchange();
}
```

The form fields may already have a value, and this value should be processed immediately. Therefore the script fires the onchange event handler immediately after the handler has been registered.

Couldn't I have executed `checkMaxLength()` and `assignStyles()` directly, without the detour through the event handlers? No. Both functions use the `this` keyword, and as we'll see in 7F, that keyword can misfire dramatically if it's used outside its proper context. We have to make sure the functions operate as methods of the correct HTML elements.

7C

Anonymous functions

The examples we've discussed until now all use a normally defined function and copy it to the correct event handler. It's also possible to use anonymous functions, and I sometimes do that with onload event handlers:

```
window.onload = function () {
    // initialize
}
```

I directly assign a function to `window.onload`. This is the same as using:

```
window.onload = init;
function init () {
    // initialize
}
```

The only difference between these two cases is that the second one defines the initialization function as a separate function `init`, while the first doesn't. In both cases, the event handler is assigned a function to be executed when the event takes place, and that's what matters.

Drawbacks of the traditional model

Although the traditional event-handler registration model is easy to use and works in all browsers, you should be aware of its drawbacks. The most important one is that, since you define the value of a method, any subsequent definition overwrites the earlier value.

For instance, in the code below, you first set onclick to the value of `doThis`, and later you set it to the value of `doThat`. As a result, only the function `doThat()` is executed when the user clicks on the element.

```
x.onclick = doThis;
   x.onclick = doThat;
```

If you want to execute both functions when the user clicks on the element, you have to do something like this:

```
x.onclick = function () {
    doThis();
    doThat();
}
```

Apart from being a bit kludgy, this syntax also causes the `this` keyword in `doThis()` and `doThat()` to refer to the wrong object, because the functions are not methods of the object `x`.

This problem can become even worse, as Site Survey shows. We already saw that that script needs an onunload event handler on the window and an onclick event handler on the document. But Site Survey may be included in any site, and the host site may already contain an onunload event handler. Therefore I may not do this:

```
window.onunload = ST_exit;
   document.onclick = ST_openPopup;
```

Now if I assign event handlers, I might overrule event handlers of the host site, or the host site's event handlers might overrule mine. The result would be that either the scripts of the host site or Site Survey would not be executed, and that's clearly undesirable.

There are two ways to solve this problem. The first is to check if the site already has a `window.onunload` and a `document.onclick`. For instance:

```
var existingClick = document.onclick || function () {};
document.onclick = function () {
    existingClick();
    ST_openPopup();
}
```

First I create a variable `existingClick` that contains either the existing `document.onclick` or, if none is defined, an empty function. Then I define an anonymous function that executes `existingClick()` and `ST_openPopup()`, and assign it to `document.onclick`. This works, but it's a bit of a kludge.

The second, and in my eyes superior, solution is to use the two advanced event-handler registration models.

W3C and Microsoft models

Both W3C and Microsoft have defined advanced event-handler registration models that effectively solve the overwrite problem. These models allow you to define as many event handlers as you like for the same event on the same element.

Let's repeat our doThis/doThat example in the advanced models. First W3C:

```
x.addEventListener('click',doThis,false);
x.addEventListener('click',doThat,false);
```

Now `doThis()` and `doThat()` are both executed when the user clicks on element x. `addEventListener()` means "add an extra event handler on this element in addition to any event handler that may already exist." Note, however, that you cannot be sure they will be executed in this order: the browser may execute doThat() first.

As you see, addEventListener() takes three arguments:

- The event name as a string, without the "on".

- The function to be executed (without parentheses (), of course; we don't want to execute it right now, but only when the event takes place).

- A boolean that states whether the event bubbles up (false) or is captured (true). We'll discuss this in 7D, but for now, know that you nearly always use bubbling, and that the third argument is therefore always false.

The Microsoft model works in a similar way:

```
x.attachEvent('onclick',doThis);
x.attachEvent('onclick',doThat);
```

Here, too, doThis() and doThat() are both executed when the user clicks on element x. As you see, attachEvent() takes two arguments:

- The event name as a string, with the "on".

- The function to be executed (without parentheses (), for the usual reasons).

> ## ADDING ONE EVENT HANDLER MULTIPLE TIMES
>
> In general, you can't add one event handler more than once to an argument. Take this code:
>
> ```
> x.addEventListener('click',doThis,false);
> x.addEventListener('click',doThis,false);
> ```
>
> If the user clicks on the element, doThis is executed only once, not twice. The exception is in Explorer, where the following code causes the function to be executed twice after one click:
>
> ```
> x.attachEvent('onclick',doThis);
> x.attachEvent('onclick',doThis);
> ```

Removing event handlers

Both advanced models contain methods for removing event handlers. Let's look at `removeEventListener()` and `detachEvent()`:

```
x.removeEventListener('click',doThis,false); // W3C
x.detachEvent('onclick',doThis); // Microsoft
```

Now the `doThis()` event handler is removed from element `x`, and only `doThat()` is executed when the user clicks on the element.

As you see, `removeEventListener()` takes the same arguments as `addEventListener()`, and `detachEvent()` takes the same arguments as `attachEvent()`.

Disadvantage

The advanced models have one disadvantage: it's impossible to find out which event handlers have been registered on an element. Among other things, that means you can't say "Now remove all onclick event handlers from element x."

In the traditional model, this is possible:

```
x.onclick = null;
```

However, the advanced models require you to name the event-handling function you want to remove. If you can't do that because you're not sure which event handlers are currently registered, you can't remove the event handler.

addEventSimple()

Unfortunately, neither of these advanced event-registration models are cross-browser. At the time of writing, Explorer supports only the Microsoft model, while Mozilla and Safari support only the W3C model. Opera supports both.

As always when different browsers support different models, we need a bit of object detection. I generally use the two helper functions `addEventSimple()` and `removeEventSimple()` to do this job for me:

[Usable Forms, lines 151-163. These functions are also used in Site Survey, Dropdown Menu and Edit Style Sheet.]

```
function addEventSimple(obj,evt,fn) {
    if (obj.addEventListener)
            obj.addEventListener(evt,fn,false);
    else if (obj.attachEvent)
            obj.attachEvent('on'+evt,fn);
}

function removeEventSimple(obj,evt,fn) {
    if (obj.removeEventListener)
            obj.removeEventListener(evt,fn,false);
    else if (obj.detachEvent)
            obj.detachEvent('on'+evt,fn);
}
```

Both functions expect three arguments: the object the event should be added to, the event name as a string without 'on,' and the function to be executed. This is a call from Usable Forms:

[Usable Forms, line 53]

```
addEventSimple(document,'click',showHideFields);
```

Differences between W3C and Microsoft models

Until now we've pretended that the W3C and Microsoft models are essentially the same, with the names of the methods to be called as the only difference. Unfortunately, that is not quite true:

- The Microsoft model does not support event capturing. Since you rarely use capturing anyway, this is not a big problem.

- The Microsoft model treats the event-handling function as a global function, not a method of the HTML element it's registered on. That means that the `this` keyword refers to the window instead of to the object the event handler is registered on. This is a serious problem that we'll discuss in more detail in 7F.

The best way

With all that said, what is the best way of registering event handlers? In the example scripts, you'll see that I use either the traditional model or my addEventSimple() function. I prefer the traditional model because it's so simple and completely cross-browser, and because the this keyword always works correctly. There are situations in which I cannot use this model, though, and in those cases I use addEventSimple().

I use the traditional model when I have complete control over all scripts in a page. Sandwich Picker, for instance, was written specifically for my client's site, and since I created the entire site I could control all event-handler registrations. Since there were no other scripts involved, it was safe to use the traditional model.

On the other hand, Usable Forms and Site Survey can be added to any page. These modules should not set event handlers through the traditional model, since those might overwrite or be overwritten by handlers of the native scripts on the host page.

Therefore I use addEventSimple() in Usable Forms and Site Survey. Using the two advanced models ensures that event handlers from my modules and from native scripts don't interfere with each other.

Another situation in which addEventSimple() may be a good choice is when you need mass initialization. For instance, Dropdown Menu and Edit Style Sheets run on the same page, but both have a separate initialization function that should be executed onload. To make sure that the two onload event handlers don't interfere with each other, I set both through addEventSimple().

So in general I use addEventSimple() when several scripts that should not interfere with each other are present (or could be present) on the same page.

Nonetheless, let's repeat it one more time: the this keyword doesn't work correctly when you use addEventSimple(). I usually solve this problem by tiptoeing around it: if my functions don't use this, then there is no problem.

7C

If you need `this` and cannot use the traditional model because of interference danger, the time has come to look into more complex event-registration functions. I recommend Dean Edwards' solution, which you can find at http://dean. edwards.name/weblog/2005/10/add-event/.

D: Event bubbling and capturing

Suppose you have a `<div>` that contains a `<form>` that contains a form field. All three elements have an onclick event handler. The user clicks on the form field. Obviously, the event handler of the form field should now fire. But what about the `<div>`'s and the `<form>`'s event handlers? Should they fire too?

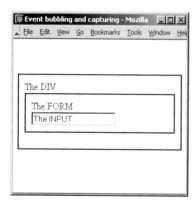

FIGURE 7.2
div, form, and input all have an onclick event handler. The user clicks on the input.

The answer is Yes. If an event takes place, and several event handlers are eligible to handle the event, all of them fire.

But which event handler fires first? The `<div>`'s, because it's the uppermost element? Or the form field's, because it's the element the user clicked on? The answer depends on whether you use event capturing or event bubbling.

Event bubbling means that the event starts on its target (the element the user clicked on, i.e., the form field), fires the target's onclick event handler, and then bubbles up through the document tree from ancestor to ancestor until it reaches the document element. For any new HTML element it encounters, it also fires any relevant event handlers, if present, and therefore the onclick event handlers of the `<form>` and the `<div>` also fire, in that order.

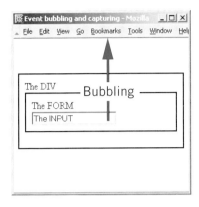

FIGURE 7.3
Event bubbling. The events fire in
the order form field, form, div.

Event capturing is exactly the opposite. It starts at the document level and
travels down the document tree to the event target (the form field). For each
HTML element it encounters, it fires any relevant event handlers. Therefore,
the handlers fire in the order `<div>`, `<form>`, form field.

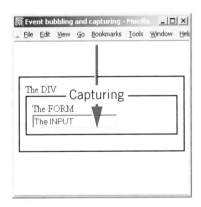

FIGURE 7.4
Event capturing. The events fire in
the order div, form, form field.

W3C model

In the W3C event model, both capturing and bubbling occur. When an event
fires, it is first captured by the document, and then travels down the document
tree to the event target. This is called the capturing phase. Once the event
arrives at its target, the bubbling phase starts, during which the event travels
back upwards to the document.

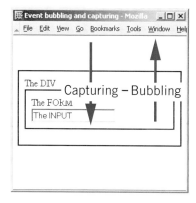

FIGURE 7.5
In the W3C event model, event capturing takes place first, followed by event bubbling.

However, an event handler is always set for only one of these phases. As we saw in 7C, addEventListener() and removeEventListener() need a boolean argument true or false. true means that the event is set for the capturing phase, and false means the event is set for the bubbling phase.

So suppose we do this:

```
var field = [the form field];
var div = [the div];
field.addEventListener('click',doThis,false);
div.addEventListener('click',doThat,false);
```

When the user clicks on the form field, the event starts at the document level and travels downwards to the form field. During that trip down, it does not encounter any event set for the capturing phase, so the first event handler that fires is the form field's own doThis(). Then the event enters the bubbling phase and travels back to the document. Now it encounters an event set for the bubbling phase, and the <div>'s doThat() event handler is fired.

Let's change the code:

```
div.addEventListener('click',doThat,true);
```

Now if the user clicks on the form field, the event starts at the document level and travels downwards to the form field. During that trip it encounters an event set for the capturing phase, and doThat() is executed. Next it travels onwards to the event target and fires the form field's own doThis(). Then the event enters the bubbling phase and travels back to the document. It encounters no events set for the bubbling phase, so no event handlers are fired.

Traditional and Microsoft models

The traditional and Microsoft models support only bubbling, not capturing. In order to avoid browser incompatibilities, it's therefore best to restrict yourself to event bubbling. Besides, in most practical cases, there is no real difference between capturing and bubbling.

The Microsoft model allows you to capture mouse events through the `setCapture()` and `releaseCapture()` methods, but this feature is hardly ever used.

Practical uses of event bubbling

Event bubbling allows you to use one event handler to service many HTML elements. See how it's being done in Dropdown Menu:

```
<ul class="menutree">
<li><a href="#">News</a>
  <ul>
    <li><a href="#">Press Releases</a>
        <ul>
                <li><a href="#">Release 1</a></li>
                <li><a href="#">Release 2</a></li>
                <li><a href="#">Release 3</a></li>
        </ul>
    </li>
    etc.
</ul>
```
[Dropdown Menu, lines 7-11]

```
var lists = document.getElementsByTagName('ul');
for (var i=0;i<lists.length;i++) {
    if (lists[i].className != 'menutree') continue;
    lists[i].onmouseover = navMouseOver;
    lists[i].onmouseout = navMouseOut;
```

When the menu is initialized, the script goes through all `<ul>`s in the document and sees if they have a class 'menutree'. If one does, the script sets onmouseover and onmouseout event handlers on this `<ul>`.

However, the actual events take place on the `<a>` elements that form the visible part of the dropdown menu. These elements themselves do not have event handlers. That's no problem, because the events bubble up and eventually reach the `<ul>`. Once they arrive there, the `navMouseOver()` or `navMouseOut()` event handler is fired, and the dropdown menu works.

Effectively, this approach allows you to concentrate events on a lot of elements in one spot. You have to set only one single event handler on one single HTML element, and then you calmly wait until the events that take place on its descendants bubble up to that element. This keeps your script administration simple.

Usable Forms uses the same trick, by the way: it defines one general onclick event handler on the document. Event bubbling makes sure that every click event in the entire document eventually reaches this handler.

[Usable Forms, line 53]

```
addEventSimple(document,'click',showHideFields);
```

CAPTURING INSTEAD OF BUBBLING

This one-handler-for-all-elements trick would also work fine with event capturing. The click event encounters the handlers on the `<ul>` in the capturing phase, fires them, moves on to the target and then back in the bubbling phase, during which it encounters no more event handlers. The net result is exactly the same.

Interface events: no bubbling

You cannot use event bubbling in all situations, because some events are not valid on some HTML elements. The most restrictive rule is that interface events such as change or submit don't work on the document or window.

Take Textarea Maxlength. Theoretically it could service an unlimited number of textareas. Therefore, setting one general event handler on the document, and waiting for the events to bubble up would seem a good idea.

Unfortunately, the change event is not allowed on the document so the change events that are initiated on textareas would be unnoticed by the document, and my script would fail:

❌ `document.onchange = checkMaxLength; // event never fires`

Therefore I'm forced to define an onchange event handler on every single textarea.

As a general rule, you can catch mouse and keyboard events on the document level, but not interface events. However, you should always test this general rule for your specific events and browsers—you might get lucky.

Cancelling event propagation

The W3C and Microsoft models allow you to cancel event capturing and bubbling. You are allowed to say, "This event should not propagate further." The traditional model does not offer a similar feature.

Obviously, the two models each need their own command. In the W3C model you should call the `stopPropagation()` method of the event object, while the Microsoft model expects you to set the `cancelBubble` property to `true`. (We already discussed this bit of code in 5J.)

```
var evt = [the event object];
if (evt.stopPropagation)
    evt.stopPropagation();
evt.cancelBubble = true;
```

To avoid odd side-effects in complicated DHTML menus, it is occasionally useful to cancel the propagation of the mouseover and mouseout events after they've been handled. Dropdown Menu is too simple to need such drastic measures, but sometimes clients ask for vastly more complicated structures, and in those cases this trick might save your bacon. Or not.

E: The event object and its properties

> **WARNING** General browser incompatibility warning throughout this section

Once you have registered an event handler for the correct event on the correct element, you can turn your attention to the event-handling function itself. Of course the exact form of this function depends heavily on the actions you want to take. Possibilities range from a simple one-line style change to complex initializations of extra functionalities that take dozens of lines.

Sometimes you need to access the event object. The browser automatically creates this object whenever an event occurs, and it contains all kinds of useful information about the event, such as the target element, the event type, the mouse position, the key the user pressed, and much more.

The event object and its properties suffer from serious browser incompatibilities. Although many of these incompatibilities are restricted to differing property names (W3C's `target` vs. Microsoft's `srcElement`, for instance), there are areas where the problems are more fundamental, and some event properties are not present in all browsers.

The event object

Before delving deeper into its properties, you first have to access the event object, which is handled differently by the W3C and the Microsoft models:

- In the W3C model, the event object is sent to the event-handling function as the first argument.
- In the Microsoft model, the event object is always `window.event`.

Fortunately, these incompatibilities are easily accommodated by a single line of code:

```
// use one of these three registrations
document.onclick = handleEvent;
document.addEventListener('click',handleEvent,false);
document.attachEvent('onclick',handleEvent);
function handleEvent(e) {
    var evt = e || window.event;
    // do something with evt, which now
    // refers to the event object
}
```

Note the `e` argument of the `handleEvent()` function. W3C-compliant browsers send the event object to the function as an argument. It's traditional to name the variable that holds this argument `e`, but of course you can use any name you like.

The first line of the function makes sure that `evt` contains the event object in all browsers. `evt` becomes `e`, or, if it's not available (i.e., if the browser hasn't sent an event object), it becomes `window.event`, the Microsoft object. We discussed the exact purpose of the `||` operator in 5G.

As you can see, accessing the event object is pretty easy. Unfortunately, as we'll see below, its properties contain many unpleasant surprises.

type

The `type` property of the event object contains the event type (mouseover, keypress, submit, and so on). Most unusually, it's supported by all browsers. In fact, it is one of the few cross-browser event-object properties.

Targeting

The event object contains various properties having to do with targeting: on which HTML element does the event take place?

7E

The W3C properties are `currentTarget`, `relatedTarget`, and `target`. The Microsoft properties are `fromElement`, `toElement`, and `srcElement`. 7F discusses `target` and `srcElement` in depth, while 7H highlights `relatedTarget`, `fromElement`, and `toElement`.

Mouse position

WARNING   Browser incompatibility alarm phase red

Sometimes you want to find the mouse position at the time the event took place. Poor you—you're in for a rough ride.

There are six mouse-coordinate property pairs. All have an X and a Y component, which give the mouse coordinates in pixels. All inform you that the mouse is X pixels to the right of and Y pixels below the reference point. A negative X means it's left of the reference point; a negative Y means it's above the reference point.

Of course the question is: what is this reference point? Here's where things turn sour. The reference points of the property pairs are as follows:

Pair	Reference point	Browser compatibility
`clientX`, `clientY`	The browser window	All but Safari
`layerX`, `layerY`	A Browser Wars-style layer (the nearest absolutely positioned ancestor, or, if it's not there, the document)	Mozilla and Safari
`offsetX`, `offsetY`	The event target	All but Mozilla
`pageX`, `pageY`	The document	All but Explorer
`screenX`, `screenY`	The computer screen	All browsers
`x`, `y`	Various small fry. Don't use it. There's always a better choice.	Totally incompatible; not supported in Mozilla

Let's start with the good news: `screenX` and `screenY` work in all browsers. Unfortunately, the information they contain is usually worthless: you rarely need to know the mouse position relative to the computer screen—well, maybe if you're writing a complicated drag-and-drop script.

Instead, you usually want to know the mouse position relative to the document. Often you need the coordinates because you want to place an element next to the mouse when the user mouses over a certain element. (Edit Style Sheet's color picker is an example of this.) You can use `pageX` and `pageY` to find the mouse coordinates relative to the document, add or subtract a few pixels, and transfer them to the `top` and `left` style properties of an absolutely positioned element, and you're ready for whatever comes next. This makes `pageX` and `pageY` is by far the most interesting and useful mouse coordinate property pair. But just to keep you on your toes, it's not supported by Explorer.

The second most useful pair is `clientX` and `clientY`, which gives the coordinates relative to the window (except in Safari, where they're relative to the document).

Fortunately, this pair gives us the possibility of working out the coordinates relative to the document in Explorer. If we add the scrolling offset of the page to the coordinates relative to the window, we can find the coordinates we need.

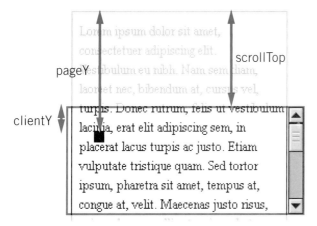

FIGURE 7.6 The user clicks at the point indicated by the black box. We want to know the coordinates relative to the document. pageY contains them, but is not always supported. Another way of finding the same information is to add scrollTop to clientY.

We'll discuss `scrollTop` fully in 9H, but this code finds the mouse position relative to the document:

```
var posx = 0;
var posy = 0;
var evt = e || window.event;
if (evt.pageX || evt.pageY) {
    posx = evt.pageX;
    posy = evt.pageY;
}
else if (evt.clientX || evt.clientY) {
    posx = evt.clientX +
    document.documentElement.scrollLeft + ➡
    document.body.scrollLeft;
    posy = evt.clientY +
    document.documentElement.scrollTop + ➡
    document.body.scrollTop;
}
```

We first try `pageX` and `pageY`. If they exist, we take their values and can move on. If they don't exist, we use `clientX` and `clientY`, add the `scrollLeft` and `scrollTop` of both `document.documentElement` and `document.body`, and we've found the same value.

`layerX/Y` and `offsetX/Y` are not supported by all browsers. They are useful only when you want to find an element's position relative to its absolutely positioned parent:

```
var x = [the element];
var pos = x.layerX || x.offsetX;
// now pos holds the horizontal position of x relative to its
// absolutely positioned parent.
```

Note that this only works if the absolutely positioned element is the direct parent of `x`. If it isn't, odd side effects may occur.

Don't do it

The chaos surrounding the mouse position is the most severe Browser War-style incompatibility still in existence, which makes the position properties rather hard to use.

Besides, any script that uses the mouse position is fundamentally inaccessible: when the user doesn't use a mouse, the mouse coordinates don't hold useful information. In fact, you might find wildly incorrect mouse coordinates because, for instance, the mouse pointer is permanently located in the middle of the computer screen.

Fortunately, finding mouse coordinates is rarely necessary, as Edit Style Sheet's color picker proves. The idea of the script is that the user clicks on the Pick color link, and that the color picker then appears at the same height as the link.

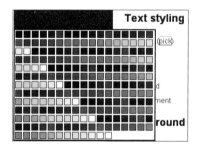

FIGURE 7.7
Clicking on the Pick color link opens the color picker at the same height as the link.

This script needs to calculate the color picker's position. This calculation could start from the mouse position ("place the color picker 200 pixels to the left of and at the same height as the current mouse position"), but a far better technique is to start from the position of the link itself ("place the color picker 200 pixels to the left of and at the same height as the link the user clicked on"). We'll discuss this in 9H.

As an added bonus, the position-finding script is accessible: it also works for non-mouse events such as focus.

90% of the scripts that calculate the mouse position could just as easily use the position of the element the user clicked on or moused over for their calculations. Therefore, my advice is not to try to find the mouse position at all. You rarely need it.

7E

Mouse button

Browser incompatibility alarm phase orange

It's also possible to read out the mouse button the user has clicked on. You can find this information in the button property. 99.9% of the mouse-button checks are about disabling the right mouse button (return false!) so that the user can't use View Source. You can use the button property to do this: if the user presses the right mouse button to bring up the context menu, button is 2.

That's the good news. The bad news is that W3C's specification for button is flat-out wrong, although many browsers have implemented it regardless. Microsoft uses a proprietary system that's much better than the standard.

Model	Left button	Middle button	Right button
W3C	0	1	2
Microsoft	1	4	2

What's wrong with W3C's system? The 0. First of all, using the value 0 to indicate that something has happened is very odd. In my opinion, 0 should mean "no button pressed."

The Microsoft system is a bitmask, which allows you to detect several buttons at once. For instance, when the user presses the left and right buttons simultaneously, button becomes $1 + 2 = 3$; when he presses the right and middle buttons, it becomes $2 + 4 = 6$.

W3C-compatible browsers don't support this bitmask. Worse: they *cannot* support it, because of the 0. Left + right buttons would become $0 + 2 = 2$, the same as when the user clicks the right button only.

I hope that a future version of the specification will use the Microsoft values, since they make sense. Fortunately, this difference doesn't matter in practice, since you want to detect a right click in order to disable the View Source option. As I said, on a right click, button is 2 in all browsers.

Key properties

Sometimes you want to know which key the user has pressed. As we saw in 7B, this is only possible on the keydown and keyup events. Some browsers don't allow it on the keypress event.

keyCode contains the code of the pressed key. The letters range from 65 (a) to 90 (z), and most other keys have their own code, too.

The altKey, ctrlKey, and shiftKey properties are true when the user presses the Alt, Control, or Shift key, false when he doesn't. In some browsers, these properties are available only when the user presses a "real" key simultaneously.

F: Targeting

When an event occurs, you often want to do something with the element on which the event took place. In order to do that, you need to find this element.

For instance, when the user mouses over a link in Dropdown Menus, you need to find out which link that is, and whether it has a submenu (i.e., a nested <ul>). If it does, the time has come to drop the menu down. If the user clicks on a form field in Usable Forms, you need to find this element and see if it has a rel attribute.

There are two important targeting properties. The first is the event object's target or srcElement property, which always refers to the element on which the event took place. The second is the this keyword, which usually (but not always!) refers to the element on which you have defined the event handler.

The difference

Take Dropdown Menu. As we saw in 7D, the script defines onmouseover and onmouseout event handlers on the <ul>, even though the actual events take place on the <a>s that make up the bulk of the menu. Let's tweak the script a

7F

bit to alert the nodeNames (see 8C) of the HTML elements the event target and
the this keyword refer to:

```
var x = document.getElementsByTagName('ul');
for (var i=0;i<x.length;i++) {
    if (x[i].className != 'menutree') continue;
    x[i].onmouseover = navMouseOver;
}
function navMouseOver(e) {
    var evtTarget = [the target];
    alert(evtTarget.nodeName);
    alert(this.nodeName);
}
```

The user mouses over an <a> element. The event bubbles up to the <ul>, and
navMouseOver() is executed. The event target is the <a> element, since that's
the element the user moused over. Therefore the first alert shows 'A'. However, the
this keyword refers to the element on which you defined the event handler,
and therefore the second alert shows 'UL'.

Which of the two you need depends on the context of your script, but in general it's best to have both references available so that you can use either one if
necessary.

this

As we saw in 5J, the this keyword always refers to the object through which a
method is invoked, and it must be enclosed in a function body in order to work.

In the traditional and W3C models, JavaScript event handlers are methods of
the HTML elements on which they're registered. Therefore, the this keyword
refers to that HTML element, and is something you can use in your event handling scripts.

Take a simple script that's supposed to change the background color of an element on which the user clicked:

```
function test() {
    this.style.backgroundColor = '#cc0000';
}
```

As we saw in 5J, any function can be seen as a method of JavaScript's global object, the window object. Since the `this` keyword always refers to the object a function is a method of, it now refers to the window object.

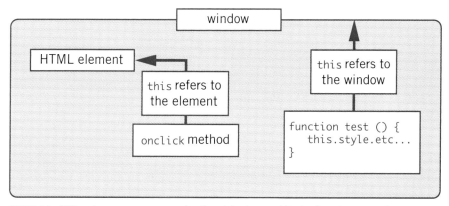

FIGURE 7.8   Without any more commands, the `this` keyword in the function `test()` refers to the window. In the onclick property of the element, it refers to the element.

If we execute `test()` without any more preparations, the function tries to set the `style.backgroundColor` of the window. Since the window has no `style` property, that action generates an error message.

If we use traditional event registration, we take a function and assign it as an object's event handler. It now becomes a method of `x`.

```
x.onclick = test;
```

Now the `this` keyword refers to `x`. If the user clicks on `x`, the function correctly sets the background color of HTML element `x` to red.

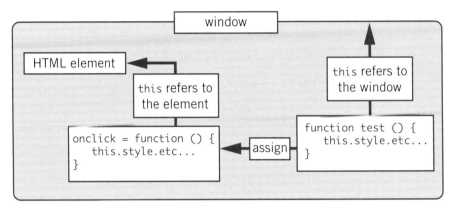

FIGURE 7.9   If we assign the function `test()` to the element's onclick property, the `this` keyword refers to the element.

Now let's change the registration a bit:

```
x.onclick = function () {
    test();
}
```

When the user clicks on x, the event handler calls `test()`. Now the function is invoked through the global object, and therefore the `this` keyword refers to the global object: the window. The function misfires once more.

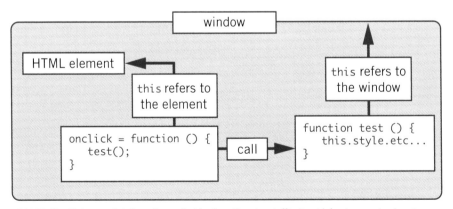

FIGURE 7.10   If the onclick function calls the function `test()`, the `this` keyword refers to the window.

Examples

If you want to use the `this` keyword, you have to be sure it actually refers to the element on which the event handler is registered.

In the following cases, the `this` keyword refers to the correct element:

```
<element onclick="this.style.backgroundColor="#cc0000">
x.onclick = test;
x.addEventListener('click',test,false);
```

But in the following cases, it doesn't; `test()` is called as a global function, and `this` refers to the window object.

```
<element onclick="test()">
x.onclick = function () {
    test();
}
x.addEventListener('click', function () {
    test();
},false);
x.attachEvent('onclick',test);
```

Note the Microsoft `attachEvent()` method in the last list. As we saw in 7C, its lack of support for the `this` keyword is the most serious problem of the Microsoft model.

Target

> **WARNING**   Browser incompatibilities ahead

The target of an event is always the element the event actually took place on, regardless of where the event handler is defined. There's a minor browser difference here: W3C-compliant browsers call it `target`, while Explorer calls it `srcElement`. Fortunately, the problem is easy to solve:

```
function handleEvent(e) {
    var evt = e || window.event;
    var evtTarget = evt.target || evt.srcElement;
}
```

7F

First you access the event object, and then try to read out either its `target` or its `srcElement` property. One of the two always works, so that `evtTarget` now contains a reference to the event target and you can start using it.

Unexpected target values

Every once in a while the event target is not what you expect it to be. The most annoying example is a bug in older Safari versions, where the target of a mouse event is not the element it took place on, but rather the text node contained by that element.

```
<a href="somewhere.html" id="test">Text</a>

document.getElementById('test').onmouseover = handleEvent;
function handleEvent(e) {
    var evt = e || window.event;
    var evtTarget = evt.target || evt.srcElement;
    alert(evtTarget.nodeName);
}
```

When the user mouses over 'Text', most browsers take its parent—the link—as the event target. Older Safari versions, however, take the text node 'Text' itself as the event target, and that can cause weird problems.

The solution is to check if the target is a text node, and if it is, to move one element upward:

```
function handleEvent(e) {
    var evt = e || window.event;
    var evtTarget = evt.target || evt.srcElement;
    if (evtTarget.nodeType == 3)
            evtTarget = evtTarget.parentNode;
    alert(evtTarget.nodeName);
}
```

Now the target is the link in all browsers. (We'll discuss `nodeType`, `parent-Node`, and text nodes in 8C, 8B, and 8H, respectively.)

In some situations, you encounter more subtle problems, especially when you use events like mouseover and mouseout, which can potentially fire a lot of times. Take Dropdown Menu. As you have seen, it works on an HTML `<ul>/<li>/<a>` structure and uses event bubbling to deliver the event to the centralized handler on the `<ul>`.

CSS-wise, a dropdown menu is usually quite complicated. While creating the CSS, you'll frequently move borders and paddings and such from the `<li>`s to the `<a>`s and back again, until your styles work in all browsers.

In my version of Dropdown Menu, all `<a>` elements are tightly fitted together. Therefore, when the user mouses over them, four mouseover events take place, one for every `<a>` element.

Mouse movement

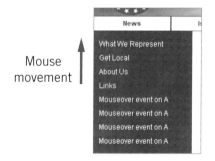

FIGURE 7.11
No CSS space between the <a> tags. When the mouse moves over the four links, four mouseover events on <a> elements take place.

However, as soon as I add a little bit of CSS padding to the `<li>`s, the situation changes dramatically.

```
#nav2 li {
    padding: 1px;
}
```

The `<li>`s now have a visible area, and the same mouse movement now causes twelve mouseover events: one on every `<a>` and two on every `<li>` (padding-top and padding-bottom).

7F

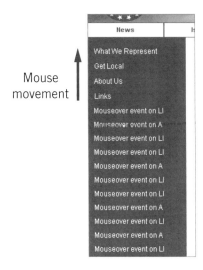

Mouse movement

FIGURE 7.12
As soon as you define li {padding: 1px} in CSS, the <li> elements are visible, and mouseover events also register on them.

If you silently expect all events to take place on <a> elements, you're in for a big shock when you add the padding. That's why I'm so careful in reading out the event target in navMouseOver():

[Dropdown Menu, lines 27-31]

```
var evt = e || window.event;
var evtTarget = evt.target || evt.srcElement;
if (evtTarget.nodeName == 'UL') return;
while (evtTarget.nodeName != 'LI')
    evtTarget = evtTarget.parentNode;
```

If the event takes place on a <ul> (i.e., on the <ul class="menutree"> itself), the script doesn't handle it at all. In all other cases it takes the event target and moves up in the document tree until it encounters an <li> element. (Incidentally, this also solves the Safari bug we noted above.) Now the script can work from the assumption that evtTarget is an <li> element.

More generally, if you use trigger-happy events like mouseover and mouseout, be sure to check and double-check the event target before you start using it. It may not be what you expect it to be.

this or target?

When do you use the `this` keyword and when do you use the event target? There are a few general rules, but there's also a lot of overlap, especially when you have registered the event on the same element that will be the event target.

- *In general,* the `this` keyword is useful when you register the same event handler on a lot of elements and/or when you want to call the event handlers directly, i.e., without an event taking place.

- *In general*, the event target is useful when you rely on bubbling to take the event upward in the document tree.

this example

Take Textarea Maxlength. The script registers event handlers on all textareas. It uses the traditional model, so `this` works as expected:

[Textarea Maxlength, lines 16-17]

```
texareas[i].onkeyup = texareas[i].onchange = checkMaxLength;
texareas[i].onkeyup();
```

When the user changes the text in the textarea, `checkMaxLength()` is called. This function needs to know which textarea the user is currently editing—and it finds it by using the `this` keyword:

[Textarea Maxlength; lines 22-30]

```
function checkMaxLength() {
    var maxLength = this.getAttribute('maxlength');
    var currentLength = this.value.length;
    if (currentLength > maxLength)
            this.relatedElement.className = 'toomuch';
    else
            this.relatedElement.className = '';
    this.relatedElement.firstChild.nodeValue = currentLength;
}
```

7F

The script now accesses the correct textarea.

But isn't the textarea the user is currently editing also the target of the event? Yes, it is. Then why doesn't the function use the target? Because of the `textareas[i].onkeyup()` statement in the initialization routine.

That statement essentially calls `checkMaxLength()` as a method of the textarea object, and in order for the function to work, it must use the `this` keyword. If it didn't—if it used the event target—the function call would give error messages, since there's no event object available.

target example

In Usable Forms, the script registers a general onclick event handler on the document, and waits for click events on form fields to bubble up. In addition, the script registers the same function as the onchange event handler of select boxes.

[Usable Forms, lines 21-23 and 53]

```
var selects = document.getElementsByTagName('select');
for (var i=0;i< selects.length;i++)
    addEventSimple(selects[i],'change',showHideFields);
// more initialization
addEventSimple(document,'click',showHideFields);
```

Obviously, when a user clicks on something, the first item on the agenda is to find out which element he clicked on, and whether the action should trigger document changes. Because I use `addEventSimple()`, the `this` keyword is useless: it doesn't work in Explorer. Besides, even if it did, it would refer to the document, since that's where I registered the onclick event handler.

In this situation, I use the event's target:

[Usable Forms, lines 70-81, condensed]

```
var evt = e || window.event;
var evtTarget = evt.target || evt.srcElement;
```

```
if (!(
    (evtTarget.nodeName == 'SELECT' && e.type == 'change')
    ||
    (evtTarget.nodeName == 'INPUT' && ➥
evtTarget.getAttribute('rel'))
)) return;
```

Now the script checks if the target is a `<select>` and the event `type` is change; or if the target is an `<input>` that has a `rel` attribute. If neither is the case, the function ends; no changes in the document structure are necessary.

Overlap

There are a few cases in which `this` and the target overlap each other, with few clear-cut advantages on either side. For instance, in Sandwich Picker I set a lot of click events on the Order buttons in the following way (the Trash button works similarly):

[Sandwich Picker, lines 49-50]

```
var extraLink2 = orderLink.cloneNode(true);
extraLink2.onclick = moveToOrderTable;
```

In order to find the link the user clicked on, I use the `this` keyword:

[Sandwich Picker, lines 145-148, condensed]

```
function moveToOrderTable() {
    var node = this.parentNode.parentNode;
    document.getElementById('ordered').appendChild(node);
```

I could also have registered a general click event on the entire document and used the event's target property for targeting. That script would look something like this:

```
document.onclick = moveToOrderTable;
function moveToOrderTable() {
```

```
        var evt = e || window.event;
        var evtTarget = evt.target || evt.srcElement;
        var node = evtTarget.parentNode.parentNode;
    }
```

There's a slight problem with this approach. The Order links need one function, and the Trash links need another one. I could have read the text in the event's target element and gone on from there:

```
function moveToOrderTable() {
        var evt = e || window.event;
        var evtTarget = evt.target || evt.srcElement;
    var linkText = evtTarget.firstChild.nodeValue;
    if (linkText == 'Order') {
            // move to order table
    }
    else if (linkText == 'Trash'); {
            // move to start table
    }
}
```

However, I decided that both buttons should have their own event-handling function, because that's clearer overall.

Nonetheless, this example shows that there is no firm, fixed line between cases where the this keyword is preferable and where the event target is better suited. You'll have to develop your own habits within the welter of restrictions we just discussed.

G: The example scripts

Let's take a look at the specific event solutions I devised for the eight example scripts. These explanations will serve as examples of selecting events, registration models, targeting, and practical uses of event bubbling.

Textarea Maxlength

Obviously, Textarea Maxlength needs a key event. Whenever the user adds another character, the script checks if the maximum length has been exceeded. I chose the keyup event for several reasons:

- It fires only once when the user releases the key, and therefore: my script is called only once per keystroke. In general, I like to call functions as infrequently as possible.

- Since we don't need to cancel the default action (i.e., prevent the pressed key's character from being added to the textarea), we don't need keypress.

- We don't need to know which key the user pressed. (If we did, we wouldn't be able to use keypress.)

Nonetheless, the keyup event is not enough. Users might also paste text into the textarea without ever pressing a key. In that case, keyup wouldn't fire. Therefore I also use the change event: if the user leaves the textarea and its content has changed, the script runs.

So my event handlers become:

[Textarea Maxlength, line 16]

```
textareas[i].onkeyup = textareas[i].onchange = checkMaxLength;
```

If either the keyup or the change event occurs, checkMaxLength() is executed. Neither are mouse events, so there shouldn't be any problem accessibility-wise.

Textarea Maxlength uses the this keyword for targeting, as we already saw in 7F. There's an extra complication, though: checkMaxLength() should change the <span> element next to the textarea. This element is neither the event target nor the element the event handler is defined on, so neither this nor the target will point to it.

Instead, the script creates a reference to the <span> on the textarea:

[Textarea Maxlength, line 15]

```
textareas[i].relatedElement = [the span];
```

Later on, checkMaxLength() uses this reference. We discussed this trick in 4C.

7G

Usable Forms

Picking the right events for Usable Forms is tricky. The script needs to know if the user has changed any form field with a `rel` attribute. A change event would seem the obvious choice, but I decided not to use it for two reasons.

The page I originally wrote Usable Forms for contained 142 form fields, and I didn't want to set a separate event on every one of them. Instead, I wanted to use event bubbling. Unfortunately, change is an interface event and cannot be registered on the document in most browsers. Therefore, I decided to use the click event. Registering an onclick event handler on the document is always possible, and therefore the event bubbles up nicely.

In addition, in Explorer the change event on radio buttons and checkboxes fires only when the user blurs them, i.e., when he clicks or tabs somewhere else. This is a serious problem in Usable Forms' interface. It should be totally clear to the user that checking or unchecking certain form fields causes the form to change. We can't postpone the form change until later, since that could confuse some users.

I use `addEventSimple()`, because Usable Forms is a module that can be added to any site, and the site may already have a document.onclick event handler:

[Usable Forms, line 53]

```
addEventSimple(document,'click',showHideFields);
```

There are no accessibility issues, since a click event also fires when the user activates form fields by hitting the space bar.

Unfortunately, the general click event doesn't cover changes to select boxes, since click events on options or selects are not supported. For select boxes I needed the change event, and its lack of bubbling capabilities forced me to add individual change events to all selects:

[Usable Forms, lines 22-23]

```
var selects = document.getElementsByTagName('select');
for (var i=0;i<selects.length;i++)
    addEventSimple(selects[i],'change',showHideFields)
```

We discussed Usable Forms' need for the event target in 7F.

Form Validation

Obviously, Form Validation needs the submit event. When the user submits the form, the script checks the content of all form fields:

[Form Validation, line 67]

```
forms[i].onsubmit = validate;
```

The `validate()` function returns either `true` or `false`, so that the event knows whether to allow the form submission or not.

I don't need `addEventSimple()`, even though Form Validation is a module. If there is another form-validation routine that also uses the submit event, only one of the two routines should be executed. Therefore, I overwrite any existing onsubmit event handlers without a qualm.

The main validation function uses the `this` keyword to find the correct form (after all, there can be multiple forms on a single page), but the real action takes place on the form's elements:

[Form Validation, lines 73-74]

```
function validate() {
    var els = this.elements;
    // validate all elements
```

I use a second event in Form Validation. When the script finds an error, it gives the offending form field special styles. When the user changes the value of the form field, I politely assume that she has corrected the error, and the special styles should be removed.

In order to remove the styles, I use the change event once more. If the user changes the value, assume there is no more error:

[Form Validation, lines 108-110 and 122-129 condensed]

```
function writeError(obj,message) {
    obj.className += ' errorMessage';
    obj.onchange = removeError;
    // administration
}
```

7G

```
function removeError() {
    this.className = this.className.replace(/errorMessage/,'');
    // administration
    this.onchange = null;
}
```

I set this event only on those form fields that actually contain an error. When the user changes the form-field value, `removeError()` is called, and it removes the class and the change event. After that's done, the event is not useful any more, and since I prefer to clean up this sort of loose ends, I therefore set it to `null`.

Dropdown Menu

In Dropdown Menu I use the same event-bubbling trick as in Usable Forms. I set a mouseover and a mouseout event for every `<ul class="menutree">`, which fire when the user mouses over or out of any link in the dropdown menu:

[Dropdown Menu, lines 6-11]

```
function initNavigation() {
    var x = document.getElementsByTagName('ul');
    for (var i=0;i<x.length;i++) {
        if (x[i].className != 'menutree') continue;
        x[i].onmouseover = navMouseOver;
        x[i].onmouseout = navMouseOut;
```

But now the menu is inaccessible without a mouse. Therefore, I also added a focus event. Unfortunately, the focus event does not bubble, so I'm forced to add it to all links inside `<li>`s that have a `<ul>` child—in other words, all links that should trigger a new dropdown menu.

[Dropdown Menu, lines 12-16]

```
var listItems = lists[i].getElementsByTagName('li');
for (var j=0;j<listItems.length;j++)
{
    var test = listItems[j].getElementsByTagName('ul')[0];
    if (test) { // li contains a nested ul
        listItems[j].firstChild.onfocus = navMouseOver;
```

Note that the event is set not on the *<li>* itself but on the *<a>* that is its first child, because *<li>*s are unable to receive the keyboard focus.

I do not use the blur event to simulate the mouseout, because it adds little to the overall user experience. If the user focuses on another link, all dropdown menus that are not children of this link are hidden anyway.

By adding the focus event, I've made Dropdown Menus as accessible as possible. Nonetheless, when you tab through the menu you'll find that it doesn't behave quite the same as when you use the mouse. Besides, in order to reach the last link in the menu, you have to tab through all other links first, while the mouse events allow you to take a shortcut.

This user experience can be vastly improved by adding arrow-key navigation to the script. I didn't do so, but the idea would be to register a general onkeydown event handler to all *<ul>*s, and then to read out the arrow key the user has pressed, and focus on the next (or previous) link.

Since Dropdown Menu uses event bubbling, all functions look for the event target and go on from there. In 7F we already discussed the extreme care you have to take when using event targets of trigger-happy events like mouseover.

Edit Style Sheet

At first glance, Edit Style Sheet seems very similar to Usable Forms. The script should run whenever the user changes any value of any form field, and I could again have opted for a general click event.

There's one important difference between the two scripts, though: Edit Style Sheet also works with text fields in which the user can enter data, while Usable Forms only works with radio buttons, checkboxes, and selects. A click event on a text field doesn't give much information, since at the time it occurs the field is most likely empty.

Therefore, in Edit Style Sheet I cannot replace the change event with the click event, and since the change event doesn't bubble up, I have to set it on every single field in the correct form:

7G

[Edit Style Sheet, lines 33-35]

```
var els = document.forms[1].elements;
for (var i=0;i<els.length;i++) {
    els[i].onchange = assignStyles;
```

The script uses the `this` keyword to find the form field the user has changed:

[Edit Style Sheet, lines 57-60, condensed]

```
function assignStyles() {
    var styleName = this.name;
    var styleValue = this.value;
```

In addition to these change events, the script also needs a few extra event handlers. The first two fields—the select that allows the user to pick a rule and the Restore Defaults button—need their own event handlers, obviously a change and a click event, respectively:

{Edit Style Sheet, lines 30-31]

```
document.getElementById('selectors').onchange = assignRule;
document.getElementById('restoreDefaults').onclick = ➡
restoreDefaults;
```

Finally, the two Pick color links need their own click events to trigger the color picker:

[Edit Style Sheet, lines 39-42]

```
var links = document.getElementsByTagName('a');
for (var i=0;i<links.length;i++) {
    if (links[i].className != 'colorPicker') continue;
    links[i].onclick = placeColorPicker;
```

Sandwich Picker

Sandwich Picker needs keyboard events for the Search box and every individual sandwich order box, and click events on all Order and Trash buttons. Setting the first event is very simple:

[Sandwich Picker, line 54]

```
document.getElementById('searchField').onkeyup = searchSandwich;
```

The script sets the other events during the general loop through all the sandwiches. The sandwich order input box is already there, but the script creates the Order and Trash links by cloning templates (we'll discuss this in detail in 8E). One annoying feature of the `cloneNode()` method is that it does not clone event handlers, so I have to set them manually on every clone:

[Sandwich Picker, lines 45, 48 and 50]

```
searchField.onkeyup = orderSandwich;
extraLink.onclick = removeSandwich;
extraLink2.onclick = moveToOrderTable;
```

All functions use the `this` keyword to find the element the user has clicked on or entered data in.

XMLHTTP Speed Meter

XMLHTTP Speed Meter also needs a key event on form fields. When the user changes his postal code or house number, the script should run. In addition, the user might press Enter to submit the form, and in that case the script should also run. Therefore, we also need a submit event:

[XMLHTTP Speed Meter, lines 24-29]

```
var formFields = document.getElementsByTagName('input');
for (var i=0;i<formFields.length;i++) {
    if (formFields[i].type != 'text') continue;
    formFields[i].onkeyup = initSendData;
}
document.forms[0].onsubmit = initSendData;
```

Since the script has to read out both of the form fields (postal code and house number), it uses neither the `this` keyword nor the event target: it just manually searches for its data:

[XMLHTTP Speed Meter, lines 41-43]

```
function sendData() {
    var postCode = document.getElementById('postcode').value;
    var number = document.getElementById('huisnummer').value;
```

Site Survey

Site Survey is a special case. It is the single example script that does not directly respond to user actions. Instead, it stores the URLs of the pages the user visits. Therefore, it has to be notified when the user goes to a new page, and to do that it needs either the load or the unload event.

An important job of Site Survey is keeping open communication with the main window, as we discussed in 6B. To do this, the script must be notified when the user leaves a page. It then starts up a script that tries to re-establish communication with the main window.

In order to run the communication script, the page needs access to the popup, and that's impossible onload, since at that time the communication has not yet been restored. Therefore, this job needs the unload event, and to keep things simple I use the same event for storing the URLs. ST_exit() handles both tasks.

Site Survey uses addEventSimple() since it's a module that can be added to any site and it shouldn't disturb the event handlers of the host site:

[Site Survey/survey.js, line 43]

```
addEventSimple(window,"unload",ST_exit);
```

In addition, Site Survey needs a click event to open the popup in the first place. Since the user may click anywhere, I use a document-wide click event:

[Site Survey/survey.js, line 56]

```
addEventSimple(document,"click",ST_openPopup);
```

H: Dropdown Menu, mouseouts, and the related target

Dropdown Menu will show you how to work with the mouseover and mouseout events, and will also show you that the last event, especially, can cause a lot of trouble if you don't use it correctly. We'll also discuss the `relatedTarget` and `toElement` properties that are vital to scripts that use mouseout a lot.

The problem is that these events can fire a lot of times even when the user makes a small mouse movement, so you have to manually distinguish between important and unimportant mouseovers and mouseouts.

Besides, neither the event target nor the `this` keyword is worth much in mouseout events. They refer to the element the mouse moves out of, and as we'll see, that's usually not very interesting information.

Mouseover

Let's delve into Dropdown Menu's bowels a bit. As we saw, the script defines general onmouseover and onmouseout event handlers for the entire menu, and relies on event bubbling to get all the events that take place on its descendants:

```
<ul class="menutree">
<li><a href="#">News</a>
  <ul>
    <li><a href="#">Press Releases</a>
          <ul>
                  <li><a href="#">Release 1</a></li>
                  <li><a href="#">Release 2</a></li>
                  <li><a href="#">Release 3</a></li>
          </ul>
    </li>
    etc.
</ul>
```

[Dropdown Menu, lines 7-21]

```
var lists = document.getElementsByTagName('ul');
for (var i=0;i<lists.length;i++) {
    if (lists[i].className != 'menutree') continue;
    lists[i].onmouseover = navMouseOver;
    lists[i].onmouseout = navMouseOut;
    var listItems = lists[i].getElementsByTagName('li');
    for (var j=0;j<listItems.length;j++) {
        var test = listItems[j].getElementsByTagName('ul')[0];
        if (test) {
            listItems[j].firstChild.onfocus = navMouseOver;
            listItems[j].relatedItem = test;
        }
    }
}
```

Note the second part of the initialization: it goes through all <li>s of the drop-down menu and finds out if they have a nested <ul>. If they do, the script gives them a custom relatedItem property to point to this <li>. This property serves two purposes:

- Its presence alerts the script that the <li> has a child menu. (I could search for a nested <ul> every time the user mouses over something, but I find this approach cleaner.)

- Its value refers to this child menu, and that makes it easy to find the <ul> that should open when the user mouses over a certain <li>.

relatedItem is used in navMouseOver():

[Dropdown Menu, lines 33-36]

```
if (evtTarget.relatedItem && !evtTarget.relatedItem.opened) {
    evtTarget.className = 'highlight';
    evtTarget.relatedItem.className = 'foldOut';
    evtTarget.relatedItem.opened = true;
```

We already discussed Dropdown Menu's targeting. We make very certain `evtTarget` is an `<li>`, and then we check if it contains a `relatedItem`, i.e., a submenu. If it does, the script changes the class names of the `<li>` and the submenu, and the submenu opens. That's not too convoluted.

Mouseout and its problems

Our problems start when we consider the mouseout event. Sacred tradition requires us to close the menus as soon as the user mouses out of them. But how do we find out if we have to close menus, and which ones?

Suppose the user mouses out of the Area 3 link by moving down. Now the dropdown menu that the link is part of should close.

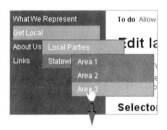

FIGURE 7.13
The user mouses out of the link and leaves the entire submenu. The sub-menu should close.

Suppose the user mouses out of the Area 3 link by moving up. Now the mouse stays within the submenu and it should not close.

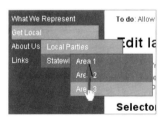

FIGURE 7.14
The user mouses out of the link but stays within the submenu. Nothing should happen.

{ **MOUSELEAVE**

Microsoft's proprietary mouseleave event would come in very handy here.
If we register it on the submenu, it only fires when the mouse moves out of
the entire submenu, while ignoring any internal mouseouts. Unfortunately,
we can't use it because of the lack of support in non-Explorer browsers. }

Solution

Working with the mouseout event can quickly become horrifically complicated.
That's why I decided to use a separate array, currentlyOpenedMenus, which
stores all menus that are currently opened. Thus I can easily go through all
opened menus and see if they need to be closed. I reached this solution independently in both my 2001 and my 2005 dropdown menu scripts, so I suppose
this approach is worthwhile.

The principle is simple. As soon as a menu is opened, a reference to this menu
is added to currentlyOpenedMenus:

[Dropdown Menu, lines 34-37]

```
evtTarget.className = 'highlight';
evtTarget.relatedItem.className = 'foldOut';
evtTarget.relatedItem.opened = true;
currentlyOpenedMenus.push(evtTarget.relatedItem);
```

When the time comes to close menus, I go through this array and decide which
of the currently opened menus should be closed.

How do I decide whether to close a certain menu? I take the element the
mouse *goes to* and see if the menu contains this element. If it does, the menu

should not be closed, since the user is still mousing over it. If the menu does not contain the element, the user has moused out of it, and it should be closed:

[Dropdown Menu, lines 47-54, condensed]

```
function foldMenuIn(targetNode) {
        for (var i=0;i<currentlyOpenedMenus.length;i++) {
            if ([the menu does NOT contain targetNode]) {
                    // close menu
            }
        }
}
```

This function is called onmouseover. When the user mouses over a new item, any menus associated with other items should close. In this case, the element the mouse moves to is easy to find—it's the mouseover's event target:

[Dropdown Menu, line 32]

```
foldMenuIn(evtTarget);
```

Obviously, we should also call this function onmouseout, since a mouseout might also trigger menu closures. But how do we find the element the mouse moves *to*? The event's target is the element the mouse moves *from*, and that information is useless.

relatedTarget, fromElement, and toElement

Fortunately, both the W3C and the Microsoft models allow you to find out which element the mouse comes from. The W3C model defines the `relatedTarget` property of the event object. This property refers to the object the mouse goes to (onmouseout) or comes from (onmouseover).

The Microsoft model has two separate properties for this information. `fromElement` refers to the object the mouse comes from onmouseover, `toElement` to the object the mouse goes to onmouseout.

This solves our problem. If we read out relatedTarget or toElement, we find the element the mouse moves to, and we can send this information on to foldMenuIn(). Therefore we need the following function:

[Dropdown Menu, lines 41-45]

```
function navMouseOut(e) {
    var evt = e || window.event;
    var relatedNode = evt.relatedTarget || evt.toElement;
    foldMenuIn(relatedNode);
}
```

This works, and DropDown Menu is ready.

Nonetheless, you'll agree that working with the mouseout event can be pretty hard sometimes. If you have the chance to avoid it, or to use the Microsoft proprietary mouseleave instead, do it.

þþ]{

DOM

JAVASCRIPT ALLOWS YOU to restructure an HTML document, for instance by adding, removing, or reordering the items shown on the page. In fact, without the possibility of restructuring the document, or at the very least providing some feedback (such as text in a form field or an image swap), JavaScript is pretty much worthless.

The example script that best demonstrates this restructuring is Sandwich Picker. Users can quickly and easily specify the sandwiches they want to order, and the script gathers the data by moving the <tr>s that contain sandwiches to the order table—in other words, by changing the document structure.

To change anything on a page, JavaScript needs access to all elements in the HTML document. Allowing this access and providing for methods and properties to query the current status of the HTML elements, or to add, move, or remove HTML elements, is the job of the Document Object Model, or DOM.

We discussed DOM history in 1C, but it's useful to repeat a few fundamentals. Since without a DOM JavaScript is worthless, the earliest JavaScript browsers already allowed limited access to a few HTML elements, most notably form fields and images. This old way of doing things is called the Level 0 DOM, and it was a part of the de facto Netscape 3 standard. Nowadays the Level 0 DOM is used only for form manipulation, for which it remains better equipped than its successor (see 8J).

In 1998, W3C published its Level 1 DOM specification, which allowed access to and manipulation of every single element in an HTML page, from the document itself to the lowliest text node. Better still, all browser vendors actually implemented this recommendation, and as a result, incompatibility problems in the DOM have almost (but not entirely) disappeared.

The W3C Level 1 DOM was created to allow any programming language to read and change XML documents. Since properly written XHTML is XML, and properly written HTML can be interpreted as such, the DOM can also be used by JavaScript to read and change HTML documents.

The greater part of this chapter discusses the Level 1 DOM, but we'll also take a look at the old Level 0 DOM, especially at its useful form-field properties.

We'll mainly use Sandwich Picker and Usable Forms as examples, since these scripts use the document-restructuring possibilities of the Level 1 DOM to the greatest effect.

{ **XML DOCUMENTS**

Remember: the W3C DOM can also be used on XML documents. We'll discuss an example of this in 10B and 10C. }

> { **W3C DOM COMPATIBILITY TABLES**
>
> As you'll notice in this chapter, the W3C DOM implementation of the browsers are occasionally incompatible. In order to guide Web developers through this maze of problems, I set up the W3C DOM Compatibility Tables at www.quirksmode.org. }

A: Concepts

Before we delve deeply into the DOM, let's discuss a few general concepts.

Nodes

To the W3C DOM, everything in an HTML document is a *node*. The entire document is a document node; every HTML tag, such as `<body>`, `<p>`, or even `<br />`, is an element node; and the texts contained in these elements are text nodes. Furthermore, HTML attributes like ID are attribute nodes, and even comments are comment nodes.

Node hierarchy

Nodes have a hierarchical relationship to each other. Take this HTML snippet:

```
<p>I am a JavaScript hacker.</p>
```

The snippet contains two nodes: one element node for the `<p>` tag, and one text node that contains 'I am a JavaScript hacker'. Since the `<p>` node contains the text node, their relationship becomes parent (`<p>`) and child (text).

In this hierarchical way, all nodes form a document tree. This tree starts at the document node itself and continues to branch out until it has reached all text nodes that reside at the lowest level of the tree.

8A

Take this simple HTML page:

```
<html>
<head>
<title>Hacking JavaScript</title>
</head>
<body>
<h1>Hello world!</h1>
<p>I am a JavaScript hacker!</p>
</body>
</html>
```

The Level 1 DOM sees it as the following node tree:

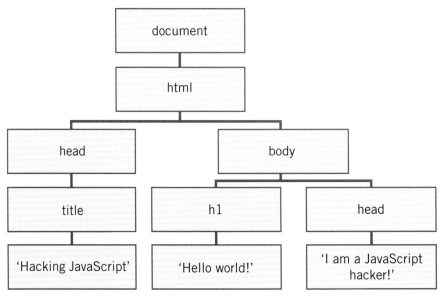

FIGURE 8.1 The DOM treeview of the HTML snippet.

Node types

Document, html, head, body, title, h1, p, 'Hacking JavaScript', 'Hello world!', and 'I am a JavaScript hacker' are all nodes. They're not all the same type of nodes, though. The document is a document node, the three texts are text nodes, and the six HTML tags are element nodes.

The node type determines what you're allowed to do with a node. For instance, text nodes cannot contain other nodes, so, unlike element nodes, they have no child nodes. On the other hand, they have a few properties for reading out the text, which is something element nodes can't do (and don't need to do).

Family tree

All these nodes have relationships to each other, and the DOM uses terminology borrowed from family trees to describe these relationships. Every node except for the document has a *parent node*. For instance, the parent node of the <body> element node is the <html> element node, and the parent node of the 'Hello world!' text node is the <h1> element node.

Most element nodes have *child nodes*. For instance, the <head> node has one child node: the <title> node. In turn, the <title> node has a text node as its child node.

Some nodes are *siblings* because they share a parent. For instance, the <h1> and <p> nodes are siblings because they're both child nodes of the <body> node.

Nodes can have *descendants* and *ancestors*. Descendants are all the nodes that are children of a node, or children of those children, etc. For instance, all text nodes are descendants of the <html> node, while the second and third text nodes are descendants of the <body> node.

Ancestors are nodes that are parents of a node, or parents of this parent, etc. All text nodes have the <html> node as an ancestor, while the second and third text nodes have the <body> element as an ancestor.

Finding elements

You can run up and down this family tree in order to find nodes. For instance, the <h1> node contains a property parentNode that refers to its parent: the <body> node.

You can also directly find an element with a certain ID (getElementById()) or all elements with a certain tag name (getElementsByTagName()).

Changing the tree

The W3C DOM allows you to change the node tree of a document. The following snippet changes the document tree:

```
var x = document.getElementsByTagName('h1')[0];
var y = document.getElementsByTagName('p')[0];
x.parentNode.insertBefore(y,x);
```

FIGURE 8.2
The DOM tree as rendered by
the browser before (above)
and after (below) the script
has run.

The <h1> and <p> nodes now trade places, both in the DOM tree and in the browser window. This shows the great power of the W3C DOM: any change to the tree is immediately rendered by the browser and becomes visible to your users.

Creating elements

The W3C DOM also allows you to create new elements and insert them in the document tree. This means that you can add anything to the document: status texts, new data obtained from an XMLHttpRequest script (see Chapter 10), or anything else that strikes your fancy.

It's even possible to completely rewrite an HTML page. Just remove all nodes in the document and append new nodes to it, including, if you wish, new style sheets and JavaScript files. This is rarely done; it's usually easier to simply load a new page, but the W3C DOM allows it.

B: Finding elements

The first step in any DOM script is finding the elements you want to do something with. There are two ways of finding elements:

- Through the `getElementById()` and `getElementsByTagName()` methods. This is the best choice for searching long-distance through the entire document.

- Through the `parentNode` and similar properties of an element. This is the best choice for short-distance travels from node to node.

Long-distance travel

When you start up your script, you usually want to find some HTML elements somewhere in the document. The two methods `getElementById()` and `getElementsByTagName()`, which we've already seen in many code examples in the previous chapters, can find any HTML element in the entire document, provided you give them correct instructions.

These two methods largely ignore the document structure. If you want to find all <p>s in the document, it doesn't really matter if they're direct children of the <body> or children of <div>s or other elements; you just want to get them all. Similarly, `getElementById()` always returns the correct element, wherever it may be hidden in the document structure. Therefore, these two methods are the ones you need for "long-distance" searching: they give you the HTML elements you need regardless of where they are in the document.

getElementById

The `getElementById()` method returns the element that has the ID specified in the argument:

```
document.getElementById('someID');
```

{ **NOT IN XML**

`getElementById()` is the single W3C DOM method that doesn't always work in XML. In an XML document, it searches through attributes that have the type (and not the name!) `id`, and this type must be defined in the XML document's Document Type Definition (DTD). }

getElementsByTagName

The `getElementsByTagName()` method returns a nodeList (and not an array!) of all elements with the desired tag name that are descendants of the element on which you use the method. We'll discuss nodeLists in detail in 8I. Once we have a nodeList, we go through all elements in it and do something with them, for instance, checking if they have a certain attribute, or setting an event handler on them.

`getElementsByTagName()` can be used on any HTML element, as well as on the document. Both of these calls are therefore valid:

```
document.getElementsByTagName('p');
document.getElementById('someID').getElementsByTagName('p');
```

The first call returns a nodeList of all <p> elements in the document, while the second one returns a nodeList of all <p> elements that are descendants of the element with ID="someID".

We usually store such a nodeList in a variable:

```
var pars = document.getElementsByTagName('p');
```

Now `pars` contains a list of all individual <p>s in the page, and we can access them by their index numbers. The first <p> has index 0, the second index 1, etc. The most common use of `getElementsByTagName()` is requesting all tags of a certain type in order to loop through them.

```
var pars = document.getElementsByTagName('p');
for (var i=0;i<pars.length;i++) {
    // do something with pars[i]; ie. with every paragraph
}
```

To access the fifth `<p>` in the page you can also say:

```
var fifthP = pars[4];
```

This syntax is useful only if you know exactly which `<p>` you want to access, and are certain that it hasn't been moved or removed by another part of your script. Therefore it isn't often used.

getElementsByTagName('*');

Finally, you can use `getElementsByTagName('*')`, which gives you all element nodes in the document in the order they appear in the source code. This method is not used often, since you rarely need all the elements in the entire document. Besides, it is not supported by Explorer 5.5 and earlier.

Examples

For an example, let's look at Usable Forms. When the script starts up, it should go through all tags of a certain kind; if they contain a `rel` attribute, they should be removed from the document. The script does this through the `getElementsByTagName()` method:

[Usable Forms, lines 1 and 25-28]

```
var containerTag = 'TR';
var containers = document.getElementsByTagName(containerTag);
for (var i=0;i<containers.length;i++) {
    if (containers[i].getAttribute('rel')) {
        // remove element
        // containers[i] refers to the <tr>
        // we're currently studying
    }
}
```

`containers` becomes a nodeList that contains all `<tr>` tags in the entire document. The script goes through them one by one and sees if they have a `rel` attribute. If so, it removes them from the document and puts them in a waiting room, where they remain until the user checks or selects the appropriate form field.

Sandwich Picker needs a slightly different approach. Initially I only want to go through all `<tr>`s in the third table on the page, the one that contains the sandwiches. The two other tables also have a few `<tr>`s, but these contain static information such as the search field and the order form.

So the script goes through the `<tr>`s in the third table, which has ID="startTable" (well, actually, its `<tbody>` has this ID, for reasons we'll discuss in 8E).

[Sandwich Picker, lines 32-33]

```
var containers = document.getElementById('startTable').➡
getElementsByTagName('tr');
for (var i=0;i<containers.length;i++) {
    // initialize
    // containers[i] refers to the <tr>
    // we're currently studying
}
```

Short-distance travel

Every node in the document has five properties and two nodeLists that allow you easy short-distance travel. The five properties are `parentNode`, `firstChild`, `lastChild`, `previousSibling`, and `nextSibling`, and they each refer to the node that is the parent node, first child, etc. of the node you use them on.

parentNode, firstChild, lastChild, previousSibling, nextSibling

Take this bit of HTML from Sandwich Picker:

```
<tr>
    <td class="number"><input /></td>
    <td class="description">Spicy roast beef</td>
    <td class="extra">With our own mix of herbs and spices</td>
    <td class="empty">home made</td>
</tr>
```

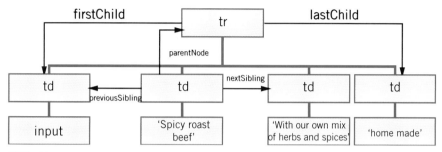

FIGURE 8.3 The DOM tree of the `<tr>` with the short-distance properties sketched in.

The first `<td>` is the `firstChild` of the `<tr>`; the last `<td>` is the `lastChild`. When we start at the second `<td>`, the `<tr>` is its `parentNode`, the first `<td>` is its `previousSibling`, and the third `<td>` is its `nextSibling`. Almost all nodes contain these five properties, although text nodes cannot have child nodes and document nodes cannot have parent nodes.

childNodes[] and children[]

Every node has two properties that contain nodeLists: `childNodes[]` and `children[]`. The difference between the two is that `childNodes[]` contains all children of a node, while `children[]` contains only those children that are element nodes themselves, and not the text nodes. `children[]` is the more useful of the two, since you're rarely interested in text nodes when you go through the children of an element, but unfortunately it is not a part of the W3C DOM specification, and at the time of writing is not supported by Mozilla.

> { **PREVIOUSSIBLING, NEXTSIBLING, AND CHILDNODES[]
> ARE USELESS**
>
> `previousSibling`, `nextSibling`, and `childNodes[]` appear to be useful properties, but unfortunately they are not nearly as handy as they seem. In the example scripts I use `nextSibling` twice, and I don't use `previousSibling` and `childNodes[]` at all.
>
> The reason is that they generally don't refer to the element nodes you'd expect, but to empty text nodes. We'll study these nuisances in 8H. }

8B

Short distance only

Although it's theoretically possible to use these properties to go from any node to any other node, that's not recommended. Take, for instance, this path:

```
var x = [a node];
var y = x.parentNode.lastChild.childNodes[2].firstChild.
nextSibling;
```

The code is unreadable; no other JavaScript programmer will intuitively understand what you're doing. Besides, even though the path may be correct at the moment you create the script, it doesn't account for changes in the document tree, and changing the document tree is the whole point of W3C DOM scripts.

Therefore, I use these properties exclusively for short-distance travel. In general I restrict myself to two, or at most three, of these properties per statement, because if you need more of them you're usually better served by `getElement-ById()` or `getElementsByTagName()`.

Examples

By far the most common use of `firstChild` is in accessing the text of an element:

```
<p>I am a JavaScript hacker.</p>
```

If you want to find the text contained by the paragraph, you have to travel to the text node it contains and read out its `nodeValue`:

```
var par = [the paragraph];
var text = par.firstChild.nodeValue;
```

You'll also use `parentNode` a lot. For instance, take this bit of Sandwich Picker:

[Sandwich Picker, lines 106-133, condensed]

```
function orderSandwich() {
    // more stuff
    var x = this.value * 1;
    if (isNaN(x) || x == 0)
            removeFromOrder(this);
    else
```

```
            moveToOrder(this);
    }

    function moveToOrder(obj) {
        obj = obj.parentNode.parentNode;
        obj.className = 'highlight';
        // more stuff
    }

    function removeFromOrder(obj) {
        obj = obj.parentNode.parentNode;
        obj.className = '';
        // more stuff
    }
```

orderSandwich() is called whenever the user enters text in a form field. The script first checks if the text is a number. If it's not a number, it calls remove-FromOrder(); if it is a number, it calls moveToOrder(). this (the form field in which the user entered data) is sent as an argument to both functions.

One of the jobs of the two functions is to highlight or un-highlight the <tr> that contains the form field, and it does so by giving its className a new value (see 9B). Before that's possible, though, the script has to access the correct <tr>. This is the HTML of one sandwich <tr>:

```
    <tr>
        <td class="number"><input /></td>
        <td class="description">English sandwich</td>
        <td class="extra">bacon, cheese, lettuce, tomato</td>
        <td class="empty">freshly fried</td>
    </tr>
```

Therefore, seen from the form field (obj), the <tr> can be accessed by parentNode.parentNode. The form field's parentNode is the <td>, and the <td>'s parentNode is the <tr>.

Since this is short-distance travel, and since the script moves entire <tr>s through the document but doesn't touch the internal structure of the <tr>s, using parentNode.parentNode is safe.

You'll also use parentNode often when you change the document structure, because, as we'll see in 8D, all methods you need for structure changes are defined on the parent node of the node you want to change. Suppose you want to remove the node with ID="testID" from the document:

```
var x = document.getElementById('testID');
x.parentNode.removeChild(x);
```

First you access the node (long range!), but in order to execute the removeChild() method, you have to move to its parent first.

Root nodes

Finally, there are two special document properties that allow access to the <html> and <body> tags: document.documentElement and document.body. The first property exists in all XML documents, since every XML document must have a root element from which all other nodes descend. In HTML pages this is obviously the <html> tag.

document.body is a special addition for HTML pages, since it is often useful to directly access the <body> tag.

C: Node information

Every node has a few properties that contain a bit of information about the node. They are nodeName, nodeValue, nodeType, and tagName.

nodeName

nodeName is the most useful property. Unsurprisingly, it contains the name of the node. The name of an element node is always the tag name, the name of an attribute node is always the attribute name, the name of a text node is always #text, and the name of the document node is always #document.

One caveat: nodeName contains the UPPERCASE tag name of an HTML element, even if you used lowercase in your HTML.

As an example, take this function from Usable Forms. It fires whenever the user clicks anywhere in the document or changes a select box, and I need to find out if this action took place on a form field or a label:

[Usable Forms, lines 70-81, condensed]

```
var evt = e || window.event;
var evtTarget = evt.target || evt.srcElement;
if (!(
    (evtTarget.nodeName == 'SELECT' && e.type == 'change')
    ||
    (evtTarget.nodeName == 'INPUT' && ➡
evtTarget.getAttribute('rel'))
)) return;
// valid click, show/hide form fields
```

First the function accesses the event target, as we discussed in 7F. Then it checks if the target is a select and the event type is 'change', or if the target is an input that has a rel attribute. If neither is true, the function ends. (We discussed this if statement in detail in 5H.) For both checks I use nodeName.

nodeValue

On text nodes, nodeValue contains the actual text:

```
<p>I am a JavaScript hacker.</p>
var x = [the paragraph];
var text = x.firstChild.nodeValue;
```

On attribute nodes, nodeValue contains the attribute value. It is not available on document and element nodes.

In Sandwich Picker, I use nodeValue to find the sandwich name:

[Sandwich Picker, lines 32-39, condensed]

```
var containers = document.getElementById('startTable'). ➡
getElementsByTagName('tr');
for (var i=0;i<containers.length;i++) {
        var cells = containers[i] getElementsByTagName('td');
        containers[i].productName = cells[1]. ➡
        firstChild.nodeValue.toLowerCase();
}
```

This function goes through all <tr>s in the start table, takes their <td>s, and then accesses the first child of the second <td>, which always contains the sandwich name. It then takes its nodeValue, sets it to lowercase to be safe, and stores it in the productName property of the <tr> object.

Reading out the content of text nodes is the only practical application of nodeValue.

nodeType

nodeType contains a number that gives the type of the node:

Element type	nodeType
Element	1
Attribute	2
Text	3
Comment	8
Document	9

There are many more node types, but they aren't important in Web development.

We saw an example of `nodeType`'s use in 7F. In Safari, the target of an event might be a text node instead of an element node. I use `nodeType` to find out if this is the case, and if so, I redirect the target to the text node's parent:

```
var evt = e || window.event;
var evtTarget = evt.target || evt.srcElement;
if (evtTarget.nodeType == 3)
    evtTarget = evtTarget.parentNode;
```

tagName

`tagName` also contains the tag name of element nodes, but it is not available on any other node type. Since it contains the same information as `nodeName` but is less versatile, I never use `tagName`.

D: Changing the document tree

The W3C DOM contains four methods for changing the document tree. You'll use `appendChild()` and `insertBefore()` often, and `removeChild()` and `replaceChild()` more rarely.

General rules

All four methods return a reference to a node they acted on. For instance, in Sandwich Picker, for each sandwich the user orders, I append a `<tr>` to the order table:

[Sandwich Picker, line 148]

```
document.getElementById('ordered').appendChild(node);
```

I could also have done this:

```
var newSandwich = document.getElementById('ordered'). ➡
appendChild(node);
```

Now the node is appended, and the return value of appendChild() is assigned to newSandwich, so that it contains a reference to the node. We rarely need this reference, and therefore usually don't assign the return value of the methods to a variable. Nonetheless, remember that these references are available; occasionally you'll need them.

The four methods are all defined on the parent node of the node you want to do something with. So if you want to remove node x, you write:

```
x.parentNode.removeChild(x);
```

The following simple HTML page will serve as an example during the explanation of the four methods:

```
<html>
<head>
<title>Hacking JavaScript</title>
</head>
<body>
<h1>Hello world!</h1>
<p>I am a JavaScript hacker!</p>
<p>And that's bloody marvellous</p>
</body>
</html>
```

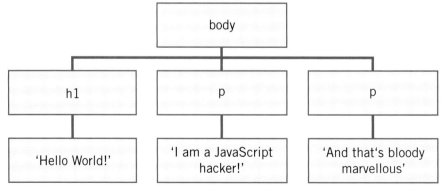

FIGURE 8.4 The DOM tree of the HTML example shows only the <body> tag and its descendants.

appendChild()

The `appendChild()` method allows you to append a node as the *last child* of an element. If the node you append is already present in the document, it is removed from its current position. The node retains all its child nodes; these are also moved to the new position.

Example:

```
var x = document.getElementsByTagName('h1')[0];
x.parentNode.appendChild(x);
```

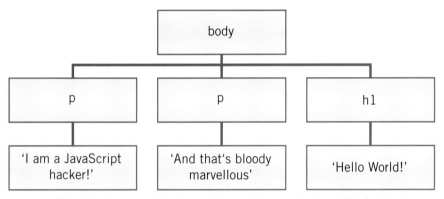

FIGURE 8.5 The <h1> is removed from its position and becomes the last child of the body. Its child node—the text node 'Hello World!'—also moves.

Of course you can also append text nodes:

```
var y = x.firstChild;
var z = document.getElementsByTagName('p')[1];
z.appendChild(y);
```

Now the text node 'Hello World!' is removed from the <h1> and appended as the last child of the second <p>.

Return value

`appendChild()` returns a reference to the appended node:

```
var x = y.appendChild(z);
```

Now x contains a reference to node z.

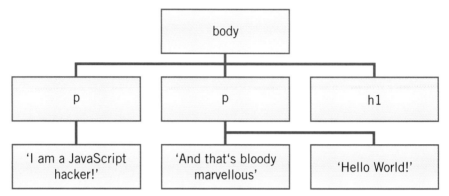

FIGURE 8.6 The <h1>'s text node has become a child of the second <p>. Note that the <p> now contains two text nodes; they aren't automatically merged.

Example

I use appendChild() many times in the example scripts. Take, for instance, this function from Sandwich Picker:

[Sandwich Picker, lines 184-186]

```
function addExtraButton() {
    document.getElementById('extraButtonTarget'). ➡
    appendChild(extraButton);
}
```

The extra button says 'Collect all orders', and it should appear when the user has ordered sandwiches but hasn't yet moved them to the order table. I prepared the extraButton node in advance (we'll discuss that in the next section), and now I append it to the <td> with ID="extrabuttonTarget".

insertBefore()

The insertBefore() method allows you to insert a node before another node, and therefore you use it every time you want to append a child but don't want it to become the last child. Just as with appendChild(), if the inserted node is

already present in the document, it is removed from its current position, and
the inserted node retains all its child nodes.

```
var x = document.getElementsByTagName('p')[0];
var y = document.getElementsByTagName('h1')[0];
x.parentNode.insertBefore(x,y);
```

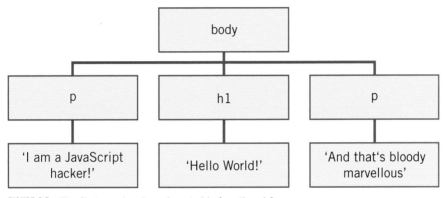

FIGURE 8.7 The first <p> has been inserted before the <h1>.

Now the first <p> becomes the <body>'s first child. The <h1> remains in the
document, but now appears between the paragraphs. As before, it retains its
child text node.

Return value

insertBefore() returns a reference to the inserted node:

```
var x = y.insertBefore(z,a);
```

Now x contains a reference to z.

Example

I use insertBefore() less often than appendChild(), but still quite a lot. For
instance, take this line from Usable Forms:

[Usable Forms, line 126]

```
insertPoint.parentNode.insertBefore(Elements[i],insertPoint);
```

When a form field that was initially hidden should return to the visible form, I insert it before its insert point. (This insert point is a marker that exists only to mark the point where the `<tr>` should be inserted, and it is a `<tr>`, too. We'll discuss markers in 8L.)

I first move to the parent node of the insert point `<tr>` and execute `insertBefore()` from there.

removeChild()

The removeChild() method allows you to remove a node and its child nodes. For instance:

```
var x = document.getElementsByTagName('p')[0];
x.parentNode.removeChild(x);
```

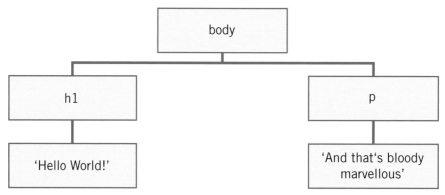

FIGURE 8.8   The first <p> has been removed entirely, and its child text node is removed, too.

Return value

`removeChild()` returns a reference to the removed node:

```
var x = y.removeChild(z);
```

Now `x` contains a reference to `z`.

Example

We already saw the addExtraButton() function from Sandwich Picker. There's also a removeExtraButton() function that removes the button if the user has moved all his ordered sandwiches to the order form:

[Sandwich Picker, lines 188-191]

```
function removeButton() {
    if (extraButton.parentNode)
            extraButton.parentNode.removeChild(extraButton);
}
```

First I check if extraButton is in the document. (Why? See 8K.) Then I move to its parentNode and remove extraButton.

replaceChild()

The replaceChild() method allows you to replace one node by another. Just as with appendChild() and insertBefore(), if the inserted node is already present in the document, it is removed from its current position. The inserted and replaced nodes retain all their child nodes.

For instance:

```
var x = document.getElementsByTagName('h1')[0];
var y = document.getElementsByTagName('p')[1];
x.parentNode.replaceChild(x,y);
```

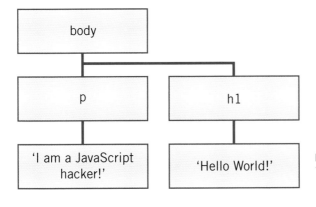

FIGURE 8.9
The second <p> has been replaced by the <h1>.

Now the `<h1>` moves to its new position, and the second `<p>` is removed from the document tree. Both take their child text nodes to their new positions.

The replaced node (y in the example) is now gone from the document, and unless you take precautions, you'll not be able to use it any more. We'll discuss this further in 8K and 8L.

Return value

`replaceChild()` returns a reference to the replaced node:

```
var x = y.replaceChild(z,a);
```

Now x contains a reference to a.

Example

I use `replaceChild()` only one single time in the example scripts, in Usable Forms's initialization function:

[Usable Forms, line 49]

```
hiddenFields[0].parentNode.replaceChild(newMarker,➥
hiddenFields[0]);
```

`hiddenFields[0]` is a `<tr>` that should be hidden. I replace it with `newMarker`, an empty marker `<tr>` (see 8L).

Removing all child nodes

Occasionally you want to wipe an element clean; you want to remove all of its child nodes before appending new ones. There are two simple ways of doing this:

```
while (x.childNodes[0])
    x.removeChild(x.childNodes[0]);
```

This simple `while()` loop continues to work as long as the element has a first child node (`childNodes[0]`). It removes this first child node, and, as we'll see in 8I, the `childNodes[]` nodeList is immediately updated. Therefore the second child node becomes the first one, and the process is repeated until x has no more child nodes. (Of course, you could also use `firstChild` instead of `childNodes[0]`.)

The other way is even simpler:

```
x.innerHTML = '';
```

Just set the innerHTML of the element to an empty string. We'll discuss this property further in 8F.

E: Creating and cloning elements

The W3C DOM allows you to create your own elements and text nodes, and add them to the document tree. In theory, you could remove all elements from the tree, create new ones, and repopulate the tree, thus changing the page completely. In practice, this feature is used in a somewhat more restrained way.

The DOM also allows you to clone existing elements, so that you can easily duplicate a certain feature and spread copies through your document.

createElement() and createTextNode()

The `createElement()` method and the `createTextNode()` do just what their names say they will:

```
var x = document.createElement('p');
var y = document.createTextNode('This is a created element');
```

x refers to the newly created <p> element, while y refers to the newly created text node. These nodes aren't inserted in the document yet. You would now use `appendChild()` or `insertBefore()` to add them to the document tree. For instance:

```
x.appendChild(y);
document.body.appendChild(x);
```

This appends the text node to the <p>, and the <p> to the document. Now the document has one extra <p> tag as its last child.

> **CREATEELEMENT('OPTION'): DON'T USE**
>
> Don't try to create option elements through `createElement()`, because Explorer doesn't support it. See 8J for the safe way to add options to a document.

Usually you create an element and insert it into the document immediately. But you can also create elements and keep them around for future use. I do this with the `extraButton` in Sandwich Picker that we already saw in the `appendChild()` and `removeChild()` examples.

Right at the start, before I even run my initialization function, I create a few elements I'll need in the rest of the script:

[Sandwich Picker, lines 4-12, condensed]

```
if (W3CDOM) {
    // create more elements
        var extraButton = document.createElement('button');
    extraButton.className = 'extraButton';
    extraButton.appendChild(document.➡
    createTextNode('Collect all orders'));
    extraButton.onclick = moveAllToOrderTable;
}
```

> **WHY CREATE THE BUTTON BEFORE INITIALIZATION?**
>
> Frankly I can't remember why I created this button before the official script initialization. These are real-world example scripts, so occasionally they contain real-world oddities.

If the W3C DOM is supported, the script creates a `<button>` element, gives it a class name for CSS purposes, appends a text node so that the user understands what the button does, and adds an onclick event handler that calls the right function.

The extra button is now ready for use, but I want it to appear only when the user orders a sandwich by entering an amount in a form field; at that moment I use `appendChild()` to actually add the button to the document. Until then it's quietly waiting in the DOM hyperspace we'll discuss in 8K; it may not ever be used.

createTextNode() and HTML entities

There's one problem with `createTextNode()`: it cannot create HTML entities like `&copy;` or `&#8212;`. Instead of the symbol you need, it creates the literal text:

```
var x = document.createTextNode('&copy; Copyrights reserved');
document.getElementById('test').appendChild(x);
```

FIGURE 8.10
createTextNode() cannot
create HTML entities.

Use `innerHTML` instead:

```
document.getElementById('test').innerHTML = ➡
'&copy; Copyrights reserved';
```

FIGURE 8.11
Solution: use innerHTML.

8E

cloneNode()

The cloneNode() method clones a node; that is, it makes a near-exact copy of the node, which you can subsequently insert in the document tree. For instance:

```
var x = document.getElementsByTagName('h1')[0];
var y = x.cloneNode(true);
document.body.appendChild(y);
```

I take the first <h1> in the document and clone it. Then I append the clone to the <body>.

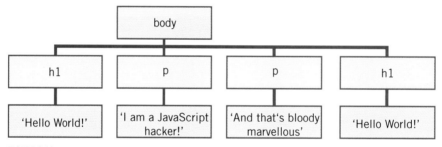

FIGURE 8.12   The last element on the page is a clone of the <h1>.

cloneNode() has a couple of features you must know about in order to use it properly:

- cloneNode() expects an argument true or false. true means "Clone the element and all its child nodes." false means "Clone the element but not its child nodes." In practice, you always use true; I have never yet encountered a situation in which you want to clone a node but not its children.

- cloneNode() does not clone event handlers. This is extremely annoying, but it's how the method was specified. (Why? I have no idea.) So every time you clone a node with event handlers, you have to redefine them on the clone.

Sandwich Picker contains a useful example of all this. Every sandwich should have its own Order and Trash buttons, and of course these dozens of buttons are exactly the same. This is a typical job for cloneNode()!

[Sandwich Picker, lines 21-28]

```
var trashLink = document.createElement('a');
trashLink.href = '#';
trashLink.innerHTML = 'trash ';
trashLink.className = 'trash';
var orderLink = document.createElement('a');
orderLink.href = '#';
orderLink.innerHTML = 'order ';
orderLink.className = 'order';
```

At the start of the initialization function, I create one trashLink and one orderLink as template nodes. Note that I use innerHTML to create the link texts: I need a   for CSS reasons, and createTextNode() doesn't allow me to insert it.

Later, when I go through all <tr>s in the order table, I clone these two templates, add the correct event handlers, and insert them into the document.

[Sandwich Picker, lines 47-52]

```
var extraLink = trashLink.cloneNode(true);
extraLink.onclick = removeSandwich;
var extraLink2 = orderLink.cloneNode(true);
extraLink2.onclick = moveToOrderTable;
searchField.parentNode.appendChild(extraLink2);
searchField.parentNode.appendChild(extraLink);
```

Every sandwich <tr> has a searchField form field. Since the buttons should appear underneath this form field, I append them to searchField.parentNode: the <td>.

Note that I assign the event handlers only after the buttons have been cloned. They would not survive the cloning process.

8E

Creating tables and form fields

Creating tables and form fields in the W3C DOM is tricky if you don't know the ins and outs.

Use <tbody>

Generating table elements like <td> or <tr> works, as long as you use a <tbody>, eschew the specialized DOM table methods, and don't use innerHTML too frequently.

Some browsers (Explorer, at the time of writing) require you to append your <tr>s to a <tbody>. If you append the <tr>s directly to the <table>, they simply don't show up.

Sandwich Picker constantly moves <tr>s to other tables. For instance:

[Sandwich Picker, lines 86-89, condensed]

```
var node = [tr that should move to search results];
document.getElementById('searchResults').appendChild(node);
```

I added the ID 'searchResults' not to the <table> tag, but to the <tbody> tag:

```
<table class="search" id="searchTable">
    <tr>
            <td colspan="4" class="searchFieldContainer">
                <h4>Search for sandwiches</h4>
            <input id="searchField"></td>
    </tr>
    <tbody id="searchResults">
    </tbody>
</table>
```

Now all <tr>s are appended to the <tbody>, and the script works smoothly in all browsers.

{ **NO CELLINDEX IN SAFARI**

At the time of writing, `cellIndex` is buggy in Safari 2.0; it always returns 0. }

W3C DOM table methods and properties

The W3C DOM defines quite a few methods and properties for working with tables. Unfortunately, they suffer from a few browser-incompatibility problems, and even if they work perfectly they're far slower than traditional `createElement()`/ `appendChild()` scripts. I advise you not to use most of these methods and properties.

The `rowIndex` and `cellIndex` properties may come in useful in some situations. They give the index number of a row in its table (`rowIndex`) or a cell in its row (`cellIndex`). There's also `sectionRowIndex`, which gives the index number of a row in its table section (thead, tbody, or tfoot).

innerHTML

`innerHTML` is badly supported for table elements other than <td>s. At the time of writing, it's not possible to set the `innerHTML` of the tbody, thead, or tfoot in Explorer or Safari.

Form fields in Explorer

Generating form fields is hard in Explorer. In theory, it seems simple:

```
var newField = document.createElement('input');
newField.type = 'checkbox';
newField.name = 'My name';
newField.value = 'My value';
document.getElementById('theForm').appendChild(field);
```

8E

Unfortunately, this code gives errors in Explorer, because the browser cannot handle the `newField.type`. If we use `setAttribute()`, the error message disappears:

```
newField.setAttribute('type','checkbox');
```

Another problem is that generated radio buttons don't work well in Explorer. Although it's possible to generate them through "pure" W3C DOM methods, the browser makes a mess of the `name` attributes of the radio buttons. Therefore, the generated radio buttons will likely not work as you expect them to.

{
HOW RADIO BUTTONS WORK

Remember: the user is allowed to check only one radio button in a group, and a group is defined as all radio buttons that share a `name` attribute. If the `name` attribute doesn't work correctly, the radio buttons won't work, either.
}

Switching to innerHTML offers a solution:

```
var newField = '<input type="radio" ➡
name="radioGroup" value="first" />';
newField += '<input type="radio" name= ➡
"radioGroup" value="second" />';
document.getElementById('theForm').innerHTML += newField;
```

Now the radio buttons work as expected.

F: innerHTML

In the previous section, I used the `innerHTML` property for certain jobs, but it's time to discuss it more formally. Even though officially it's a Microsoft proprietary property, it is supported by all modern browsers, and is a required item in the bag of tricks any JavaScripter should carry.

{ INNERHTML AND THE SPECS

`innerHTML` is not a part of the W3C DOM specification. For some people, that's reason enough not to use it. Personally, I disagree sharply: as we'll see in this section and the next, `innerHTML` is excellently suited for some tasks, and it has perfect browser compatibility.

You'll have to decide this for yourself, but I don't see any good reasons for refusing to use `innerHTML`. Instead, we should try to find out in which situations `innerHTML` will work better than pure DOM methods, and in which situations the pure methods will have the advantage. }

innerHTML gives the HTML content of an element as a string, and it also allows you to write new HTML content into an element. Take this example:

```
<p id="test">This is a <strong>bold</strong> bit of text.</p>
var x = document.getElementById('test');
alert(x.innerHTML);
```

Now the alert faithfully says 'This is a bold bit of text.'

You can also italicize the text:

```
x.innerHTML = 'This is an <em>emphasized</em> bit of text.';
```

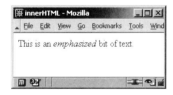

FIGURE 8.13
Setting the innerHTML immediately changes the document
tree, too.

Garbage in, garbage out

Since innerHTML is so powerful, you should take care to always pass it correct HTML. Garbage HTML can cause very weird effects. Take this example:

```
x.innerHTML = 'This is <em>badly <strong>nested</em> HTML.';
alert(x.innerHTML);
```

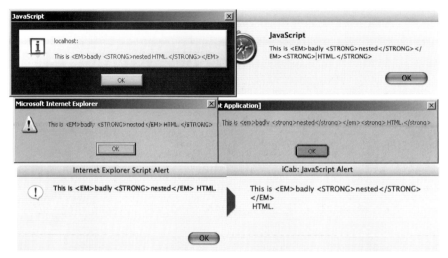

FIGURE 8.14 Browsers disagree sharply on the interpretation of the malformed HTML.

The browsers must solve the problem of the missing `</strong>` tag somehow. Each finds its own solution, and likely none of these solutions are what you want. Obviously, you should avoid this by making sure you always pass correct HTML to the `innerHTML` property.

Speed

`innerHTML` is noticeably faster than pure DOM methods in the current browsers. When you append one or two children to an element, the speed difference isn't really important; the user hardly distinguishes between, say, a 7- and a 12-millisecond delay. However, once you start creating complicated structures such as tables, using `innerHTML` instead of `createElement()/appendChild()` is a noticeable improvement.

The speed difference between `innerHTML` and pure DOM methods goes from three times as fast (Mozilla, Opera) to thirty times as fast (Explorer).

Examples

I don't often use innerHTML in the example scripts. None of them appends large
structures to the document tree, and that's where innerHTML is most useful.
Nonetheless, let's review two examples where I do use innerHTML.

In Site Survey, I want to show a text that warns the user that a popup is about
to appear. I wrote a standard message, but of course any site owner should be
able to change that message. Therefore, I put it in a global variable at the top
of my script, and later use innerHTML to add the message to the page:

[Site Survey/survey.js, lines 6 and 52]

```
var ST_pageText = 'At the moment we\'re conducting a survey about
the use of our site. For this reason a <strong>popup</strong> will
be opened shortly.'
// during initialization
text.innerHTML = ST_pageText;
```

If the site owner wishes to add a bit of HTML to the message, he should be
free to do so, and not be bothered having to write lots of extra appendChild()
lines.

I also use innerHTML in Textarea Maxlength to add the counter to the page:

[Textarea Maxlength, line 13]

```
counterClone.innerHTML = '<span>0</span>/'+textareas[i].➡
getAttribute('maxlength');
```

8F

This is a clear example of innerHTML's simplicity and power. If I'd restricted myself to pure W3C DOM methods, I'd have to do this:

```
var newSpan = document.createElement('span');
newSpan.appendChild(document.createTextNode('0'));
counterClone.appendChild(newSpan);
counterClone.appendChild(document. ➡
createTextNode('/'+x[i].getAttribute('maxlength')));
```

Not impossible, but the first example is more concise and easier to understand.

innerHTML and pure DOM cooperation

innerHTML and pure DOM methods cooperate perfectly; any changes you make by means of the one are immediately available to the other.

Textarea Maxlength shows that any change to the innerHTML of an element is immediately available as part of the document tree:

[Textarea Maxlength, lines 13-15, condensed]

```
counterClone.innerHTML = '<span>0</span>/'+ ➡
textareas[i].getAttribute('maxlength');
textareas[i].relatedElement = counterClone. ➡
getElementsByTagName('span')[0];
```

First, I set the counterClone's innerHTML. Two lines later, I enter counterClone by the pure DOM getElementsByTagName() method to find the <span> element. This works fine; the browsers understand that counterClone now contains a <span>, and they make it available to normal DOM methods.

The reverse also works fine. Suppose the element with ID="test" is empty:

```
var x = document.getElementById('test');
x.appendChild(document.createTextNode('Test text'));
alert(x.innerHTML);
```

Now the alert shows 'Test text'.

outerHTML, innerText, outerText

Together with innerHTML, Microsoft created three other properties: outerHTML, innerText, and outerText. outerHTML works as innerHTML, but also shows the outer tag of which it is a property. innerText and outerText show the text (non-HTML) contained in the tag (and no, I don't have the faintest idea how outerText should differ from innerText).

Take this code example:

```
<p id="test">This is a <em>test</em> text.</p>
var x = document.getElementById('test');
alert(x.innerHTML);
alert(x.outerHTML);
alert(x.innerText);
alert(x.outerText);
```

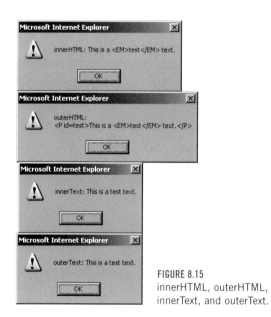

FIGURE 8.15
innerHTML, outerHTML,
innerText, and outerText.

> { **INNERTEXT AND TEXTCONTENT**
>
> Occasionally it's useful to treat `innerText` as a way of reading or writing texts without going to the trouble of creating text nodes. In that case, you also need the `textContent` property, which is the W3C DOM equivalent of `innerText`.
>
> ```
> element.innerText = element.textContent = 'The new text.';
> ```
> }

These three properties are rarely used in practical Web development, partly because Mozilla doesn't support them, but mostly because the information they offer isn't very useful.

innerHTML vs. DOM

So when do you use `innerHTML`, and when do you use the pure DOM? In the end, this depends on your personal coding style, and it's hard to give general rules. Nonetheless, there are some advantages to using `innerHTML` for the creation of large amounts of HTML.

The power of `innerHTML` lies in the ease with which you can create complicated tree structures with just one line of code. None of the example scripts contains a case in which I have to add really huge swaths of HTML to the document, so here's a contrived example of adding a slightly more complicated structure than the ones we've seen until now:

```
var x = document.getElementById('writeroot');
x.innerHTML = '<ul><li>First option</li>➥
<li>Second option</li></ul>';
```

Compare this to the following script that uses pure DOM methods:

```
var x = document.getElementById('writeroot');
var y = document.createElement('ul');
var z = document.createElement('li');
z.appendChild(document.createTextNode('First option'));
```

```
y.appendChild(z);
var a = document.createElement('li');
a.appendChild(document.createTextNode('Second option'));
y.appendChild(a);
x.appendChild(y);
```

This is rather more cumbersome, especially when you want to add a static structure.

When you work with dynamic structures, however, DOM methods become more interesting. Suppose you have an array with an unknown number of message texts. All of these texts should be shown in their own <li>s.

This is the innerHTML version:

```
var x = document.getElementById('writeroot');
var msg = [array with messages];
var writeString = '<ul>';
for (var i=0;i<msg.length;i++) {
    writeString += '<li>' + msg[i] + '</li>';
}
writeString += '</ul>';
x.innerHTML = writeString;
```

This is the pure DOM version:

```
var x = document.getElementById('writeroot');
var msg = [array with messages];
var root = document.createElement('ul');
for (var i=0;i<msg.length;i++) {
    var newLI = document.createElement('li');
    var newMsg = document.createTextNode(msg[i]);
    newLI.appendChild(newMsg);
    root.appendChild(newLI);
}
x.appendChild(root);
```

The innerHTML version is still shorter than the pure DOM version, although the difference is not nearly as large as in the first example.

8F

Now let's make this example a bit more complicated. There's also an array that contains the class names the `<li>`s should get. With `innerHTML` we get this:

```
var x = document.getElementById('writeroot');
var msg = [array with messages];
var classes = [array with class names];
var writeString = '<ul>';
for (var i=0;i<msg.length;i++) {
    writeString += '<li class="' + classes[i] ➡
+ '">' + msg[i] + '</li>';
}
writeString += '</ul>';
x.innerHTML = writeString;
```

With pure DOM methods we get this:

```
var x = document.getElementById('writeroot');
var msg = [array with messages];
var classes = [array with class names];
var root = document.createElement('ul');
for (var i=0;i<msg.length;i++) {
    var newLI = document.createElement('li');
    newLI.className = classes[i];
    var newMsg = document.createTextNode(msg[i]);
    newLI.appendChild(newMsg);
    root.appendChild(newLI);
}
x.appendChild(root);
```

For me personally, this is about the breaking point at which pure DOM methods become more attractive than `innerHTML`. I find the following line becoming unreadable, and it's getting easier and easier to make mistakes in the quotes and brackets:

```
writeString += '<li class="' + classes[i] + ➡
'">' + msg[i] + '</li>';
```

Some of you will have started using pure DOM methods much earlier, while others will feel `innerHTML` is still the easier option. There is no simple right or wrong here; you should try to find your personal border between these two ways of working.

G: Attributes

Attributes are a bit odd. Although officially they're nodes, they are not fully-fledged parts of the document tree and do not appear in, for instance, the `childNodes[]` list of their parent node. Furthermore, many common HTML attributes, like the `src` of an `<img>` or the `href` of an `<a>`, are also JavaScript properties, which means you don't need the W3C DOM attribute methods to read or change them. Finally, the handling of attributes is the area of the W3C DOM that contains most browser incompatibilities, and only about 20% of this part of the specification actually works correctly in all browsers.

Attributes are always name/value pairs. Take a well-known attribute:

```
<img src="pix/theImage.gif" />
```

The name of the attribute is src, and its value is "pix/theImage.gif". Unsurprisingly, all attributes have a `name` and a `value` property that give the name and value of the attribute.

8G

> **{** **ATTRIBUTES, PROPERTIES, AND BROWSER COMPATIBILITY**
>
> I do not treat any W3C DOM attribute method or property except for `getAttribute()` and `setAttribute()`, because most of them are subject to one browser bug or another (and therefore useless). You can study the W3C DOM browser-compatibility tables at www.quirksmode.org. **}**

Getting and setting attributes

The W3C DOM has two more or less reliable attribute methods: getAttribute()
and setAttribute(). The first one is used often, the second rather less.

getAttribute() requires an attribute name and returns the value of that
attribute. setAttribute() requires an attribute name and value, and sets that
attribute to the new value. Take this example.

```
<img src="http://www.quirksmode.org/pix/logo.gif" id="test" />
var imgEl = document.getElementById('test');
alert(imgEl.getAttribute('src'));
imgEl.setAttribute('src',➥
'http://www.quirksmode.org/pix/logo2.gif');
```

You access the <img> and ask for its src attribute. The browser returns the
value of this attribute, and therefore the alert says 'http://www.quirksmode.
org/pix/logo.gif'. Then you set the src attribute to a new value, and the image
changes.

If an attribute does not exist, getAttribute() returns null.

Custom attributes

getAttribute() and setAttribute() work on any attribute an HTML tag contains, even custom ones, i.e., attributes that are not officially a part of any
(X)HTML specification. I take advantage of this fact in Textarea Maxlength,
Usable Forms, and Form Validation. All three scripts require the HTML coder to
use custom attributes to give the script instructions. We already discussed the
use and dangers of custom attributes in 4B. In this chapter it's enough to say
that any HTML attribute is available through getAttribute().

Limitations

WARNING   Browser incompatibilities ahead

Unfortunately, these methods have a few problems in Explorer 6 and earlier.
Many HTML tags have special attributes to store their inline styles (style) and

their event handlers (onclick, onkeydown, etc.). In Explorer, these attributes cannot be read or set through getAttribute() and setAttribute(); in fact, weird bugs may occur if you try it.

The solution is to use the JavaScript properties style, onclick, onkeydown, etc. to read or set these attributes. In order to completely understand this, we first have to discuss the subtle difference between HTML attributes and JavaScript properties.

HTML attributes and JavaScript properties

Although superficially they might seem the same, and there is in fact considerable overlap, HTML attributes are not always equal to JavaScript properties.

Let's dissect a few lines from Sandwich Picker. Each <tr>in the document contain one sandwich. I need to know the price of this sandwich to calculate the total price when the user orders it. Because the purpose of the script is to change the placement of these <tr>s in the document, I want to attach the price of a sandwich to its <tr>. In that way, the price always remains easily available, wherever the <tr> may happen to be at a certain time.

FIGURE 8.16
All sandwiches below this header are priced at 2,00.

Sandwich prices are located in the header <tr>s of the third table. I put them in a custom attribute in the HTML. Note that this is an HTML attribute; it's hard-coded in the page's HTML.

```
<tr price="2.00">
    <th colspan="5" class="header">&euro; 2,00</th>
</tr>
```

> {
> **BROWSER INCOMPATIBILITIES**
>
> Some browsers (Explorer and Safari at the time of writing) equate HTML attributes and JavaScript properties, and allow you to use `x[i].price` and `x[i].getAttribute('price')` indiscriminately.
>
> Other browsers see HTML attributes and JavaScript properties as different things. To keep your scripts cross-browser compatible, it's best to treat attributes and properties as distinct entities.
> }

When the script encounters the `price` attribute, it sets this price to all following sandwiches, until it encounters a new `price` attribute.

[Sandwich Picker, lines 34-40, condensed]

```
if (containers[i].getAttribute('price'))
    currentPrice = containers[i].getAttribute('price');
containers[i].price = currentPrice;
```

The first two lines read the HTML custom *attribute* `price` and then set `currentPrice` to its value. The third line sets the JavaScript `price` *property* of the `<tr>` to the value of `currentPrice`.

Even though they share a name, the HTML custom attribute and the JavaScript property are different things. The HTML attribute is located in the document tree as an attribute node of the `<tr>`, while the JavaScript property belongs to the object that represents the `<tr>` and is not present in the document tree.

This is the general rule. There are, however, numerous exceptions.

Attribute/property mappings

Before W3C specified the DOM, JavaScript needed a way to access a few important HTML attributes, like the `value` of a form field or the `src` of an image. In order to do this without the as-yet-unspecified `getAttribute()` method, JavaScript's inventors decided to map certain properties of JavaScript objects to HTML attributes.

For instance, all image objects would have a JavaScript `src` property that was equal to the HTML `src` attribute. Therefore these two lines are the same, though only the second one works in older browsers:

```
imgEl.setAttribute('src',➡
'http://www.quirksmode.org/pix/logo2.gif');
imgEl.src = 'http://www.quirksmode.org/pix/logo2.gif';
```

It's important to note that this is *not* a general rule, but that the browser vendors have hand-picked certain important attributes and created JavaScript properties to match them. These attribute/property mappings are most often found in the areas that have been open to scripting influences since the beginning: form fields, links, and images.

Later on, the `style` attribute that holds all inline styles of an element, as well as all event handlers (like `onclick` and `onkeydown`), were added to this list of special attributes/properties.

Although the W3C DOM now offers general and unrestricted access to all attributes, these special properties have never been removed from JavaScript, since that would mean that old scripts would stop working.

The best way of getting and setting attributes

With all this theoretical knowledge, we can discuss the best way of getting and setting attributes. I myself use these guidelines:

8G

- If there is an attribute/property mapping, I use it. This especially goes for `style` and event handlers, since Explorer cannot get or set them through the W3C DOM methods.
- If there is no attribute/property mapping, I use `getAttribute()` and `setAttribute()`.
- Under no circumstances do I use the `attributes[]` nodeList, which is supposed to contain all attributes but differs significantly per browser, or any other W3C DOM method. Their browser implementation is currently too buggy.

H: Text nodes

In general, text nodes are easy to work with. The W3C DOM defines a few methods for getting and changing texts, but the Core string methods and properties we discussed in 5F are more useful and versatile.

nodeValue

Many element nodes hold a text node:

```
<p id="test">I am a JavaScript hacker.</p>
```

Often you want to read or change the text in the text node. You generally do this through the nodeValue of the text node, which is usually the firstChild of an element node:

```
var x = document.getElementById('test');
alert(x.firstChild.nodeValue);
x.firstChild.nodeValue = 'I never hack text nodes.';
```

You access the correct element node, move to its first child (the text node), and then access its nodeValue. The alert shows the text 'I am a JavaScript hacker.' The third line assigns a new value to the text node, and of course this change is immediately visible in the browser.

The x.firstChild works only if the text node is actually the first child of the element. If that's not the case, accessing the text node is somewhat harder:

```
<p id="test"><br />I am a JavaScript hacker.</p>
```

> **DATA METHODS**
>
> See the W3C DOM compatibility tables at www.quirksmode.org for the W3C DOM data methods. In general, the Core string methods are better suited to working with text nodes.

Now `x.firstChild` is the `<br />` element node, which doesn't have a `node-Value`. You have to access the text node as `x.lastChild` or `x.childNodes[1]`.

Fortunately, this is a rare case; most common text containers like `<p>`, `<li>`, or `<a>` contain exactly one node: a text node.

Empty text nodes

Normal text nodes are easy to work with. Unfortunately, there are also empty text nodes. They are by far the most useless and annoying feature of the W3C DOM, but you'll encounter them in every HTML document you work with.

Consider this HTML snippet:

```
<body>
<h1>Hello world!</h1>
<p>I am a JavaScript hacker!</p>
</body>
```

How many child nodes does the `<body>` have? Two, right? The `<h1>` and the `<p>`?

Wrong.

The `<body>` has five child nodes. Two of them are element nodes, the other three are empty text nodes. There is text between the tags: a hard return between the `<body>` and the `<h1>`, between the `</h1>` and the `<p>`, and between the `</p>` and the `</body>`. Since spaces, hard returns, and tabs are text content, the W3C DOM creates text nodes to hold them.

{
NO EMPTY TEXT NODES IN EXPLORER

Explorer Windows does not support empty text nodes. This is an excellent idea, but unfortunately all other browsers disagree, and thus incompatibilities are born.
}

> {
> **EMPTY TEXT NODES ARE NOT EMPTY**
>
> Empty text nodes are not really empty; they contain whitespace characters. Nonetheless, they are useless in an HTML document, since HTML interprets a sequence of whitespace characters as either a space or a hard return—whichever suits the document best.
>
> As far as their practical usefulness goes, these text nodes might as well be empty.
> }

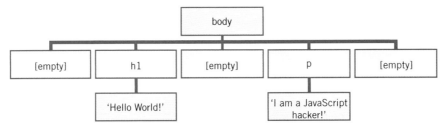

FIGURE 8.17 DOM tree with empty text nodes.

I purposely omitted empty text nodes from the DOM overview in 8A because they would have made my explanations too complicated and dense. In fact, they make working with the DOM complicated and dense, too.

For instance, take this script:

```
var x = document.getElementsByTagName('p')[0];
x.parentNode.insertBefore(x,x.previousSibling);
```

This seems simple, right? Take the paragraph and insert it before its previous sibling: the <h1>. It works fine in Explorer.

Unfortunately, in all the other browsers, the <p>'s previous sibling is not the <h1> but the empty text node between the </h1> and the <p>. The DOM tree changes, but not the way you'd like it to change.

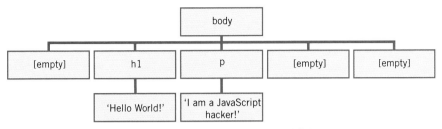

FIGURE 8.18   The DOM tree has changed, but the change is invisible.

One way to remove these incompatibilities is to turn all empty text nodes off. This could be done by removing all whitespace from your HTML:

```
<body><h1>Hello world!</h1><p>I am a JavaScript hacker!</p></body>
```

Now the <body> really has only two child nodes. Nonetheless, working in HTML files without any whitespace becomes annoying in a hurry.

Living with empty text nodes

Therefore, effectively empty text nodes are here to stay, and we have to learn to live with them. Their first victims are the previousSibling and nextSibling properties, which are rather useless since they usually refer to empty text nodes. The same happens to childNodes[]. This nodeList, too, is riddled with empty text nodes and therefore rarely used.

Let's try to get the previousSibling in the last code example to work. We want to insert the <p> before the <h1>. We already saw that this works in Explorer, but not in the other browsers:

```
var x = document.getElementsByTagName('p')[0];
x.parentNode.insertBefore(x,x.previousSibling);
```

Similarly, this works in the other browsers but not in Explorer:

```
var x = document.getElementsByTagName('p')[0];
x.parentNode.insertBefore(x,x.previousSibling.previousSibling);
```

The following has a better chance to work across the board:

```
var x = document.getElementsByTagName('p')[0];
var previousElement = x.previousSibling;
while (previousElement.nodeType == 3)
    previousElement = previousElement.previousSibling
x.parentNode.insertBefore(x,x.previousElement);
```

We take the element's `previousSibling`. If this turns out to be a text node, we take the previous sibling of the `previousSibling`, and we continue this check until we encounter a non-text node.

There's a hidden assumption here: the parent node of the `<p>` (the `<body>` here, but it might be another node in other situations) never contains real text nodes that actually contain text. If you're absolutely certain that this is the case, the last example will work. But as soon as any Web developer or CMS accidentally adds a real text node as a sibling of the `<p>`, the script will misfire.

By far the safest solution is not to use `previousSibling` at all:

```
var x = document.getElementsByTagName('p')[0];
var y = document.getElementsByTagName('h1')[0];
x.parentNode.insertBefore(x,y);
```

This makes sure that your script always uses the correct elements, regardless of empty text nodes.

In fact, the best defense against empty text nodes is to not use `previousSibling`, `nextSibling`, and `childNodes[]`. In the eight example scripts, I use `nextSibling` only twice (and `previousSibling` and `childNodes[]` not at all). In both cases I use `nextSibling` when I add a new element to the document, and it doesn't really matter whether it's inserted before an empty text node or not. In cases where I have to change the order of elements that are already in the document, I always search for all relevant elements through `getElementsByTagName()`.

> ## CONSTRUCTED DOM TREES
>
> The only situation in which properties like `nextSibling` are useful is when you construct a document tree, or a portion of one, entirely in JavaScript. Then it contains no empty text nodes, and all properties work as you expect them to work.

I: nodeLists

Some W3C DOM methods and properties return nodeLists: lists of all nodes that meet a certain criterion. Of these, `getElementsByTagName()` is by far the most important. It returns a nodeList that contains all elements that have a certain tag name. Let's take a close look at nodeLists and their dangers.

Superficially, nodeLists look like arrays. They accept an index number between square brackets, and return the node with that index number. For instance:

```
var x = document.getElementsByTagName('p')[1];
```

`x` is the second paragraph (with index 1) in the document.

> ## ITEM() NOT NECESSARY
>
> All nodeLists also have an `item()` method. It requires an index number, and returns the node with that index number. These two calls do exactly the same thing:
>
> var fourthP = x[3];
>
> var fourthP = x.item(3);
>
> `item()` is meant for other languages in which nodeLists don't behave as arrays. In JavaScript you never need it.

All nodeLists also have a `length` property that gives the length of the nodeList:

```
var x = document.getElementsByTagName('p').length;
```

`x` is the number of paragraphs in the document.

These two features combined mean that we often use nodeLists as arrays:

```
var x = document.getElementsByTagName('p');
for (var i=0;i<x.length;i++) {
    // do something with each paragraph
}
```

In 5L I said that nodeLists can be seen as read-only arrays. The time has come to amend that definition somewhat. It's true that you cannot directly add or remove elements to or from a nodeList. For example, if I run the following script, nothing happens, not even an error message:

❌ `x[1] = 'Test!';`

But nodeLists are not static. In fact, they're dangerously dynamic, because they immediately reflect all changes in the document. For instance, take this code:

```
var x = document.getElementsByTagName('p');
alert(x.length);
var par = document.createElement('p');
document.body.appendChild(par);
alert(x.length);
```

This creates a nodeList that holds all paragraphs in the document and alerts its `length`. Then another paragraph is added to the document, and again the script alerts the `length` of the nodeList. The nodeList has now increased by one because there's one more paragraph in the document. The nodeList is updated automatically, and doesn't require a new `getElementsByTagName()` call to see the changes.

The danger

To explain why this is dangerous, let's take another look at Usable Forms. When the script starts up, it has to go through all <tr> (or <div>) tags in the document and move those elements with a rel attribute to the waiting room. Superficially, this seems simple:

[Usable Forms, lines 1, 11, and 25-34 condensed and changed]

```
var containerTag = 'TR';
var waitingRoom = document.createElement('div');
var containers = document.getElementsByTagName(containerTag);
for (var i=0;i<containers.length;i++) {
    if (containers[i].getAttribute('rel'))          {
            // do some administration
            waitingRoom.appendChild(containers[i]);
    }
}
```

Note that the waiting room is not a part of the document. Say that the second <tr> in the document is the first one with a rel attribute. When the script reaches the second <tr> (with index 1), it sends it to the waiting room, i.e., outside the document. Then it moves on to index 2 and checks again.

The problem is that the nodeList immediately updates and therefore the index numbering of the <tr>s has changed! We removed the second <tr> (x[1]), but this means that the former third <tr> (x[2]) has now become the second one (x[1]). Since the script moves on to index 2, it never checks this <tr>, and continues with the former fourth <tr> (which was x[3], and is now x[2]).

That's why nodeLists are so dangerously dynamic. While looping through all elements of a nodeList, you should *never* add or remove these elements to or from the document, or even move them, because doing so messes up your for() loops and results in very odd bugs.

18

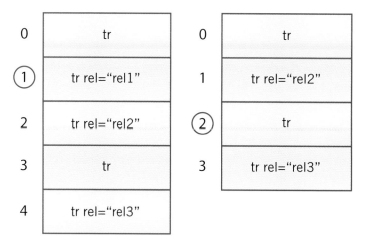

FIGURE 8.19   The former third `<tr>`, which has a `rel` attribute, never gets checked.

Helper arrays

Helper arrays are a good and easy solution to the nodeList problem we just discussed. I always use them if I have to go through a nodeList and remove certain of its elements. The principle is simple: if a certain element should be removed, I add it to the helper array. When the `for()` loop through the nodeList has ended, I start up a new loop to go through this array and remove the `<tr>`s from the document.

When working with the helper array, I always use `push()` and `shift()`, the two array methods that I promised an example of in 5L. In addition, it's useful to note that the helper array does not have to survive the second loop: by the end, it has done its duty.

[Usable Forms, lines 25-51, condensed]

```
var containers = document.getElementsByTagName(containerTag);
var hiddenFields = new Array;
for (var i=0;i<containers.length;i++) {
    if (containers[i].getAttribute('rel')) {
        // more stuff
        hiddenFields.push(containers[i]);
```

```
        }
    }
    while (hiddenFields.length) {
        // administration, including the creation of newMarker
        hiddenFields[0].parentNode.➡
        replaceChild(newMarker,hiddenFields[0]);
        waitingRoom.appendChild(hiddenFields.shift());
    }
```

The script goes through all <tr>s and, if one has a rel attribute, pushes it into the helper array hiddenFields. When it has looped through the entire nodeList, hiddenFields contains pointers to all <tr>s that should be removed.

Then the script starts up a while() loop that sees if the array still has a length, i.e., if it still contains elements. Each loop works on hiddenFields[0], i.e., the first array element that's still available.

After some administration, the script replaces the <tr> with a marker (see 8L) and then appends it to the waitingRoom. This causes it to be removed from the document, but it doesn't disappear from hiddenFields. hiddenFields, after all, is a real array, not a nodeList, and is therefore not updated automatically.

That's why the script uses shift() in the last line: this method returns the first element in an array and simultaneously removes it from the array. Therefore the <tr> is removed from the array, and this causes the next element to become hiddenFields[0], and the loop is repeated until hiddenFields doesn't contain any more elements (i.e., its length is 0).

J: Forms and the Level 0 DOM

Until now, we've discussed the W3C Level 1 DOM. All browsers, however, also support the Level 0 DOM, which is part of the de facto Netscape 3 standard. This DOM is more limited than the W3C Level 1 DOM, and it has been almost completely superseded by the newer one, which is far more versatile and generalized. There's one exception: the Level 0 DOM remains better equipped for working with forms and form fields than the W3C DOM.

Level 0 DOM nodeLists

The Level 0 DOM also works with nodeLists, but they differ from Level 1 DOM nodeLists in four important respects:

- Level 0 DOM nodeLists are available only for a limited number of elements, most importantly form fields, images, and links.

- Level 0 DOM nodeLists allow you to search for an element by name or ID, in addition to the index numbers we already discussed in 8I.

- One Level 0 DOM nodeList, `options[]`, allows you to create and remove option elements. It is effectively a read/write array.

- The Level 0 DOM nodeList `elements[]` has no counterpart in the Level 1 DOM.

Take this HTML snippet:

```
<body>
<img src="someImg.gif" name="firstIMG" />
<img src="someOtherImg.gif" id="secondIMG" />
</body>
```

The Level 1 DOM allows us to access these images by `document.getElements ByTagName('img')`. The Level 0 DOM allows the same through the `document. images[]` nodeList. `document.images[0]` is the same as `document.getElements ByTagName('img')[0]`.

In addition, the Level 0 DOM allows `document.images['firstIMG']` and `document.images['secondIMG']`. It searches for the image with the given name or ID. That can occasionally be quite useful, especially if you have to find a specific image and are not sure of the exact document structure (because other scripts might have changed it, for instance). Just as Level 1 DOM nodeLists do, `document.images[]` reflects all changes in the document, so it presents the same dangers.

`document.images[]` is nothing more than a convenient alternative to `document. getElementsByTagName('img')`. The other common Level 0 DOM nodeLists are somewhat more than that.

{

DOCUMENT.FIRSTIMG

The Level 0 DOM even allows you to say `document.firstIMG`, i.e., to use the name of the image (or form field or whatever) as a property of `document`.

Even back in the Netscape 3 days I didn't like this syntax, because it obscures what you're doing. Take this: `document.income`. Is this an image, a form, a link, or what? Other JavaScript programmers who have to work with your scripts won't know right away, whereas `document.forms['income']` is totally clear to everyone.

Therefore, I advise you not to use this syntax.

}

First of all, there are `document.links[]` and `document.anchors[]`. These contain all `<a href>` and `<a name>` tags in your pages, respectively. In contrast, `document.getElementsByTagName('a')` contains both kinds of tags. Although I've never needed them, it's still remotely possible that these old nodeLists may come in useful in a few situations.

Form fields

`document.forms[]` is equivalent to `document.getElementsByTagName('form')`. Apart from being able to access forms by name or id, there is little difference between these two nodeLists.

Every form has an `elements[]` nodeList. This is the one Level 0 DOM nodeList we still use often, because it has no counterpart in the Level 1 DOM and is so useful we cannot do without it.

`document.forms[0].elements[]` contains all form fields in the first form in the document. The trick is that these form fields can have different tag names (input, select, or textarea), so there is no single `getElementsByTagName()` call that delivers us all of them. Of course you can use three calls for the three tag names, but even then you don't get the form fields in the order they appear in the document—something that can be important in, for instance, form validation.

Once you have accessed form fields, you usually want to read out their values.

Form field properties

Every kind of form field has its own quirks, but before we discuss these we'll take a look at five properties any form field possesses: `type`, `form`, `disabled`, `name`, and `value`.

The `type` property of a form field gives its type: text, hidden, textarea, checkbox, radio, select-one, select-multiple, file, submit, or reset. It is possible to change the `type` of a form field, but this does not work in all browsers, and is counter-indicated.

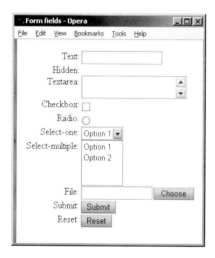

FIGURE 8.20
Form fields.

The `form` property of a form field refers to its parent form, and because the `<form>` tag is usually not the `parentNode` of a form field, this simple property can be quite useful, as we'll see when we discuss radio buttons.

The `disabled` property contains a boolean that says whether the form field is disabled (`true`) or not (`false`). You can set `disabled`, and this will disable the form field so that the user cannot change it. Note, however, that a disabled form field is not sent back to the server, even if it contains a value.

The last two properties are rather obvious: they give the name and the value of the form field.

```
<input name="test" value="This is a test value" />
```

This form field has name "test" and value "This is a test value". Of course the value is also the text contained in the form field, and if the user types a new text, the value changes. It is also possible to set the value:

```
document.forms[0].elements['test'].value = 'Changed value!';
```

The text in the form field is immediately updated. Changing the name of a form field is not possible in all browsers, and I advise against it.

text, hidden, and textarea

When you access a text field, hidden field, or textarea, you usually want to read out its value, which is contained in the value property.

checkboxes

Checkboxes have a value, too, but usually you want to know if the user has checked the box. This information can be found in the checked property, which gives a boolean true (checked) or false (not checked).

radios

Radios have a checked property, too, and it works the same as with checkboxes. Nonetheless, radios are slightly more complicated than checkboxes, because you usually need to go through an entire array of radio buttons and see which one of them is checked.

In order to work properly, all radio buttons that belong together should have the same name attribute. The Level 0 DOM conveniently creates a nodeList keyed to this name so that you can easily access a group of radio buttons.

Take this group:

```
<input type="radio" name="income" value="10" /> &euro; 10 or
lower<br />
<input type="radio" name="income" value="100" /> &euro; 11-100<br
/>
```

```
<input type="radio" name="income" value="1000" /> &euro; 101-
1000<br />
<input type="radio" name="income" value="10000" /> &euro; 1001-
10000<br />
```

They are accessible through this DOM call:

```
var radios = document.forms[0].elements['income'];
```

Now radios is a nodeList that contains all radio buttons with name="income" and you can loop through them to see if one of them is checked:

```
var radios = document.forms[0].elements['income'];
for (var i=0;i<radios.length;i++) {
    if (radios[i].checked)
            // do something
}
```

It's when you work with radio buttons that the form property of all form fields is very useful. Suppose you catch all click events on radio buttons and you want to go through all other radio buttons in the same group, just as we did above. Before you can do that, you have to gather the relevant radios:

```
function handleEvent(e) {
    if (!e) var e = window.event;
    var tg = e.target || e.srcElement;
    var allRadios = tg.form[tg.name];
    for (var i=0;i<allRadios.length;i++) {
            // do something with all radio buttons
    }
}
```

First we determine which radio button is the event target, as discussed in 7F. Then we take all radio buttons in the same group by going to the form property of the target, i.e., the form it's part of (tg.form), and taking the radio button nodeList (tg.form[]) that's keyed to the name of the target (tg.form[tg.name]).

selects and options

Remember that common select boxes have type 'select-one', not 'select'. This serves to distinguish them from multiple selects, which are never used.

Selects also have a `value` property, which takes the value of the selected option. Furthermore, they have a `selectedIndex` property that contains the number of the option the user has selected. Finally, they have an `options[]` nodeList that contains all options of the select.

`options[]` is a unique nodeList because you're allowed to add or remove elements, and these options are added to or removed from the visible select box. Therefore, `options[]` is *not* equal to `getElementsByTagName('option')`, which is a normal read-only Level 1 DOM nodeList.

In order to remove an option, simply set the correct element of the `options[]` nodeList to `null`:

```
var x = [a select box];
x.options[1] = null;
```

Now the second option is removed from the select box, and of course all other options move one step up to accommodate this change. Therefore, a new `x.options[1]` is immediately available: this is the old `x.options[2]`.

Adding an option is slightly more complicated. You must first create a new option object and add that to the `options[]` array:

```
var newOpt = new Option('text','value');
x.options[1] = newOpt;
```

Note that the new option requires two arguments: the text and the value. Once it's created, you insert it in the `options[]` array, and of course the old `x.options[1]` now becomes `x.options[2]`, etc.

File uploads

File-upload fields are protected by JavaScript security. No script is allowed to enter a value in a file upload, since that could lead to a serious security risk:

```
fileUploadField.value = '/my/password/file.txt';
fileUploadField.form.submit();
```

> ### NO CREATEELEMENT(), NO ADD()/REMOVE()
>
> Options should not be created by using `createElement()`, because Explorer doesn't support that. Explorer 5.0 even crashes when you try it.
>
> The W3C DOM defines two methods, `add()` and `remove()`, to add and remove options, but since they work differently in different browsers you should avoid them.

If this were allowed, malicious site owners could easily download your password files or other system-critical files. Therefore, the only thing you can do with a file upload is read out its `value`.

Submit and reset

Submit and reset buttons that are `<input>` tags also have a `value`, which represents the text that's on the button:

```
<input type="submit" value="Submit form" />
<input type="reset" value="Reset  form" />
```

`<button>` tags work differently: they contain a bit of text, and obviously this text is a separate text node as far as the W3C DOM is concerned. It is not accessible through the Level 0 DOM:

```
<button id="submit">Submit form</button>
```

Example script

This script from Form Validation determines whether the user has entered anything in a required form field:

[Form Validation, lines 15-32]

```
function isRequired(obj) {
    switch (obj.type) {
        case 'text':
        case 'textarea':
        case 'select-one':
            if (obj.value)
                return true;
            return false;
        case 'radio':
            var radios = obj.form[obj.name];
            for (var i=0;i<radios.length;i++) {
                if (radios[i].checked) return true;
            }
```

```
                         return false;
                 case 'checkbox':
                         return obj.checked;
         }
     }
```

The script uses a `switch()` statement (see 5H) that uses the `type` of the field to determine which bit of code should be executed. If the required field is a text field, textarea, or select box, it must have a `value`. If it doesn't, the script returns `false`: required field not filled out.

Required checkboxes should be checked, while one radio of a required group should be checked. For checkboxes, the script simply returns the `checked` property, since that's `true` or `false` anyway. For radios, it goes through all radios in the same group (`obj.form[obj.name]`), and if one of them is `checked` it returns `true`, otherwise `false`.

K: DOM hyperspace

Now that we've discussed the most important parts of the W3C DOM and the Level 0 DOM, it's time to look at a few related subjects. The first is what I call the "DOM hyperspace." It plays a vital role in Usable Forms.

Take this code:

```
<p id="test">I am a JavaScript hacker!</p>
var x = document.getElementById('test');
x.parentNode.removeChild(x);
```

The paragraph is removed from the document. But it's not gone. Where is it? I say that it floats in the DOM hyperspace. Since variable `x` still refers to it, it's still accessible. For instance, this works fine:

```
x.appendChild(document.➥
createTextNode(' I never hack text nodes.'));
document.body.appendChild(x);
```

The text node is appended to the paragraph, and the revised paragraph is reinserted into the document.

It's important to realize that the element remains available only as long as a pointer to it exists; in that respect it's similar to cross-window communication, as we discussed in 6B. If I wrote the following, the connection would be lost, and could not be re-established:

```
var x = document.getElementById('test');
x.parentNode.removeChild(x);
x = null;
x = document.getElementById('test');
```

The last line doesn't work, since the element with ID="test" cannot be found in the document. The element is lost forever.

Every new element you create starts in the DOM hyperspace:

```
var x = document.createElement('div');
// append more stuff to the div
document.body.appendChild(x);
```

The new <div> element is created in the hyperspace, more elements and text nodes are added to it, and only when it's ready do we insert it into the document.

Storing elements in hyperspace

It's possible to store large numbers of elements in hyperspace, and Usable Forms does so. Taking a closer look at this part of the script is instructive.

In 8I, we saw that the script first gathers pointers to the <tr>s that should be removed. After that's done, the script goes through the hiddenFields array and moves the <tr>s to the DOM hyperspace.

However, moving them to hyperspace is not enough. The <tr>s should remain available for reinsertion into the document, and as we just saw, that requires that a variable or an array element continues to point to the element so that it isn't lost.

8K

This part of Usable Forms takes care of that:

[Usable Forms, lines 14 and 41-51, condensed]

```
var hiddenFormFieldsPointers = new Object();
while (hiddenFields.length) {
    var rel = hiddenFields[0].getAttribute('rel');
    if (!hiddenFormFieldsPointers[rel])
            hiddenFormFieldsPointers[rel] = new Array();
    var relIndex = hiddenFormFieldsPointers[rel].length;
    hiddenFormFieldsPointers[rel][relIndex] = hiddenFields[0];
    // create newMarker (see section L)
    hiddenFields[0].parentNode.➡
replaceChild(newMarker,hiddenFields[0]);
    waitingRoom.appendChild(hiddenFields.shift());
}
```

The script creates an object—hiddenFormFieldPointers—that functions as an associative array (see 5K). As the name suggests, this associative array contains pointers to the <tr>s that aren't currently displayed (the ones that are floating in hyperspace.) In addition to providing a lookup table (see below), it also makes sure that pointers to all hidden form fields continue to exist, so that they're not lost.

hiddenFields[0] is the <tr> that's currently being removed from the document. The script takes the value of its rel attribute and checks if hiddenForm-FieldPointer already has a key with this value. If not, it creates this key and assigns an empty array as its value:

```
var rel = hiddenFields[0].getAttribute('rel');
if (!hiddenFormFieldsPointers[rel])
    hiddenFormFieldsPointers[rel] = new Array();
```

It's possible to have several <tr>s with the same value of the rel attribute; they should all be shown or hidden when the user selects the appropriate form fields. Therefore, the script has to find out how many `<tr>`s with this `rel` attribute are already in hyperspace. The array already points to all of them, so its `length` gives this number. I add a pointer to the `<tr>` as the last element of the array:

```
var relIndex = hiddenFormFieldsPointers[rel].length;
hiddenFormFieldsPointers[rel][relIndex] = hiddenFields[0];
```

Now I can safely remove it from the document and send it to hyperspace; a pointer exists, so it is not lost.

```
waitingRoom.appendChild(hiddenFields.shift());
```

When the time comes to reinsert form fields into the document, I use `hidden-FormFieldPointers` as a lookup table for quick and easy access to the relevant `<tr>`s. Suppose the user clicks on this checkbox:

```
<input type="checkbox" name="country_other" rel="othercountry">
```

Now the `<tr>`s with rel="othercountry" should be reinserted into the document. That's easy: `hiddenFormFieldsPointers['othercounty']` contains the correct `<tr>`s:

[Usable Forms, lines 121-136, condensed]

```
function intoMainForm(relation) {
    var Elements = hiddenFormFieldsPointers[relation];
    for (var i=0;i<Elements.length;i++) {
        // find insert point
    insertPoint.parentNode.insertBefore(Elements[i],insertPoint);
    }
}
```

This script uses the `rel` value as a key to `hiddenFormFieldsPointers`, and finds an array. It goes through this array and reinserts all the `<tr>`s in the page. (We'll get back to finding the insert point in 8L.)

8K

Hyperspace and innerHTML

WARNING   Browser incompatibilities ahead

The same principles should apply when you work with innerHTML:

```
var x = document.getElementById('test');
document.body.innerHTML = '';
x.appendChild(document.➡
createTextNode(' I never hack text nodes.'));
document.body.appendChild(x);
```

In most browsers, the changed paragraph is reinserted into the document. Unfortunately, in Explorer the original text of the paragraph is lost, and only the newly appended text node is visible. Therefore, these techniques are not usable in combination with innerHTML.

Is an element in hyperspace?

Occasionally you're not sure if a certain element is in hyperspace or not. You can check its position by seeing if the element has a parentNode. Generally, elements in hyperspace don't have one, since they're currently "free-floating." On the other hand, every HTML element in the page has a parentNode.

I use this trick in Sandwich Picker:

[Sandwich Picker, lines 188-191]

```
function removeButton() {
    if (extraButton.parentNode)
            extraButton.parentNode.removeChild(extraButton);
}
```

This function removes the extra button 'Collect all orders', and as we saw in 8D, removeChild() requires us to go to the element's parentNode first. However, if the element is already in hyperspace, it doesn't have a parentNode, so executing extraButton.parentNode.removeChild would give an error. That's why the function first checks if extraButton has a parentNode.

L: Markers

There is one more aspect of Usable Forms I'd like to present: markers. Unlike all other topics in this chapter, markers are not "native" W3C DOM features, but rather a structuring trick I use in Usable Forms and Sandwich Picker.

First, consider the problem. Usable Forms hides form fields until the user takes a certain action: checks a radio button, selects a new option, whatever. Then the script retrieves the correct <tr>s from hyperspace and reinserts them into the document.

But where in the document? Correct placement is absolutely vital to Usable Forms' user experience. When creating the HTML, we put the form fields in an order logical to the user (we hope), and when form fields return from hyperspace they should once again take up this logical place in the form.

To a lesser degree, Sandwich Picker has the same problem. If a user discards a sandwich, that sandwich should return to the start table at the bottom of the page. Although its exact placement is not as vital as in Usable Forms, it should at least go under the right price header.

The solution to this placement problem is to use markers. The principle is very simple: I create one new, empty, hidden <tr> for each <tr> that will be hidden or moved, give it a unique ID, and insert it just before or after the <tr> I'm going to remove. When the <tr> has to return to its original position, I insert it before the marker.

Thus I keep the placement information where it belongs: in the HTML structural layer. I could also use a complicated JavaScript object, array, or hash to hold this information, but I find relying on the document structure much safer and more elegant.

Choosing a simple ID-naming scheme is important in using markers:

[Usable Forms, lines 1, 18-19, and 41-51]

```
var containerTag = 'TR';
var marker = document.createElement(containerTag);
marker.style.display = 'none';
```

```
while (hiddenFields.length) {
    var rel = hiddenFields[0].getAttribute('rel');
    if (!hiddenFormFieldsPointers[rel])
            hiddenFormFieldsPointers[rel] = new Array();
            var relIndex = hiddenFormFieldsPointers[rel].length;
    var newMarker = marker.cloneNode(true);
    newMarker.id = rel + relIndex;
    hiddenFields[0].parentNode.replaceChild(newMarker,hiddenFields
[0]);
    waitingRoom.appendChild(hiddenFields.shift());

}
```

The script first creates a template marker and stores it in variable `marker`.
Then, while the `<tr>`s with a `rel` attribute are removed from the document, the
script replaces with a marker with a unique ID. This unique ID consists of the
value of the `rel` attribute plus the index number of the `<tr>` in the `hidden-
FormFieldPointers` array.

Of course it uses the same information when retrieving the `<tr>` to get the correct marker. It inserts the `<tr>` before its marker:

[Usable Forms, lines 121-136, condensed]

```
function intoMainForm(relation){
    if (relation == 'none') return;
    var Elements = hiddenFormFieldsPointers[relation];
    for (var i=0;i<Elements.length;i++) {
            var insertPoint = document.getElementById(relation+i);
        insertPoint.parentNode.insertBefore(Elements[i],insertPoint);
    }
}
```

Because the ID scheme is so simple, it's easy to find the correct marker and
insert the returning `<tr>` just before it.

CSS modification

JAVASCRIPT ALLOWS YOU to modify the CSS presentation layer of your site. A style change is an excellent (and very common) way to draw your users' eyes to the page element on which you want them to focus.

In fact, seven of the example scripts use some form of CSS modification. For instance, Form Validation changes the styles of the incorrect form field, and XMLHTTP Speed Meter uses animations (i.e., many changes to the same style in a short time) to draw the eye of the user to the speed data. (Also, to be honest, as a bit of eye candy.) Dropdown Menu uses style changes to show and hide menu items. These changes all have the same purpose: to draw the eye of the user to these elements.

JavaScript can modify CSS in four ways:

- By modifying the `style` property of an element (`element.style.margin = '10%'`).

- By changing the class or id of an element (`element.className = 'error'`). The browser automatically applies the styles defined on the new class or id.

- By writing new CSS instructions in the document (`document. write('<style>.accessibility {display: none}</style>')`).

- By changing the style sheet of the entire page.

Most CSS modification scripts use either the `style` property or a class/id change. The `document.write` method is used only in specialized situations to enhance the page's accessibility. Finally, changing entire style sheets is rarely useful, both because it's not supported by all browsers, and because usually you want to single out specific elements for style changes.

However, I use all four methods in the example scripts. We'll look at all of them, and their proper context, in this chapter.

A: The style property

The first, and best-known, way of modifying CSS is through the `style` property that all HTML elements possess, and that accesses their inline styles. `style` contains one property for every inline CSS declaration. If you want to set an element's CSS `margin`, you use `element.style.margin`. If you want to set its CSS `color`, you use `element.style.color`. The JavaScript property always has a name similar to the CSS property.

> **INLINE STYLES!**
>
> Remember: the style property of an HTML element gives access to the inline styles of that element.

Let's review a bit of CSS theory. CSS offers four ways to define styles on an element. You can use inline styles, where you put your CSS directly in the `style` attribute of the HTML tag:

```
<p style="margin: 10%">Text</p>
```

In addition, you can embed, link to, or import a style sheet. However, since an inline style is more specific than any other kind of style, inline styles over-rule styles defined in an embedded, linked, or imported style sheet. Because the `style` property gives access to these inline styles, it will always overrule all other styles. That's the great strength of this method.

However, when you try to read out styles, you might encounter problems. Take this example:

```
<p id="test">Text</p>
p#test {
    margin: 10%;
}
alert(document.getElementById('test').style.margin);
```

The test paragraph doesn't have any inline styles. Instead, the `margin: 10%` is defined in an embedded (or linked or imported) style sheet, and is therefore impossible to read through the `style` property. The alert remains empty.

In the next example, the alert will return a result of "10%", because `margin` has now been defined as an inline style:

```
<p style="margin: 10%" id="test">Text</p>
alert(document.getElementById('test').style.margin);
```

Thus, the `style` property is excellently suited for setting styles, but less useful for getting them. Later we'll discuss ways to get styles from an embedded, linked, or imported style sheet.

9A

Dashes

Many CSS property names contain a dash, for instance `font-size`. In JavaScript, however, a dash means "minus," and therefore it cannot be used in a property name. This gives an error:

❌ `element.style.font-size = '120%';`

Does the browser have to subtract the (undefined) variable `size` from `element.style.font`? If so, what does the `= '120%'` bit mean? Instead, the browser expects a camelCase property name:

```
element.style.fontSize = '120%';
```

The general rule is that all dashes are removed from the CSS property names, and that the character after a dash becomes uppercase. Thus `margin-left` becomes `marginLeft`, `text-decoration` becomes `textDecoration`, and `border-left-style` becomes `borderLeftStyle`.

Units

Many numerical values in JavaScript need a unit, just as they do in CSS. What does `fontSize=120` mean? 120 pixels? 120 points? 120 percent? The browser doesn't know, and therefore it doesn't do anything. The unit is necessary to clarify your intent.

Take the `setWidth()` function, which forms the core of the animations in XMLHTTP Speed Meter:

[XMLHTTP Speed Meter, lines 70-73]

```
function setWidth(width) {
    if (width < 0) width = 0;
    document.getElementById('meter').style.width = width + 'px';
}
```

The function is handed a value, and it should change the width of the meter to this new value. After a safety check that allows only 0 or larger numbers, it sets

{

DON'T FORGET YOUR 'PX'

Forgetting to append the `'px'` unit to a width or height is a common CSS modification error.

In CSS quirks mode, adding `'px'` is not necessary, since the browsers obey the old rule that a unitless number is a pixel value. In itself this is not a problem, but many Web developers have acquired the habit of leaving out units when they change widths or heights, and encounter problems when they work in CSS strict mode.

}

the `style.width` of the element to the new width. Then it adds + `'px'`, because without that, the browsers wouldn't know how to interpret the number, and would do nothing.

Getting styles

WARNING   Browser incompatibilities ahead

As we saw, the `style` property cannot read out styles set in embedded, linked, or imported style sheets. Because Web developers occasionally need to read out these styles nonetheless, both Microsoft and W3C have created ways of accessing non-inline styles. The Microsoft solution works only in Explorer, while the W3C standard works in Mozilla and Opera.

Microsoft's solution is the `currentStyle` property, which works exactly like the `style` property, except for two things:

- It has access to all styles, not just the inline ones, and therefore reports the style that is actually applied to the element.

- It is read-only; you cannot set it.

9A

For instance:

```
var x = document.getElementById('test');
alert(x.currentStyle.color);
```

Now the alert shows the current `color` style of the element, regardless of where it's defined.

W3C's solution is the `window.getComputedStyle()` method, which works similarly but with a more complicated syntax:

```
var x = document.getElementById('test');
alert(window.getComputedStyle(x,null).color);
```

`getComputedStyle()` always returns a pixel value, even if the original style was, for instance, `50em` or `11%`.

As always when we encounter incompatibilities, we need a bit of code branching to satisfy all browsers:

```
function getRealStyle(id,styleName) {
    var element = document.getElementById(id);
    var realStyle = null;
    if (element.currentStyle)
            realStyle = element.currentStyle[styleName];
    else if (window.getComputedStyle)
            realStyle = window.➡
            getComputedStyle(element,null)[styleName];
    return realStyle;
}
```

You use this function as follows:

```
var textDecStyle = getRealStyle('test','textDecoration');
```

Remember that `getComputedStyle()` will always return a pixel value, while `currentStyle` retains the unit specified in the CSS.

Shorthand styles

WARNING   Browser incompatibilities ahead

Whether you get inline styles through the style property, or other styles through the function we just discussed, you'll encounter problems when you try to read out shorthand styles.

Take this border declaration:

```
<p id="test" style="border: 1px solid #cc0000;">Text</p>
```

Since this is an inline style, you'd expect this line of code to work:

```
alert(document.getElementById('test').style.border);
```

Unfortunately, it doesn't. The browsers disagree on the exact value they show in the alert.

- Explorer 6.0 gives `#cc0000 1px solid`.
- Mozilla 1.7.12 gives `1px solid rgb(204,0,0)`.
- Opera 9 gives `1px solid #cc0000`.
- Safari 1.3 doesn't give any border value.

The problem is that `border` is a shorthand declaration. It secretly consists of no less than twelve styles: width, style, and color for the top, left, bottom, and right borders. Similarly, the `font` declaration is shorthand for `font-size`, `font-family`, `font-weight`, and `line-height`, so it exhibits similar problems.

9A

> **RGB()**
>
> Note the special `color` syntax Mozilla uses: `rgb(204,0,0)`. This is a valid alternative to the traditional `#cc0000`; and you can use either syntax in CSS and JavaScript.

How is the browser supposed to handle such shorthand declarations? The example above seems pretty straightforward; you would intuitively expect the browser to return `1px solid #cc0000`, exactly as the inline style attribute says. Unfortunately, shorthand properties are more complicated than that.

Consider the following case:

```
p {
    border: 1px solid #cc0000;
}
<p id="test" style="border-color: #00cc00;">Test</p>
alert(document.getElementById('test').style.borderRightColor);
```

All browsers report the correct color, even though the inline style doesn't contain a `border-right-color` but a `border-color` declaration. Apparently the browsers consider the color of the right border to be set when the color of the entire border is set; not an unreasonable line of thought.

As you see, browsers have to make rules for these unusual situations, and they have chosen slightly different approaches to handle shorthand declarations. In the absence of a specification for the exact handling of shorthand properties, it's impossible to say which browsers are right or wrong.

B: Changing classes and ids

JavaScript allows you to change the class or id of an element. When you do that, the browser automatically updates the styles of the element.

After the welter of tricky details and browser differences we encountered while discussing the `style` property, class and id changes are a quiet oasis of logic and perfect browser harmony. Consider this example:

```
p {
    color: #000000; /* black */
}
p.emphasis {
```

{ **CLASSNAME, NOT CLASS!**

Note that JavaScript uses `className`, because `class` is a reserved word, kept apart for a future in which JavaScript might start to support Java-like classes. }

```
    color: #cc0000; /* red */
}
<p id="test">Test</p>
```

Initially, the paragraph doesn't have a class, and its color is therefore black. However, one line of JavaScript is enough to change its styles:

```
document.getElementById('test').className = 'emphasis';
```

Instantly the text becomes red. To change it back, you do the following:

```
document.getElementById('test').className = '';
```

You remove the class, and the paragraph reverts to the standard `p{}` rule.

For a practical example, take a look at Textarea Maxlength. The counter has this structure and presentation (the structure is generated by JavaScript, but that doesn't matter):

```
<div class="counter"><span>12</span>/1250</div>

div.counter {
    font-size: 80%;
    padding-left: 10px;
}
span.toomuch {
    font-weight: 600;
    color: #cc0000;
}
```

9B

When the script sees that the user has exceeded the maximum length, it changes the class of the counter span to `toomuch`:

[Textarea Maxlength, lines 20-23]

```
if (currentLength > maxLength)
    this.relatedElement.className = 'toomuch';
else
    this.relatedElement.className = '';
```

Now the counter `<span>` becomes bold and red.

An id change works exactly the same way:

```
p {
    color: #000000; /* black */
}
p#emphasis {
    color: #cc0000; /* red */
}

<p>Test</p>

document.getElementsByTagName('p')[0].id = 'emphasis';
```

Again, the paragraph becomes red. Nonetheless, I advise you not to change ids too much. Apart from serving as CSS hooks, often they are also JavaScript hooks, and changing them may have odd side effects. In practice you can implement every CSS modification you need as a class change, and you don't have to work with ids.

Adding classes

Often you do not *set* the class of an element to a new value. Instead, you *add* a class value, because you don't want to remove any styles the element might already have. Since CSS allows for multiple classes, the styles of the new class are added to the element, without removing any instructions that already-existing classes give it.

The `writeError()` and `removeError()` functions of Form Validation are good examples. I generally use a few classes for form fields, because the graphic design often uses two or even three widths for input fields. When a form field contains an error, I want to add a special warning style, but I don't want to disturb any style that the element might already have. Therefore, I cannot simply overwrite the old class value; I'd lose my special widths.

Take this situation:

```
<input class="smaller" name="name" />
input.smaller {
    width: 75px;
}
input.errorMessage {
    border-color: #cc0000;
}
```

Initially, the input has a width of 75px. If the script *sets* the class to 'errorMessage' and discards the old value, the form field would get a red border color but lose its width, and that would be very confusing to the user.

Therefore I *add* the class errorMessage:

{Form Validation, lines 105-106]

```
function writeError(obj,message) {
    obj.className += ' errorMessage';
```

This code takes the existing `className` and adds the new class to it, preceded by a space. This space is meant to separate the new class value from any class value the object might already have. Now the form field gets a red border color in addition to its 75px width—exactly what we want. The form field now applies both classes, as if the HTML were:

```
<input class="smaller errorMessage" name="name" />
```

9B

> { **CLASS NAMES AND SPACES IN MOZILLA**
>
> You may have noticed that `removeError()` removes the class value
> "errorMessage" without the leading space. That's because of a browser
> bug. When you add " errorMessage" to a class that *doesn't* have a value
> yet, Mozilla discards the leading space. If we subsequently do `replace(/`
> `errorMessage/,'')`, Mozilla doesn't remove the class; it can't find the
> string " errorMessage" because the leading space is not there. }

Removing classes

Once the user has corrected her mistake, the class `errorMessage` should be
removed, but any original class, such as `smaller`, should not be touched. The
`removeError()` function provides this functionality:

[Form Validation, lines 119-120]

```
function removeError() {
    this.className = this.className.replace(/errorMessage/,'');
```

It takes the class of the element and replaces the string `'errorMessage'` by
`''` (an empty string). The `"errorMessage"` bit is taken from the class value,
but other values are not touched. The form field loses its red border color, but
retains its 75px width.

C: Writing CSS into the page

The third method of CSS modification is a rather specialized one that should
be used *only* to enhance the accessibility of a page. It works as follows:

```
document.write('<style>element {property: value}</style>');
document.write('<link rel="stylesheet" ➥
href="specialstyles.css" />');
```

The purpose of this method is to define styles that should only be used when
JavaScript is enabled. If JavaScript is disabled, or if the browser fails its

{ **ALTERNATIVE: ADDING A <LINK /> TAG**

You can also use the W3C DOM to create an extra element that holds the special styles. For instance, you could create a new `<link />` tag, give it the correct `href`, and add it to the document. Since it avoids the use of a `document.write`, some people prefer this method.

However, it has its drawbacks, too. It's impossible to add a `<link />` tag to the document when it hasn't yet been loaded completely; the `<head>` element, to which you must append the `<link />`, is not yet available. Therefore, you must either wait until after the load event, which may cause elements to flicker, or add an extra hard-coded `<link />` tag and give it its proper `href` when JavaScript turns out to be supported.

I leave it to others to decide on the semantic value of empty `<link />` tags, but personally I don't like these potentially useless elements. I prefer the `document.write` method. Feel free to use `<link />` tags, though, if you like them better. }

object-detection checks, the `document.write` is never executed, and the styles are never applied.

Dropdown Menus uses this method:

[Dropdown Menus, lines 1-4]

```
var compatible = (document.getElementsByTagName && ➡
document.createElement);
if (compatible)
    document.write('<link rel="stylesheet" ➡
    href="navstyles.css" />')
```

These are the first lines of the script. Note that they are not contained within any function; they are executed as soon as the browser has parsed them, and as we'll see in a moment this is a vital part of such CSS modifications.

96

The script checks whether the browser supports the W3C DOM, as discussed in 3C. If the browser survives the check, the `document.write` line adds a special style sheet, navstyles.css, to the page. The reason for this special construction is accessibility.

This is the most important part of that style sheet:

```
ul.menutree ul {
    display: none;
    position: absolute;
}
```

When applied without checking the browser support, these styles are actively dangerous. `display: none` hides the submenus, and without JavaScript there's no way to make them visible. The menu becomes inaccessible.

Even if this problem were somehow solved, noscript users would see a confused jumble of submenus, because they're all positioned absolutely in their parent `<li>` and overlap each other when they're all visible. Therefore, I also want to hide the `position: absolute` until I'm certain the browser supports the necessary JavaScript to handle the submenus properly.

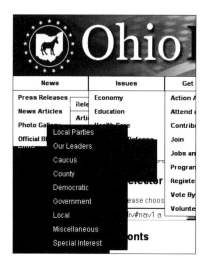

FIGURE 9.1
Even without `display: none`, the `position: absolute` makes for inaccessible and unusable dropdown menus. We have to hide this style.

Sandwich Picker does the opposite. The Sandwich Picker page contains this paragraph:

```
<p class="noscript">Unfortunately your browser doesn't support
(enough) JavaScript to use the advanced form. You can always
<a href="mailto:correct@address.nl">mail</a> us to order some
sandwiches.</p>
```

This provides noscript users with a way to order sandwiches. Obviously, this text should be hidden if the browser supports the script, since it'd only confuse "scripted" users. Therefore, the script adds an extra style:

[Sandwich Picker, lines 4-7, condensed]

```
if (W3CDOM) {
    document.write('<style>.noscript{display: none}</style>');
```

If the browser supports sufficient JavaScript, the noscript text is hidden.

As we discussed in 2G, the usability of this solution is not all that it could have been. Nonetheless, technically it's a correct example of hiding elements from the advanced, scripted interface.

Execute immediately

When using this method, it's very important that you apply the special styles *as soon as possible*. If you don't, because you wait for the load event, your users might see an ugly flickering when elements that were visible are suddenly hidden, or vice versa. By adding the special styles up front, the styles are already there when the browser starts loading the HTML, and all elements have the right show/hide instructions at the moment they're created and rendered.

That's why `document.write` is right at the top of the JavaScript file, outside any function. I want it executed while the browser parses the JavaScript file, and before it starts loading the HTML.

6C

{ **DOCUMENT.WRITE AND PAGE LOADING**

It's important to repeat a feature of `document.write` from 6F: if you use it *after* the page has been loaded completely, the browser must create a new page to contain the new content, and it destroys the old page in the process. Therefore, the user sees a blank page with a cryptic line of code instead of your carefully crafted interface.

This is another reason to execute the `document.write` immediately. }

Incidentally, XMLHTTP Speed Meter does it wrong. The script should hide the form's Submit button when sufficient JavaScript is supported, but it does so only at onload, which is too late:

[XMLHTTP Speed Meter, lines 19-22]

```
window.onload = function () {
    var supportCheck = [check support];
    if (!supportCheck) return;
    document.getElementById('submitImage').style.display = 'none';
```

If the page is slow in building, visitors will first see the submit image, but then all of a sudden it's hidden. That is confusing, and I should have used the `document.write()` trick here, too.

Used correctly, this method is a powerful accessibility tool. Used incorrectly, it can cause serious trouble. Always think out all the scenarios before using `document.write` to add styles, and test your pages with JavaScript disabled.

D: Changing entire style sheets

WARNING   Browser incompatibilities ahead

Changing entire style sheets works in Internet Explorer for Windows and Mozilla, and in no other browsers. Therefore this technique isn't ready for prime time yet, apart from the fact that editing an entire style sheet rarely makes sense. However, we'll take a look at it anyway, since I use this technique in Edit Style Sheet.

Theory

A document contains one or more style sheets, each of which contain one or more rules. Every rule contains one selector and an unlimited number of style declarations. Just as with the inline styles, these style declarations are accessible through the `style` property of the rule.

```
stylesheet ⎡
           ⎢  rule ⎡ selector {
           ⎢       ⎢      property: value[;]   } declaration
           ⎢       ⎣ }
           ⎢
           ⎢  rule ⎡ selector {
           ⎢       ⎢      property: value;     } declaration
           ⎢       ⎢      property: value;     } declaration
           ⎢       ⎢      property: value[;]   } declaration
           ⎣       ⎣ }
```

FIGURE 9.2 Every style sheet contains one or more rules. Every rule contains a selector and one or more declarations, each of which consists of a name/value pair.

In addition, Explorer and Mozilla support the addition and removal of entire rules from the style sheet. Although Edit Style Sheet doesn't use this feature, we'll treat it below.

Although the addition and removal of rules has been specified by W3C, Explorer supports only its own version. So a bit of object detection is necessary when you want to use these features.

document.styleSheets

The first requirement for successful style-sheet editing is support for the `document.styleSheets` nodeList. If the browser doesn't support that, the script won't work.

Therefore, Edit Style Sheet's `initStyleChange()` function starts by checking support:

[Edit Style Sheet, lines 5-7]

```
function initStyleChange() {
    if (!document.styleSheets) return;
    var sheets = document.styleSheets;
```

If the browser doesn't support `document.styleSheets` at all, the function ends immediately. Otherwise, the script creates a `sheets` variable that refers to the `document.styleSheets` nodeList.

`document.styleSheets` contains all style sheets in the document, whether they're embedded or linked. Take this bit of HTML:

```
<head>
<link type="text/css" rel="stylesheet" href="main.css" />
<link type="text/css" rel="stylesheet" href="colors.css" />
<style type="text/css">
.specialCase {
    color: #cc0000;
}
</style>
</head>
```

Now `document.styleSheets` contains three style sheets: the linked main.css, the linked colors.css, and the embedded .specialCase rule. As usual, they're numbered in the order they appear in the source code, and the first one has index 0. Therefore, the embedded style sheet is `document.styleSheets[2]`.

Edit Style Sheet has to search for the style sheet that users are allowed to edit. In my example script, it's called colors.css:

[Edit Style Sheet, lines 8-13]

```
for (var i=0;i<sheets.length;i++) {
    var ssName = sheets[i].➥
    href.substring(sheets[i].href.lastIndexOf('/')+1);
```

```
      if (ssName == 'colors.css')
              var currentSheet = sheets[i];
    }
    if (!currentSheet) return;
```

The script goes through all style sheets and searches to their href property to find the style-sheet name after the last slash. If this name is equal to colors.css, the script has found the correct style sheet, and stores it in currentSheet.

If currentSheet doesn't have a value after this loop, colors.css is missing, and the function ends.

cssRules[] and rules[]

Browser incompatibilities ahead

Edit Style Sheet needs access to all the rules in the style sheet. Mozilla uses the W3C-specified cssRules[] nodeList, while Explorer needs the Microsoft-proprietary rules[] nodeList. Fortunately, these two nodeLists are exactly the same except for their names:

[Edit Style Sheet, lines 14-18]

```
    if (currentSheet.cssRules)
        sheetRules = currentSheet.cssRules;
    else if (currentSheet.rules)
        sheetRules = currentSheet.rules;
    else return;
```

Therefore, a simple object detection is enough. If the browser supports css-Rules[], store this nodeList in sheetRules; if it supports rules[], store that nodeList in sheetRules. If the browser supports neither, the script won't work, and it ends.

Note that sheetRules is a global variable; other functions will need this information, too.

06

selectorText

Every rule has a `selectorText`, which contains, unsurprisingly, the rule selector as a string.

When the user selects a new rule to edit from the first select, the `assignRule()` function searches for this rule and opens it for editing:

[Edit Style Sheet, lines 48-55]

```
function assignRule() {
    var selector = this.value;
    for (var i=0;i<sheetRules.length;i++)
            if (sheetRules[i].selectorText.toLowerCase() ➡
            == selector.toLowerCase())
                    currentRule = sheetRules[i];
}
```

It takes the desired selector (i.e., the select box's `value`), and then goes through all the rules in `sheetRules`. When it finds a rule with a matching `selectorText`, it points `currentRule` to this rule. `currentRule`, too, is a global variable, since other functions need access to the rule that's currently being edited.

One word of warning: some browsers (Explorer and Safari at the time of writing) return an UPPERCASE selector text. Therefore, the above function compares `selectorText.toLowerCase()` to `selector.toLowerCase()`.

style

Every rule has a `style` property that works exactly like the `style` property of individual HTML elements we discussed in 9A. If we wanted to change the `color` of `currentRule` to green we could do this:

```
currentRule.style.color = '#00cc00';
```

Now all elements that take their style information from this rule will change their color to green.

The `assignStyles()` function is called whenever the user changes a style declaration through the main form. It sets the correct style of the current rule to the correct value:

[Edit Style Sheets, lines 57-64]

```
function assignStyles() {
    if (!currentRule) return;
    var styleName = this.name;
    var styleValue = this.value;
    if (this.type == 'checkbox' && !this.checked)
            styleValue = '';
    currentRule.style[styleName] = styleValue;
}
```

First it checks for a `currentRule`, and if there is none, it exits. Then it takes the name and value of the form field the user has changed:

```
<input type="checkbox" name="fontWeight" value="bold" />
```

Checkboxes need special treatment: if they are not checked, the CSS property value they set should be empty. We already discussed the last line of this function in 5G. It sets the correct style property of the current rule (`currentRule.style[styleName]`) to the correct value.

Now the browser implements the revised styles, and the user immediately sees the effect of her changes.

cssText and submitting the style sheet

Since Edit Style Sheet never left the prototype phase, I never devised a way to send the edited style sheet back to the server. Nonetheless, the script is useless without some sort of submission that allows the server to store and use the updated style sheet.

The simplest way would be to copy the entire text content of the style sheet, store it in a hidden textarea, and send it to the server. A server-side program would create a neat file and store it as colors.css. Thus the style sheet would become available to all users of the site.

> **WARNING** Browser incompatibilities ahead

The problem is that there's no simple cross-browser way of reading the entire text of the style sheet. The W3C DOM CSS module contains the `cssText` property, but the browsers don't entirely agree on the scope of this property.

`cssText` contains style declarations as a string. But which style declarations? There are three ways to use `cssText`:

1. `document.styleSheets[0].cssText;`
2. `document.styleSheets[0].cssRules[0].cssText;`
3. `document.styleSheets[0].cssRules[0].style.cssText;`

The first example would give the entire style sheet as a string; that's exactly what we need for Edit Style Sheets. If we pasted `document.styleSheets[0].cssText` into a hidden text area, we'd be ready.

Unfortunately, Mozilla doesn't support this use of `cssText`. For this reason, I was sorely tempted to restrict this script to Explorer Windows, but its implementation was delayed several times, and in the end I didn't solve this conundrum.

{
BROWSER COMPATIBILITY

At the time of writing, the first use of cssText was supported only by Explorer (Windows and Mac), the second one only by Explorer Mac and Mozilla, while only the third one is supported by all browsers. These compatibility patterns may change, though.
}

Inserting and deleting rules

You can insert new rules into a style sheet, or remove rules from it. This feature is not used in Edit Style Sheet—I definitely don't want a user who knows little of CSS to insert new rules that might mess up the entire page.

> **WARNING**   Browser incompatibilities ahead

Nonetheless, inserting and deleting rules is important enough to treat. Unfortunately, this area of JavaScript again contains some browser incompatibilities. Mozilla uses the W3C-specified `insertRule()` and `deleteRule()` methods, while Explorer uses the Microsoft-proprietary `addRule()` and `removeRule()` methods. Safari and Opera don't support these actions at all.

As soon as you insert a rule, the style declarations in it are immediately applied to all relevant elements. Deleting a rule immediately removes these style declarations from all relevant elements.

insertRule() and addRule()

When you are inserting a new rule, the browsers expect three bits of information:

1. The selector of the new rule.

2. The style declarations of the new rule, as a string.

3. The position of the new rule (first rule of the style sheet, last rule, somewhere in between?).

The W3C `insertRule()` and Microsoft `addRule()` methods need this information, but they differ in the way they want it delivered.

W3C's `insertRule()` expects two arguments:

1. The entire rule (selector + declarations) as a string.

2. The position of the new rule (0 = first rule in the style sheet, etc.).

9D

Example:

```
var x = document.styleSheets[0];
x.insertRule('PRE {font: 0.9em verdana}',2)
```

Now this CSS rule is added to the first style sheet of the page, as the third rule (with index 2).

```
pre {
    font: 0.9em verdana;
}
```

Microsoft's addRule() expects three arguments:

1. The selector as a string.

2. The declarations as a string.

3. The position of the new rule.

Example:

```
var x = document.styleSheets[0]
x.addRule('PRE', 'font: 0.9em verdana',2)
```

This gives exactly the same result as the previous code example: the same CSS rule is added as the third rule in the style sheet.

deleteRule() and removeRule()

If you want to delete a rule, you should specify which one by giving its index number. So in order to delete the rule we just inserted, we should do this:

```
var x = document.styleSheets[0]
x.deleteRule(2); // W3C
x.removeRule(2); // Microsoft
```

Now the third rule in the first style sheet is deleted.

Helper functions

In order to defeat these rule-related browser incompatibilities, we have to create two helper functions. Deletion is easy:

```
function deleteCSS(sheet,index) {
    if (sheet.deleteRule)
          sheet.deleteRule(index);
    else if (sheet.removeRule)
          sheet.removeRule(index);
}
```

Inserting a rule is slightly more complicated because of the different arguments the functions expect:

```
function insertCSS(sheet,selector,declarations,index) {
    if (sheet.insertRule) {
          var toBeInserted  = selector + ➡
          ' {' + declarations + '}';
          sheet.insertRule(toBeInserted,index);
    }
    else if (sheet.addRule)
          sheet.addRule(selector,declarations,index);
}
```

E: Comparison

Now that we have studied all four CSS-modification methods, we can ask ourselves which one is the best. The document.write method should be used only in specialized accessibility-related cases. Changing an entire style sheet is rarely useful. Therefore two methods remain. Should you use the style property, or change class or id values?

To get some answers, let's take a look at the example scripts. Site Survey doesn't modify CSS at all, Edit Style Sheet changes the entire style sheet, and Usable Forms uses the document.write method. Only XMLHTTP Speed Meter changes style properties, while four scripts—Textarea Maxlength, Sandwich

Picker, Form Validation, and Dropdown Menu—use class changes. As you might guess, I feel the class change is usually the superior CSS-modification technique.

In my opinion, excessive reliance on the `style` property violates the separation of presentation and behavior, and besides it's more complicated to code. Styles belong in the CSS presentation layer—their natural habitat—not in either the HTML structural layer or the JavaScript behavior layer.

When you change a style, you are saying, "Give this element a new presentation." Giving this command is obviously a job for JavaScript. However, *defining* the new presentation is a job for CSS. The new styles of the element, as well as the old ones, should therefore be defined in the CSS file.

Thus presentation and behavior remain separate: JavaScript gives the command to change styles, but it's up to the CSS to define the new styles.

Example

Let's take a look at a practical example. Suppose I'd used the `style` property instead of a class change in Form Validation:

[Form Validation, lines 105-6 and 119-120, changed]

```
function writeError(obj,message) {
    obj.style.border = '1px solid #cc0000';


function removeError() {
    this.style.border = '';
```

Of course this works fine. But suppose later on the graphic designer decides the text also has to become red. You'd have to add two lines to your script:

```
function writeError(obj,message) {
    obj.style.border = '1px solid #cc0000';
    obj.style.color = '#cc0000';


function removeError() {
    this.style.border = '';
    this.style.color = '';
```

And so on. Each extra style for form fields with errors would take two lines of JavaScript. In contrast, a class-change script is easier to maintain, since an extra style requires only one line of CSS.

Of course, adding two lines of JavaScript hardly counts as complex programming. Nonetheless, implementing these changes would still require someone who knows his way in the JavaScript code. A graphic designer/CSS wizard without any JavaScript experience would not be able to do it.

CSS developers who know nothing about JavaScript *are* able to edit a style sheet, and this is not an inconsiderable advantage in a larger company, where people tend to have more specialized jobs. As a JavaScript developer, you don't want every tiny style change to have to go through you. Therefore, decreasing the complexity of the JavaScript layer is to your own advantage, too.

So there are a few reasons why I believe that in general a class change is superior to a `style` property change. Nonetheless, like any good general rule, this one has exceptions. The two most important ones are simple show/hide scripts and animations.

F: Showing and hiding elements

In many cases, you want to show and hide elements based on user actions. These cases may be complicated, like Usable Forms, or they may be extremely simple, such as a menu that folds in or out when the user clicks on a header.

9F

{ HIDE ELEMENTS IN JAVASCRIPT! }

As we saw in 2F, for accessibility's sake we should give the initial commands to hide content *in JavaScript*. That way, if a visitor to your site doesn't have JavaScript enabled, the content is never hidden, and although the page may lose some usability, it's still perfectly accessible.

Simple show/hide scripts

Simple show/hide scripts display or conceal only one element per user action. Most of these scripts change the `style.display` property of the element.

Mostly this method is used out of tradition: when people started writing show/hide scripts, class changes weren't yet possible in Netscape 4 (an important browser back then). Besides, show/hide scripts generally change only one CSS property: `display`.

Therefore, this is a typical example of a show/hide script. It uses style-property changes throughout, and doesn't touch the class names of the elements:

```
<h3>Header</h3>
<div class="content">
    <p>Content</p>
    <p>Content</p>
</div>

window.onload = function () {
    var x = document.getElementsByTagName('div');
    for (var i=0;i<x.length;i++) {
            if (x[i].className != 'content') continue;
            x[i].style.display = 'none';
            var header = x[i].previousSibling;
            if (header.nodeType != 1)
                    header = header.previousSibling;
            header.relatedTag = x[i];
            header.onclick = openClose;
    }
}
function openClose() {
    var currentValue = this.relatedTag.style.display;
    var newValue = (currentValue == 'none') ? 'block' : 'none';
    this.relatedTag.style.display = newValue;
}
```

The script goes through all `<div>`s in the document, and ignores those that don't have a class="content". Then it sets their `display` to `none` (styles that hide content should be set in JavaScript!).

Then the script finds the header the `<div>` is related to. In principle, this is the `previousSibling` of the `<div>`, but as we saw in 8H there may be empty text nodes between the header and the `<div>`. Therefore, the script goes back through the document tree until it finds a node with `nodeType` 1 (i.e., an element node). This is the header it's looking for.

Once it finds this header, it sets its `relatedTag` property to point to the `<div>`, and the header gets an onclick event handler.

When the user clicks on the header, the `openClose()` function reads out the current display of the header's `relatedTag` (i.e., the `<div>` that should be opened or closed), and sets its `display` to the opposite value.

GENERATING THE DIVS

Sometimes you don't want the extra `div class="content"` in your HTML code. It has no semantic meaning, and editors of the HTML page could suddenly add extra headers. In addition, if the page is updated through a CMS, it would have to generate an extra `div class="content"` around the correct content. You'd just have to hope the CMS you're working with could do that.

Enter the W3C DOM. Don't put any divs in your HTML, but generate them when the page has been loaded. Go through all children of the `<body>`. As soon as you find a header, append a new div after it. Then move all nodes you find after the header to this generated div, until you encounter a new header. Then generate a new div, and continue with the content after the new header.

Try expanding the show/hide script with this new functionality. It's a useful DOM exercise.

9F

Note a few important points:

- The crucial `display: none` is set in JavaScript, not in CSS. If a noscript browser visits the page, all blocks remain open and accessible.

- We set the inline style of the `<div>` to `display: none` so that we can read out the current `display` of the block through `style.display`.

- When the script has loaded (`onload`) we relate every header to the content block it should open. We discussed the creation of such relations in 4C.

This simple example of a show/hide script can be used in many circumstances.

Showing and hiding table rows

In my script I used `<div>`s as example tags, but of course you can write a show/hide script for any tag you like. Showing and hiding `<ul>`s or `<li>`s in a navigation could also be useful; in fact, Dropdown Menu does exactly that (though in a more complicated way than the simple script we just reviewed).

> **WARNING**   Browser incompatibilities ahead

One case deserves special attention: showing and hiding table rows. Hiding table rows is done through `display: none`, obviously, but how do you show them? Table elements ought to have the special `display` value `table-row`, but unfortunately Explorer uses `display: block` instead.

> **TABLE DISPLAY VALUES**
>
> According to the CSS specification tables, table rows and table cells should not use `display: block`, but rather `display: table`, `display: table-row`, and `display: table-cell`, respectively. However, Explorer uses `block` throughout.

All browsers are strict about what they allow. If they expect `table-row`, they'll choke on `block`, and vice versa. For instance, the following line makes Explorer restore the `<tr>` to view, but the other browsers literally make the `<tr>` a block that doesn't pay attention to the rest of the table:

```
var tr = [the tr you want to show];
tr.style.display = 'block';
```

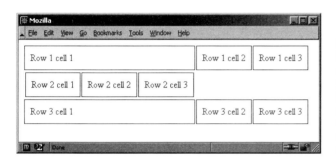

FIGURE 9.3
I gave the middle `<tr>` display: block. Mozilla takes me at my word; it makes the `tr` a block, and the vertical alignment of `<td>`s is lost.

Conversely, if you use the correct `table-row` value, the other browsers restore the `<tr>`, but Explorer Windows gives an error:

```
tr.style.display = 'table-row';
```

What now? Do we have to use a browser detect to decide between `block` and `table-row`? Fortunately, no. Every browser has a default style sheet that declares all default styles of all elements, and this style sheet includes the default `display` value of a `<tr>`.

This default style sheet contains either `block` or `table-row`, depending on the browser. If you allow this sheet to take over once more, the problem is solved; all browsers will restore the `<tr>` to view.

How do you do this? As we saw at the start of this chapter, the `style` property sets the inline style of an element. If we remove the inline value entirely, the browser once again takes its `display` instructions from the default style sheet, and the problem is solved:

```
tr.style.display = '';
```

9F

By removing the inline style entirely, the default style sheet takes over and the `<tr>` becomes visible in all browsers. Better still, you don't have to know whether the browser needs `'block'` or `'table-row'`.

G: Animations

Animations draw the eye of the user to the element that's animated. If that's a good thing, the animation serves a good purpose; but if not, it doesn't.

XMLHTTP Speed Meter is the only example script that uses an animation. Although it's there to provide some eye candy, it also serves a real purpose. By making the animation fluctuate within a range of download speeds, the interface conveys the message "Your download speed will be somewhere around here," without specifying an exact speed. This is very important to the client—an ISP who simply cannot guarantee an exact speed, and wants its clients to be aware of that fact.

How animations work

Animations are repeated changes to the same style of the same element. With a bit of luck, the style changes follow each other so rapidly that the user perceives the animation as one continuous movement instead of a lot of small steps.

Nonetheless, JavaScript animations may become jerky for several reasons: the script isn't fast enough; the user's computer is slow; the page has many scripts running in addition to the animation; or the animation uses too many tiny steps. If perfect animations are an absolute requirement for your site, Flash remains the best tool.

Animations are one area in which changing the `style` property is better than a class change. If XMLHTTP Speed Meter used class changes, I'd have to define dozens of classes: one for each possible animation step. That would make the CSS presentation layer extremely complicated.

XMLHTTP Speed Meter uses two nested `<div>`s. The outer one contains the grey background image, and the inner one the black image. Initially, the inner

<div> has width: 0 and is thus invisible. The animation script changes the width of the black <div>, and since its background has exactly the same position as the outer background, it appears to become a black meter running over a greyed background:

```
<div class="grey">
    <div id="meter">
    </div>
</div>
div.grey {
    background: url(pix/bg_meter_grey.gif); // grey bg
    height: 23px;
    width: 280px;
}
div#meter {
    background: url(pix/bg_meter_black.gif); // black bg
    height: 23px;
}
```

[XMLHTTP Speed Meter, lines 70-73]

```
function setWidth(width) {
    if (width < 0) width = 0;
    document.getElementById('meter').style.width = width + 'px';
}
```

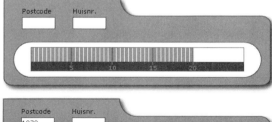

FIGURE 9.4
Initially, the meter has width: 0 (invisible); later, it has width: 56px and obscures part of the grey background.

Changing the `width` is pretty easy (as long as you remember to append a correct unit). However, the `width` shouldn't change once, but many times over. How do we cleanly issue a lot of commands to change the `width`?

setTimeout and setInterval

In order to create a proper animation, you need either `setTimeout` or `set-Interval`. Before discussing the use of these methods, let's take a peek at the problem they solve.

If you command the browser to change widths multiple times without any pause, it will change the on-screen rendering only after the entire script has been run. Suppose we want to animate a change from 0 to 56px width, with 14px intervals:

```
function changeWidths() {
    setWidth(14);
    setWidth(28);
    setWidth(42);
    setWidth(56);
}
```

Now the browser faithfully changes the `width` of the element to 14, 28, 42, and 56 pixels. However, it doesn't show any of these changes until the function has ended. Therefore, as far as the user is concerned, the black bar is invisible at first (`width: 0`), and then all of a sudden it has a substantial size (`width: 56px`), without any steps in between. This is no animation—you might just as well have set `width: 56px` immediately.

We have to pause between the steps to give the browser the chance to catch up and to show every single step on the screen before proceeding to the next one. We have to time our commands: do `setWidth(14)`, wait, do `setWidth(28)`, wait, etc.

As we discussed in 6E, JavaScript contains two methods that allow you to time your commands: `setTimeout` and `setInterval`. They come in especially handy in animations.

Using setTimeout

We're going to use `setTimeout` to define a slight waiting period between the `width` changes. (Why not `setInterval`? We'll discuss that later.)

```
function changeWidths() {
    setTimeout('setWidth(14)',100);
    setTimeout('setWidth(28)',200);
    setTimeout('setWidth(42)',300);
    setTimeout('setWidth(56)',400);
}
```

Now the animation works. The browser is commanded to run `setWidth()` four times: once with argument 14 after 100 milliseconds, once with argument 28 after 200 milliseconds, etc. As far as the browser is concerned, after executing the function once, it considers the function ended, and shows the results on-screen.

Now the user sees a simple animation, each step of which makes the black bar 14 pixels wider, with a 100 millisecond pause between each step. The style change has become a true animation.

{ **USING THE RIGHT INTERVAL TIME**

An important part of creating a good animation is choosing an appropriate interval for your steps. In theory, the smaller the time, the better the animation, since small steps make an animation more fluid. Unfortunately, if you make your steps too small, browsers start to have trouble.

10 milliseconds seems to be a practical limit; it's about the smallest delay time browsers can handle. But even if you stay above this limit—setting, say, 500 animation steps with a 20-millisecond interval—your script may use too many browser resources, since it runs 500 times in a 2-second period. Of course, the exact behavior of the browser depends on the speed of the computer it runs on, so some browsers might still show such an animation correctly.

I generally use a delay time of 50 milliseconds at minimum, and restrict the number of steps to a moderate amount, say 10 to 50. }

When creating an animation, I always allow the client to set the exact animation time. Clients frequently think an animation is slightly too slow or too fast,
and by allowing them to modify one variable by themselves, I save myself valuable development time.

So let's add a variable moveTime, which defines the pause between the animation steps:

```
var moveTime = 100; // in milliseconds
function changeWidths() {
    setTimeout('setWidth(14)',moveTime*1);
    setTimeout('setWidth(28)',moveTime*2);
    setTimeout('setWidth(42)',moveTime*3);
    setTimeout('setWidth(56)',moveTime*4);
}
```

That's a useful addition, but the function is still quite ugly. Looking for ways
to further sanitize it, we see that what we're really doing is giving a repetitive
command, and such commands can be worked into a for{} loop:

```
var moveTime = 100; // in milliseconds
function changeWidths() {
    for (var i=1;i<5;i++) {
            setTimeout('setWidth(' + (i*14) + ')',moveTime*i);
    }
}
```

This is much better. i loops from 1 to 4. The width that the black meter
should be set to is always i*14 (14, 28, 42, 56), and the timeout time is
always moveTime*i (100, 200, 300, 400). Now the animation function has
become much more standardized, and all timeouts are set at once, reducing
the clutter in your script.

setTimeout or setInterval?

Why do I use `setTimeout`, not `setInterval`? In my opinion, the two methods, though similar, are meant for different situations, especially when it comes to animations. Before continuing, let's review the difference:

```
setTimeout('theFunction()',100);
setInterval('theFunction()',100);
```

The first line means "Execute function `theFunction()` 100 milliseconds from now." The second line means "Execute function `theFunction()` 100 milliseconds from now, and *continue* executing it every 100 milliseconds."

`setInterval` is best for animations that continue for an indefinite time (for instance, until the user does something). `setTimeout`, on the other hand, is best suited for animations that have a fixed start and end point.

The animation that moves the speed meter to a new value has a fixed start point (the old value) and a fixed end point (the new value.) Therefore this animation requires `setTimeout`.

Once the XMLHTTP Speed Meter has arrived at its new value, however, a second animation kicks in. This is the fluctuation that continues until the user does something. Since the fluctuation doesn't have a fixed start and end point but should continue until further notice, this animation requires `setInterval`.

Examples

XMLHTTP Speed Meter initializes the two kinds of animations. When a new speed arrives from the server, `moveToNewSpeed()` is called. We'll ignore the calculations and focus on setting and cancelling the timeouts and intervals:

[XMLHTTP Speed Meter, lines 78-86, condensed]

```
function moveToNewSpeed(Mbit) {
    for (var i=0;i<animationSteps.length;i++)
            clearTimeout(animationSteps[i]);
    animationSteps.length = 0;
    // calculations
    clearInterval(fluctuationInterval);
```

As soon as moveToNewSpeed() is called, it clears all timeouts and intervals that may exist; all animations should stop what they're doing and await new orders.

All timeouts are stored in the animationSteps[] array. This is done in order to easily remove them in the clearTimeout routine at the start of this function. The function cannot be sure in advance of the exact number of timeouts, since this varies with the start and end points of the desired animations. Storing them in an array is therefore the best solution; the array can become as long as necessary.

[XMLHTTP Speed Meter, lines 90-94]

```
do {
        animationSteps[timeoutCounter] = ➡
        setTimeout('setWidth(' + (pos*7) + ')', ➡
        timeoutCounter*moveTime);
        timeoutCounter++;
} while ([perform some calculations])
```

Now it calls the necessary setTimeouts in a way similar to the changeWidths() function we discussed previously. timeoutCounter counts the timeouts that are already set, so that every timeout gets its own entry in the animationSteps array. pos*7 is the desired width, so we feed this value to setWidth(). We already discussed the do/while() loop in 5H.

[XMLHTTP Speed Meter, lines 96-97]

```
        setTimeout('initFluctuation()',timeoutCounter*moveTime);
}
```

Then the script sets a last timeout to initialize the fluctuation. timeoutCounter has increased since the last timeout, so initFluctuation() is called after the last time setWidth() has been called, and the fluctuation takes over seamlessly:

[XMLHTTP Speed Meter, lines 102-107, condensed]

```
function initFluctuation() {
    // calculations
    fluctuationInterval = ➡
    setInterval('fluctuate()',fluctuationTime);
}
```

initFluctuation() performs some calculations, and then sets an interval that calls fluctuate() every once in a while. The exact time between fluctuations is set by the client and stored in fluctuationTime:

[XMLHTTP Speed Meter, lines 109-116, condensed]

```
function fluctuate() {
    // calculations
    setWidth(currentFluctuation*7);
}
```

fluctuate(), finally, performs some more calculations and calls setWidth(). This function continues to be called until new data arrives from the server and the interval is cancelled by moveToNewSpeed().

In this way, both animations are set and cleared in the most efficient way possible.

H: Dimensions and position of elements

To wrap up this chapter, we will discuss how you can find an element's real dimensions and position in pixels.

Element dimensions

In some situations, you need to find the exact dimension of an element—and that includes the browser window. You can use a few properties that, though not part of any standard, are defined for all HTML elements in all browsers. They all yield a width or height in pixels.

- The clientWidth and clientHeight properties give the width and height of the visible part of an element (i.e., CSS width + padding). They don't take borders or scrollbars into account, nor any possible scrolling.

- The offsetWidth and offsetHeight properties give the total width and height that the element takes up in the page. The only difference from the previous property pair is that these two take into account the borders and scrollbars of an element.

H6

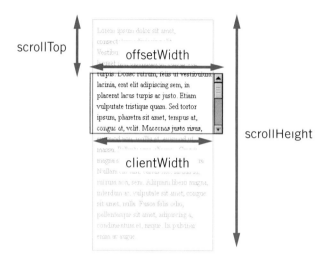

FIGURE 9.5
What scroll-Top, offsetWidth, scrollHeight, and clientWidth measure. (scrollLeft, off setHeight, scroll-Width, and client-Height work the same, but in the other dimension.)

- The scrollWidth and scrollHeight properties give the total width and height of the element as if it had overflow: visible. If this width and height are larger than the clientWidth and clientHeight, the element needs scrollbars.

- The scrollTop and scrollLeft properties give distance (in pixels) that the element has scrolled. When you set these properties, the page scrolls to the new coordinates.

Therefore, the following gives the real width in pixels of the element with id="test":

```
document.getElementById('test').clientWidth;
```

To get the width of the borders and the scrollbars, use offsetWidth instead.

Finding the browser window's dimensions

Since these measurement-related properties are defined for all elements, they also work on <body> and <html>. In fact, it's on these elements that they're most commonly used. If you take the clientWidth and clientHeight of <body> or <html>, you find the visible width and height of the browser window, and that's useful in many scripts (though not in any of the example scripts).

As we saw in 8B, the `<html>` and `<body>` tags are represented by
`document.documentElement` and `document.body`. Therefore, one of these
lines will give you the browser window's width (without the scrollbars):

```
document.documentElement.clientWidth;
document.body.clientWidth;
```

The second line is meant for Explorer versions earlier than 6, while the first
line is meant for all other browsers. The difference is the interpretation of the
`<body>` tag. In ancient times, the `<body>` element was the topmost visible
element, and the `<html>` element remained hidden. However, modern browsers
made `<body>` a normal block-level element, while `<html>` encompasses the
entire browser window.

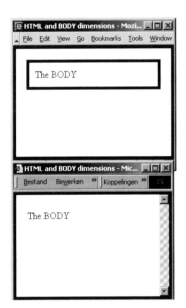

FIGURE 9.6
In Mozilla, the `<html>` element encompasses
the entire browser window, while the `<body>`
element is a normal block-level element. In
Explorer 5.5, the `<body>` element encompasses the browser window, while the `<html>`
element is invisible.

Hence, to read out the window's width and height, you have to query the
`clientWidth` of the `<html>` element in modern browsers, but of the `<body>`
element in older ones. Fortunately, that's simple:

```
var windowWidth = document.documentElement.clientWidth
        || document.body.clientWidth;
```

{ **OLDER PROPERTIES**

In all browsers but Explorer, the older property pairs `window.innerWidth/`
`Height` and `pageXOffset/pageYOffset` give the browser window's width
and height and the scrolling offset, respectively. However, since all these
browsers also support the `clientWidth/Height` and `scrollTop/Left`
properties, there's no more need to use the old ones. }

The window width is `document.documentElement.clientWidth`, but if that
property is 0 or doesn't exist, we take `document.body.clientWidth`.

Element position

Occasionally, you want to find an element's position in the window. Edit Style
Sheet needs this information when it wants to position the color picker right
next to the link that says 'pick'; it has to know the position of this link.

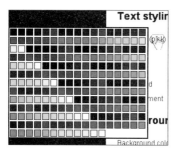

FIGURE 9.7
The color picker should be positioned next to
the link the user clicked on. To do this, the
script needs to find the position of this link in
the browser window.

Any element has two properties, `offsetLeft` and `offsetTop`, that give the offset of the element in pixels. The question is, of course, the offset relative to
which element? The browsers disagree sharply on this. Explorer calculates the
position of the Pick link relative to its `parentNode` (the `<label>` tag), while
Mozilla calculates it relative to the `div#container`, because that's the first
ancestor to have a CSS `position` other than `static`.

At first, this seems to be one of those unsolvable cross-browser incompatibilities. Fortunately, all browsers agree that the property `offsetParent`

{ **PARENTAL PROBLEMS**

The `offsetParent` function is not perfect, and although it'll work fine in 90% of the cases, sometimes it needs a bit of help.

One drawback is that the `<body>` and `<html>` elements don't have an `offsetParent` themselves, and thus no `offsetWidth/Height`. If you give either element a CSS `margin` or `padding`, this value may not be added to the calculated offset. Fortunately, I did not define any `margin` or `padding` to the `<body>` or `<html>` element in Edit Style Sheet.

In addition, the function doesn't work perfectly on elements with `position: relative` in Explorer.

See http://www.quirksmode.org/js/findpos.html for an overview of the problems you can expect, as well as a few test cases. }

refers to the element relative to which the offset is calculated. In Explorer, the link's `offsetParent` refers to the `<label>`, but in Mozilla it refers to the `div#container`.

That means that we can jump from `offsetParent` to `offsetParent` without having to worry about their exact identity. We just follow the trail of `offsetParent`s until we end up at the `<body>` or `<html>` tag.

We first calculate the link's offset relative to its `offsetParent`, and then we go to this `offsetParent` and add its offset relative to its own `offsetParent`, etc. When we're finished, we've found the link's offset relative to the `<body>` or `<html>` tag.

The `findPos()` function does so:

[Edit Style Sheet, lines 181-191]

```
function findPos(obj) {
    var curleft = curtop = 0;
    if (obj.offsetParent) {
        while (obj.offsetParent) {
```

H6

```
                    curleft += obj.offsetLeft;
                    curtop += obj.offsetTop;
                    obj = obj.offsetParent;
                }
            }
        return [curleft,curtop];
    }
```

The return value of this function is an array (see 5L). The function first sets curleft and curtop to 0. If the offsetParent property does not exist, it returns [0,0]: calculation impossible.

Otherwise it enters a while() loop. While the current object has an off-setParent, it adds the offsetTop/Left of the current object to curleft and curtop, and then moves on to the offsetParent of the current object. The while() loop makes sure that it continues to do so until there is no more offsetParent.

Once this loop has ended, we find the element's offset relative to the <body> or <html> element.

findPos()'s results are used as follows:

[Edit Style Sheet, lines 138-142, condensed]

```
    function placeColorPicker() {
        var coors = findPos(this);
        colorPicker.style.top = coors[1] - 20 + 'px';
        colorPicker.style.left = 0;
```

findPos() returns an array, so coors becomes an array. In this specific example, the color picker ignores any left value but instead sets its left to 0. The element's top, though, is taken from findPos()'s results, 20 pixels are subtracted, and the 'px' unit is appended. Now the color picker appears to the left of the link the user clicked on.

Data retrieval

MOST WEB SITES are collections of HTML documents. These documents are connected by hyperlinks, and clicking on such links causes the browser to discard the old page and load the new one, a process that may take a few seconds.

This is fine as far as it goes, but occasionally you want a spiffier interface that doesn't change or flicker while new data is being fetched from the server, and where the new data is integrated seamlessly into the existing page. Usually this is called a Single Page Interface, since the users enter a certain page, and all actions they take result in new data being shown within that page.

From a JavaScript perspective, the question is one of data retrieval: how do you retrieve data from the server without reloading a page? Simple: you use the XMLHttpRequest object, which all modern browsers support.

Throughout this chapter we'll discuss XMLHTTP Speed Meter, since it's the only example script that uses data retrieval. Note from the outset, however, that it is the simplest possible data-retrieval script, because it fires just one data query. More complicated data-retrieval applications need many more features than this chapter discusses. After all, this book is not about application design, but about basic JavaScript.

Note that you're allowed to retrieve XML data files only from the same domain as the page. This is due to JavaScript's same-source policy, discussed in 1B.

A: Sending the request

Sending an HTTP request through the XMLHttpRequest object requires the following minimum steps:

1. Create an XMLHttpRequest object (this is browser dependent).

2. Instruct the object to open a specific file (the open() method).

3. Tell the object what to do with the data the server will return (an onreadystatechange event handler).

4. Give the object the command to send the request (the send() method).

There are more actions you can take, but we'll focus on these required steps first.

The XMLHttpRequest object

WARNING   Browser incompatibilities ahead

In order to send an XMLHttpRequest request and receive a response, you first have to create an XMLHttpRequest object that's capable of performing these actions. Unfortunately, creating this object requires a few browser-dependent workarounds, since in Explorer 6 and earlier the object is an ActiveX object, while in all other browsers (including Explorer 7) it's a native object.

This is XMLHTTP Speed Meter's object-creation function:

[XMLHTTP Speed Meter, lines 140-145]

```
var XMLHttpFactories = [
    function () {return new XMLHttpRequest()},
    function () {return new ActiveXObject("Msxml2.XMLHTTP")},
    function () {return new ActiveXObject("Msxml3.XMLHTTP")},
    function () {return new ActiveXObject("Microsoft.XMLHTTP")}
];
```

First, we create an array, XMLHttpFactories, that contains one function for every possible way to create an XMLHttp object. The first one (new
XMLHttpRequest()) tries to create a native object, while the remaining ones
try to create ActiveX objects. Msxml2.XMLHTTP, Msxml3.XMLHTTP, and
Microsoft.XMLHTTP are all possible names for that ActiveX object; which
one is supported depends on the user's Windows configuration, not on the
browser.

[XMLHTTP Speed Meter, lines 147-160]

```
function createXMLHTTPObject() {
    var xmlhttp = false;
    for (var i=0;i<XMLHttpFactories.length;i++) {
        try {
                xmlhttp = XMLHttpFactories[i]();
        }
        catch (e) {
                continue;
        }
        break;
    }
    return xmlhttp;
}
```

The createXMLHTTPObject() function first sets the xmlhttp variable to false
(no support). Then it goes through all factory methods and tries them. The
problem is, of course, that if a factory method is not supported, executing it
gives an error message.

Hence the use of a try/catch statement (see 5H). We try to execute each factory method. If that succeeds, we have an XMLHttpRequest object, the function skips the catch, and encounters the break that immediately ends the for
loop. If a factory method gives an error, the function executes the catch statement and continues the for loop.

10A

Afterwards, `xmlhttp` either refers to an XMLHttpRequest object that we can use, or it's still `false`, which means that the user's browser doesn't support XMLHttpRequest at all. We return this value to the function that asked for it.

The first time I call `createXMLHTTPObject` is during the overall object detection at the start of the script.

[XMLHTTP Speed Meter, lines 19-21]

```
window.onload = function () {
    var supportCheck = document.createElement && ➥
    document.getElementsByTagName && createXMLHTTPObject();
    if (!supportCheck) return;
```

The advanced interface should start up only if the browser supports both the W3C DOM and XMLHttpRequest. In addition to the normal W3C DOM check, the script tries to create an object. If that fails, the initialization function ends, and the user gets the noscript interface.

open

The next step is to open a new request, which means preparing it for sending. The actual send command is given later.

The basic syntax is as follows:

```
xmlhttp.open(method,url,true);
```

`method` defines the method of the request: GET, POST, or HEAD. The first two work as always: With GET the (form) data is appended to the URL as a query string; with POST the data is sent along in the HTTP request's body.

A HEAD request returns only the HTTP headers of the response, not the file itself. This is occasionally useful, for instance if you want to display the last modification date of a file.

{ **POSTING YOUR REQUEST**

Note that if you want to POST your data you must set the 'Content-Type' header of the request to 'application/x-www-form-urlencoded'. }

`url` is the URL of the file to be downloaded. The last argument tells the browser whether to handle the request asynchronously (`true`) or synchronously (`false`). You generally use `true`.

Practical example:

```
xmlhttp.open('GET','some.xml',true);
```

Now the file some.xml is loaded by GET in an asynchronous way.

{ **ASYNCHRONOUS VS. SYNCHRONOUS**

Asynchronous means that the browser does not wait for the response, but immediately allows more JavaScript commands or user actions. In contrast, if you send a synchronous request, all browser activity is stalled until the response arrives.

The problem is, of course, that if all activity stalls, the browser stops responding to the user's actions. Especially when it takes more than a few seconds to download the data, the user may think that the browser has crashed, and this is something to be avoided at all costs. Therefore, synchronous requests are rarely useful. }

10A

readystatechange

After you've called the open() method, you should specify what happens when the response to your request arrives at the browser. For this you use the (originally Microsoft-proprietary) readystatechange event, which fires whenever the "ready state" of a request changes.

Personally, I'd rather use a simple load event ("when the response has loaded, do this"), but unfortunately Explorer doesn't support that event on XMLHttpRequests.

readystatechange is a curious event. There are five ready states: 0, 1, 2, 3, and 4.

Value	Meaning	Description
0	Uninitialized	The object has been created, but the open method has not yet been called.
1	Loading	The object has been created, but the send method has not yet been called.
2	Loaded	The send method has been called, but the status and headers are not yet available.
3	Interactive	Some data has been received.
4	Completed	All data has been received.

The first four values contain a few obscure browser incompatibilities and are very rarely used in practice. (I've never understood their purpose.) Ready state 4 (all data has been received) is the state generally used.

The basic syntax is as follows:

```
xmlhttp.onreadystatechange = function () {
    if (xmlhttp.readyState != 4) return;
    // do something with the response
}
```

When the ready state of the request changes, the handler fires. Its first point of action is seeing if readyState is 4. If it isn't, the function ends immediately. If it is, you can start doing something with the response. We'll get back to "doing something with the response" in 10B.

Oddities

Although onreadystatechange seems a normal event handler, there are some oddities. First of all, the event type is load in Explorer, instead of the readystatechange you'd expect. Secondly, only Safari creates an event object for this event. Therefore, the following code doesn't work:

```
xmlhttp.onreadystatechange = handleResponse;
function handleResponse(e) {
    var evt = e || window.event;
    // now evt is only defined in Safari
    // IE, Mozilla and Opera can't find the event object
}
```

Fortunately, access to the event object is rarely necessary when using onreadystatechange.

send

Once you've called the open() method and set an onreadystatechange event handler, you can send the request. The syntax is as follows:

```
xmlhttp.send(data);
```

The send() method requires an argument. If you POST your data, the argument is the post data; if you use GET, the argument is null.

When the request is sent, you wait for the response to arrive. When it arrives, the onreadystatechange event handler kicks in and does what you instructed it to do.

10A

setRequestHeader

The four features we've discussed so far are required. There are two more methods of the XMLHttpRequest object that can come in handy in some situations.

{ **REQUEST HEADERS**

You can find an overview of HTTP request headers at: http://www.w3.org/
Protocols/HTTP/HTRQ_Headers.html. }

The `setRequestHeader()` method allows you to set one of the HTTP request
headers. Its syntax is as follows:

```
xmlhttp.setRequestHeader('Header-name','value');
```

I commonly set the User-Agent header to 'XMLHTTP' so that server-side programs are able to distinguish between XMLHttpRequests and other requests.

```
xmlhttp.setRequestHeader('User-Agent','XMLHTTP');
```

This allows you to write server-side scripts that serve up one document for
advanced browsers and another one for browsers that don't support (sufficient)
JavaScript. In 10D we'll see that this can occasionally be a useful accessibility tool.

If you want to POST your data, you *must* set another header:

```
req.setRequestHeader('Content-type','application/x-www-form-
urlencoded');
```

sendRequest function

Let's bring all this wisdom together in one function: the `sendRequest()` function I use in all my XMLHttpRequest projects (including XMLHTTP Speed Meter).
It requires the `createXMLHTTPObject()` function we discussed earlier.

[XMLHTTP Speed Meter, lines 120-138, condensed]

```
function sendRequest(url,callback,postData) {
    var req = createXMLHTTPObject();
    if (!req) return;
    var method = (postData) ? "POST" : "GET";
```

```
    req.open(method,url,true);
    req.setRequestHeader('User-Agent','XMLHTTP');
    if (postData)
          req.setRequestHeader('Content-type', ➥
          'application/x-www-form-urlencoded');
    req.onreadystatechange = function () {
          if (req.readyState != 4) return;
          if (req.status != 200 && req.status != 304) {
                alert('HTTP error ' + req.status);
                return;
          }
          callback(req); }
    if (req.readyState == 4) return;
    req.send(postData);
}
```

It's called like this:

```
sendRequest('some.xml',handleResponse); // GET
sendRequest('some.xml',handleResponse,postData); // POST
```

some.xml is the file you need, handleResponse is the function that should run when the response becomes available, and the optional argument postData contains the POST data.

First the function tries to create a new XMLHttpRequest object and store it in req. If that's not possible, the function ends. Otherwise, it checks if a postData argument exists: if so, it sets the request's method to POST; if not, it sets it to GET.

It opens the request with method, url, and true and sets the User-Agent header to 'XMLHTTP'. If the request should be POSTed, it sets the Content-type header to 'application/x-www-form-urlencoded'.

Then it creates an onreadystatechange event handler, which we'll discuss in the next section.

10A

The function next checks if the request's `readyState` is already 4. If so, the document is already in the browser's cache, and the request does not need to be sent. This is important for Explorer, since if you request a file that's already cached in this browser, it may fire the onreadystatechange event handler before the request is officially sent, and that could cause weird problems.

Finally, the function sends the request with `postData` (either the POST data or `null`) as an argument.

abort

WARNING   Browser incompatibilities ahead

The `abort()` method allows you to abort an ongoing request. This is rarely necessary. When you take an XMLHttpRequest object that's already downloading data and give it other instructions, it forgets about its previous orders and starts downloading the new data. The only exception to this rule is Mozilla: This browser may require you to use the `abort()` method first.

Note that if you use `abort()` you should first remove the onreadystatechange event handler, since Explorer and Mozilla also fire this event handler when the request is aborted:

```
xmlhttp.onreadystatechange = function () {};
xmlhttp.abort();
```

Note further that Explorer requires you to assign an empty function to onreadystatechange. If you give it a `null` value, weird errors ensue.

B: Handling the response

The request is sent to the server, which returns a document. In 10C we'll take a closer look at what format this document should be (XML, HTML, JSON); in this section we'll treat the nuts and bolts of handling the response.

status

Let's first return to the onreadystatechange event handler used in sendRequest():

[XMLHTTP Speed Meter, lines 120-138, condensed]

```
function sendRequest(url,callback,postData) {
        // more administration
        req.onreadystatechange = function () {
            if (req.readyState != 4) return;
            if (req.status != 200 && req.status != 304) {
                    alert('HTTP error ' + req.status);
                    return;
            }
            callback(req);
        }
    }
```

First of all, note that this function, which is defined within the body of sendRequest(), has access to its parent function's variables req and callback. This is a practical example of JavaScript's variable scope, which we discussed in 5I.

> **WARNING** Browser incompatibilities ahead

When the response's readyState has become 4, the function checks its status property. This property contains the HTTP status code that the server has returned. What we want is status 200: OK. Opera, though, sometimes returns status code 304: Not Modified. Therefore we see if the status code is 200 or 304; if it isn't, the function shows an alert, and ends.

{ HTTP STATUS CODES

Here's a list of all HTTP status codes: http://www.w3.org/Protocols/HTTP/ HTRESP.html **}**

Callback function

If the document has been received normally, the callback function is called. This function was defined in the original sendRequest() call:

[XMLHTTP Speed Meter, lines 46 and 120]

```
sendRequest('ajax_endpoint.php'+queryString, catchData);
function sendRequest(url,callback,postData) {
```

XMLHTTP Speed Meter sends a request for ajax_endpoint.php and appends the user's postal code and house number as a query string. Furthermore, this call sets catchData() as the callback function, which means that catchData() is called when the document has been loaded.

This callback function receives the entire XMLHttpRequest object, which by now includes the response, as an argument:

[XMLHTTP Speed Meter, lines 134 and 52-53]

```
callback(req);
function catchData(req) {
    var returnXML = req.responseXML;
```

responseText and responseXML

It's up to the callback function—catchData(), in the case of XMLHTTP Speed Meter—to do something with the response, and obviously the first step is to read it. For this purpose, an XMLHttpRequest object has two properties: responseText and responseXML. The first holds the document as one text string, while the second holds the document as an XML document; such documents are accessible to the W3C DOM.

The format of the returned data determines whether you need responseText or responseXML, and we'll take a closer look at this question in 10C. XMLHTTP Speed Meter has XML as its response format, and therefore uses responseXML.

{ **RESPONSEXML AND ABORT() IN MOZILLA**

Occasionally, when you use the abort() method, the responseXML goes missing in Mozilla. I have no idea how to solve this curious bug; your only line of defense is not to use abort() at all.

If this bug occurs, Mozilla also skips readyState 3. }

Example: catchData()

The catchData() function of XMLHTTP Speed Meter starts by extracting the responseXML.

[XMLHTTP Speed Meter, lines 52-59]

```
function catchData(req) {
    var returnXML = req.responseXML;
    if (!returnXML) return;
    var speed = parseInt(returnXML. ➡
    getElementsByTagName('speed')[0].firstChild.nodeValue);
    if (speed != currentSpeed)
            moveToNewSpeed(speed);
    currentSpeed = speed;
    var error = returnXML.getElementsByTagName('message')[0].
firstChild;
```

If there is no responseXML for whatever reason, the function ends. If there is responseXML, returnXML now points to its document node.

The script uses a normal getElementsByTagName() call to read out the download speed. After all, the document is an XML document, so all W3C DOM methods and properties work fine (with the exception of getElementById).

The script takes the speed from the XML, and if it's different from the currently shown speed it sends it to the moveToNewSpeed() animation function discussed in 9G. Finally, it sees whether a <message> tag exists in the XML. The server-side programmer and I agreed that any error message would be contained in this tag. If the tag is present, the script shows the text contained in it.

10B

responseXML needs an XML document

responseXML is available only when the returned document actually is XML, i.e., when its MIME type proclaims it to be XML. That means that if you fetch an HTML page or a text file, responseXML is not available.

However, if you make sure that your server sets the MIME type of HTML pages to text/xml, these pages are considered XML documents (provided they're well-formed), and responseXML will be available.

Unfortunately, if you serve all your HTML pages as text/xml, you'll definitely encounter problems, since normal, non-XMLHttp requested HTML pages should be text/html in order for the browser to properly show them.

Here is where setting the User-Agent header of the request to 'XMLHTTP' can come in handy: a server-side script could send HTML pages as text/xml when it encounters this header, but as text/html otherwise.

getResponseHeader

The getResponseHeader() method allows you to read out individual HTTP response headers. The syntax is as follows:

```
var lastModified = req.getResponseHeader("Last-Modified");
```

getAllResponseHeaders

The getAllResponseHeaders() method gives you a complete list of all HTTP response headers that the server sent back. The syntax is as follows:

```
var allResponseHeaders = req.getAllResponseHeaders();
```

C: The response format

An XMLHttpRequest allows you to retrieve any sort of data format from the server. In practice, most Web developers restrict themselves to XML, HTML,

JSON (JavaScript Object Notation), CSV (comma-separated values), or another form of plain text.

In this section we'll discuss the advantages and disadvantages of all of these formats. I'll use the return values of XMLHTTP Speed Meter as examples. The script expects XML, but it could easily be changed to accommodate JSON or CSV. HTML, as we'll see, is much harder to use in this specific case.

XML

Because of the name *XML*HttpRequest, many developers select XML as their return format. There's nothing wrong with that, but you should bear in mind that other formats are possible, and that sometimes they're more useful.

The big advantages of XML are that most programmers know what it is, and that XML files can be read and used by a variety of programming languages. If you announce to other developers that you're going to use XML they'll nod sagely, while announcing any of the other formats may cause a few raised eyebrows and requests for further explanations. Socially, XML is the most acceptable format.

What about its technical advantages and disadvantages? The most obvious advantage is that you can use nearly all W3C DOM methods and properties on an XML file—you don't have to learn any new programming tricks.

The disadvantage of XML is that both the server response and the script that interprets it can become quite verbose. You have to read out every interesting XML element separately, and you have to create every HTML element you need separately, too. This can make for quite lengthy scripts that become hard to read and maintain.

10C

Example
Let's look at XMLHTTP Speed Meter's response:

```
<?xml version="1.0" encoding="utf-8"?>
<wanadoo>
```

```
<distance>2495</distance>
<speed>15</speed>
<message/>
<error>0</error>
</wanadoo>
```

The `<distance>` and `<error>` elements are not used by my script. They might come in useful in other situations, and their presence does not hinder my script in any way, so I don't mind them being there.

If the postal code is incorrect, we get an error message like this:

```
<?xml version="1.0" encoding="utf-8"?>
<wanadoo>
 <distance>0</distance>
 <speed>0</speed>
 <error>1</error>
 <message>Your postal code and/or house number are incorrect.</
message>
</wanadoo>
```

We already saw the script that reads out the relevant data and does something with them:

[XMLHTTP Speed Meter, lines 52-59]

```
function catchData(req) {
    var returnXML = req.responseXML;
    if (!returnXML) return;
    var speed = parseInt(returnXML. ➡
    getElementsByTagName('speed')[0].firstChild.nodeValue);
    if (speed != currentSpeed)
            moveToNewSpeed(speed);
    currentSpeed = speed;
    var error = returnXML.getElementsByTagName('message')[0].
firstChild;
```

Since we're only reading out two tags and don't generate any HTML, this is a pretty simple function. Be warned, however, that as soon as you start generating HTML, such a function becomes much, much more complicated.

HTML

In certain respects, HTML is the best choice for importing data to a Web site. The reason is, of course, that Web sites already work with HTML, and that adding extra bits of it is extremely simple:

```
function catchData(req) {
    var newHTML = req.responseText;
    document.getElementById('someID').innerHTML = newHTML;
}
```

You read out the `responseText`, i.e., the response as a text string. Since this text is already HTML, you can simply paste it into some element's `innerHTML`, and the page will contain the new data.

But if you want to read out bits of data and write them into several elements, or pass them on to other functions, as I do in XMLHTTP Speed Meter, HTML becomes hard to work with.

Showing error messages is easy; if the server-side script returns something like this, we just paste it in the appropriate HTML element:

```
<p>Your postal code and/or house number are incorrect.</p>
```

10C

HTML AND FORMS IN EXPLORER

Explorer seems to be unable to add HTML snippets that contain a `<form>` tag to a page. It also refuses to cooperate when you want to load HTML snippets into a `<form>` element.

However, reading out the speed is another thing. The script does not want to print out the speed, but instead needs to send it on to another function that starts up the animation. In theory this is possible, but it's not really intuitive or easy:

```
// returned data
15

// script that does something:
function catchData (req) {
    var response = req.responseText;
    var speed = parseInt(response);
    if (speed != currentSpeed)
            moveToNewSpeed(speed);
}
```

This method would work. The disadvantage is that the returned data is just "15", and that doesn't really count as HTML. Besides, it doesn't make use of HTML's main advantage: pasting the response into an element.

All in all, the HTML response format is not suited for XMLHTTP Speed Meter, or for any script that needs to manipulate the server data instead of just printing them on the screen. On the other hand, as we'll see in 10D, HTML is the most accessible format.

JSON

The JavaScript Object Notation format returns a string that should be interpreted as a JavaScript object. This string contains a JavaScript object literal (see 5J).

JSON INTRODUCTION

JSON was invented by Douglas Crockford. See http://www.json.org/ for an extended introduction to the format.

This would be the JSON equivalent of XMLHTTP Speed Meter's XML response:

```
{
    distance: 2495,
    speed: 15,
    message: null,
    error: 0;
}
```

Or, in case of an error:

```
{
    distance: 0,
    speed: 0,
    message: "Your postal code and/or house number are ➡
    incorrect.",
    error: 1;
}
```

The advantage of JSON is that it's slightly more in line with JavaScript's internal structure than XML.

The disadvantage is that the syntax is very precise and unique to JavaScript, which means that developers without experience in JavaScript will not be able to create JSON strings on the fly. Besides, the script you need to create an HTML structure to hold the data is roughly as verbose as a script that reads out XML.

How do we interpret such a JSON string? For example, catchData() would become something like this:

```
function catchData(req) {
    var responseObject = eval('(' + req.responseText + ')');
    var speed = responseObject.speed;
    if (speed != currentSpeed)
            moveToNewSpeed(speed);
    var error = responseObject.message;
    // handle error
}
```

10C

CSV

NOTE   CSV is the only plain-text format we'll cover here, but others are similar
enough that this will serve as an adequate example.

Comma-separated values (or values separated by another character) is one
of the oldest data-retrieval systems in use. It simply sends back a string, within
which the commas denote where one bit of data ends and another one starts.

The advantages of CSV are that it's the shortest and most efficient data format,
it has a venerable pedigree, and it's well-known by developers in all sorts of
languages.

The disadvantage is that the file doesn't contain any clue about the interpretation
of the data. Files in other formats contain some sort of pointer (be it an XML or
HTML tag or a JavaScript property name) that tells you what sort of data they hold.

For instance, if I swap the `speed` and `message` tags (XML) or properties (JSON),
the XML and JSON scripts would continue to function, since they access the
speed and message data by tag or property name, not by their position in the
response file. However, in a CSV file we can only access them by their position,
and this requires client-side and server-side developers to be very disciplined in
generating and reading the output.

These are CSV files for XMLHTTP Speed Meter:

```
2495,15,null,0
0,0,Your postal code and/or house number are incorrect.,1
```

The data is read out and used in the following way:

```
function catchData(req) {
    var data = req.responseText.split(',');
    var speed = data[1];
    if (speed != currentSpeed)
            moveToNewSpeed(speed);
    var error = data[2];
    // handle error
}
```

As you see, the relevant data are being read by `data[1]` and `data[2]`, so the function expects to find the speed at the second place, and the error message at the third. If a server-side programmer accidentally reversed the speed and message data, the JavaScript would not be able to extract the data it needs.

The best format?

It won't surprise you that there is no best format—only formats that are best suited to a specific type of application or situation. In general, I decide on a response format in the following way:

- If I want to add large chunks of data to a page, I opt for HTML, since it allows me to easily add data with only a few lines of script.

- If the project is large and complicated and requires close cooperation with several programmers, I opt for XML, because this format is the most likely to be known and understood by all parties involved.

- If I need to go through a lengthy response in search of the few bits of data I really need, I opt for either XML or JSON, since only these formats allow quick searches.

- I never use CSV files, since I dislike the lack of metadata such as a `speed` or `message` tag or property name.

Of course you should feel free to disregard this advice and pick your own response format. Especially when you'll be doing both the client-side and the server-side coding, you should choose what comes naturally to you.

D: Accessibility

Complicated, script-heavy, XMLHttpRequesting applications have a problem when it comes to accessibility. Making such an application accessible without JavaScript is definitely a tough job. However, it's something that simply has to be done. The main problem is that many application developers refuse to consider the issue, which of course makes finding answers even more difficult.

10D

Unfortunately, the definitive guide on XMLHttpRequest and accessibility has not yet been written. I try to provide some hints in this section, but you should always temper the guidelines below with common sense; chances are that you'll find yourself in a situation in which none of them apply.

Accessibility with HTML

One (and only one) format is accessible in and of itself, and that's HTML. Anyone who surfs the Web has a program that is able to interpret HTML. Therefore, working with HTML files is the key to keeping an XMLHttpRequest application accessible.

Let's start with a simple example: you want to import a bit of data and paste it into your page as is, without modifying it or searching for specific data. As we saw in 10C, the HTML response format is best suited for this.

So let's create a link list with a JavaScript hook, and an element to hold the returned data:

```
<ul id="xmlhttp">
    <li><a href="data.html">Data</a></li>
    <li><a href="moredata.html">More data</a></li>
    <li><a href="stillmoredata.html">Still more data</a></li>
</ul>
<div id="writeroot"></div>
```

These simple links will work in any HTML-capable user agent. Your application is accessible.

> **HIJAX**
>
> The methodology I describe here was developed by Jeremy Keith, who calls it Hijax. Read about it at http://domscripting.com/blog/display/41.

If a browser happens to support XMLHttpRequest, you can enhance these links. You could do the following (using the `createXMLHTTPObject()` and `sendRequest()` functions we already discussed):

```
var XHRsupport = createXMLHTTPObject();
window.onload = function () {
    if (!XHRsupport) return;
    var linkList = document.getElementById('xmlhttp');
    var links = linkList.getElementsByTagName('a');
    for (var i=0;i<links.length;i++) {
            x[i].onclick = getPage;
    }
}

function getPage() {
    sendRequest(this.href,showPage);
}

function showPage(req) {
    var HTMLPage = req.responseText;
    // paste HTML into page
}
```

Now whenever the user clicks on a link, the `getPage()` function kicks in and fetches the required HTML page through XMLHttpRequest.

However, if the browser supports the advanced interface, you don't want to receive the entire HTML page, but only the part of it that contains the actual content. After all, you may not paste a second <html>, <head>, or <body> tag into your page, and besides you probably don't want to show the site navigation and other overhead, either.

Instead, you want to show only the actual content of the HTML page you're importing. The first step is to mark up this content:

```
// data.html
<html>
<head>[…]</head>
```

10D

```
<body>
<ul class="navigation">[…]</ul>
<div id="content">
    <h2>Page content</h2>
    […]
</div>
</body>
</html>
```

Now the problem becomes one of importing or showing *only* `<div id="content">`, without the rest of the HTML. One solution would be a server-side script that extracts this `<div>` from the requested HTML page and sends it and its content back to the browser:

```
function getPage() {
    sendRequest('extractScript.php?page=' + this.href,showPage);
}


function showPage(req) {
    var newData = req.responseText;
    document.getElementById('writeroot').innerHTML = newData;
}
```

Of course, you could also use the reverse solution: create HTML snippet files on your server to import with XMLHttpRequest, and also create a template file that's used to give these snippets a "coating" of overhead HTML in case the browser requests the pages without XMLHttpRequest. In this case you can distinguish between XMLHttp and non-XMLHttp requests by checking if the User-Agent header is 'XMLHTTP'.

If a server-side solution is not possible, the simplest client-side solution is to use an iframe, and load the HTML pages into that iframe:

```
<iframe id="writeroot"></iframe>
function getPage() {
    document.getElementById('writeroot').src = this.href;
}
```

Accessibility with other response formats

Unfortunately, XML, JSON, and CSV files are not accessible by themselves, so as soon as you use one of these response formats, accessibility gets more complicated. There are two ways to reconcile non-HTML responses and accessibility, but sometimes neither can be used.

The first way is simply to make sure that any XMLHttpRequested content consists of nice extras. That leaves the basic functionality in the HTML page accessible to anyone. While the requested extra bits should make your page more usable, they shouldn't contain any essential elements. Choose this solution if you can, since it keeps things simple. Often, however, it is not a viable alternative.

The second way is to create two server-side programs: one to deliver the XML (or JSON or CSV) to the XMLHttpRequest, and another to deliver plain HTML pages to older browsers. These programs must make a distinction between XMLHttpRequest and normal requests; they could do so by checking whether or not the User-Agent header is 'XMLHTTP'.

The disadvantage to this method is that the server-side programmers have to create and maintain two applications instead of one, which of course makes the project more complex and expensive.

Unfortunately, I have no other accessibility hints for XMLHttpRequest applications that do not work with HTML snippets. This only goes to show that we've barely scratched the surface of this complicated topic, and that more research is necessary.

If you build a data-retrieval application, please take an hour to think about accessibility. Especially when you don't work with HTML, chances are that you won't find a solution, but I have the secret hope that somebody (maybe you!) will think of a viable approach that will take us one step nearer to accessible XMLHttpRequest applications.

10D

Afterword

The future of JavaScript

THAT CONCLUDES OUR journey through JavaScript. I hope that this book enables you to grow and improve in your day to day scripting.

Remember, though, that what you've read is not a complete overview of all JavaScript features and functionalities, but a selection of features that you're most likely to need in your scripts, or that are so fundamental that it's impossible to understand JavaScript without knowledge of them.

This book is the start of your learning process, not the end.

To finish in style, let's take a short peek into our crystal balls and try to predict the future of JavaScript. I see three important developments that will change JavaScript over the next few years or so.

The most important one is the end of the Ajax hype. I'm not sure when it will happen, but I know that it will. What goes around comes around—what once was cool and modern will become old hat and boring.

The hype has taught us a lot—even if only by setting bad examples. If we study the difference between unsuccesful and successful Ajax applications we'll gain more insight into the limitations of the users' comprehension of complicated interfaces, and thus JavaScript's overall purpose. We might even be able to define that purpose in a way that will survive the next few alternations of fat and thin phases.

Despite these possible long-term benefits, the disappearance of the hype will cause one short-term change that has disadvantages as well as advantages: many developers who came from "hard" programming will once again return to their original languages once JavaScript is no longer cool.

The disadvantage is that these programmers have a lot of knowledge of advanced programming structures that the average Web developer lacks, and once they're gone they can't explain application design to us. I hope some of them will stick around to teach us.

The advantage is that the disappearance of the "hard" programmers will allow JavaScript developers to focus on accessibility more than is the case now. One of the prime problems of JavaScript accessibility is that many programmers who create Ajax applications are largely unaware of it. It remains an issue that Web developers are better equipped to deal with than "hard" programmers; and the disappearance of the hype will give Web developers their chance to do so.

The second important development is the emergence of the Core 2.0 standard. It will bring JavaScript closer in line with other programming languages—although right now it seems that this change will come too late to help the Ajax developers. Nonetheless, Core 2.0 might help programmers to take JavaScript more seriously, which will benefit the entire language and all its users.

The third important development is that all browser vendors, including Microsoft, are now firmly committed to Web standards. Even though browser incompatibilities have not yet disappeared, they'll gradually grow less in scope and severity—except of course for those problems that are caused by a human programming error: these will never disappear.

In short, I feel that with a little bit of luck the coming years will see a better definition of JavaScript's purpose (which may include a serious attempt to integrate accessibility into common scripting practices); the emergence of a better programming style thanks to Core 2.0 and the lessons of "hard" programmers; and less browser problems.

JavaScript is on the move. The best is still to come.

Index